AN INTRODUCTION TO PUBLIC RELATIONS

OXFORD
UNIVERSITY PRESS
AUSTRALIA & NEW ZEALAND

AN INTRODUCTION TO PUBLIC RELATIONS
FROM THEORY TO PRACTICE

Joy Chia   Gae Synnott

OXFORD
UNIVERSITY PRESS

Oxford University Press is a department of the University of Oxford.
It furthers the University's objective of excellence in research,
scholarship, and education by publishing worldwide. Oxford is a registered
trademark of Oxford University Press in the UK and in certain other
countries.

Published in Australia by
Oxford University Press
253 Normanby Road, South Melbourne, Victoria 3205, Australia

National Library of Australia Cataloguing-in-Publication data

Chia, Joy
An introduction to public relations: from theory to practice / Joy Chia, Gae Synnott.

ISBN 978 0 19 556465 5 (pbk.)

Includes index.
Public relations.
Synnott, Gae

659.2

Edited by Sandra Goldbloom Zurbo
Text design and typeset by Norma van Rees
Proofread by Kate McGregor
Indexed by Karen Gillen
Printed by in China by Sheck Wah Tong Printing Press Ltd.

*Links to third party websites are provided by Oxford in good faith and for information only.
Oxford disclaims any responsibility for the materials contained in any third party website
referenced in this work.*

CONTENTS

CONTRIBUTORS

Coordinating authors

Dr Joy Chia, FPRIA

Dr Joy Chia is a senior lecturer and program director of the public relations undergraduate and postgraduate programs at the University of South Australia, a Fellow of the Public Relations Institute of Australia (PRIA), past PRIA (SA) president, and member of PRIA's National Education Committee. In 2008, she and her research partner Associate Professor Margaret Peters were awarded a Canada–Asia Program Award from the International Council for Canadian Studies to undertake research into employee commitment to social capital investment in Australian and Canadian credit unions. This work in progress has resulted in publication in international journals, which has added to the scholarly contributions on relationship management and relational theory developed in previous national research. Joy enjoys the international context of public relations and has extensive experience developing and delivering public relations courses in Southeast Asia.

Dr Gae Synnott, FPRIA, MIMC, IAP2

Dr Gae Synnott is the director of Synnott Mulholland Management Services (SMMS), a Perth-based management and communications consultancy. She has a strong communication and social sciences background, and works primarily in the areas of community engagement, sustainability engagement, communications, social research, and strategic planning. SMMS, which has been in operation since mid 1997, provides advice mainly to state and local government, as well as to the resources sector in Western Australia. Gae uses a values-based approach in her work and loves to get involved in participatory sustainability projects with complex journeys and outcomes. As part of a virtual network, Gae is keen to explore new mechanisms to engage with individuals and communities, and approaches every new project as an opportunity to improve and prove the value of working jointly.

Contributors

Dr Nigel De Bussy is public relations course coordinator at Curtin University of Technology, Western Australia. He is a Fellow and past state president of the Public Relations Institute of Australia. Before joining Curtin, he spent more than a decade in public relations consultancy in the United Kingdom and Australia. His current research interests include stakeholder management, the link between corporate social responsibility and corporate reputation, as well as new media and public relations.

Kate Fitch is a senior lecturer in public relations at Murdoch University, Western Australia. She has worked in public relations roles for local and state government and arts companies in Australia, and in book publishing in the United Kingdom. Her research interests include public relations in Southeast Asia and public relations theory.

Dr Gwyneth Howell has fifteen years' experience in corporate marketing and communications, in practice and in education. She has extensive global corporate and consulting experience in business, marketing, and public relations. Her public relations experience has been gathered inhouse within public and private organisations of various sizes, and in agencies, all of which provided expertise in media relations, event and issues management and production. She is currently a senior lecturer in Public Relations at the University of Western Sydney, New South Wales.

Melanie James worked as a public relations manager in the government and financial services sectors prior to joining the University of Newcastle, New South Wales, as a lecturer in public relations in 2006. She is a member of the Public Relations Institute of Australia and has won state and national awards for her campaigns. She is currently enrolled in a PhD program. Her research interests include public relations strategy and public relations education.

Hamish McLean, after more than ten years as an editor and senior reporter for metropolitan and regional newspapers, ventured into the discipline of public relations where he worked at senior levels in police, emergency services, and corrections for ten years before starting his own agency, Maddison PR. He currently consults to corporations, mainly in the legal, law enforcement, health, aviation, and technology sectors, and provides specialised risk communication and crisis management workshops for senior executives and corporate boards. He holds an MA with first-class honours (Griffith) for which he twice earned a Griffith Award for Academic Excellence (2004 and 2006). He is the principal teaching fellow (Public Relations) at Bond University, Queensland.

Amisha Mehta is a lecturer and public relations subject area coordinator in the School of Advertising, Marketing and Public Relations at Queensland University of Technology, Queensland. She is currently enrolled in a PhD program. Her research interests include organisational change, crisis communication, legitimacy, and public relations education.

In August 2008, Amisha Mehta and Robina Xavier received a citation from the Australian Learning and Teaching Council for contribution to student learning.

Dr Richard Phillipps was at the Australian Broadcasting Corporation from 1965 to 1986, for ten years as a journalist, and then, from 1974, as senior information officer at head office, where he edited its annual reports to parliament and a fortnightly staff magazine, *Scan*. In 1986, he joined MMA Public Relations in Sydney as senior public relations consultant. In 1987, he founded the teaching of public relations at University of Western Sydney, where he taught until 2004, before moving to Bond University, Queensland. He is research fellow in Public Relations and Journalism and edits Bond's *Humanities and Social Sciences Faculty News*. In 2003, he completed a PhD at the University of Sydney; his thesis was on political media advisers.

Dr Marianne D Sison is discipline head, communication and senior lecturer at the School of Applied Communication at RMIT University, Victoria. She has been teaching public relations, organisational communication, and communication research in the undergraduate and postgraduate programs. Her research interests include organisational culture and communication, diversity and public relations, and public relations education. She has a Bachelor of Arts (Broadcast Communication) from the University of the Philippines, Master of Arts in Mass Communication (Public Relations) from the University of Florida, and her Doctor of Philosophy is from RMIT University.

Dr Richard Stanton is a senior lecturer in the Department of Media and Communication at the University of Sydney, New South Wales. He is a former journalist, editor, publisher, and public relations practitioner. He is also the author of several books, including *Media Relations* (2006) and *All News is Local: The failure of the media to reflect world events in a globalised age* (2007). He is the editor of *Political Communication Report*.

Dr Elspeth Tilley is a senior lecturer in the Department of Communication, Journalism and Marketing at Massey University, Wellington, New Zealand. She has a professional background in journalism and public relations, and has been teaching public relations and communication management to undergraduates and postgraduates in Australia and New Zealand since 2001. She has published refereed scholarly articles on a wide range of public relations topics, particularly ethics, and is founding editor of *PRism: Online journal of refereed public relations & communication research*.

Robina Xavier is head of the School of Advertising, Marketing and Public Relations at Queensland University of Technology, Queensland. She is also deputy president of the Public Relations Institute of Australia and chair of its National Education Committee. She is currently enrolled in a PhD program. Her research interests include crisis communication and public relations education. In August 2008, Robina Xavier and Amisha Mehta received a citation from the Australian Learning and Teaching Council for contribution to student learning.

PREFACE

It has been fascinating to see the way that public relations education and practice are changing in Australia, New Zealand, and many parts of Asia. New public relations programs are developing in the tertiary sector at the same time as new public relations positions are emerging in all sectors—government, not-for-profit, and corporate, but the authors are not sure that public relations is understood and recognised for what it is. An invitation to conduct a workshop for thirty public relations directors, 'Managing Public Relations for the Twenty-first Century', indicated to Joy Chia that public relations is often squeezed into a box labelled 'this is how we do it'. Sometimes, little attempt is made to think about the possibilities of managing and exploring public relations as a diverse, dynamic, and creative profession. The seminar and the discussion that followed left the participants wondering what was needed to extend the horizons of public relations thinking, to move away from not only considering what public relations does but also to understanding why practitioners practise in the way they do, why new ways of engaging with different audiences and communities need to be thought about, and how a resourceful, vibrant profession that makes a difference to organisations and the community can be developed.

This book is not a how to book that attempts to cover every aspect of public relations practice. It is a book that will help students to make sense of the profession and gradually build awareness, understanding, and appreciation. A stronger appreciation of the context and theory will develop practitioners who are better prepared and capable of adding value to their organisations.

The springboards for sense-making in this book include our discussions about the rationale for practice, what the profession is, why it works in the way it does, theories that are critical to practice, ethical considerations for practice, management and organisational issues that affect practice, research that directs practice, a discussion of the new and traditional media essential to practice, and the strategies and tactics as a function of practice.

This book's reflections on the professional diversity of public relations are underpinned by strong theoretical frameworks that impact the function, relationships, communication processes, and communication management of public relations.

Case studies and examples throughout the book will take you into the life of public relations practitioners and give you an understanding of the importance of the public relations role to organisations, the community, and society.

Starting from the premise that the role of public relations is to contribute to organisational reputation and relationship management, there are some key themes that must have a place in how practitioners make sense of their role.

Issues management is the constant awareness of, and sensitivity to, the views of stakeholders and the growth of public opinion. Dealing with multiple stakeholders who support or contest your organisation's mission, means that actions and attitudes are constantly on the move. When communication breaks down and organisations and communities find that issues are escalating and cannot be managed, crisis public relations becomes important. One of the key components of public relations practice is to manage an issue before it becomes a crisis, so the understanding of issues and crisis management in an introductory scholarly work is very important.

Social responsibility and social responsiveness depict an organisational approach that acknowledges the inter-relatedness of organisations and communities, and the need for organisations to consider themselves as part of a network in which everyone has a commitment, in some sense, to everyone else.

Community relations and community engagement are areas of practice that are growing because of the need to understand and engage at a grassroots level.

Research provides the means of connecting organisations to their communities, to understand issues and expectations, and to assess the current or likely response to organisational policies and actions.

People interact in many ways and increasingly, *social media* are the media people use to communicate. Social media change the way people source information and share ideas, change the dialogue and who is involved in the conversation, and have many implications for the practitioner who is charged with trying to achieve good relationships and positive reputations.

Further, when you practise internationally, often in different cultures, public relations may be understood differently in the country where you are practising from the way that you understand it. Whether your audience is your own staff or outside the organisation, the human element determines that public relations is not prescriptive but part of constantly changing organisational, community, and societal environments in which adaptation to change is critical to its effectiveness.

During a breakfast conference meeting in Bournemouth in 2003, one of the conference participants handed Joy Chia a book about public relations in the participant's post-communist country. The woman recounted how most people in her part of the world had lost trust in all communication to them, so public relations was mainly about working out ways to begin to communicate with small community groups who would then communicate to their larger communities. This is one of many stories the authors have heard in the last ten years about public relations moving at a different pace in different parts of the world, or where the expectations of local communities are reflected in social and political conditions and opportunities, or the lack of them.

This book takes you through scholarly, academic contributions from Australian, New Zealand, and international scholars, and gives you a glimpse of the experiences of practitioners. Each offers a way to uncover the most effective public relations practices and how they can be considered and improved. The Reflect and Discuss points in each chapter are where the theory is matched with the practice. To gain the most from this book, embrace the theory and have lively discussions with your friends about each of the topics, meet practitioners, attend seminars run by your professional public relations associations and institutes, become involved, and begin to grasp the importance of networking and building relationships that are so important to public relations.

When the lines of theory and practice become blurred between the rationale for practice and the practice itself, then it is time to celebrate twenty-first century public relations.

———

Chapter 1 introduces the public relations profession, with a focus on public relations values and ethos. The profession is understood and defined more broadly as international, where it reflects the intercultural contexts that frame the theory and practice constantly changing and adapting to changing social needs globally. The professional structure and associations are introduced, and components of practice begin to define what it is that public relations practitioners do. The rationale for theory and core theoretical concepts set the scene for further theoretical engagement that is central to this book.

Chapter 2 introduces you to the influences on the public relations profession. Reflections from the Commission on Public Relations Education frame some of the early discussion on challenges to the profession around accountability and ethical practice and the need to communicate and engage with publics, audiences, and the community. New and emerging media are changing practice. As professional lines straddle, and broader communication management practices frame public relations practice, public relations is taking a key role in social responsiveness and community engagement. This is an introduction; the book moves on from this chapter to encapsulate the essence of public relations theory and practice.

Chapter 3 is an indepth discussion on core communication, public relations, and organisational theory that affect and underpin practice. The steps of the ladder— functionalist/systems, interpretive/rhetorical, critical/dialectical—need to be studied one by one; examples in each of the sections need to be carefully considered. It is most important to understand the rationale for practice, so time taken to work through theoretical concepts and what they mean will make this book come alive. It will also make your public relations career rich and meaningful.

Chapter 4 is central to the ethos and philosophy of public relations as it situates the profession within the ethical professional context in which it practises. This is an intriguing chapter that tells you what it means to be ethical, a captivating and important consideration. Codes of practice and ethics theories important to public relations provide considerable food for thought and time to work through what matters to you in your public relations career.

Chapter 5 begins to move into the specifics of making public relations relevant, workable, and strategic. The rationale for research and why it is important is discussed and examples of research being conducted demonstrate the need for varied research techniques. New tools of research are emerging and research is becoming part of community grassroots engagement. Without research, the public relations practitioner cannot plan in an informed way or understand issues; knowing what to research, why we need to, what is effective, and how to measure and monitor, are critical to a strategic and ethically managed profession.

Chapter 6 tells you where public relations practitioners work and what they do. It also provides a very good understanding of the way corporate public relations might work with not-for-profit organisations. Corporate community investment and grassroots public relations are becoming more important; they are given further consideration in Chapters 7 and 8. Public relations is not always understood or appreciated, and the challenges for the practitioner are clearly pointed out.

Chapter 7 is about the practice of public relations in organisations, the way organisational culture can affect the practice. The management role of public relations is discussed within a systems theory perspective; the internal and external communication challenges include managing and developing employee relations, working with human resources and the legal department, and having workable relationships with other organisations, stakeholders, and communities that are also part of social responsiveness and responsibility.

Chapter 8 focuses on the corporate public relations role and the development of corporate reputation. The role of stakeholder theory and stakeholder management in the development of reputation are discussed. As you begin to understand the difference between image, brand, and reputation and find that organisations have personality and identity, you will also see that corporate public relations is becoming active in giving back to the community as part of social responsibility.

Chapter 9, as well as being a chapter about strategies and tactics, also situates strategy within the contested space, intentional representation, and intended meaning of strategies. You will find how to make strategy effective, what tactics work and why, and how you can monitor your tactics and their effectiveness. More importantly, the contested spaces of practice direct your thinking into the possibilities of strategic thinking and planning.

Chapter 10 defines what an issue is, how to understand it, and what happens when an issue cannot be managed. Crisis management, the cycles and phases, and the way to manage crisis are clearly set out, and theory important to sound crisis management is fully articulated. This scholarly perspective would not be complete without a solid crisis analysis, as an introduction to public relations must take you from knowing what the profession is to what it does and what it needs to do when things do not work—it is only then that the cycle of public relations activity is complete.

Chapter 11 focuses on traditional media relations but also includes aspects of emerging media, which are discussed in more detail in Chapter 12. New media are so much a part of all media management that one cannot function without the other, yet it is important to understand the role of traditional media, the theories important to traditional media, the intercultural perspectives, the way relationships with journalists can be developed, and why that matters. The how of media releases and other media tactics are discussed, together with the legal and ethical considerations.

Chapter 12 presents the ever-changing world of new media and the struggles for public relations practitioners to keep up with new media relationships. As social media are making publics active in communicating and maybe opposing what an organisation is doing, this chapter looks at the impact on public relations, and the reality that practitioners have to catch up and be part of this new media world.

Chapter 13 concentrates on the theory and practice of public relations in Asia. Whether you want to walk through the countries and examine their definitive public relations traditions or simply to understand what makes public relations important, this chapter clearly indicates why the theories and trends presented in earlier chapters suggest that internationalisation and intercultural contexts are now central to the practice of public relations.

Chapter 14 sets you on the path to a sound public relations career. To make the most of your studies and your experience, use this chapter to begin your career journey to a profession that has so much to offer and that you can make even more dynamic and meaningful.

Our best wishes for a productive and enjoyable future.

Joy Chia and Gae Synnott

AUTHORS' ACKNOWLEDGMENTS

We would like to thank the commissioning editors at Oxford University Press, Lucy Mcloughlin who began it all, and Karen Hildebrandt who ably took on the task of guiding and supporting us.

We thank the contributors and the public relations practitioners who told their stories and shared their experiences so willingly.

We also thank our families who have been incredibly patient through the times of edits and research—it is their book as much as ours.

Joy Chia and Gae Synnott

PUBLISHER'S ACKNOWLEDGMENTS

The author and the publisher wish to thank the following copyright holders for reproduction of their material.

Bond University, for the news release on page 316, 'Bond to Shine Light on Future ICT Careers', 11 May 2009; Copyright Clearance Center, for the table on page 74, 'Mixed motive', in Dozier, Grunig & Grunig 1995, *Manager's Guide to Excellence in Public Relations and Communication Management*, Lawrence Erlbaum, Mahwah; IAP2, for the table on page 143, 'Steps in the IAP2 Public Participation Spectrum', copyright IAP2, all rights reserved; John Wiley & Sons Inc., for the table on page 282, 'Crisis clusters', in Pauchant & Mitroff 1992, *Transforming the Crisis-prone Organisation: Preventing Individual, Organizational, and Environmental Tragedies*, Jossey-Bass, San Francisco; Jock Macneish, for the cartoon on page 83, 'Claes Janssen's Four Room Apartment model' by Jock Macneish; Nestlé Australia, for the logos on page 242, Milo, Carnation and Kit Kat are registered trademarks of Société des Produits Nestlé S.A., Vevey, Switzerland and are used with permission; the Procter & Gamble Company, for the logos on page 243; Sage Publications Ltd, for the table on page 206, 'Public relations and marketing activities and their overlap', reproduced with the permission of Sage Publications, from Cornelissen 2004, *Corporate Communications*, copyright © Cornelissen 2004; University of Illinois Press, for the table on page 65, 'Shannon and Weaver mathematical model of communication', from *The Mathematical Theory of Communication*, copyright 1949, 1998, by the Board of the Trustees of the University of Illinois, used with permission of the author and the University of Illinois Press.

Every effort has been made to trace the original source of copyright material contained in this book. The publisher will be pleased to hear from copyright holders to rectify any errors or omissions.

Part **1**

THE RATIONALE FOR PRACTICE

Chapter **1**

UNDERSTANDING TWENTY-FIRST CENTURY PUBLIC RELATIONS

Joy Chia

PRACTITIONER PROFILE \ TRACY JONES

As national president of the Public Relations Institute of Australia (PRIA), Tracy Jones believes public relations professionals have the capacity to contribute to the development of business, government, and the community. 'Our role involves so much more than just writing media releases these days,' said the Darwin-based public relations consultancy principal. 'When we do our job well, we can change the way people think, feel, and act.'

Tracy has worked in public relations since 1988, having started her career seven years earlier as a journalist. While she loved the immediacy and pace of journalism, she moved to public relations because it gave her the opportunity to take a more strategic role in her work. 'I wanted to look past tomorrow's headline,' she says.

As a public relations professional consulting to business and government, Tracy says she is often in a position to recommend fundamental change in organisations.

Much of our work is involved with managing reputation, and you cannot do that with a bit of gloss and a lick of paint. Organisations need to change the way they do things if they want to impact their reputation. It's wonderful when you are working with people and they make that realisation. It's like a light going on.

Her advice to new public relations graduates is to work with people they admire and 'learn, learn, learn'.

The best people in our profession understand the difference between promotion and real public relations. The term *public relations* implies that a relationship is formed—and that only happens in an environment of honesty and trust. That says a lot about how we should go about our work.

CHAPTER **AIMS**

By the end of this chapter, you should be able to:

➤ define public relations

➤ demonstrate an understanding of public relations

➤ understand the structure of the public relations profession, with a focus on Australia and including examples from New Zealand and Asia

➤ understand why theory is important to practice and what theory is important to public relations practice

➤ understand the activities and functions of public relations within the varied roles of public relations practice and the values that underpin practice.

Introduction

What is public relations and how is the profession responding to twenty-first century challenges?

These are inspiring times for public relations educators, practitioners, and students because the public relations profession is starting to be recognised for the significant contribution it makes to organisations, the community, and to society as a whole. Understanding the profession and having a working knowledge of what it does and how it is practised is as important as appreciating and understanding the values, ethos, and professional philosophy of public relations.

Public relations practitioners actively engage in all levels of organisational and community life as they develop ways to work with the community and other publics and audiences and adapt their practice to changing societal needs and demands. The media often portray public relations as spin, hype, and propaganda but this is an outdated view and no longer appropriate to or reflective of contemporary practice. Public relations developments worldwide are changing perceptions and understanding of the profession.

David Guth and Charles Marsh (2007: 8) suggest that perception needs to catch up with reality as 'public relations is big business' and more practitioners are engaging in organisational decision making, taking an active role in management, and engaging in grassroots campaigns, all of which directly support organisations to achieve their business goals. The case study in this chapter focuses on motorists and the role of public relations in helping them to cope with escalating fuel costs, which exemplifies the grassroots approach to public relations practice and the opportunity to make a difference to society through the work we do. This is public relations of the twenty-first century.

Public relations is evolving and changing with 'porous boundaries to a range of other disciplines; marketing, management, organization studies, communications, journalism, media studies' (L'Etang 2008: 7), as practitioners liaise and collaborate with other disciplines and, simultaneously, define their practice and position in organisations.

In this chapter, we begin to understand what is shaping the profession as we consider what public relations is, how it is understood in different cultures, how it has developed, and how it is practised. The theories that provide the rationale for practice are also introduced so that an appreciation of the profession as a whole is developed and understood.

REFLECT AND DISCUSS

➤ Visit the Global Alliance public relations website to become familiar with developments worldwide and begin to grasp the significance of growth in all public relations sectors.

➤ Visit the International Public Relations Association website. Become familiar with your professional public relations institute, such as the Public Relations Institute of Australia, the Institute of Public Relations of Singapore, and the Public Relations Institute of New Zealand (see Web resources on page 27 for addresses).

➤ When you visited these websites, what was your first impression of public relations?

➤ List three words that describe public relations.

Historical origins: an overview

To make sense of what public relations is and to understand its historical origins, two important terms require explanation: publics and stakeholders.

Public is any group of people who share common interests or values in a particular situation—especially interests and values they might be willing to act upon. When a public has a relationship with your organisation, the public is called a stakeholder, meaning that it has a stake in your organisation or in an issue potentially involving your organisation (Guth & Marsh 2007: 5).

Joy Chia

Publics include internal publics such as the employees of an organisation, in addition to publics who are external to an organisation. Public relations activity also involves communication with audiences or those who might receive or listen to our messages but may not be stakeholders or specific publics. In this book we use the term 'publics and audiences' to refer broadly to those people who organisations interact with through communication programs. The term 'stakeholder' refers to internal and external stakeholders who might include members of an organisation's board or an external sponsor of an organisation, each having a stake in the organisation for very different reasons (see Chapter 8).

To understand public relations and gain knowledge of its practice, principles, and standards, a brief introduction to the profession's historical developments is a good first step. Public relations has always been part of society. The 'practice of using communication to influence the public is hundreds of years old, with its roots in ancient civilisation, including the Greek and Roman empires' (Edwards 2006: 7).

Lee Edwards also points out that much has been written about the development and history of public relations in the USA but developments in many parts of the world have not been as prominent. Developments in other regions are important and will become more important to student education and to practitioners as public relations becomes increasingly global (Sriramesh & Vércîc 2003; Tilson & Alozie 2004; Parkinson & Ekachai 2006).

We begin with developments in the USA, where Ivy Ledbetter Lee was regarded as the 'first practitioner of modern style public relations' (Newsom, Turk & Kruckeberg 2007: 22). In 1906 Lee began in a publicity role, the forerunner of the media relations role of public relations. In thirty-one years of practice, Lee contributed a great deal to the development of public relations as it moved from a publicity to a counselling role. Edward Bernays was one of the first public relations practitioners to use the term 'public relations counsel'. By 1923 Bernays' persuasive techniques had begun to change US public opinion. Public opinion is a most important concept: it refers to expressions of attitudes as 'derived from evaluations that the public make about what is happening in society' (Seitel 2007: 66). It reflects publics' sentiments about issues such as youth homelessness, binge drinking, and obesity and fast food consumption.

According to Doug Newsom, Judy Turk, and Dean Kruckeberg (2007) the US public relations profession moved through five main stages:

1 *press agentry and publicity*, in which tactics, or public relations devices such as press agentry, were publicity dominated
2 *communicating and initiating* at a time of press agents, promoters, and propagandists promoting organisations' achievements
3 *reacting and responding* at a time where writers were hired to deal with special interests as the profession began to look at its performance and how it related to society

4   *planning and prevention*, which was viewed as the maturing of the profession as it became part of a management role

5   *status of professionalism development*, which widened the profession and in which international perspectives became important.

These developments are similar to the way aspects of professional public relations have progressed in Australian, New Zealand, and Asian public relations (see Chapter 13 for a detailed analysis of Asian public relations and its practice), but the process of development cannot be tracked as succinctly. Public relations is developing in different stages according to social, political, and economic circumstances, and to the developments of countries and regions, and is underpinned by ideologies that often reflect dominant cultures. As Richard Stanton (2007) points out, public relations in countries such as China will be influenced by the government's control of the media. Political change in China and other Asian countries influences the direction of public relations making their practice a little different to that reported in the USA (Newsom, Turk & Kruckeberg 2007; Cutlip, Center & Broom 2006; Seitel 2007; Wilcox, Cameron, Ault & Agee 2007).

In Australia Candy Tymson and Peter and Richard Lazar (2002: 35) indicate that George Fitzpatrick was the first person to practise public relations, initially as an organiser of public charities. Others, such as Eric White, a former journalist who established public relations consultancies in Australia with offices in New Zealand, Asia, and London, made a significant contribution to the development of the public relations profession (Tymson, Lazar & Lazar 2002). The Australian Public Relations Institute (PRIA) had its first meeting in 1949, when Noel Griffiths was elected as its first president. At that time thirty-five members enrolled in the Institute. By 2008, PRIA membership was approximately 2648. Practitioners actively engage in the institute's activities, its annual conference, and planned professional development programs, and are recognised for excellence and best practice through Golden Target Awards (see the PRIA website) in a range of categories such as crisis and issues management, event management, community program management, investor relations, and financial management.

Some practising professionals are not PRIA members, but the gap is closing between those affiliated with PRIA and those who function independently and are not part of the institute.

REFLECT AND DISCUSS

Should it be compulsory for all public relations practitioners to be PRIA members or members of a professional body in order to practice?

Joy Chia

The evolution of professional associations in other countries includes:

➤ The Public Relations Institute in New Zealand, which 'can be traced to an historic meeting in the Auckland Star Hotel in 1954 when a group of demobilized military press officers formed what was to become the Public Relations Institute of New Zealand' (Motion & Leitch 2003: 123).

➤ The Institute of Public Relations of Singapore, which began in 1970 and continues to have a strong emphasis on providing training for members with a focus on lifelong learning; however, development of public relations in Singapore can be traced to the late 1940s (Tan & Soh 1994) when the British military began a department of policy and training there.

➤ The Malaysian Institute of Public Relations, which was founded in 1962 and has experienced strong growth. Multinational companies, such as Edelman Public Relations and Ogilvy Public Relations, have been at the forefront of public relations, but local public relations practitioners are increasingly taking charge of Malaysian programs and leading public relations initiatives.

➤ The China International Public Relations Association (CIPRA), which is growing; professional numbers are soaring as the profession is changing and developing. Chen and Culbertson (2003: 42) indicate that public relations in China 'is a new field, is changing rapidly as it defines itself. Western practices do not sit well with the Chinese people' and the acceptance of the profession and what it is, is constantly changing.

Public relations at the crossroads

While public relations practitioners understand the scope and contribution of their role within organisations, others may not fully understand what the role offers, including sometimes the organisations they work for. The profession needs to take its place in society. Guth and Marsh (2007) suggest that it is useful to focus on planning and research as these elements of public relations convey a more precise understanding of the profession. These scholars emphasise that research, evaluation, planning and communication (RACE)—the traditional four step model of the public relations process—are only relevant if they are also central to the values and ethos of the organisations that public relations plans for.

REFLECT AND DISCUSS

➤ What is the most prominent characteristic of a public relations role?

➤ Are the stages of public relations development that Newsom, Turk & Kruckeberg (2007) outlined in this chapter evident in the public relations you observe in your society?

➤ What do you think sophisticated public relations practitioners might do?

Defining and understanding public relations

As the profession develops, definitions may not be useful if they too narrowly describe public relations or if they include descriptions of what is ideal rather than what is possible. It is also important to define the profession in terms of its practice, values, and cultural context. The definitions discussed here come from a range of perspectives:

➤ the USA, the United Kingdom, and Asia, and the global context of these definitions within the common threads of practice across the cultures
➤ this author's definition, which offers a composite view of the profession
➤ a perspective according to the values of the profession.

The US perspective

Robert Heath and Coombs (2006: 7) define public relations as:

> the management function that entails planning, research, publicity, promotion, and collaborative decision making to help any organisation's ability to listen to, appreciate, and respond appropriately to those persons and groups whose mutually beneficial relationships the organization needs to foster as it strives to achieve its mission and vision.

This definition encompasses the profession in its management role and outlines the core functions of public relations, such as planning and research, that inform and direct the profession. These functions are successful if the profession attentively and appropriately responds to and collaborates with those who will benefit from public relations efforts. Mutual benefit might mean that the community 'utilizes institutional resources' where 'organizational and community interests are advanced' (Bruning, McGrew & Cooper 2006:129) as relationships are developed through organisations and community members respecting and valuing each others' contributions. Public relations practitioners set up networks and connections within the community so that relationships become meaningful and have long-term value for all relational parties. It has been fascinating to see the way credit union public relations teams establish community relationships with young carers, for example, so that they can continue their education (Chia & Peters 2009) as these carers would not otherwise have the opportunity to manage their education successfully.

The United Kingdom perspective

The Chartered Institute of Public Relations (CIPR) has made significant changes to the profession as members take an active role in the Institute's activities and extensive professional training programs.

The institute describes public relations in a similar way to Heath and Coombs, as a:

discipline which looks after reputation, with the aim of earning understanding and support and influencing public opinion and behaviour. It is the planned and sustained effort to establish and maintain goodwill and mutual understanding between an organisation and its publics (Edwards 2006, 6).

The sustained effort required in public relations practice to maintain goodwill between organisations and publics is central to relationship management (Chia 2006; Hung 2008) where strategic intent is as important as developing, maintaining, and initiating relationships. Maintaining good relationships with internal and external publics means that practitioners are aware of employee discontent or public sentiment, and they know and understand how to respond to issues that matter to employees, or change public opinion as they work collaboratively with diverse publics important to organisations and society.

The Asian perspective

Public relations is understood and practised in different way in different cultures. In defining Malaysian public relations Professor Dato Mohd Hamden Haji Adnan (2004: 20) refers to the concept of the nation state as important, as communication is primarily from government 'where government assumes responsibility for national development'. Malaysian public relations is described as a 'scarce resource that is used within a set of rigid requirements' that reflect the way public relations is understood in Malaysia and in some Asian cultures, where governments' power and control, especially of media, considers what is permissible and acceptable communication to the public. There may be restrictions about what can be promoted and who can gain publicity for certain public relations initiatives. Private services are emerging in Malaysia.

The role of government is no longer as prominent in countries such as Korea, where a more diversified public relations profession is moving into many new areas of practice. The way relationships between government and media and key constituents are understood and managed affects public relations publicity, planning, and strategic intervention to generate a different environment in which public relations functions (see Chapter 13 to understand more about the context of public relations in the Asian region).

Author's definition

Building on our understanding of the profession, the subtlety of public relations practice demands that practitioners operate at many levels. Among their many attributes practitioners have the ability to support delicate negotiations with diverse publics and clients, and to launch campaigns at precisely the right time that publics are ready for public relations collaboration.

I would define public relations as a profession that:

➤ collaborates with diverse publics through dialogue and multiway discussion, networking, and relationship monitoring and management

➤ researches and evaluates its practice to understand how to work well with majority and minority groups in organisations and society, and to explore mutual objectives

➤ is creative and innovative, yet flexible in its practice, as it constantly adapts to changing needs and changing circumstances. The profession thrives on its creative edge and its ability to make a difference. Examples might include engaging with coastal care communities to preserve coastlines and empowering communities and schools to take a role in revegetation and tree planting programs in their localities, thereby improving the landscape and local environment.

Although the profession is complex, the complexity of public relations practice opens up the potential for practitioners to be creative as they adapt their practice and change their program plans in response to changing societal needs (Chia 2006, 2008; Ströh 2007). A public relations response to petrol price hikes, changing driver habits, and choices of transport requires proactive programs and campaigns that encourage taking a bus or riding to work as part of budget saving measures and being a responsible citizen.

The profession is open and responsive to different points of view, it embraces transparency and accountability, and respects cultural, political, economic, and social differences. There is a time and place for public relations input and leadership and there may also be many barriers to change that require a considered effort by all parties who contribute to public relations planning and program management. Public relations practitioners respond to, facilitate, and encourage rigour in debate about issues. They need to be prepared to accept conflict, dissent, and different points of view as the notion of 'interdependent yet opposing tensions' (Hung 2007: 452) exists in public relations relationships, where change and tension are present in relational exchanges between organisations, between government and the public, between local and state government, and between the not-for-profit and private sectors. Practitioners respond by facilitating the most effective ways to listen and respect varying points of view and by undertaking research that informs and directs practice.

Counsel, or giving advice and working through the best and most appropriate alternatives in public relations planning and programming, is important as practitioners become the facilitators of communication that may not always be popular for all parties involved in negotiation. Issues around the impact of global warming, for example, where whole communities are affected by change in weather that affects their lifestyles, livelihood, and ways of managing their businesses, can be sensitive. Public opinion is affected by what is being communicated and what is important to communities; it may sway like a pendulum as the public receives mixed messages about climate change and their contribution to global warming and what they should be doing about cutting carbon emissions and saving the planet.

Joy Chia

This is best understood through the South Australian publics' response to government water restriction campaigns during the 2008 drought. South Australian media reports indicated that some residents did not comply with these restrictions as they did not want to lose their gardens, restrict water usage in their homes, or otherwise make adjustments to their water consumption. An alternative approach, through community engagement, empowered local residents to take ownership in managing the issue.

REFLECT AND DISCUSS

> ➤ In response to global warming, what local activities are evident in your city that might reduce carbon emissions?
> ➤ What public relations campaigns are you aware of that have made a difference to energy consumption?
> ➤ What is your response to global warming?

Defining public relations values

The profession has been described by some scholars as being values driven (Guth & Marsh 2009) and as having a values-based approach. This means that when you are employed as a government, not-for-profit, corporate, or consultant practitioner your practice will be underpinned by:

➤ emphasis on transparent, two-way communication where listening and taking ideas on board is as important as informing, giving your ideas, and promoting your plans
➤ representing the interests and needs of your organisation and your endeavour to work for what is best for society as there is an ethical obligation to do so
➤ ethical and responsible practice that becomes part of community engagement or corporate social responsibility where the moral fibre of organisations goes beyond serving the community to giving back to the community
➤ plans and activities of organisations and their values and goals that are in line with the values and goals of publics and audiences, which is critical to relational development between organisations and their publics—public relations activity and planning will be successful if it is also formally and informally researched so that there is complete understanding of the context in which public relations is managed
➤ public relations taking an active role in organisations to give counsel to and develop strong internal relationships with decision makers and employees, and have input to policy development and the way organisations are managed.

These values shape practice because ethically managed communication underpins all aspects of public relations. It is through this type of practice that the profession gains respect and dignity within the community at large.

Why theory is important

A public relations student returned to class frustrated by her experience of her previous week at work. After developing a position paper about the need for her organisation's involvement in a community program to support a new teens' skate park, her executive director said that she should focus on real public relations. She reported to the class that she found it very disappointing to see that there was so little response to her hard work and creative public relations approach. This student, who was in a middle management role, found that her public relations plans and ideas were often limited by her organisation's narrow view of public relations possibilities.

To practice public relations you need knowledge and skill. You also need the rationale and understanding of why you manage in certain ways, thereby giving context to your decision making and practice. This chapter introduces you to theoretical terms and gives a brief overview of theory.

Theories underpin communication, organisational practice, the process of public relations, and critical thinking about public relations. When it comes to public relations, theories are so extensive and the profession draws from so many different theoretical bases that some help is needed to search for and come to terms with theory that directs public relations across all areas of practice. A grasp of theory by itself will not prepare a student to run public relations campaigns, manage a crisis, or develop a position paper to manage an issue; however, attempting to implement campaigns without understanding why we plan and manage in certain ways creates an imbalance in the way public relations is conducted. As Okay and Okay (2008: 303) put it, it is no longer about whether theory is important to practice, but rather it is about which theory works.

Theories are developed from research that informs practice and develops principles for practice as 'theory is the application of knowledge that has been verified and confirmed to consistently "work" in consistent situations' (Center, Jackson, Smith & Stansbury 2008: 13).

Theory helps us because:

➤ it draws from what has been tested and researched and found to be beneficial; it can also point to what has to be avoided
➤ understanding theory and applying it to practice is critical to a profession that is at the forefront of communication exchange and management
➤ theory development is robust, and publications that are specific to theory development can be followed up as students extend their scholarly enquiry.

Joy Chia

REFLECT AND DISCUSS

Read one article from the following journals that gives you a good understanding of why theory might be important to practice:

➤ *Public Relations Review*
➤ *Journal of Public Relations Research*
➤ *Journal of Communication Management*
➤ *PRism Online PR Journal,* through Massey University New Zealand
➤ *Asia Pacific Public Relations Journal.*

Although the development of public relations theory is in its early stages, it will 'someday provide a foundation for the merging profession and its practice' (Broom 2006: 141) that incorporates intercultural perspectives, global relevance, and applicability, but this will take time.

Theory and its application seem to have been dominated by a Western worldview (Gower 2006) that has been central to the normative approach of public relations theory (Grunig & Hunt 1984; Deatherage & Hazleton 1998; Holtzhausen 2005; Kent & Taylor 2007) and that has emphasised how public relations should be understood and practised rather than how it is practised. Gower's view, and that of other scholars such as Kreps (2008) and Murphy (2000), indicates that theory needs to address the complexity of public relations practice so that it facilitates understanding of the vibrant and dynamic role of the practitioner and constantly responds and adapts to change in all areas of public relations practice.

Becoming familiar with theoretical terms

There seems to be a lot to comprehend when one begins to consider theory. Each area of organisational theory, communication theory, public relations theory, and other theoretical frameworks presents concepts that are important to practice, yet each demands a depth of analysis that students may find a little daunting. The important thing is to start the process of grasping the theories that frame practice.

Watson and Noble's (2007: 7) assessment of public relations theory is that it is 'fragmented and not unique as a discipline' and that there is still a way to go in the theorisation of public relations. European scholars have had considerable input to theorisation and its relevance to public relations as they 'have interpreted sociologists and communication theorists such as Weber, Habermas, Foucault and Bourdieu when setting public relations perspective' (Watson & Noble, 9). Philosopher Jürgen Habermas, for example, suggests that 'PR has the ability to set the agenda and thus intervene and disrupt the bottom flow from citizens to those in power' (L'Etang 2008: 107), thereby framing public relations as manipulating and setting the agenda for public debate. Each theorist presents arguments that can be debated and disputed; the key point for your introduction to theory is to be aware of the way in which theory informs practice, how to consider it, and why it is practised in certain ways.

Core theoretical perspectives

Some of the key terms important to a theoretical understanding of public relations practice are now examined.

Critical theory, with its 'origins in Marxist analysis' (Tench & Yeomans 2006: 168–80), points to the application of theory to public relations practice as 'inherently tied to corporate interests'. Critical theorists review what is happening in organisations as part of sense-making, understanding organisational dynamics, and working out ways to manage effectively (Kreps 2008).

A rhetorical perspective, the premise of Heath's theoretical stance, is about the discussion and discourse between parties, which includes verbal and non-verbal communication and where the objective, or end goal, is part of the discourse. Heath and Coombs (2006) posit that the rhetorical view of public relations assumes that factual evidence is reasoned argument, where ethical judgment is crucial to effective communication and establishing solid relationships.

Systems theory, relevant to all public relations practice (see Chapters 3 and 7), is described as a 'set of parts (or subsystems) which impact on each other and which together interact with the organisation's environment' (Gregory 2008: 51). Organisations are understood as being part of a 'social system', which involves the management of these systems, adapts to changes in the systems and subsystems, and produces 'products or services of the organisation'. Systems and boundary spanning also depend on practitioners' roles that may or may not be in positions of power or authority to carry out the necessary boundary spanning to influence internal and external publics. Public relations practitioners as boundary spanners 'are the go-betweens, explaining the organization to its stakeholders and interpreting the environment to the organization' (Lattimore, Baskin, Heiman, Toth & Leuven 2004: 48).

Relationship management and relational theory focus on the way that relationships develop, how they are challenged, and how they sometimes collapse. Even though scholars (Ledingham & Bruning 1998, 2000; Bruning & Ledingham 1999; Grunig & Huang 2000; Grunig & Hon 1999; Taylor 2004; Taylor & Doerfel 2005) have put forward the notion of relational characteristics such as satisfaction, commitment, control mutuality, or control and power in relationships as important to effective relationships, relationships are very complex and constantly changing so we need to understand the context of relationships and manage them according to changing relational dynamics (Chia 2005, 2008). Scholars (Hung 2007; Ströh 2007: 452) contend that amidst uncertainty and tension public relations relationships and relational exchanges react and respond to relational dynamics from their point of view. Chia (2008) argues that relational sense making means that relational partners together work out ways to continue relationships where the relational expectations are reviewed and constantly reframed so that they can be effective and meaningful.

Communication theory, from the basics of Osgood and Schramm's model of communication, contends that 'each party has to interpret the message and shape a response before sending it out or back' (Theaker 2008: 22). The way that parties or publics interpret public relations messages also needs to be carefully monitored according to the circumstances and context in which they are sent.

Agenda setting theory maintains that the media determine what people think or have an interest in: 'The term agenda setting refers to the variable degrees of attention the mass media give to certain ideas, issues or themes, lending them more or less significance' (Newsom, Turk & Kruckeberg 2007: 139). Constant reports about global warming, for example, set the agenda for further reporting to the public as global warming is on the public agenda.

The *behavioural change model* (Center et al. 2008: 14–16) proposes that public relations activity aims to increase awareness, call the public to action so that they do not remain latent and inactive to the messages they hear, and trigger participation and behavioural change. The example of fast food consumption is one that is faced each day as messages across a wide range of media communicate information about eating healthy food and exercising for good health. Unless special conferences, campaigns, and community programs also target publics, a response to these messages may not be apparent (see Chapters 5 and 9).

FIGURE 1.1 | Changing fast food habits

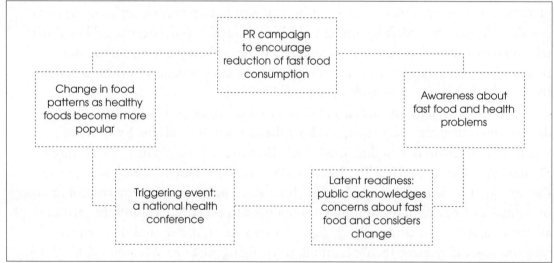

Source: Newsom, Turk & Kruckeberg 2007: 121

REFLECT AND DISCUSS

➤ Think about the messages you hear about fast food. Would you consider giving up fast food? Why?

➤ What triggering event might change your views about fast food consumption?

➤ What message about fast food would reach your group of friends and how would you communicate that message?

Public relations theory

The premise of James Grunig and Todd Hunt's theory is that it is more about the communication process than the communication itself (Center et al. 2008: 19). Grunig and Hunt propose the following:

➤ *Press agentry*: propagandistic; seeks media attention; focus is on promotion; a one-way communication model.

➤ *Public information*: disseminates accurate information but does not volunteer negative information or seek input; a one-way communication model.

➤ *Two-way asymmetrical:* identifies those messages most likely to gain support from targeted publics without having to change the behaviour of the organisation; thus it is manipulative. Change benefits the organisation but not necessarily the publics.

➤ *Two-way symmetrical*: uses bargaining, negotiation, and conflict resolution strategies to effect change in ideas, attitudes, and behaviours of both the organisation and its publics for mutual benefit.

This theory, or model, of public relations was integral to the excellence study in which 'Grunig and colleagues continued the quest to understand and improve public relations with a three-country, long-term study of public relations practice, in conjunction with the International Association of Business Communicators' (Edwards 2006: 147).

In later developments, Grunig (2001) acknowledged that the mixed-motive model includes a mix of asymmetric and symmetric communication in which dialogue and negotiation are part of a win–win but where publics' and dominant coalitions' perspectives may dominate in an asymmetrical mode. The five models of practice are found in most textbooks and even though critics of the model have pointed to its limitations, the Grunig and Hunt model has a place in framing thinking and rationale for public relations. It is suggested that the normative model of practice proposed by Grunig and Hunt has been the catalyst for much theoretical development and discussion wherever public relations is practised, and that is valuable.

Joy Chia

Practising public relations

'I have always wanted to be a public relations practitioner because I love working with people.'

This is a comment frequently made by those aspiring to be public relations practitioners. When prompted as to what public relations might include, or what they think about public relations practice, they have a limited understanding of public relations sectors, roles, and activities and what 'I love working with people' might actually mean.

A further observation is that students often ask for public relations experience in a public relations consultancy or agency as that seems to be the most familiar area of practice to them. Less well known is the fact that a public relations practitioner might be responsible for such events as:

➤ a campaign to increase blood donations to a blood bank
➤ managing a speedway racing event with a focus on families and family involvement
➤ developing a position paper on climate change for a government department.

REFLECT AND DISCUSS

> ➤ Why do you want to be a public relations practitioner?
> ➤ What do you expect you will be doing in your career?

New public relations roles and positions are emerging. One of the most rewarding experiences for an educator is to see graduates breaking new ground by being the first public relations practitioner in an organisation or changing the public relations role in an organisation. In Australia, New Zealand, and Asia, organisations exist that have never before employed a public relations practitioner, so it is heartening to see these organisations begin to appreciate the need for such a position and expand their view of what public relations is, its resourcefulness and creativity.

As public relations grows, 'small business people and managers need to know what public relations is today and how it works' (Saffir 2007: 12), and every sector—government, not-for-profit, corporate, and private—needs to be alert to the profession's diversity. Development of new positions and ways to manage public relations are integral to the ingenuity and positioning of the profession on its path to maturity and professionalism.

Internal or inhouse public relations is the most common role, described by Seitel (2007: 94) as 'a staff professional in a public relations department of a corporation, university, hospital, sports franchise, political campaign, religious institution, and so on whose task is to support the primary business of the organisation'. The inhouse practitioner has the opportunity to develop expertise about their organisation and develop long-term relationships with stakeholders and the community.

Consultants are 'a line professional in a public relations agency, where the primary task is to help the organization' (Seitel 2007: 94). In a consultancy or agency, practitioners work for one or more clients for a fee and these fees vary according to the experience of the consultant; senior consultants will command much more than junior staff. Fees and charges are either billed by the hour, through a fixed project fee, or through a retainer. In retainer contracts or those that 'retain the services of a professional consultant, usually exclusive of competitors' (Franklin 2000: 86), clients know that they are in a long-term relationship, which is good, but consultants cannot assume that the client is satisfied with their work, no matter how it is carried out. Freelance individuals work for themselves and are often employed short-term by an inhouse practitioner but could continue with this working relationship for many years.

Consultants offer both generalised services and niche market expertise, which they have developed from experience gained through working with a diversity of clients on many and varied communication scenarios. As a result, they often develop specialisations in particular areas. This means that part of their role may be knowledge transfer to get the client up to speed but most important is the need to manage the expectations so there is no gap between what clients expect and what the consultant can deliver. Consultants need to:

➤ understand the culture of the organisation that hires them
➤ challenge perceptions of the client about themselves and their target publics
➤ be transparent and open in their dealings with clients so that understanding of each other's perspective is central to the development and growth of the consultant–client relationship.

In whatever capacity public relations practice takes place there are many similarities in all sectors and there is, across all these sectors, a need for:

➤ sound ethical practice guided by codes of ethics that are relevant and active
➤ open, transparent, two-way or multiway internal and external communication
➤ acknowledgment of the need for good relationships with key publics and audiences, and sustaining and building these relationships
➤ recognition and support of management in public relations campaigns and public relations programs
➤ good understanding of research
➤ the skill to manage new and traditional media
➤ local and global understanding of public relations, with sensitivity to and awareness of intercultural matters.

The roles and the practice of public relations in government, not-for-profit and private sectors are followed up in Chapter 6, and discussed further in Chapters 7 and 8.

Joy Chia

REFLECT AND DISCUSS

➤ List ten organisations that employ public relations practitioners.

➤ List ten skills that these practitioners would need for effective practice.

➤ List ten functions they might perform.

Public relations sectors and positions

As the following statistics show, most graduates will be employed in internal public relations positions rather than as consultants.

FIGURE **1.2** \ Public relations practice sectors: results from the 2006 trends survey

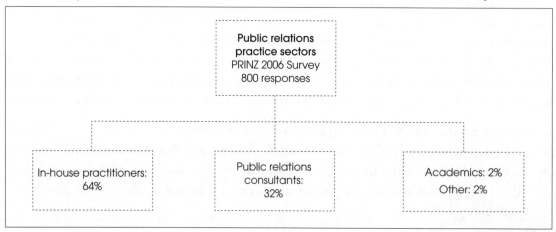

Source: *PRINZ Annual Report 2007*

The 2006 New Zealand PRINZ survey, which collected 800 responses, indicated that six out of ten practitioners or 64 per cent work inhouse, 32 per cent are consultants, and 2 per cent are academics; the remaining 2 per cent, 'other', might include freelance and private practitioners.

A 2004 survey by the Hong Kong Public Relations Professionals' Association found that of the 257 respondents, 33 per cent were consultants, 6.3 per cent worked in the not-for-profit sector, 5 per cent in transportation, manufacturing, and education, 12.5 per cent in government, 8.6 per cent in financial services, 16 per cent were others, and 1.2 per cent worked in professional services.

In a 2005–6 survey conducted in Singapore, of 501 practitioners, 70 per cent were from the private sector, 17 per cent were government practitioners, and 13 per cent were consultancies, with the main consultancy services being media relations, strategic planning and counselling, writing and editing, and event planning.

Australian statistics indicate that the majority of practitioners work inhouse for organisations. In 2008, of the 2648 members of the Public Relations Institute of Australia, 26 per cent worked inhouse in the corporate sector, 19 per cent in government, 13 per cent in the not-for-profit sector, and 31 per cent worked for consultancies; 11 per cent were academics or students studying public relations.

What do public relations people do?

In this introductory chapter we also become familiar with the components or the fundamentals of public relations practice and what a practitioner might do. We have begun to explore this in the definitions of the profession but the specifics of practice include the diverse skills outlined in Table 1.1 below.

TABLE **1.1** \ Practising public relations

Public relations components	Understanding public relations practice
Internal communication management	• Internal publications, managing bulletin boards, managing organisations' blogs, collaborative website management, position papers for management, writing speeches. • Employee relations, working with HR and management to keep employees informed, included and motivated in all aspects of an organisation's public relations programs, policy development, and decision making. • Developing media relations, placement of appropriate communication to media.
External networking and multifaceted communication, relationship building	• Managing online communication through interactive websites, blogging, and new media initiatives. • Meeting and collaborating with community leaders and stakeholders and organising events to celebrate organisations' success and role in the community. • Promoting corporate social responsibility in partnerships with other organisations. • Promotion and publicity for organisations.
Issues management/crisis management, reputation and brand management	• Monitoring issues, or the ongoing matters of concern to the organisation and/or society as a whole, providing media training for crisis management, and taking a leading role at the time of the crisis to inform, manage the crisis team, and support management, and managing an organisation's reputation.
Research	• Conducting interviews, focus groups, and internal audits, requesting market research for strategic thinking and planning, evaluating and reviewing all programs and campaigns.

Public relations components	Understanding public relations practice
Public affairs	• Lobbying, preparing position papers, putting forward proposals for new government campaigns, and promoting government initiatives. • Developing white papers and opening up communication for community consultation.
Investor relations and financial public relations	• Promoting financial services in a way that can be understood by those who access the service of credit unions, banks, and other providers of financial service and promoting these services. • Shareholders are one stakeholder group who expect service and support.
Developing a new public relations position for an organisation	• Recognising the need for public relations in an organisation and establishing public relations functions and components of public relations.

These components make up much of this book, although investor relations and financial public relations can be followed up in more advanced public relations studies, and the ethics and codes of practice underpin all areas of practice. The nuts and bolts of practice are sometimes part of marketing public relations or integrated marketing communication as the two disciplines have much in common. Chapter 2 unravels some of the developments in these disciplines as Harris and Wheelen (2006: 3) suggest that 'public relations has driven spectacularly successful marketing programs' and this has had a considerable impact on both professional fields.

This is the beginning.

Your introduction to public relations has opened up the links between the layers of theory and practice; now you need to take time to research, read as many magazines, articles, and updates about public relations as possible, visit websites important to contemporary practice, and keep in touch with public relations developments through meeting other practitioners and getting to know what public relations means to them, why it is important, and what is making the profession so important to organisations and society.

CHAPTER **SUMMARY**

➤ Public relations is a dynamic profession that is expanding its areas of practice.
➤ Public relations is understood and practised differently in different cultures but there are also many similarities between cultures.
➤ Public relations is underpinned by ethical and transparent practice.
➤ Publics and audiences are groups of people with common interest or needs; stakeholders have a stake or interest in an organisation.

➤ Public relations theory underpins and directs practice.

➤ Public relations practitioners practise primarily as inhouse practitioners; about one-third are public relations consultants hired by organisations for specific projects and programs.

➤ Public relations components or fundamentals of practice range from public affairs to internal and external public relations, research, and counselling, to financial public relations management.

➤ Many new public relations positions are emerging and are sometimes part of marketing communications and other interdisciplinary practice.

CASE STUDY 'BOYCOTT THE VILLAINS' CAMPAIGN

During 2008, fuel costs skyrocketed. During this period, the 'Boycott the Villains' campaign was developed by Adam Thomson, public relations manager of the Royal Automobile Association of South Australia (RAA). Community engagement was critical to this campaign and is an indication of how the role of public relations is changing.

The RAA is a member-based organisation dedicated to providing roadside assistance to more than 571 000 SA motorists. It also provides security, travel, and touring services as part of a broad range of member benefits and is the motorists' advocate as it continues to lobby state and federal governments on legislative change, petrol, infrastructure funding, road maintenance, and safety issues.

GOAL

The overarching goal of the campaign was to highlight the previous trend of unexplained fuel price increases in the metropolitan area in the lead-up to the Easter long weekend, and to ensure oil companies were held accountable.

OBJECTIVES

This campaign had three primary objectives, namely:

1 to reinforce to consumers that the discount cycle results in Tuesday being the cheapest day for purchasing fuel

2 to educate motorists who were unable to buy fuel during the cheapest part of the discount cycle as to what was a reasonable price to pay on any other day

3 to put petrol companies on notice that fuel prices would be monitored in the lead-up to and over the Easter weekend.

Joy Chia

RESEARCH

➤ The RAA monitors and tracks petrol prices daily, and fields an average of 1000 fuel-related enquiries per week.

➤ The RAA was concerned that fuel prices would be inflated pre-Easter to capitalise on the increased road usage; over the preceding twelve months it also identified erratic pricing behaviour by the Australian oil industry, particularly price hikes prior to long weekends.

➤ Pre-campaign community engagement was a crucial aspect of the research phase, with data indicating that motorists did not generally make an informed purchase decision when buying petrol.

➤ Pre-campaign media coverage identified that often media failed to grasp the complexity of petrol pricing arrangements. Inaccurate information served to further confuse the market and create blanket scaremongering and panic buying among motorists. One important consideration of this campaign was not to encourage media to engage in price speculation (that is, how high petrol could rise) because operators increase pump prices to fall in line with incorrect media predictions.

PUBLICS AND AUDIENCES

Primary publics and audiences were identified as:

➤ RAA members
➤ SA motorists
➤ petrol companies
➤ service station operators/proprietors
➤ metropolitan media
➤ key industry stakeholders, including the Motor Trade Association and UniGas.

Secondary publics and audiences included:

➤ state and federal politicians
➤ RAA staff and contractors
➤ other Australian motoring clubs and the Automobile Association of Australia (AAA).

COMMUNICATION STRATEGY

➤ The campaign provided information to consumers of LPG, and unleaded and diesel fuel types.

➤ Planning began six weeks prior to Easter; the campaign commenced three weeks out.

➤ Campaign briefings were conducted with key industry stakeholder groups, including the Motor Trade Association and national bodies such as UniGas and BP, as well as to the Australian Automobile Association and other motoring clubs.

➤ On the start date, 14 March 2007, *The Advertiser* ran a page three article titled 'RAA sets fuel targets' and explained the daily fuel price targets that would be provided to consumers. This was followed up the next day in the *National Nine News* evening bulletin with a regular price graphic and live read to promote the target prices for the following day.

➤ At 7 a.m. each morning, metropolitan media were provided with that day's fuel targets designed to target morning peak commuters and, via media coverage, to maintain pressure on the fuel industry to set reasonable pump prices.

➤ Drivers were encouraged to adapt their purchase behaviour to take advantage of the cheaper Tuesday discount prices rather than wait until the Thursday prior to Easter to fill up.

➤ An initial fact sheet, followed up by daily price updates, was provided to RAA's front line office and call centre staff, who were in the ideal position to answer basic fuel-related questions from members, as well as being able to advise what the target fuel prices for the day were.

➤ Predicting target fuel prices was an unprecedented move by RAA, and in many respects this was a test campaign to gauge member reaction about the association providing this degree of information and whether it was of use.

IMPLEMENTATION

The RAA wrote to all major oil companies operating in Australia, demanding that they 'do the right thing' with regards to Easter fuel prices; it also wrote to the ACCC requesting that additional resources be allocated to monitor pre-Easter fuel prices and investigate recent unexplained increases in refinery profit margins.

Channel Nine and the *Advertiser* were engaged as media partners, with Channel Nine screening the next day's pricing targets in its evening news bulletin; the *Advertiser* printed them in the daily newspaper.

Media releases were sent out each morning to metropolitan media with the daily target prices; the releases resulted in outstanding media coverage.

The RAA website was updated daily with price targets, and media releases included promotion of the website as a viable source of consumer information.

Fuel price boards with magnetic numbers were installed in all metropolitan RAA offices; numbers were changed daily by staff to reflect that day's fuel targets.

A number of underpinning public relations activities also occurred, including proactive engagement of talkback shows with key topics of interest regarding fuel and fuel pricing to further educate the community and encourage informed debate.

Key RAA staff received daily information bulletins on the campaign, along with the daily price targets.

Joy Chia

BUDGET

The decision was made to draw on inhouse public relations and graphic design skills, which resulted in the campaign being developed and implemented without external assistance or cost.

RESULTS AND EVALUATION

FUEL PRICES

Leading up to and over Easter, Adelaide recorded some of the lowest fuel prices nationally; this continued into the following month.

INDUSTRY REACTION

On the campaign launch day, a number of petrol outlets were spotted by media winding back price boards to fall in line with the RAA's price targets. Later, Caltex made the unprecedented move of publicly committing itself to responsible pricing over Easter.

The Australian Institute of Petroleum (AIP) sought information on the methodology employed in setting the target price. A detailed response was sent with an invitation to contact the Public Affairs department if the AIP was not satisfied with the response or required further clarification: no further correspondence was received.

MEMBER FEEDBACK

The RAA received approximately 600 letters, emails, and website responses from motorists who praised the campaign and urged an expansion to become a daily activity. Many comments flagged a better understanding of fuel pricing and the weekly discount cycle.

FEDERAL GOVERNMENT REACTION

One highlight occurred when the federal treasurer echoed the RAA's call for the ACCC to monitor pre-Easter petrol prices, and take action against any operators found to be profiteering.

MEDIA COVERAGE

Metropolitan media coverage was outstanding. Every television network sought daily RAA comment on fuel pricing issues during this campaign.

Fifty items that made a direct reference to the target fuel price campaign were noted in a three week period. When syndicated broadcasts are included, this figure increased to 93 items.

Over the campaign period, an additional 81 items were featured on fuel pricing, making 174 items in total.

Strong media take-up followed the campaign announcement. Radio station 5AA led AM radio coverage; it promoted the daily target fuel price on nine occasions. ABC Radio 891 made mention of the campaign only twice but, through syndication, was responsible for ten mentions.

A GREAT RESULT

The campaign resulted in a State Golden Target Award for the RAA, and, most importantly, satisfied members as part of successful community engagement.

FURTHER READING

Broom, G, Cutlip, S & Center, A & 2009, *Effective Public Relations*, 10th edn, Prentice Hall, Englewood Cliffs.
Theaker, A 2008, *The Public Relations Handbook*, 3rd edn, Routledge, Abingdon.

WEB RESOURCES

Global Alliance, at www.globalpr.org.
Hong Kong Public Relations Institute, at www.prpa.com.hk.
International Public Relations Association, at www.ipra.org.
Institute of Public Relations of Singapore, at www.iprs.org.sg.
Public Relations Global Alliance, at www.globalpr.org.
Public Relations Institute of Australia, at www.pria.com.
Public Relations Institute of New Zealand, at www.prinz.org.nz.
Royal Automobile Association of South Australia, at www.raa.net.

REFERENCES

Berger, B 2007, 'Public Relations and Organizational Power', cited in E Toth, *The Future of Excellence in Public Relations and Communication Management. Challenges for the Next Generation*, Lawrence Erlbaum, Mahwah, 221–34.
Bruning, S & Ledingham, J 1999, 'Relationships Between Organizations and Publics: Development of a Multi-Dimensional Organization–Public Relationship Scale, *Public Relations Review*, 25(2): 157–70.
Bruning, S, McGrew, S & Cooper, M 2006, 'Exploring University–Community Engagement from the Perspective of Community Members and Satisfaction Evaluations', *Public Relations Review*, 32(1): 125–30.
Center, A, Jackson, P, Smith, S & Stansberry, F 2008, *Public Relations Practice. Managerial Case Studies and Problems*, 7th edn, Prentice Hall, Upper Saddle River.

Chia, J 2005, *Relationship Management: Developing Relationship Management Parameters Critical to the Effective Management of Relationships Between Public Relations Consultants and Their Clients*, PhD thesis, University of South Australia, Adelaide.

Chia, J 2006, 'Measuring the Immeasurable', *PRism Online Journal*, 4(2), available at http://praxis.massey.ac.nz/evaluation.html, for PRism Special Edition on Measurement and Evaluation.

Chia, J 2008, 'Managing Complexity as Relational Opportunity', paper presented at the International Communication Association Conference, Montreal, 21–6 May.

Chia, J & Peters, M 2009, 'Making a Difference. Employees as Social Capital Investors', paper presented at the European Conference on Intellectual Capital, Holland University of Applied Sciences, The Netherlands, 28–29 April.

Cutlip, S, Center, A & Broom, G 2006, *Effective Public Relations*, 9th edn, Prentice Hall, Englewood Cliffs.

Dato Mohd Hamden Haji Adnan 2004, *Government Public Relations*, Asian Pacific Public Relations Academy, Selangor.

Deatherage, C & Hazleton, V 1998, 'Effects of Organizational Worldviews on the Practice of Public Relations: A Test of the Theory of Public Relations Excellence', *Journal of Public Relations Research*, 10(1): 57–71.

Edwards, L 2006, 'Public Relations Origins: Definitions and History', in R Tench & E Yeomans, *Exploring Public Relations*, Prentice Hall, Harlow.

Fawkes, J 2008, 'Public Relations and Communication', in A Theaker, *The Public Relations Handbook*, 3rd edn, Routledge, Abingdon.

Franklin, B 2000, 'Do I Need a PR Consultancy?', in F Jefkins, *Public Relations for Your Business*, Management Books, Chalford, 86–95.

Gower, K 2006, 'Public Relations Research at the Crossroads', *Public Relations Review*, 18(2): 177–90.

Gregory, A 2008, 'Public Relations and Management', in A Theaker, *The Public Relations Handbook*, 3rd edn, Routledge, Abingdon, 51–69.

Grunig, J 2001, 'Two-way Symmetrical Public Relations, Past, Present and Future', in R Heath, *Handbook of Public Relations*, Sage, Thousand Oaks.

Grunig, J & Hon, L 1999, *Guidelines for Measuring Relationships in Public Relations*, Institute for Public Relations Commission on PR Measurement and Evaluation, University of Florida, retrieved from www.instituteforpr.com, 13 June 2004.

Grunig, J & Huang, Y-H 2000, 'From Organisational Effectiveness to Relationship Indicators: Antecedents of Relationships, Public Relations Strategies, and Relationship Outcomes', in J Ledingham & S Bruning, *Public Relations as Relationship Management: A Relational Approach to the Study and Practice of Public Relations*, Lawrence Erlbaum, Mahwah.

Grunig, J & Hunt, T 1984, *Managing Public Relations*, Harcourt Brace, Fort Worth.

Guth, D & Marsh, C 2007, *Public Relations. A Values-Driven Approach*, cases edition, 3rd edn, Allyn & Bacon, Boston.

Guth, D & Marsh, C 2009, *Public Relations. A Values-Driven Approach*, cases edition, 4th edn, Allyn & Bacon, Boston.

Harris, T & Whalen, P 2006, *The Marketer's Guide to Public Relations in the Twenty-First Century*, Thomson Higher Education, Mason.

Heath, R & Coombs, T 2006, *Today's Public Relations. An Introduction*, Sage, Thousand Oaks.

Holtzhausen, D 2005, 'Public Relations Practice and Political Change in South Africa', *Public Relations Review*, 31: 407–16.

Hung, C-J, 2007, 'Toward the Theory of Relationship Management in Public Relations: How to Cultivate Relationships', in E Toth, *The Future of Excellence in Public Relations and Communication Management, Challenges for the Next Generation*, Lawrence Erlbaum, Mahwah, 443–76.

Kent, L & Taylor, M 2007, 'Beyond Excellence: Extending the Generic Approach to International Public Relations. The Case of Bosnia', *Public Relations Review*, 33: 10–20.

Kreps, G 2008, 'A Weickian Approach to Public Relations and Crisis Management', in T L Hansen-Horn & B Neff, *Public Relations: From Theory to Practice*, Allyn & Bacon, Boston, 20–30.

Lattimore, D, Baskin, O, Heiman, S, Toth, E & Leuven, J 2004, *Public Relations: The Profession and the Practice*, McGraw Hill, New York.

L'Etang, J 2008, *Public Relations, Concepts, Practice and Critique*, Sage, London.

Ledingham, J & Bruning, S 2000, 'A Longitudinal Study of Organization–Public Relationship Dimensions: Defining the Role of Communication in the Practice of Relationship Management', in J Ledingham & S Bruning (eds), *Public Relations as Relationship Management: A Relational Approach to the Study and Practice of Public Relations*, Lawrence Erlbaum, Mahwah.

Ledingham, J & Bruning, S 1998, 'Relationship Management in Public Relations: Dimensions of an Organization–Public Relationship', *Public Relations Review*, 24(1): 55–65.

Mackey, S 2004, 'Public Relations Theory', in J Johnston & C Zawawi, *Public Relations, Theory and Practice*, Allen & Unwin, Sydney, 41–63.

Matera, F & Artigue, R 2000, *Public Relations: Campaigns and Techniques*, Allyn & Bacon, Boston.

Motion, J, Leitch, S & Cliff, S 2003, 'Public Relations in Australasia: Friendly Rivalry, Cultural Diversity, and Global Focus', in K Sriramesh & D Vércîc 2003, *The Global Public Relations Handbook*, Lawrence Erlbaum, Mahwah, 121–41.

Murphy, P 2000, 'Symmetry, Contingency, Complexity: Accommodating Uncertainty in Public Relations Theory', *Public Relations Review*, 26(4): 447–62.

Newsom, D, Turk, J V & Kruckeberg, D 2007, *This is PR: The Realities of Public Relations*, 9th edn, Thomson Wadsworth, Belmont.

Okay, Aydemir & Okay, Alya 2008, 'The Place of Theory in Public Relations', in T L Hansen-Horn & B Neff, *Public Relations: From Theory to Practice*, Allyn & Bacon, Boston, 281–96.

Parkinson, M & Ekachai, D 2006, *International and Intercultural Public Relations: A Campaign Case Approach*, Allyn & Bacon, Boston.

Saffir, L 2007, *PR on a Budget: Free, Cheap, and Worth the Money Strategies for Getting Noticed*, Kaplan Publishing, New York.

Seitel, F 2007, *The Practice of Public Relations*, 10th edn, Prentice Hall, Upper Saddle River.

Sriramesh, K & Vércîc, D 2003, *The Global Public Relations Handbook*, Lawrence Erlbaum, Mahwah.

Stanton, R 2007, *Media Relations*, Oxford University Press, Melbourne.

Stark, K & Kruckeberg, D 2003, 'Ethical Obligations of Public Relations in an Era of Globalisation', *Journal of Communication Management*, 8(1): 29–40.

Joy Chia

Ströh, U 2007, 'An Alternative Postmodern Approach to Corporate Communication Strategy', in E Toth, *The Future of Excellence in Public Relations and Communication Management, Challenges for the Next Generation*, Lawrence Erlbaum, Mahwah, 199–219.

Tan, Y S & Soh, Y P 1994, *The Developments of Singapore's Modern Media Industry*, Times Academic Press, Singapore.

Taylor, M 2004, 'Exploring Public Relations in Croatia Through Relational Communication and Media Richness Theories, *Public Relations Review*, 30: 145–60.

Taylor, M & Doerfel, M 2005, 'Another Dimension to Explicating Relationships: Measuring Inter-organizational Linkages', *Public Relations Review*, 31: 121–9.

Theaker, A 2004, *The Public Relations Handbook*, 2nd edn, Routledge, Abingdon.

Theaker, A 2008, *The Public Relations Handbook*, 3rd edn, Routledge, Abingdon.

Tilson, D & Alozie, E 2004, *Toward the Common Good, Perspectives in International Public Relations*, Pearson, Boston.

Tymson, C, Lazar, P & Lazar, R 2002, *The New Australian and New Zealand Public Relations Manual*, Tymson Communications, Sydney.

Watson, T & Noble, P 2007, *Evaluating Public Relations. A Best Practice Guide to Public Relations Planning, Research and Evaluation*, 7th edn, Chartered Institute of Public Relations, with Kogan Page, London.

Wilcox, D, Cameron, G, Ault, P & Agee, W 2007, *Public Relations. Strategies and Tactics*, 8th edn, Allyn & Bacon, Boston.

Wu, M-Y 2005, 'Can American Public Relations Theories Apply to Asian Cultures?', *Public Relations Quarterly*, 50(3): 10–16.

Chapter **2**

TRENDS AND DEVELOPMENTS

Joy Chia

PRACTITIONER PROFILE   PUBLIC RELATIONS TRENDS

Corporate Conversation, based in South Australia, is a high-energy media and corporate communications firm that specialises in helping fast-growing businesses communicate effectively with key target audiences. Managing Director Chris Doudle and Senior Consultant Louise Close talk about what they see as the latest trends in public relations.

Australia's evolving business environment is driving change in companies' communication and public relations needs. In recent years, the widespread skills shortage and increasing demand for organisations to be good corporate citizens have been responsible for a shift in communication priorities. For any public relations strategy to be effective, it must be based on an organisation's key business needs.

Increasingly, our clients are telling us that their most urgent business need is to find and attract the best staff. Many businesses are struggling to keep up with customer demand so they are seeking communication strategies that will position

them as employers of choice. They want communication outcomes that promote and reinforce the strength of their employer brand.

Highlighting a company's achievements and workplace philosophies sends positive messages to potential recruits and makes existing employees feel good about their organisation. Demonstrating good corporate social responsibility is also moving higher on the public relations agenda.

The companies we work with are focused on doing the right thing by their customers, employees and the broader community. They seek our assistance to help communicate their efforts to minimise their environmental impact, be accountable for their actions, and conduct their business in an open and transparent manner.

Other trends in public relations include a maturing of the profession in line with a growing understanding of the importance of a strategic approach. For companies looking to grow their bottom line, activity that does not meet specific needs and objectives is a waste of time and resources.

Public relations must be strategic, targeted, and results driven, whether helping companies to attract new staff, expand into new markets, or raise corporate profile among key decision makers. As public relations professionals, this means ensuring that our activity remains focused on opportunities that help build our clients' businesses.

CHAPTER **AIMS**

By the end of this chapter you should be able to:

➤ understand what is shaping the profession
➤ understand the international and local context of the public relations profession
➤ develop an understanding of some ways to respond to changing environments in the profession.

What is shaping twenty-first century public relations?

The fact that the public relations profession is growing is exciting. Why it is growing and what could affect the increasing demand for practitioners and public relations educators is the focus of this chapter. Global and local trends will continue to change the operating environment for public relations, in the same way that societal demands have already shaped it. The profession will remain relevant if it continues to adapt its practice to respond to new ways to capture the publics' attention, and to be collaborative with multiple parties and stakeholders to achieve the best possible outcomes for organisations and society.

One of the main factors to shape the profession is the realisation described by Stark and Kruckeberg (2003: 39) that the 'most important stakeholder is society itself' and that organisations do not exist as individual entities surviving in a vacuum with little need to respond to society and the community. This mandates twenty-first century public relations to take a critical role in proactively engaging with society and the community. Public relations professionals have an ethical obligation to act responsibly 'because of their influence on society' (Starck & Kruckeberg 2003: 37) and, in doing so, need to be guided by their professional values and beliefs if their input to corporations' social aspirations is going to be relevant and meaningful. Stark and Kruckeberg emphasise that there is a need for public relations leadership to make communication transparent, so that practitioners are able to help develop productive organisational culture and positively influence organisational outcomes.

Organisations' expectations for timely, effective, and creative public relations programs have an impact on practitioners, who are working hard to meet the requirements of project managing and scheduling multiple public relations activities while also acting ethically and responsibly. In addition, ask any public relations practitioner about their daily demands and they will tell you that emails, text messages, and endless online communication exchanges have changed the way that they manage public relations activities and programs. Public relations practitioners' influence and relevance is challenged by the changing context of the communication environment of practice as we are facing very challenging times. As Devito (2008: 11) suggests:

> The American worker is exposed to more messages in one year than a person living in 1900 was in his or her entire life. The average employee now receives more than 50 emails daily. And in one day the average manager sends and receives more than 100 documents.

Not surprisingly, the PRIA website describes the profession of public relations as 'mentally and physically demanding and deadline driven', and points to the reality of practice where practitioner demands have increased because of the multimedia environment in which the profession functions. Edelman's senior vice-president, Christopher Hannegan, indicates that blogging, for example, has developed 'grassroots relationships with customers that simply did not exist before' (Flynn 2006: 180); these extensive relationships need monitoring, development, and careful management, which adds to the demands of public relations practice. These changing circumstances present opportunities and prospects for creative and innovative practice and even better project management skills.

REFLECT AND DISCUSS

➤ Find some references on time management and create a list of ten work practices that will help you avoid wasting time on the job.

➤ If you were blogging about a public relations program concerned with binge drinking, organ donation, or the rapid rise of salmonella poisoning cases, who might be engaging with you online?

What is influencing public relations practice?

This chapter explores the rationale for public relations practice as it responds to global and international trends and influences, online communication changes and new ways to communicate, and changing professional demographics. The public relations profession retains its strong corporate role and is now becoming more involved in community relations and supporting not-for-profit programs with an emphasis on corporate responsibility and community engagement.

These may be 'turbulent times' (Davis 2003: 162) for public relations as organisations find themselves 'repeatedly challenged by a variety of constituencies or publics to demonstrate that they are socially responsible'. As organisations are questioned about their programs and organisational activities, and when issues-specific publics (publics who advocate and campaign for or against a particular issue) oppose an organisation's programs, practitioners deliberate how to work with these publics and how to manage diverse public interests responsibly and transparently. Practitioners are aware of the considerable effort required to work with clients, constituencies, and stakeholders so that the best possible outcomes are achieved for all parties.

Harris and Fleisher facilitate our understanding of global trends and why we need to be conversant with the way these trends influence public affairs globally. Public affairs is defined as the 'totality of government affairs or relations' and 'the policy formulation process of public and corporate stakeholder programs' (2005: xxxii) that impacts public relations practice at all levels.

Harris and Fleisher put forward the following key points:

➤ Public policy and government involvement is something that more publics want and yet many do not want governments to be too involved in policy formulation and regulation. Practitioners hired to consult and advise governments on matters of public concern, or public affairs managers working for government, would be aware that the public often cries out for change to health and transport policies and services and yet they do not want governments to be too powerful or to regulate excessively.

➤ Effective communication management means that 'transparency and disclosure are now the norm' (9). In the past, information was disseminated to the public on a need to know basis, which was considered adequate as publics were informed about what was thought to be necessary for them to know. Publics in many parts of the world are now better informed than ever before and they demand accountability from all sectors: corporate, government, private, and not-for-profit organisations. When information is withheld, organisations may suffer severe consequences, such as the collapse of Enron. When Enron ceased trading it was the end of an organisation that had communicated poorly to its publics and audiences, especially shareholders. Enron's public relations department was ignorant of the organisation's affairs so they had no opportunity to communicate openly and accurately to the community and their stakeholders (Lattimore et al. 2004: 281).

➤ Fleisher and Harris emphasise that ethical practice is paramount to public relations professionalism and best practice. Transparency and accountability affect codes of practice and the way they are administered by the professional body managing and directing communication, public affairs, and private practice. These codes are important because, as corporate scandals become more common, there is a growing 'distrust of business' (9). The trust barometer (see Edelman's trust barometer in the next Reflect and Discuss activity) indicates that many publics are sceptical of business.

There is also criticism about the effectiveness of codes of practice. Having a code of ethics is often perceived as an ineffective way to ensure ethical practice and responsible behaviour. Gower (2008) indicates that many codes of practice emphasise that clients' confidentiality is essential, yet public relations practitioners must be open and honest in their communication to the public, which could mean client confidentiality cannot be maintained. Codes can be too general, which makes it difficult to know what is ethical and what is expected practice. One way to address this is to include case studies and examples of ethical practice or ethical responses that guide the practitioner to ethical decision making when it comes to contentious issues (see Chapter 4 for a more detailed discussion about ethical issues).

Another influence on public relations practice is the international context and increased tension between local–global perspectives. As the internet and other forms of media inform publics worldwide, activity at the local level is growing simultaneously as citizens become passionate about local issues and what is important to them. Activists may take a local and global position as they pressure local governments and influence wider public opinion. In these environments, public relations efforts can be effective if there is an understanding of local issues that has been developed by working with local experts and grasping the cultural perspective of local community issues.

Community engagement means that organisations take a proactive interest by identifying communal interests (Davis 2007), whose aim is to promote these interests for the benefit of the community. Heath and Coombs (2006: 83) contend that this is central to the 'rhetorical challenge' as the words that are used to say what organisations intend to do need to be reinforced in the process of developing community relationships and in putting organisations' desires into action.

Joy Chia

The key point in examining societal trends and their impact on public relations practice is to be aware of much of the discussion and research about ethics, ethical behaviour, accountability, and trust. Morley (2002: 31) suggests that public scrutiny of organisations has been fuelled by the 'global voice' as the reach of communication is increasingly global. This means that expectations in one part of the world could become the expectations of constituents worldwide. It is in this vast environment that public relations is practised and where examples such as the asbestos case referred to in Chapter 8 alert all practitioners to the far reaching consequences of failings in organisational accountability.

REFLECT AND DISCUSS

Visit www.edelman.com and read about the *Edelman Public Relations Report: Trust Barometer.*

➤ What findings in its most recent report might be relevant to your public relations practice?

➤ What does it mean to trust an organisation?

Key points from the Commission on Public Relations Education

In the same way that Harris and Fleisher put forward their viewpoints about trends impacting publics relations and communication management, the *Report of the Commission on Public Relations Education* (2006: 6) recommends that there be:

> more emphasis on ethics and transparency, new technology, integration of messages and tools, interdisciplinary problem solving, diversity, global perspectives and research and results measurement.

The commission puts forward the need for a synthesis of education and practice as the profession requires theoretical and practical credentials to manage in complex environments. The commission's findings, derived from research undertaken primarily in the USA, have relevance to our understanding of international public relations trends as the surveys, interviews, and research conducted for the report provide insight into changing professional paradigms or conceptions of the profession.

The points considered by the commission affect all organisations and communities. There is no doubt that public relations is at the forefront of communication management, leading and directing communication to diverse publics in whatever culture it is practised. The commission's findings indicate that the value of public relations to an organisation is increasing.

Key points for consideration from the commission about ways to better understand and respond to public relations trends include the following:

➤ Public relations is a global profession so practitioners need to understand the impact of varying cultural values and beliefs on their practice. The commission suggests that there should be more opportunity for international exchange programs so that students can be exposed to different ways to manage public relations and understand how communication is translated and communicated in different environments.

➤ The commission points out that the internal needs of organisations and their internal audiences (and the peculiarities of academic settings and their internal audiences) affect public relations education and practice. There is considerable variation in organisations' development. The commission recognises that public relations has an increasing role in internal communication management wherever it is practised and it may need to manage organisations in crisis, or those going through a phase of internal disruption. The commission found that there is recognition of public relations practice and its value to organisations as many more organisations are appointing internal communication managers. Recent research suggests that employees are social capital investors as they are integral to organisations' decision making and success (Chia & Peters 2009). As such, employees are a key audience for communication about an organisation's business developments and plans. As transparency and accountability are important in all communication exchanges, the commission suggests that a focus on ethics should be integral to all aspects of public relations education, as it prepares students for ethical practice at each point of practice. The commission also recognised that public relations functions in an increasingly difficult ethical environment, so even though it appreciates the need for ethical, transparent public relations practice, it acknowledges that this may be difficult to achieve.

➤ The commission recognises that educators and practitioners need to encourage diversity in the workforce and in training and recruiting, thereby enabling a diverse 'mix of talent' (29) that has the skills to engage with diverse internal and external publics. An emphasis on diversity ensures that the profession is open, willing to consider a variety of points of view, and can manage public relations programs according to the needs of diverse publics. The Commission's perspective is much broader than that put forward by Harris and Fleisher as it points to the trend to develop new public relations positions to manage diverse and changing needs at every level of society. From researching with new tools, to social media developments that seem to be making the public gatekeepers of communication, the word 'public' has taken on new meaning. The public might include an online group of people who are passionate about saving whales but who have never met, and only communicate through YouTube. The public relations engagement with this group is likely to also be online. Others on the ground will be putting forward their point of view from a grassroots perspective. These changes are subtle but constant. Sense needs to be made of what is happening—the trends need to be seen—to bring them into our programs and public relations plans.

The commission suggests that internships focus on preparing students to manage new media, but this will only be successful if the profession is conversant with the latest technology. There is considerable evidence that the public relations profession has been very slow to develop the skills required to manage new media. Cutlip, Center and Broom (2006) and Seitel (2007) point out that more time is spent online than communicating offline and to an increasingly diversified audience, which makes communication management challenging as considerable effort and skill are required to effectively utilise online technology.

REFLECT AND DISCUSS

Read more about new media from one of the scholars mentioned in the following section and review an article on new media in the *Public Relations Review*.

➤ Identify three key points important to public relations management of new media.
➤ What are some of the challenges of new media management for the practitioner and the educator?

Might new media be obsolete tomorrow?

The commission's findings and its suggestions for public relations management point to the significant contribution that public relations can make and how new media can be part of that contribution. As Duhé, (2007: 58) puts it, 'In an era when so much information is stored, transmitted, and accessed electronically, organizations are transparent whether or not they choose to be'. Organisational websites, online annual reports, e-zines, and e-letters (online magazines and newsletters) may have large circulations or cater to specialised groups as webcasting and multimedia capabilities (Yale & Carothers 2001) take communication to varied publics, but many publics have only fleeting contact with organisations. Numerous short-term relationships develop as there are so many more exchanges with different publics than were in traditional forms of communication, such as face-to-face meetings or letting writing. Chia (2007) found that in public relations–client relationships these associations require two-way, multiway communication that has the potential to build connections online and offline. It seems, though, that the demands of online immediacy and the savvy, educated publics who some scholars (Seitel 2006; Chipchase & Theaker 2007) contend have changed public relations practice, might also make relationships transitory and less able to be managed.

Public scrutiny takes place online amid the complexity and uncertainty of online communication exchanges as messages are accessible to known and unknown constituents, clients, and customers. As Bates (2002: 329) points out, practitioners need to be:

> more sophisticated in knowing when and how to use technology more efficiently and effectively in order to avoid problems such as over-communicating (going to too many people with too many messages) and adding unnecessary time and expense to the process.

New communication tools will continue to emerge that will present some exciting ways to open up communication that is inclusive and welcoming. Even so, blogs, for example, or 'weblogs that communicate personal views on any topic imaginable' (Seitel 2007: 385) communicate endless points of view that may or may not be of value to organisations. Organisations are not yet ready for the extent of online communication that is important to straddle the international boundaries. The pace of online development requires investment in staff and an organisation's finances in order to realise the potential of new media for the benefit of organisations and publics (Gregory 2004).

As more publics become involved in environmental issues and changing social dynamics, the challenge for practitioners and educators worldwide is to be astute and skilled in managing new media as part of collaborative engagement with wide-ranging and often volatile publics. Gregory cautions (2004: 246) that 'activists groups who use the web to galvanise support, organise actions and propagate particular views through, for example rogue web sites' push their agenda as their stories reach the media, often representing only one point of view. Many organisations have not developed the interactive skills important to practice, (Hallahan 2008) skills that need to be constantly upgraded if they are to be effective.

As new media are changing at such a fast pace this book focuses on the possibilities and demands of new ways to communicate. Some of the tools include:

➤ *intranets* or internal communication, which targets internal publics
➤ *extranets*, which target external audiences and which require skilled management to not overload receivers, as Bates has suggested
➤ *podcasts* that have audio programs available online, 24 hours a day
➤ *YouTube* and *MySpace*, which increase online networking and exchange.

REFLECT AND DISCUSS

➤ As a practitioner managing tourism for your state or country, what new media tools would be important to your campaign to attract 10 per cent more tourists?
➤ What media, if any, do you think might become obsolete in the next five years and therefore may no longer be relevant to a tourism campaign or other public relations campaign?

International, intercultural public relations

Public relations on the international stage

When you walk into your office and access your computer you are part of an international communication network. When you are conducting an anti-smoking campaign in Australia or Singapore you are part of a wider network of public relations professionals managing a similar issue in many countries. Comparisons noted by the author on her visit to and participation in three anti-smoking campaign launches in Singapore, Australia and Canada included:

➤ Singapore public relations practitioners used mass media, including a front page article in the *Straits Times* to target a wide audience. They posted graphic pictures of a smoker's infected lungs and pasted graphic posters in the tunnels of the Singapore underground transport systems to promote the message about the health consequences of smoking. In this way many people were targeted and exposed to the messages.
➤ The Australian launch targeted young smokers and began to focus on passive smoking and an awareness campaign about smoking in cars and around children. The family focus was personalised and targeted.
➤ The Canadian campaign emphasised multiple health issues and the costs to the health system. Canadians were urged to take a responsible approach to smoking, alcohol, diet, and life management.

Each of these campaigns reflected what was relevant to each country at the time of the launch. The aims of these public relations campaign launches were similar as they intend to reduce smoking, but their goals and target groups were different.

When reference is made to global context and global perspectives it is important to understand a little more about global–international perspectives. Stephen Banks' (2000: 105) definition of international 'as a way of referring to communication activities that are performed in nations and multinational regions' suggests that international is 'not the same as global' as a global concept is broad and all encompassing, and includes myriad cultures and many different ethnic groups. To understand the internationalisation of public relations practice it is best understood as increasingly having global reach, as communication opens up between countries and within countries. Practising public relations in India, for example, is challenging, as there are twenty-five ethnic identities and 1652 mother tongues. Muslims, Sikhs, Hindus, and Christians represent many different ethnic groups, languages and religions that will interpret messages and communicate and respond to each other within the context of their particular ethnic group.

Changing economic, social, and political environments direct the way that we, as practitioners, manage communication to and from publics, stakeholders, and organisations. Countries that were part of communist or restrictive regimes, for example, suddenly find themselves needing to be open and accountable. The post-communist era comment mentioned in the preface represents a major adjustment from the previous regime in which people were told what to do and felt they could not trust either the government or party members. These days, organisations in those countries are employing public relations practitioners to assist them in communicating *with* target publics rather than *to* target publics. Changes to government and changing ideology in many countries suggest the need for communication and dialogue to reframe the way communication is disseminated and the need to work with these communities for the benefit of organisations and society (Matera & Artigue 2000: 236). A sudden change of government may not be readily accepted by diverse publics, who will continue to question the credibility of new and more open ways to communicate. In the 2008 global financial crisis, a change in economic circumstances changed the way governments responded to rapidly declining budgets. Communication about what was happening became more difficult because of the high level of concern on the part of all sectors of society, such as concerns about whether bank savings were safe and about the future of jobs.

Some scholars (Sriramesh & Vércîc, 2003: 17) indicate that 'when the media of a society are accessible to individuals or groups with different points of view, the resulting publicity will increase the fluidity of the environment for organizations', but they also point out that when various viewpoints are not considered (such as would be the case in a restrictive regime), then public relations will not be a necessary part of that culture or society. There might also be continued government control of the media and limited freedom of speech (Newsom, Turk & Kruckeberg 2007: 381), evident in some countries, such as China, which means that public relations messages need to be managed within these restrictions.

The increase in public relations positions and in public relations education providers in China, India, and many other parts of Asia suggests that as economies and political infrastructures open up increased communication will result, but this is likely to be in the form of information to society rather than through consultation and dialogue.

As public relations grows and internationalises its activities, consideration of cultural perspectives becomes critical to effective practice. The 'collectivistic' (Wu 2005: 12) rather than individualistic cultures (that is, cultures with an emphasis on the individual rather than on the team or group, or on the collective view point) prominent in many Asian cultures influence public relations activity in terms of the messages and channels used and the values espoused. Multicultural Australian and New Zealand societies are essentially individualistic but sections within the population have collectivist orientations, which is one reason why communication programs with Indigenous communities require a different approach. Public relations practitioners practising in any society will be more effective if they undertake research to better understand societal trends and developments and make themselves open to new and more appropriate ways to manage and communicate public relations programs beneficial and relevant to all publics.

Multinational companies that spread through many regions, embracing many cultures find that they represent 'multinational corporations at home' (Lattimore et al. 2004: 379) and that they 'help bridge the communication gap that inevitably exists between foreign operations and top management in the world headquarters'. Simultaneously, many more local public relations agencies are representing their respective regions and ethnic groups so that public relations programs can be managed appropriately.

Global or local: which is more important?

Communication at the local or global level might be:

➤ mediated communication, or communication that goes through a channel such as television or print media
➤ unmediated communication, or direct communication to the public such as communication on a website where publics have the opportunity to engage with organisations and key decision makers.

Even though there may be restrictions on mediated and unmediated communication, global awareness about issues has a way of empowering public opinion (Sharpe & Pritchard 2004) at the local and wider level, which in turn influences the need for public relations. In this way the profession grows worldwide and has a greater impact on organisations and community programs across the world. The concept of think global, act local requires:

➤ careful review of all public relations and marketing material that has been prepared
➤ an understanding of the operational procedures and protocol of the countries where brands are launched and public relations programs are developed
➤ an understanding of the country, region, and ethnic particularities
➤ respect for and observation of customs and cultural manners, as they are essential to good business
➤ awareness that technology might be convenient but time zones may be very different. Public relations practitioners find that their international counterparts are often working at times of the day that mean they cannot expect, for example, immediate responses to email.

In this chapter we have become aware of the internationalisation of public relations (see Chapter 13 for the specifics of public relations in Asia).

REFLECT AND DISCUSS

➤ If you are promoting recycling in China, Australia, and Malaysia what would your key message be?
➤ Would it be the same in each culture?

The public relations–marketing mix and broader perspectives

When we discuss trends impacting public relations practice, communication integration is prominent as the public relations–marketing mix attempts to unify its strategies for the best possible outcomes. For some practitioners and educators the public relations–marketing mix is integral to all practice; however, it is important to grasp how marketing and public relations complement each other and to know what is peculiar to public relations so that its distinctiveness can be retained within the integrated approach.

The interdisciplinary response to communication management is important and the strength of each profession is dependent on the synthesis of ideas and practices, and the recognition of the unique components of each profession.

Marketing, for example is defined as 'the management process whose goal is to attract and satisfy customers (or clients) on a long-term basis in order to achieve an organisation's economic objectivity' (Wilcox et al. 2007: 18). Marketers emphasise measured outputs that make their role in an organisation tangible. Public relations measurement and evaluation of public relations outputs is also becoming increasingly important.

The history of marketing education programs in Australian universities indicates that marketing has established itself as a discipline more so than public relations; public relations programs are sometimes situated within schools of business and marketing, others in humanities and arts schools. Public relations has been viewed as a subsidiary of marketing but this is no longer so. In the education sector the discipline is establishing scholarship and recognition at the same time as the value of public relations to organisations becomes well understood, an important finding of the Commission on Public Relations Education.

Various terms are used to describe the public relations–marketing mix, including 'marketing communications', 'marketing public relations', or 'integrated communication management', where inkind promotion, 'services, product or other consideration in exchange for publicity exposures offered' (Seitel 2007: 367) or using spokespeople to promote a product become part of the mix. A public relations activity to promote, target media, and develop online resources about a product will not actually sell the product but it assists in the marketing of it. Scholars (Harris & Whalen 2006: 8) suggest that public relations is now very important to strategic marketing, and that 'marketing public relations is the largest and fastest growing segment of a fast growing industry'. This is especially so since the measurement of public relations effectiveness has become more important to the profession. Even though Australian research (Watson & Noble 2007) indicates that there is insufficient focus on evaluation and measuring outputs directing public relations planning, it is developing.

One reason why 'public relations is of growing importance to companies' (Pelsmacker, Geuens & Van den Bergh 2007: 295) is the fact that organisations need a more sophisticated relationship with their publics and audiences. The messages about products and services—the traditional marketing messages—are only one part of the full range of communication tasks to be undertaken. As 'public relations messages often try to reach several key publics, beyond customers or potential customers' (Swann 2008: 14), their focus might be on internal communication, or on a group of activists who oppose organisations' profit-only focus and demand a socially responsible approach to the community. For the public relations practitioner to have a sound knowledge of marketing practice and principles makes public relations relevant and significant, and enables good support to be provided to the marketing–communication mix. Public relations, however, will continue to take a key role in every aspect of an organisation's function and life and it is taking a greater management and leadership role the more the profession is understood and respected (see Chapter 8).

Customers and clients need to be approached differently because they are tired of 'overload caused by the ever increasing number of customer messages' (Blythe 2006: 54). Public relations plays a subtle role in developing relationships with customers and clients. This is especially important as:

➤ customers are irritated by mass advertising as well as the minor differences between brands that no longer attract them
➤ there is considerable dissatisfaction with the value of products and the number of recalls and the concerns about being taken for a ride as product claims cannot be substantiated (Seitel 2007)
➤ customers also question the ethics and the social contribution of organisations.

In credit union research it was found that credit unions no longer refer to the people who use their services as 'customers'; their focus is now on 'members': engaging them, supporting them, and providing honest advice (Chia & Peters 2009). This is likely to be the case broadly across the financial services and other sectors. Employees are motivated to continue to work for an organisation that gives back to the community because a culture of giving back is embedded in its business practice. The context of an organisation's motivation to give back and engage with community involves 'three dimensions of social capital: structural, relational and communication' (Hazleton, Harrison-Rexrode & Kennan 2007: 94):

➤ The structural dimension is the way that relationships are set up and networks and connections developed with community.
➤ The relational dimension is where relationships are developed and reciprocal components of relationships become important.
➤ The communication dimension makes these relationships function, as organisations communicate to the community recipients and vice versa.

According to Chia and Peters (2009), credit unions are focusing more on the relationships dimension of their business as the narrow focus on marketing of their products was neither successful nor central to their ethos and organisational philosophy.

It seems that the societal demand for strategic communication is best delivered as part of ethical, socially responsible practice within the domain of public relations rather than marketing. The marketing–communications mix is related more 'to the commercial and the short term' (L'Etang 2006: 292). The public relations role is important in making the communication and marketing efforts acceptable and appropriate to consumers' needs so that these efforts are also responsible. Corporate social responsibility is part of a 'rights-based approach' (L'Etang 2006: 406) in view of the emphasis on responsibility and 'the rights and duties' (406) to others and, according to L'Etang, public relations practitioners are increasingly taking a lead in promoting and developing socially responsible programs. Public relations is concerned about long-term goodwill with the focus more on an organisation's contribution to society than the need to make a profit and run a viable business (Pelsmacker, Geuens & Van den Bergh 2007: 292). Christina Hazleton, Jill Harrison-Rexrode and William Kennan (2007: 92) contend that 'for public relations professionals, the ability to effectively and strategically use various communication strategies to develop personal and public relationships is essential for organizational success' so that the investment in organisations' social capital has the potential to develop as relationships and networks add value to organisations. Throughout this book you will find the strong theme that as relationships are developed, communities engaged and responsible practice emphasised, every part of public relations is about developing relationships internally and externally that are meaningfully managed with integrity and valued by organisations and society. The role of marketing is therefore recognised as an integrated approach to ethical communication management.

REFLECT AND **DISCUSS**

Think about bottled water and current debates about its necessity as a product. Endless media reports indicate that bottled water is unnecessary and expensive. The *Advertiser* (2008: 5) describes bottled water as a 'global social phenomenon'. In this report we are alerted to the fact that 180 billion litres of water is sold worldwide, a 60 per cent increase since 1998. The problem, according to US critics, is that 20 million barrels of oil are required to process the plastic bottles that contain the water and another 50 million barrels of oil are necessary to transport, process, and refrigerate bottled water. The report goes on to say that many of the plastic bottles end up in landfill. The integrated public relations–marketing approach needs to achieve sales of product while also recognising the environmental impacts of the product. If organisations want to promote a product they need to do so responsibly; increase in landfill is not responsible behaviour.

Search the internet and read other newspaper articles on bottled water.

➤ What does the public need to know about bottled water?
➤ What public relations initiatives and ethical responses would be appropriate when marketing bottled water?
➤ What is the key message?

Women taking the lead

One of the trends apparent in many cultures is that public relations students and practitioners are primarily female. About 80 per cent of students in classes in Australia, Singapore, Malaysia, and Hong Kong are female.

In the United Kingdom this proportion reaches 90 per cent (L'Etang 2006: 162) but L'Etang's account of development of the United Kingdom public relations profession indicates that this has been a recent development. In the 1950s the representation of women in the public relations profession was only 10 per cent, indicating a significant change in the profession in the past sixty years. The same pattern emerged in the USA where, over the past ten years, there has come to be an overrepresentation of women in public relations positions. However, Wilcox et al. (2007) note that there continues to be a gap in salaries of men and women, which is a matter of concern for all women contemplating a public relations career. These scholars indicate that women are often assigned technical positions that attract a lower salary whereas men are more readily appointed to managerial positions that attract better salaries. There is continued debate about the role of women in public relations practice and their need to be recognised as equals. Wilcox et al. (65) emphasise the following:

➤ Women find the communication environment more welcoming than, for example, newspaper or other media work.
➤ Women make more money in public relations than comparable female-dominated fields such as teaching.
➤ Women can begin a public relations consultancy without a great deal of capital.
➤ Women tend to be more proficient listeners and communicators than men.
➤ Women are more sensitive in managing dialogue and consultation.

As more women in the public relations profession have the opportunity to move into management roles it is hoped that the gender gap in terms of salary and opportunity will begin to close. Women may take a greater or lesser leadership role depending on their education, opportunities for advancement, and the cultural, political environment in which they function. Aldoory (2006) suggests that much of the focus on relationship management in public relations practice can be attributed to the key role women play as relationship specialists; women also manage two-way symmetric communication more effectively than men. However the understanding of the 'feminization' (Aldoory 2006: 400, cited in Toth) of public relations has not been well researched and more needs to be explored in this area. Women entering the field need to embrace professional opportunities, continue life-long learning with a view to lead, innovate, and develop practice skills and acumen. In the next ten years the gender balance may change as the public relations profession continues to change and grow.

Professionalism, accreditation, and formal recognition

While some people argue that public relations is not a profession (Newsom, Turk & Kruckeberg 2007), the discipline of public relations and developments in education and practice indicate that public relations is advancing its professional status. A profession, such as medicine or dentistry, is recognised when it 'has prescribed standards of educational preparation' (Wilcox et al. 2001: 55). Public relations has not as yet designated or prescribed qualifications for its practice although the accreditation requirements set by professional associations are leading to more practitioners who meet the accreditation requirements than those who do not. The move to accreditation as formal recognition to practice public relations is contentious as it prescribes a point of entry to the profession that has not previously been there. But more employers are hiring accredited practitioners and this trend is likely to continue as more accredited programs develop. This is a world-wide phenomenon: China, Malaysia, Singapore, New Zealand, Australia, Canada, the USA, and many other countries are developing accreditation programs and promote them as critical to ethical and effective, professional practice. Growing Asian markets such as China and India urgently need more graduates from accredited public relations programs but the profession seems to be moving ahead of the education sector's ability to provide graduates.

The view taken in this text is that accredited practitioners who have completed recognised, accredited public relations programs or exams have the skills for professional practice that are developed further on the job. It seems counterproductive for public relations to constantly be assessing whether it is a profession at a time when the profession is advancing and taking its place at the forefront of communication management. Further, the view that it is more important to 'act like a professional in the field' (Wilcox 2001: 55) is a positive and encouraging way to approach the understanding of professionalism as it implies ethical, accountable, and competent behaviour where practitioners adhere to the principles and standards of practice as part of a values-based profession.

In Australia the number of PRIA accredited programs that have been assessed and approved by the PRIA is increasing. A visit to the PRIA website will direct you to the complete list of accredited Australian degrees. There has been a strong focus on PRIA accreditation, with regular reviews and updates of accreditation requirements. PRIA's National Education Committee, a voluntary committee made up of academics and practitioners representing each Australian state and territory, has developed a solid basis for high standards of education. The same formal and rigorous process of PRIA accreditation is not as evident in New Zealand as Judy Motion and Shirley Leitch (2003: 125) point out:

> Although programs offered in any discipline by New Zealand universities and polytechnics must undergo a stringent approval process, this process is largely overseen by other educationalists, and there are only informal, limited piecemeal opportunities for industry input.

However, PRINZ has introduced the Accreditation in Public Relations (APR) program and there is a strong commitment to professional development and training for its 1200 members.

In addition to developments in accreditation, the profession is also developing a significant body of knowledge as public relations research, scholarly endeavour, and theorisation are now more refined. The flurry of emerging public relations journals and the array of literature that is now available on a diverse range of public relations practice indicates that the profession is making a noteworthy contribution to the knowledge and understanding of all aspects of communication management.

Taking a management role

Public relations sees itself as a management function, taking a more strategic role in organisations by being part of the dominant coalition, and taking an active role in decision making as it 'counsels management and makes policy decisions' (Gregory 2007: 610, cited in Theaker). Ströh (2007) cautions that this might also isolate public relations practitioners and suppress openness and the free flow of communication within organisations if public relations is viewed as part of the hierarchy.

Public relations management is also beginning to be part of the management of the 'corporate conscience' (Seitel 2007: 85) of an organisation, as public relations is in the position of promoting the whole organisation, or a whole service to the community such as cancer care or youth programs for street kids. The role of public relations is to promote integrity by taking an objective, well-researched view on organisational activities so that practitioners can advise and be valuable to management. Its position as a social conscience regulator is one that separates it from marketing or advertising management because the focus is on what an organisation needs to do and how it should practice, not on what it sells, markets, and promotes.

REFLECT AND DISCUSS

➤ When you graduate, what makes you a professional public relations practitioner?

➤ Trends will be constantly pointing you in a new direction. What is the latest trend that you have observed in public relations practice?

CHAPTER **SUMMARY**

➤ Public relations practice constantly adapts to support organisations to effectively and appropriately respond to changes in society's expectations. It is critical to keep an eye on the trends.

➤ Practitioners should be aware of the local–global context, and be aware that local actions may have a global audience.

➤ Transparency and disclosure are critical to ethical, accountable public relations practice.

➤ Cultural awareness is important to effective practice.

➤ New media management is constantly changing, which indicates the need for ongoing upgrading of skills, budgeting for new media management, and understanding the public relations context of social media and emerging media.

➤ The public relations–marketing mix is important where public relations defines itself through its focus on relationships and engagement across a broad range of publics and audiences.

➤ Managing and taking a management role is important to public relations practitioners to enable them to provide effective input.

➤ The dominance of women in public relations is a worldwide trend.

➤ Public relations professionalism and the recognition of the profession is more about how the profession is conducted than how it is defined. Accreditation with public relations professional associations is becoming more important to practice.

CASE STUDY \ INTERNATIONAL PERSPECTIVE: THAILAND

This case study is about a public relations program undertaken in Thailand to increase awareness of depression and its effect on individuals and families. It is equally relevant to campaigns about diabetes, obesity, cancer prevention, or other health issues and is included in this chapter to focus on the international and global context of public relations. The case is based on documentation of the program (Hanpongpandh 2006).

Joy Chia

It is not reported in full; rather, the discussion is on the cultural aspects that should be considered when an international public relations consultancy manages a campaign, especially ways to emphasise cultural awareness and understanding of the campaign's main audience. Burson-Marsteller, a public relations consultancy with considerable international public relations experience, found that conducting a public relations campaign without sound local understanding of its acceptance and understanding, did not achieve the best results for the intended publics.

AIMS

The aims of the campaign were:

➤ to educate the public about the effect of depression on families and Thai society
➤ to encourage the public to seek assistance for depression
➤ to increase awareness among medical staff about the effects of depression so that they would refer and encourage treatment and follow-up.

SITUATION ANALYSIS

During 2000–5, there was a need to increase awareness about depressive disorders in the Thai community. The awareness campaign was important as '50 to 70 per cent of all suicides are caused by depressive disorder' (Hanpongpandh 2006: 347) and the prevalence of suicide in teenagers and children was very high.

Hanpongpandh (2006: 353) suggests that it 'would have been helpful for the campaign planners to know more about the existing attitudes toward and knowledge about depression' in Thailand, so that public relations efforts could be of greatest benefit to the Thai people.

TACTICS

Feature stories about depression were placed in Thai magazines, interviews were arranged with 'prominent medical authorities and Thai media representatives' Hanpongpandh (351), and for 'each of these interviews the public relations staff recruited media representatives and pitched the interviews' (351). A World Mental Health Day seminar was organised and the seminar gained good media coverage.

EFFECTIVENESS AND WHAT ELSE COULD HAVE BEEN DONE

Even though aspects of the campaign were successful and media coverage about depression increased, the impact of such a campaign could have been enhanced through local knowledge and understanding of what was particular to this part of the world that needed a different public relations approach to a widespread problem. Ideas for specific consideration of cultural influences include the following points:

➤ It takes time to establish community confidence and understand what is being promoted in a public relations campaign so that, in this case, magazine feature articles on depression, seminars, and media releases could have been supplemented by grassroots discussion and consultation about this delicate and serious problem.

➤ The campaign needed to recognise local practices and plan an awareness campaign that acknowledges that this is the norm. Thus, for example, if Thais go to the temple or visit faith healers and fortune tellers for advice about depressive disorder, then this should have been recognised and incorporated.

➤ The campaign needed to point to other possible ways that Thais could access counselling or advice, as that was central to normalising the problem. In the past, the stigma about depressive disorders resulted in families and individuals wanting to hide and seek help away from public scrutiny.

➤ The communication about alternate ways to seek help needed to be understood within accepted Thai practices. The international consultancy focused on awareness of the disorder, expecting that this would result in Thais seeking help for it. The focus of the communication needed to be about the treatment of this disorder as though it were a treatment of any Thai health problem, making it clear that help was available through reliable, trusted sources that the Thai people were willing to consult.

➤ The campaign objectives were broad. This campaign needed a pilot study in one village, then a review, discussion with the families and community leaders, and to focus on specific aims to manage depression. This is central to contemporary public relations practice and results in progressive, relevant, and meaningful community engagement, which, in the case of depression management, would focus on overall health management.

➤ The response is similar to the publics' response in Australia and New Zealand, where the stigma of depression has also hidden the problem away. The campaign needed a sensitive, step-by-step approach to increasing awareness and response to a serious problem.

The key points about this case are that:

➤ multinational public relations consultancies need to take time to work with local experts and local practitioners, this is integral to the success of public relations planning and successful implementation of campaigns

➤ this was a serious problem that needed to be communicated effectively and with relevance to the culture where the public relations campaign was delivered

➤ the experience in managing a public relations program in one country cannot be replicated in another.

Think about the response to diabetes campaigns or binge drinking. What is important to the public's response to such campaigns? What makes these campaigns successful in your country or region?

Joy Chia

FURTHER READING

Lattimore, D, Baskin, O, Heiman, S, Toth, E & Van Leuven, J 2004, *Public Relations: The Profession and the Practice*, McGraw Hill, Boston.

Seitel, F, 2007, *The Practice of Public Relations*, 10th edn, Prentice Hall, Upper Saddle River.

WEB RESOURCES

Edelman Public Relations, at www.edelman.com.

Report of the Commission on Public Relations Education 2006, at www.commpred.org.

REFERENCES

Aldoory, L 2007, 'Reconceiving Gender for an "Excellent" Future in Public Relations Scholarship', in E Toth, *The Future of Excellence in Public Relations and Communication Management, Challenges for the Next Generation*, Lawrence Erlbaum, Mahwah, 399–412.

Banks, S 2000, *Multi-cultural Public Relations, A Social-Interpretive Approach*, 2nd edn, Iowa Sate University Press, Ames.

Bates, D 2002, 'Public Relations', in J Straubhaar & R LaRose, *Media Now, Communications Media in the Information Age*, 2nd edn, Thomson Wadsworth, Belmont, 312–45.

Blythe, J 2006, *Essentials of Marketing Communication*, 3rd edn, Prentice Hall, New York.

Chia, J 2007, 'Changing Dynamics of Relationship Management in Contemporary Public Relations Practice', paper presented at the 14th BledCom Global Public Relations Symposium, Lake Bled, Slovenia, 5–7 July.

Chia, J & Peters, M 2009, 'Making a Difference. Employees as Social Capital Investors', paper presented at the European Conference on Intellectual Capital, Holland University of Applied Sciences, The Netherlands, 28–29 April.

Chipchase, J & Theaker, A 2004, 'Using the Internet Effectively in Public Relations', in A Theaker, *The Public Relations Handbook*, 2nd edn, Routledge, Abingdon.

Cutlip, S, Center, A & Broom, G 2006, *Effective Public Relations*, 9th edn, Prentice Hall, Englewood Cliffs.

Davis, A 2003, *Everything You Should Know About Public Relations: Direct Answers to Over 500 Questions*, Kogan Page, London.

Davis, A 2007, *Public Relations*, 2nd edn, Palgrave Master Series, London.

Devito, J 2008, *Interpersonal Messages. Communication and Relationship Skills*, Allyn & Bacon, Boston.

Duhé, S 2007, *New Media and Public Relations*, Peter Lang, New York.

Flynn, N 2006, *Blog Rules. A Business Guide to Managing Policy, Public Relations, and Legal Issues*, AMACOM, New York.

Gower, K 2008, *Legal and Ethical Considerations for Public Relations*, 2nd edn, Waveland Press, Long Grove.

Gregory, A 2008, 'Public Relations and Management', in A Theaker, *The Public Relations Handbook*, 3rd edn, Routledge, Abingdon.

Gregory, A 2004, *Public Relations in Practice*, 2nd edn, Kogan Page, London.

Hallahan, K 2008, 'Organizational–Public Relationships in Cyberspace', in T Hansen-Horn & B Neff, *Public Relations: From Theory to Practice*, Allyn & Bacon, Boston, 31–44

Hanpongpandh, P 2006, 'Burson-Marsteller's Depression Awareness Campaign in Thailand', in M Parkinson & D Ekachai, *International and Intercultural Public Relations. A Campaign Case Approach*, Allyn & Bacon, Boston, 346–57.

Harris, T & Whalen, P 2006, *The Marketer's Guide to Public Relations in the Twenty-First Century*, Thomson, Mason.

Hazleton, V, Harrison-Rexrode, J & Kennan, W 2007, 'New Technologies in the Formation of Personal and Public Relations', in S Duhé, *New Media and Public Relations*, Peter Lang, New York.

Heath, R & Coombs, T 2006, *Today's Public Relations. An Introduction*, Sage, Thousand Oaks.

Lattimore, D, Baskin, O, Heiman, S, Toth, E & Van Leuven, J 2004, *Public Relations: The Profession and the Practice*, McGraw Hill, Boston.

L'Etang, J 2008, *Public Relations. Concepts, Practice and Critique*, Sage, London.

Matera, F & Artigue, R 2000, *Public Relations: Campaigns and Techniques*, Allyn & Bacon, Boston.

Morley, M 2002, *How to Manage Your Global Reputation. A Guide to the Dynamics of International Public Relations*, Palgrave, London.

Murphy, P 2000, 'Symmetry, Contingency, Complexity: Accommodating Uncertainty in Public Relations Theory', *Public Relations Review*, 26(4): 447–62.

Newsom, D, Turk, J V & Krukeberg, D 2007, *This is PR: Practice*, 9th edn, Thomson Wadsworth, Belmont.

Pelsmacker, P, Geuens, M & Van den Bergh, J, *Marketing Communications. A European Perspective*, 3rd edn, Prentice Hall, Harlow.

Seitel, F 2007, *The Practice of Public Relations*, 10th edn, Prentice Hall, Upper Saddle River.

Sharpe, M & Pritchard, B 2004, 'The Historical Empowerment of Public Opinion and its Responsibility to the Emergency of Public Relations as a Profession', in D Tilson & E Alozie, *Toward the Common Good, Perspectives in International Public Relations*, Pearson, Boston, 13–36.

Sriramesh, K & Vércîc, D 2003, *The Global Public Relations Handbook*, Lawrence Erlbaum, Mahwah.

Ströh, U 2007, 'An Alternative Postmodern Approach to Corporate Communication Strategy', in E Toth, *The Future of Excellence in Public Relations and Communication Management, Challenges for the Next Generation*, Lawrence Erlbaum, Mahwah.

Swann, P 2008, *Cases in Public Relations Management*, McGraw Hill, New York.

Theaker, A 2008, *The Public Relations Handbook*, 3rd edn, Routledge, Abingdon.

Toth, E 2007, *The Future of Excellence in Public Relations and Communication Management, Challenges for the Next Generation*, Lawrence Erlbaum, Mahwah.

Watson, T & Noble, P 2007, *Evaluating Public Relations. A Best Practice Guide to Public Relations Planning, Research and Evaluation*, 7th edn, Chartered Institute of Public Relations, with Kogan Page, London.

Wilcox, D, Ault, P, Agee, W & Cameron, G 2001, *Essentials of Public Relations*, Addison Wesley Longman, New York.

Wilcox, D, Ault, P, Agee, W & Cameron, G 2007, *Public Relations. Strategies and Tactics*, 8th edn, Addison Wesley Longman, New York.

Wu, M-Y 2005, 'Can American Public Relations Theories Apply to Asian Cultures?', *Public Relations Quarterly*, 50(3): 10–16.

Yale, D R & Carothers, A J 2001, *The Publicity Handbook*, McGraw Hill, New York.

Joy Chia

Chapter 3

THEORETICAL CONTEXTS

Marianne D Sison

You do not know what you've got until you enter the workforce and are forced to apply your theoretical learning in a practical workplace setting. The moment of truth comes when you realise that what you do or say in this world actually counts for something. Professional ability starts with education. It certainly doesn't start when you get a job.

That's the opinion of Richard Amos, a 1988 graduate from RMIT's Public Relations (BA) degree course, PRIA Fellow, and now managing director of the Melbourne-based business and communication strategy firm, Royce.

Amos says that too many public relations graduates and undergraduates discount what they've learnt when it comes to professional practice.

The reality is that they are in the box seat. Most have the world at their feet and presumably the talent to prosper in a mega-exciting yet 'talent-light' industry. My advice to entry-level practitioners is to embrace their educational strengths and make it work for their employer or client, from day one.

He believes that the same advice could be applied to the profession as a whole.

Our profession must *learn to learn* if it is to innovate, grow and be relevant. After 14 years in consultancy, it's all about these things.

Above all it's about learning to seize opportunity. There are four key factors driving production or output within the intangible economy: knowledge, engagement, collaboration, and responsiveness.

Today, opportunity sits in all four areas, particularly as they relate to public relations as the creator and protector of market and stakeholder relationships.

The profession and its front-line practitioners need to be more vigilant in chasing down these opportunities. The public relations profession missed the opportunity to 'own' corporate social responsibility; it lost considerable ground as the external world 'gatekeeper' with the introduction of the internet; its reputation continues to be maligned by journalists, marketeers and other business professionals caught up in outmoded constructs of what public relations is, or does, and the profession is still paying the price for lack of accountability.

My 'PR Utopia' is where new, seasoned, young and old practitioners are aware of the challenges, are able to turn them into opportunities and actively apply their professional knowledge and understanding of our transforming society to win back lost ground and open up new horizons for both themselves and the profession.

CHAPTER **AIMS**

By the end of this chapter, you should be able to:

➤ understand the various theoretical contexts that apply to public relations
➤ know the key communication and organisational theories that have influenced public relations scholarship
➤ understand systems theory, communication theory, public relations theory, rhetorical theory, cultural theory, and critical theory
➤ describe examples of professional practice in which communication or public relations theory may have been applied.

Marianne D Sison

Introduction

There is nothing so practical as a good theory.

Kurt Lewin

Why understanding theory is important

In practical terms, the benefits to you of a good theoretical foundation include the ability to contextualise and sometimes predict outcomes, and to decide when and why certain strategies and tactics need to be developed and implemented. But beyond its practicality, understanding theory will challenge you to think more deeply about what and where your assumptions about public relations come from. Examining the different theoretical frameworks that underpin public relations practice allows you, as a future practitioner, to embark on a journey of enquiry—to learn about previously held assumptions, reflect upon these assumptions as they apply to various situations, and to question their advantages and disadvantages, strengths and weaknesses, which can result in further theory development and will certainly help you to develop a better grasp of the role of public relations. While theories are used as a guide to practice, theories need, by and large, to be tested and retested, questioned and challenged. In your professional work you will develop a set of systems and processes that work for you, and as you become more aware of your own perspective as a practitioner, you will develop a better understanding of how to apply your skills and what you are trying to achieve on your organisation's behalf.

Where does public relations theory come from?

Public relations scholarship is in a healthy state of growth and development. A recent analysis (Sallot, Lyon, Acosta-Alzuru & Jones 2008) of public relations scholarship revealed that between 2001 and 2003, 50 per cent of the articles in two key public relations journals focused on theory development.

Early approaches to public relations theory developed with influences from psychology, sociology, social science and management disciplines, and, obviously, communication. In contrast to many of these areas, public relations is a much newer discipline. Van Leuven (1989) lists five communication and social sciences models—persuasion/learning effects, social learning, low involvement, cognitive consistency, and value change—that underpin the design of public relations campaigns and their influence can be seen in a number of ways:

➤ Most communication campaigns that follow the cognitive–attitudinal–behavioural effects (awareness, attitude change, behaviour change) are grounded from social psychology's learning traditions (Van Leuven 1989).

➤ Psychology is helpful in understanding how individuals and audiences think, feel, and behave so that communication messages and strategies can be made more effective.

➤ Sociology is useful in understanding how people behave within their groups or between other groups, particularly if the public relations campaigns will affect several stakeholders who may not necessarily agree on the issue or issues.

➤ Understanding management theories helps public relations managers to work with their CEOs, other managers, colleagues, subordinates, and other employees.

These early approaches to public relations theories have been referred to as 'modern', 'structural/systems-functionalist', and 'managerial' because of their view that public relations is a function of management. Most developed from a largely US-centric literature with a focus on the structural or functionalist perspective.

More recently, public relations theory has developed from a range of perspectives drawing from rhetorical, critical, and postmodern approaches. In 1992, US scholars Elizabeth Toth and Robert Heath published *Rhetorical and Critical Approaches to Public Relations* to address and expand on these theoretical perspectives. A few years later, British scholars Jacquie L'Etang and Magda Pieczka published *Critical Perspectives in Public Relations* (1996). Unlike the earlier approaches, which seem to focus on roles, structures, effectiveness, and efficiency of public relations, rhetorical approaches focus on how public relations practitioners create, interpret, and shape messages. Critical perspectives focus on the power and influence inherent in relationships established and managed by practitioners. Meanwhile, postmodernism—which some scholars view within the rubric of critical theory—offers an alternative lens by which to study public relations. Postmodern approaches question the links between knowledge and power, dissensus and consensus, power and resistance, power and ideology, and the representation of minorities and marginalised groups (Holtzhausen 2000). Dissensus, a term meant as a counterpoint to consensus, is described as an orientation that considers struggles, conflicts, and tensions (Deetz 2001: 15). For an extensive discussion on the consensus–dissensus dimension see Deetz 2001: 11–15.

TABLE **3.1** \ Multiple perspectives framework

Perspective	Focus of analysis
Functionalist/systems	Practitioner roles, reporting relationships, organisational structures and systems, responsibilities, activities, organisational profiles, practitioner focus on effectiveness and efficiency, managerial bias, alignment of an organisation's needs with the needs of publics.
Interpretive/rhetorical	Practitioners as producers of symbols, discourse, meaning, as corporate advocates, as shapers and creators of organisational culture, and as receivers and interpreters of organisational symbols.
Critical/dialectical	Practitioner views of their power, control, and influence in the organisation, involvement in process and dialogue, practitioners' ability to effect organisational change.

Source: Marianne D Sison 2006, adapted from Trujillo & Toth 1987

Marianne D Sison

As outlined in the table above, it is not sufficient, in these current times, to have only a singular perspective on public relations theory. You might ask why. Carl Botan and Vincent Hazleton (2006) have recognised that the future of public relations scholarship lies in its internationalisation. In the USA, for example, the Labor Department estimates that by 2014, ethnic minorities (defined in the USA as African American, Hispanic American and others) will comprise 20 per cent of the workforce. In Australia, the 2006 Australian Bureau of Statistics census reports that one in four Australians have one parent born overseas. Despite the USA and Australia having developed from an immigrant history, cultural diversity seems to have achieved belated recognition only as its statistical impact permeated the workforce.

Another diversity factor that requires a multiple perspective lens is that of generational diversity. Again, while multi-age workforces are not necessarily new, the economic impact of the various age groups, particularly Generation Y, on organisational productivity and staff turnover, for example, make generational diversity a factor in public relations practice.

In 1987, organisational communication scholar Nick Trujillo and public relations scholar Elizabeth Toth developed a multiple perspectives approach to public relations. Following organisational scholars Burrell and Morgan, they categorised theoretical perspectives as 'functionalist, interpretive, and critical' (Trujillo & Toth 1987). More recently, McKie and Munshi (2007), in their critique of the dominant symmetric paradigm, called for a more pluralistic approach to theory to allow innovative and alternative theoretical perspectives to test and develop the existing body of knowledge.

Some scholars (Deetz 2001) have criticised the use of a multiple perspective approach because, in their view, it weakens the researcher's focus. However, the multiple perspectives approach is a useful framework in public relations because of the various publics and audiences with whom practitioners need to work. Combined with the increased diversity resulting from global workplaces, a multiple perspective approach almost becomes a necessity.

REFLECT AND DISCUSS

Research the characteristics of baby boomers, Generation X and Generation Y. Develop some ideas about the different ways you might need to convey company news about a proposed merger with each of these generational groupings. What is the rationale for your recommendations?

A key theoretical trend from functional to co-creational

In discussing the state of public relations theory, Botan and Taylor (2004: 651) posit that the main development in public relations theory is the move from a 'functional perspective to a co-creational one'. A functional perspective 'sees publics and communication as tools or means to achieve organisational ends', while a co-creational perspective sees publics 'as partners in the meaning-making process' (Botan & Taylor 2004: 651–2). A co-creational perspective acknowledges that public relations practitioners working, for example, on an organisation's new environmental initiatives need to understand the perspectives and goals of their employees, clients, and community residents so they can work together and collaborate on effectively implementing the policy (see Chapter 9).

The development of public relations theory somehow parallels the development of communication theory. The structuralist–functionalist paradigm favoured by dominant US-centric scholarship has been characterised by a bias towards empirical, generally quantitative types of research in which 'empirical artefacts and relationships' can be studied and measured using scientific approaches (Burrell & Morgan 1979: 26). This research approach attempts to explain what is happening and why, by, for example, using survey results to measure employees' views about their new organisational structure. Such quantitative research is not sufficient to completely understand employee perceptions and predict employee behaviour. A qualitative approach, perhaps indepth interviews or focus groups, will supplement the survey results for a more thorough and complete picture of employee views and behaviours. In Chia and Peters' qualitative research (2008), credit union employees' engagement with the community uncovered employees' varied points of view. Even though quantitative surveys suggested that most employees were satisfied with credit union community programs, the qualitative semi-structured interviews uncovered a desire for change, to focus on the credit union philosophy to be members of the community making community engagement meaningful rather than community involvement being a symbol of 'organisational rhetoric'.

The functionalist approach also reflects the earlier effects and transmission approaches in communication studies because it assumes that much of people's behaviours are influenced solely by their exposure to messages from the media.

More recently, public relations theory development has slowly embraced the influence of European cultural studies, critical and postmodern approaches (see, for example, Berger & Reber 2006; L'Etang & Pieczka 1996; Motion & Weaver 2005; Roper 2005; Toth & Heath 1992). Australian scholarship tends to integrate both approaches although there is a lot of opportunity to further the newer approaches in public relations research.

Practitioners always prefer research and theory that they can apply to their day-to-day work. Because public relations practitioners still have to justify their roles and budgets to management, measurement and evaluation studies, such as return on investment (ROI) research, are always in demand. Tensions between academic and practitioner research will ensure that more scholarship is required at different levels so that theoretical and applied knowledge complement each other. If, for example, you are working on your organisation's corporate social responsibility (CSR) program, it helps to understand why it is important to your organisation to support Trees for Life or Salvation Army programs for the homeless. A combination of academic knowledge and lessons learnt from academics and practitioners will help you develop a more effective program.

This chapter has the potential to be overwhelming—there is so much theory that is useful to public relations. Consider yourself to be taking steps up a ladder where the first steps provide the basic framework for how organisations are structured (systems theory), how people communicate (communication theory), and provide frameworks for the public relations role (public relations theory). As you keep moving up the ladder you will come across some different influences that ask you to view the public relations role through different sets of lenses. Every part of this chapter is designed to help you build your own constructs about public relations and develop some working theories that you will test out in your working life. As you start working, the puzzle pieces will begin to fit into place, more of your ideas about public relations will take shape, and you will develop more professional confidence. Take time to uncover the theoretical layers: in doing so you will be prepared for a deeper and more meaningful grasp of public relations and be taken from the 'This is how we do it' phase to the 'This is making sense' phase.

Step 1: let us take the first step with systems theory

Systems theory

What is systems theory?

Systems theory is the dominant framework used in public relations scholarship and practice. Its application in public relations management is discussed in detail in Chapter 8. It is helpful to think of an organisation as a system, made up of a number of different parts (or subsystems) such as manufacturing, marketing, finance, human resources, and public relations.

System theory, popularised by Ludwig von Bertalanffy (Littlejohn 1999), traces its beginnings from biological roots. A system is defined as 'a set of things that affect one another within an environment and form a larger pattern that is different from any of the parts' (Littlejohn 1999: 41) and is characterised by:

> ➤ being part of a whole where its parts may be interdependent
> ➤ a hierarchy which undergoes self-regulation and control
> ➤ its interaction with its environment where it strives for balance so that it can maintain itself
> ➤ its adaptability to change so that it can achieve its end goal through different means (Littlejohn 1999: 41–45).

The theory's premise is that an organism is a member of a system. In order to survive, the organism has to adapt to its environment. Applied to organisations, systems theory focuses on the elements within the group and how they relate to each other through the network of subsystems within it. At the same time, the organisation exists within an operating environment, as one organism within a bigger system. A change in environmental conditions (for example, consumer trends or an emerging issue) will lead to some response by the organisation and its various subsystems as it adapts to the new environmental conditions.

How much the organisation adapts is determined by whether the system is open or closed. Applied to organisations, open systems are those that regularly interact with their environment, such as their audiences or publics, while closed systems are those that are isolated and do not interact with their environment. Open systems organisations regularly ask, for example, for feedback from their audiences or publics regarding their products or services so they can improve their product design and service delivery. Virgin, in all facets of its operation, is a prime example of an open organisation (see Chapter 7). Because we use systems to understand how processes work, effectiveness and productivity become an essential purpose. From this perspective, the elements of the organisation are perceived as undertaking a function for the survival of that system, which is known as the functionalist approach.

REFLECT AND DISCUSS

> ➤ Is it possible for any system, or organisation, to be completely closed?
> ➤ Can you give an example? Or are systems closed only in varying degrees?

Cybernetics

Within systems theory is the concept of cybernetics, which refers to the 'study of regulation and control in systems' (cited in Littlejohn 1999: 52). Originating from mechanical systems, cybernetics primarily deals with how systems adjust to feedback received to determine the changes and adjustments needed for the system to stabilise and/or be effective. Public relations practitioners apply cybernetics when they provide and respond to feedback between their organisations and their publics and audiences. In an organisational context, the main way that senior management knows whether their employees are well informed about and satisfied with the new structure comes through opportunities to comment on the change. If feedback is not possible, then when the system parts (employees) cannot handle the change, the system might experience a stoppage (strike) or might implode (employees resign en masse).

As an example, let us apply the cybernetics concept to a community relations situation in which a new commercial development is being planned in a residential area. After being notified of the proposal by the proponent, the community residents provide the council with their opinions, comments, and complaints through a community consultation process. The public relations practitioner or government relations officer then advises the local council about the feedback and makes recommendations on how the council should adjust the project to address the concerns of the community.

Burson (1987, cited in Cutlip, Center & Broom 2000) suggested that a public relations practitioner should become a 'sensor of social change' and a corporate monitor, along with being the corporate conscience and a communicator (see Chapters 4 and 9).

Requisite variety

Related to the knowledge of systems theory and cybernetics is the concept of requisite variety. Developed by W Roland Ashby and applied in organisational studies by Karl Weick (Dayrit Sison 2007), requisite variety suggests that organisations will be better prepared to withstand the effects of change if they comprise members (employees) with different points of view. An organisation's adaptability to change, especially within a complex and turbulent environment, is its key to survival. Open systems are characterised by this adaptability to change, and most contemporary organisations would reflect this type of system. The important thing to remember with requisite variety is that the more representative organisations are of the diverse members of their communities, the more likely they are to adapt to and survive the change. The reasoning behind this is that these diverse members of communities will enable the organisation to access information and insights that may provide competitive advantage.

What requisite variety avoids are the consequences of groupthink, in which people in the organisation all think alike and do not allow for different opinions or dissent. According to Irving Janis, groupthink is a quick and easy way of thinking 'that people engage in when they are deeply involved in a cohesive ingroup, when members striving for unanimity override their motivation to realistically appraise alternative courses of action' (cf. Littlejohn 1999: 288). Ingroup pressures to think alike can cause members to err in their judgment.

BOX **3.1** \ EXAMPLE

Groupthink has often been blamed for the 1986 Challenger space shuttle disaster (Conrad & Poole 2005; Tompkins 2005). In the investigation that followed the Challenger disaster, it was revealed that one of the engineers had cautioned about the safety of the O-rings after an extremely frosty night in Florida. However, since everyone at the command centre was determined to continue with the launch, anyone who suggested a delay might be necessary was convinced to either keep silent or to ensure that they had a good reason why the flight should not go ahead.

Boundary spanning

Another important concept within systems theory is that of boundary spanning (see also Chapter 8). Miles (1980) refers to the organisational boundary as a 'region in which elements of organisations and their environments come together and in which activities are performed of such a nature as to relate the organisation more effectively to the outside world' (p. 317). Boundary spanning is what organisational members (employees) do when they operate in the internal and external environments or across organisations. Miles (1980) has developed a typology for the boundary spanner that includes:

➤ representation
➤ scanning and monitoring
➤ protecting
➤ information processing
➤ gatekeeping
➤ transacting
➤ linking and coordinating.

These activities largely characterise the work that public relations practitioners do. Other organisational roles that also span the boundaries are sales and marketing, legal, and customer service, all of which deal with the organisation's clients. Because they operate across two environments, boundary spanners are characterised as knowledgeable, articulate, responsive to change, and sensitive to the preferences of the external organisation with which they are dealing.

A public relations practitioner who is, for example, working on a disability project with a not-for-profit organisation would act as a boundary spanner by:

➤ gathering and analysing information on disability statistics in Australia
➤ representing the organisation in meetings with funding bodies, government, corporate partners, and to the media
➤ maintaining those linkages for the benefit of the organisation.

As such, they may face conflict between the needs of their organisation and the external group, or have to deal with competing agendas. Further, public relations practitioners, who are charged with developing and protecting corporate identity, face difficulties with clearly defined organisational identities because of the blurring of organisational boundaries (Cheney & Christensen 2001: 243; Cheney, Zorn & Ganesh 2004: 119). Within some organisations boundaries are already blurred, with communication functions being housed either in marketing or human resources departments.

Why is systems theory important?

Systems theory is very useful in providing public relations with a context. Public relations practice is part of a much larger operation (the business of the organisation), and understanding that it works with other elements inside and outside the organisation will allow practitioners to work to their optimum (see Chapter 8).

REFLECT AND DISCUSS

> ➤ Think about yourself as being part of a larger system, either at work or in the university. How does your knowledge of the system in which you work assist you to function more effectively?
>
> ➤ Using some of the high-profile organisations in your state or country, discuss how these organisations have responded to changes in the environment. What specific changes in their environment did they respond to? What programs or policies did they develop?

Step 2: communication theories

There are numerous communication theories that are applicable to the practice of public relations. Communication theory as a whole has evolved from simplistic transmission and effects (functionalist) traditions to the textual and reception traditions (see Littlejohn & Foss 2008). Textual and reception studies refer to research that examines how audiences read and receive media messages or events within social, political, and economic contexts. In Australia in particular, communication theory development is influenced largely by British cultural studies scholarship (Turner & Cunningham 2006).

The communication theories applicable to public relations range from the transmission models popularised by Shannon and Weaver, and by Schramm, to media effects models and theories of persuasion.

Information transmission models

Shannon's mathematical theory of communication triggered the development of the information transmission model, which looks at information as a mechanical process that excludes meaning and interpretation.

As Figure 3.1 shows, this model is appropriate for the transmission of electronic signals via a medium. For a mobile phone to send an SMS message, the information source will be the person using the mobile phone, the transmitter converts the letters on the mobile phone pad to signals, which will then be sent via the airwaves through one of the mobile phone towers and sent to the receiver's mobile phone, which will reconvert the signals into a message for the receiver to read.

FIGURE **3.1** \ Shannon and Weaver mathematical model of communication

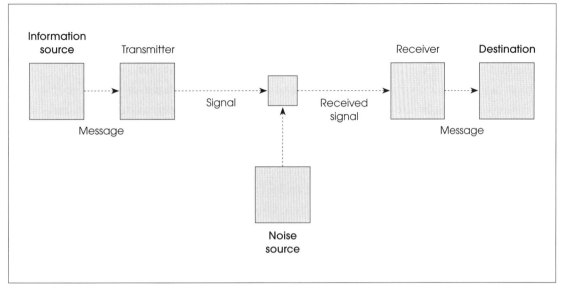

Source: Shannon & Weaver 1998

Schramm (1954, cited in Severin & Tankard 1992) developed three models in which he introduces several concepts: source, encoder, interpreter, decoder, message, and fields of experience. While these classical models have been critiqued for their weaknesses, the encoder–interpreter–decoder process identified by Schramm resonates with the contemporary sense-making, meaning-making, and rhetorical approaches suggested by public relations scholars. Similarly, the concept of field of experience suggests that if the sender's and receiver's fields of experience overlap, they are more likely to understand each other and thus, effective communication is more likely to take place.

Persuasion

In attempts to legitimise public relations as a management function, scholars such as Grunig have labelled persuasion as an unethical practice within public relations. Persuasion has been seen as synonymous with propaganda and Edward Bernays' public relations activities were described as 'scientific persuasion with imbalanced effects' and 'manipulation of the publics for the organisation's benefit' (Grunig & Hunt 1984). However, after much critique of Grunig's initial assertion, persuasion has now been included in the excellence theory as an element of dialogue (Botan & Hazleton 2006: 10). So in persuading drivers to keep to the speed limit or to not drink and drive, the communication messages are not manipulative but protective of the drivers, their passengers, and the community at large.

As we look at some of these theories of persuasion, let us examine how they are applicable to contemporary public relations practice.

Attitude vis-à-vis behaviour change

Attitude has been described as having three main components: cognitive (thinking), affective (feeling), and the behavioural (doing). The argument is that to achieve attitude change you must understand the facts of the case in a rational manner, and feel and believe the merits of the case before you will change your behaviour.

In other words, a change in attitude must happen before behaviour is changed. For many years, this linear process of behavioural change was seen as the norm, but some scholars (Krugman, cf. Severin & Tankard 1992) suggest that behavioural change can precede attitudinal change, especially in the case of television advertising where information processing occurs with low to no involvement. Krugman suggests that when people see a television commercial for a product such as a new mobile phone, they store the information in their memories, and then, when they go to the retail outlet, they act on the information and possibly purchase the product. After they buy the product they will then decide whether they have a favourable attitude towards it.

REFLECT AND DISCUSS

> One example where behaviour precedes attitude change is the legislation of the use of car seat belts. Can you think of another public relations campaign where attitude change occurs after behavioural change?

Source credibility

The believability of the communication source is an essential component of many public relations and media messages, especially within celebrity-infused media campaigns. Chapter 14 describes how celebrity public relations is part of the international landscape in which celebrities seem to fall in and out of grace, depending on media reports and YouTube videos that may make fun of or deride them. Because of the use of sports, entertainment, political, and business figures as spokespeople on a wide variety of issues, it is inevitable that credibility becomes an issue. Some of the dimensions used to measure credibility include expertness (also referred to as competence), trustworthiness, dynamism, objectivity, and charisma.

REFLECT AND DISCUSS

> Who, among the personalities you see in the media, appear to you to be credible? Why?

Two-step and multistep flow

These concepts stem from early works by Daniel Katz and Paul Lazarsfeld on voting behaviours that suggest that every group has an opinion leader who receives information from the media and passes it on to their peers (Littlejohn & Foss 2008). Further research revealed that while friends and opinion leaders are influential in decision making, individuals may also listen to information from other sources or directly access the information themselves.

BOX **3.2** \ INSIGHT

Many public relations campaigns use entertainment and sports celebrities as spokespeople, which demonstrates how opinion leaders are used to generate media attention and influence public opinion. A recent community protest organisation in Melbourne against the St Kilda Triangle development project, for example, used Australian actor Rachel Griffiths to voice the concerns of the community residents.

While celebrity spokespeople attract media coverage and increase public debate and awareness of the issue, using celebrities is not always successful. Aside from celebrities, there are also informal opinion leaders such as school teachers and community elders who exercise influence among a group. Opinion leaders change and can be influential on one topic or a variety of topics.

REFLECT AND **DISCUSS**

➤ Whose opinions are influential in your decision to buy a computer, in your choice of clothes, or in which movie to watch. Why?

➤ Do you depend on one person's view to make a decision or do you combine this view with your own research from other sources?

Emotional appeals

Persuasion theory suggests that using fear appeals in media messages is effective in making people change their behaviour.

An example of this is Australia's 2006 QUIT smoking campaigns, which featured graphic images of smokers with mouth cancers or amputated limbs to show the consequences of smoking. While these media campaigns are only a part of QUIT

Victoria's mission of 'eliminating the pain, illness and suffering caused by tobacco', it reports that smoking among adults has declined since the 1970s.

But some have questioned the effectiveness of fear appeals, especially when audiences become desensitised by so many negative or fear-based messages.

REFLECT AND DISCUSS

> ➤ How do you react when you view the graphic television commercials showing the dangers of drinking and driving, such as the Victorian Transport Accident Commission (TAC) commercials?
>
> ➤ Does it make you a more careful driver?
>
> ➤ Does it stop you from driving home when you have had more than the recommended alcohol limit?
>
> ➤ Do the advertisements make you simply aware of the consequences of drink driving or do they make you change your behaviour?
>
> ➤ In Australia, as in other countries, there are severe penalties for drinking and driving. Is it the television commercial or the penalties that convince you to not drink and drive?

Coorientation theory

When we consider the multiple stakeholders we need to communicate with in a public relations program, it is useful to apply coorientation theory by Newcomb, McLeod and Chaffee (1973). Consider the situation in which two individuals interact over a similar concern, such as hoon drivers. More often than not, the two individuals are likely to have differing perspectives or 'worldviews' (Littlejohn & Foss 2008: 258). One might see the problem as young drivers out of control, the other thinks that the age for driving needs to be increased. Acknowledging that different individuals have different viewpoints relates to the notion of requisite variety discussed earlier. Coorientation suggests that practitioners need to recognise these differences and find some agreement in dealing with their concerns. Basically, coorientation theory is about how an individual must recognise and be aware of how the other person or people in the relationship might think about or perceive an issue. One cannot assume that even if the two people in the relationship come from similar backgrounds they will perceive something in the same way.

As the model denotes, persons A & B have certain ideas (cognition) about an issue (X). Each person has some knowledge of what the other's idea about the issue is, and if they have similar or congruent views, then they could achieve consensus. The variables in the coorientation model include:

> ➤ accuracy: the degree to which one person's perception of another's cognitions matches the other's actual cognitions

➤ understanding: the degree to which both share a common definition of the situation regardless of their evaluations of it

➤ agreement: the degree to which each person holds the same summary evaluations about an object

➤ congruence: the degree of similarity between the person's cognitions and his or her perception of the other person's cognitions.

FIGURE **3.2** \ McLeod and Chaffee's coorientation model (1973)

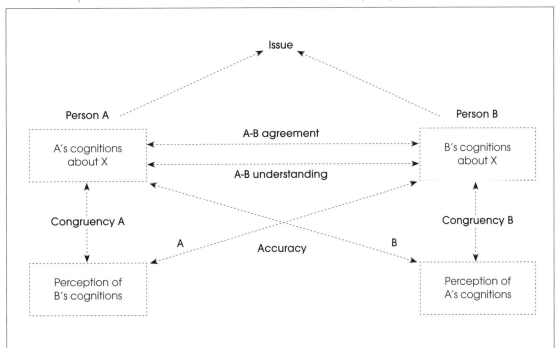

Source: McLeod & Chaffee 1973

BOX **3.3** \ EXAMPLE

Becton Corporation is a leading Australian property development company that supervised the development of a housing project over the Jolimont railyards in Melbourne. Its approved plans were challenged at the Victorian Civil and Administrative Appeals Tribunal (VCAT) by the Melbourne City Council (MCC) and existing Eastside community residents. Becton employed Socom to develop an issues management strategy to gain approval to develop the remaining land under a new proposal.

To gain approval, Socom undertook three stages of research: it reviewed media coverage of the VCAT decision, interviewed officers from the MCC and the Department of Sustainability and Environment (DSE), and surveyed the residents. Knowing how the different stakeholders viewed the development, Socom organised meetings with the affected residents that sought to clarify the consultation process and design concerns. Socom updated DSE and MCC on the agreed process, and then met with Becton to develop an information pack that included illustrations of the new and old designs. The residents were asked to review the proposals and mark their preferences on a form. Eastside's body corporate executive developed a new design brief for Becton and many of the residents' views were incorporated into the new design. The plans for the revised proposal were approved with 87 per cent support from the Eastside residents.

This case highlights the importance of understanding the concerns of all stakeholders. It was this knowledge, along with a willingness to listen and act on the concerns, that helped the company eventually achieve its goals.

Source: PRIA Golden Target Awards 2005

Agenda setting

The notion of agenda setting suggests that the media 'establish the salient issues or images in the minds of the public' (Littlejohn & Foss 2008: 293). Communication scholars Donald Shaw and Maxwell McCombs contend that the media shape our realities; however they qualify that mass media 'may not be successful in telling us what to think, but they are stunningly successful in telling us what to think about' (1977, in Littlejohn & Foss 2008: 293).

Our view about hospitals, say, will be influenced by media coverage of horror stories of patients left to die in hospital corridors, viruses out of control, and malpractice cases. Some of these issues are indeed important and their exposure in the media lends the issue an air of urgency and priority that we accept as true. But they are unlikely to represent the complete picture of what is happening in health care.

Public relations practitioners work with media to ensure that the corporate messages will be given media exposure. While public relations practitioners can attempt to set the agenda by undertaking a comprehensive campaign involving a media blitz and lobbying on a particular issue, they will require cooperation from media practitioners.

Framing

Framing refers to how individuals organise and package information, and is critical to how we construct our reality (Hallahan 1999). In public relations practice, we make a conscious decision about how to present the information on behalf of our organisation. We think about what to include and what not to include, and what is important to be communicated. Kirk Hallahan contends that framing involves 'inclusion and exclusion as well as emphasis' and cites Robert Entman in suggesting that framing is about selection and salience, determining what is important to be included in a message (Hallahan 1999: 207).

Hallahan (1999) identified seven ways that framing is used in public relations. These seven types of framing involve situations, attributes, choices, actions, issues, responsibility, and news. How these seven dimensions are framed affects relationships between public relations practitioners and their stakeholders, communities, and diverse publics. How messages, events, and situations are framed relates to the notion of coorientation, which was discussed earlier.

Originally developed by sociologist Erving Goffman, framing is one way individuals make sense of the events in their lives. By trying to make sense of a situation, one tends to interpret it based on the individual's contextual framework. A situation is defined by reducing it to strips and frames, where frames provide meaning.

The concept of framing is important in public relations because developing mutual relationships with our stakeholders or community partners requires our understanding of how they frame or view the issues. Without knowing how the other thinks and feels about key issues, it will be difficult to engage them in dialogue. Furthermore, understanding what is salient or important to your publics and audiences will help practitioners prioritise their approaches. Understanding framing as a key concept in public relations practice is the first step to acknowledging that there are perspectives, perhaps more important, beyond those of our employing organisation.

Step 3: putting the pieces together
Public relations theory
The Excellence Theory

The Excellence Theory of public relations resulted from a study funded by the International Association of Business Communicators Foundation (IABC) and undertaken by James Grunig, Larissa Grunig, and David Dozier. The study, which began in 1985, initially started out as an enquiry into how public relations contributes to organisational effectiveness (Grunig, Grunig & Dozier 2006).

The Excellence Study generated several books and journal articles. The study comprised a quantitative survey of 327 organisations in the USA, Canada, and the United Kingdom, as well as qualitative interviews of up to three people in twenty-five organisations whose scores represented the highest and lowest scores on the excellence scale.

A key outcome of the Excellence Study is confirmation that public relations is a 'unique management function that helps an organisation interact with the social and political components of its environment' (Grunig, Grunig & Dozier 2006: 55). Furthermore, the study confirmed that symmetrical communication results in more effective communication. The study also revealed that for communication functions such as marketing, advertising, and public relations to be excellent, they should be integrated through a senior communication executive or public relations department. And finally, the study recognised that activism is good for the organisation because it allows a dialogue with the activist publics and therefore addresses issues before they escalate any further than they already have.

The Excellence Theory suggests that organisations with excellent public relations have:

➤ participative rather than authoritative organisational cultures
➤ a symmetrical system of internal communication
➤ organic rather than mechanical structures
➤ programs to equalise opportunities for women, men and minorities
➤ high job satisfaction among employees (Grunig, Grunig & Dozier 2006: 53).

Botan and Hazleton (2006) said that the Excellence Theory is a good example of how critiques and debates on its merits and weaknesses led to its refinement and redevelopment. One of the key differences in the latest iteration of the Excellence Theory is that it now acknowledges that 'excellent public relations organisations use all four models of public relations practice' (Botan & Hazleton 2006: 10).

In 1984, James Grunig and Todd Hunt introduced the four models of public relations that primarily trace the evolution of public relations practice. These models have become the basis for how we categorise public relations practice.

Grunig and Hunt's four models

The four models, introduced in Chapter 1 and detailed here, are:

1 press agentry
2 public information
3 two-way asymmetric
4 two-way symmetric.

According to Grunig and Hunt (1984), *press agentry* involves one-way communication and is reflective of the publicity model. The information disseminated in this model may stretch the truth. It is a model that is still used by many organisations that perceive public relations as publicity or media relations and employ publicists. This model is often used by film companies to promote their movie releases, or publishing houses who want to gain media mileage for their latest books.

The *public information model* also uses one-way communication, but unlike press agentry, it is meant to provide truthful information. The first practitioner referred to as practising this model is Ivy Lee. This model is useful for practitioners who want to provide factual information to an audience. When, for example, the Victorian Road Authority (VicRoads) instituted the 40 kph speed zones near schools, it developed an information campaign that included a news conference, guest spots on television and radio programs, and advertising.

The *two-way asymmetric model* refers to the use of scientific information to persuade audiences, thereby influencing them to behave the way the organisation wants. It is two-way because information gathered about audience expectations is used in the development of material. It has been suggested that this model is prone to being 'manipulative' (Dozier, Grunig & Grunig 1995).

The *two-way symmetric model*, initially described as the ideal form of public relations practice, aims to establish mutual understanding between organisations and their publics. Many scholars and practitioners have taken this as the normative model, despite some criticisms from other scholars. The main criticisms of this model revolve around the assumptions of equal power between organisations and publics when they meet face to face. But this is not the case when applied to situations in which well-funded corporations are in a dialogue with community groups.

Variations to the four models

Since the models were conceptualised, they have been widely tested and critiqued. As a result, several variations and extensions to the four models have been offered. Here are a few additions worth noting.

Personal influence. In testing whether the models are applicable in other cultural contexts, several University of Maryland scholars undertook research in India, Greece, and Taiwan. The results of their combined studies revealed that in addition to the four models being practised in their respective countries, a model of personal influence was also in place (Grunig, Sriramesh, Huang & Lyra 1995). While the personal influence model may be construed by some as bordering on unethical practice, the reality is that most relationships developed in the practice of public relations depend in large part on one's interpersonal communication skills. As such, the authors' discussions revealed that this model was not found to be unique to countries outside the US. Rather, this model was also employed by many lobbyists in Washington D.C.

Mixed motive. The mixed motive model arose after Murphy (1991) applied game theory in suggesting that organisational public relations is a mixed motive game. As Dozier and colleagues (1995) suggest, both sides 'pursue their own interests, but both sides also realize that the game's outcome (the relationship in this context) must be satisfactory to both sides' (47). The benefit of this approach is that public relations practitioners are able to get their senior managers to see their organisation's behaviours through the publics' viewpoints. Moreover, the mixed motive model allows practitioners to assess their capabilities to gain a 'win–win' outcome for their organisation and the stakeholders involved in the process. The mixed motive model presents the possibility that organisations and the publics have different positions on issues and can hold conflicting interests.

FIGURE **3.3** \ Mixed motive

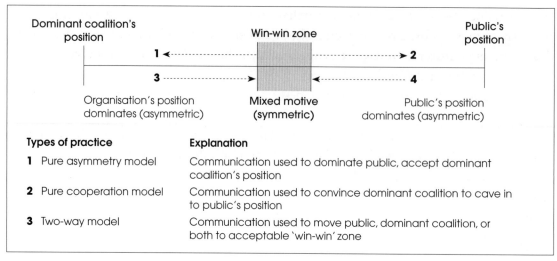

Source: Dozier, Grunig & Grunig 1995: 48

Situational theory of publics

The situational theory of publics has been integrated into the Excellence Theory to explain why and how publics communicate. The theory posits that there are three variables that predict communication behaviour, attitude change and behavioural change (Aldoory & Sha 2006: 340–1):

1   *Level of involvement*: how personally relevant a problem can be for an individual.
2   *Problem recognition*: the extent to which individuals recognise a problem is facing them.
3   *Constraint recognition*: the extent to which individuals perceive factors that inhibit their ability to move to action or change behaviour.

This theory of publics is important in prioritising which key publics and audiences need to be targeted for specific key messages, especially in the case of crises, when timely and sound responses are required (see Chapter 10). Publics and audiences who are highly likely to be affected by an issue are—or should be—highly involved and are very important in the communication program.

Relationship management

John Ledingham and Stephen Bruning developed relationship management theory in 2000. Drawing from Mary Ann Ferguson's 1984 paper, in which it was suggested that relationships should be at the heart of public relations, Ledingham (2006: 467–8) traces the emergence of the relational perspective to four key developments:

1   recognition of the central role of relationships in the study and practice of public relations
2   reconceptualising public relations as a management function

3 the emergence of measurement strategies, relationship components and types of organisation–public relationships, and linkage of organisation–public relationships to public attitudes, perceptions, knowledge, and behaviour
4 the construction of models that accommodate relationship antecedents, process, and consequences.

Critical to the concept of relationship management is the shift from thinking about public relations as a focus on message production to a management function. The organisation–public relationship is defined as 'the state which exists between an organisation and its key publics, in which the actions of either can impact the economic, social, cultural or political well being of the other' (Ledingham & Bruning 1998: 62).

Initially, Ledingham and Bruning's (1998) research revealed a two-step process for organisations wishing to apply public relations as relationship management:

1 organisations must focus on the relationships with their key publics
2 to build relationships with key publics, organisations must let their key publics know about the activities or programs that are being implemented.

They also found the following dimensions to be necessary for relationship management: building trust, demonstrating involvement, investment, commitment, and maintaining open, frank communication.

REFLECT AND DISCUSS

If relationship management is underpinned by the notion of organisation–public relationships, it requires a clear identification of who the key publics and audiences are.

➤ How are these key publics identified?
➤ How do we determine who is a key public and who is not?
➤ What criteria determine these distinctions?
➤ Who decides who is a key public to whom?

Trust is a useful component in relationship management if it is understood by both parties on the same terms (Chia 2005). Trust is important to cultivating the relationship outcomes. Chia (2008) indicated that trust is but one relational component and is the measure or outcome of sound relationship management; the relational context needs to be understood within every exchange, including exchanges online, that takes place between public relations practitioners and their clients, all publics or audience exchanges and exchanges between organisations. In many ways, public relations may as well be called 'personal' relationships, as the development and maintenance of relationships largely depends on the strength of the personal relationships between relational partners. As such, it is useful for public relations practitioners to consider re-examining interpersonal relationships and interpersonal communication in their practice and to understand how relationships can be managed effectively within the diversity of online and offline communication. Social media, for example, are changing the context of personal relationships and how they are understood because they may be conducted totally online. Public relations is constantly reframing its practice in line with the demands of emerging media so that relational theory also needs to be understood as part of emerging media (see Chapter 12).

Step 4: rhetorical and interpretive perspectives

Using our ladder analogy, the three areas—or rungs—of theory already discussed provide the basics. From this point on, every additional step will provide some new ideas that you can use to build on the basics and develop your own constructs about useful theory for public relations. This next area of theory, rhetorical and interpretive perspectives, feeds directly into important areas such as understanding how people generate and respond to ideas, how to attract their attention and interest, and how to achieve shared meaning, all of which, if successfully achieved, will support reputation and relationships.

In public relations, where words, images, actions, and context are tools of the trade, practitioners are working with very powerful means of creating meaning among the organisation's multiple publics and audiences. Rhetorical and interpretive perspectives refer to ways that people construct meaning, and these areas of theory are important because they help to explain more about the public relations role.

In the earlier example about credit unions, Chia and Peters (2008) found that credit union employees were concerned about their organisations' rhetoric and tokenistic responses; the employees wanted to be involved in doing the right thing, not just to be seen to be doing the right thing. These employees wanted to make a difference to young carers lives, rather than give a donation because it felt good to do so.

Stephen Littlejohn (1999: 199) defines interpretation as 'an active, discipline process of the mind, a creative act of searching for possible meanings'. According to Trujillo and Toth (1987), the interpretive approach examines 'the symbolic aspects of organisational life' (209) and 'interpretive approaches invite public relations researchers and professionals to understand how organisations use symbols and how publics assign meaning to organisational life and to society' (210). They posit that sense-making, rhetorical, and cultural approaches fall within the interpretive perspective. The interpretive perspective is what Botan and Taylor (2004) refer to as the co-creational perspective, mentioned earlier in this chapter.

Sense-making focuses on the creation of meaning and includes context as integral to a richer and more nuanced analysis of organisational publics (Trujillo & Toth 1987). The rhetorical approach examines organisational discourse created by public relations and communication practitioners and explores the ways in which the techniques of argumentation, persuasion, and influence are used in communication materials. The cultural approach examines how public relations and communication practitioners not only transmit but also shape organisational cultures (see next section).

As Andrej Skerlep (2001) lamented, rhetorical theory has yet to be integrated into public relations theory, unlike organisational communication theory, which has embraced it. The hesitancy to integrate rhetorical theory has been attributed to rhetoric's relations with persuasion, which, as discussed earlier, has been equated to manipulation (1989, cited in Pfau & Wan 2006).

Heath (1992) discussed the use of rhetorical perspectives in public relations from a historical and managerial point of view. Of particular interest is rhetorical enactment theory, which 'reasons that all of what an organisation does and says is a statement' (Heath 2001: 4). Following this view, public relations practitioners charged with writing a media statement or developing a community relations program are, in effect, expressing what their employing organisations stand for. This also means that practitioners are regularly involved in constructing their organisation's corporate rhetoric. Asbestos manufacturer James Hardie's corporate rhetoric (and others highlighted in Chapter 9) indicated that organisations give mixed messages about what they stand for and what they do.

Rhetorical studies examine individual and organisational discourse as symbols of meaning (Heath 1993). As Robert Putnam and Gail Fairhurst (2001) explain, rhetorical and literary studies in organisations incorporate discourse analysis, argumentation, and advocacy. They define discourse analysis as 'the study of words and signifiers, including the use of language in context, and the meanings or interpretations of discursive practices' (Putnam & Fairhurst 2001: 79). In public relations, where practitioners are often valued for their ability to use words, images, actions, and context to create shared meaning and achieve results, practitioners need to recognise the complexities involved when working with an organisation's multiple publics and audiences. For example, the 2008 financial crisis and climate change considerations changed the social acceptability of many words and meanings as discussion about fast cars, expensive and luxury items became less acceptable than small, inexpensive, frugal, and environment friendly.

REFLECT AND **DISCUSS**

Your CEO has committed to reduce energy consumption in your organisation for two reasons—as a commitment to environmental sustainability and to minimise business costs. Think about how you, as an internal communication practitioner, will develop a communication strategy aimed at engaging employees to reduce energy consumption in their workplace.

➤ What will you include in your plan?

➤ Who will you use to help bring about a change in behaviour in the workplace?

➤ What words, images, and actions will you develop to achieve your objective?

Cultural theory

Public relations practitioners have been attributed as co-creators of or partners in the creation of culture (Botan & Hazleton 2006; Cheney & Christensen 2001). As such, it is useful to discuss the schools of thought on organisational and national cultures that may impact public relations scholarship.

One school of thought that provides good direction for public relations is the area of cultural theory or cultural studies, developed through the influence of British scholar Stuart Hall. Cultural studies explores political economy, communication, social theory, philosophy vis-à-vis ideology, nationality, ethnicity, social class, and gender. A cultural studies approach focuses on the meaning of cultural artefacts and argues that producers of these artefacts exercise power and control over that culture.

Applying the cultural studies perspective to public relations gives the student and practitioner a macro-level appreciation of the power relationships that occur and how public relations may be used in perpetuating hegemony or power and authority. During a community consultation involving an organisation and community residents, for example, if the organisation representative is a high-level business executive armed with financial information who meets with a resident of a migrant community where English is a second language, there is already a sense of power imbalance. To address this imbalance, the organisational representative might suggest meeting with a community leader who is able to articulate the concerns of the migrant community the leader represents and stands up for the issues of the community.

The other important aspect to understanding cultural theory is its application to organisations. Edgar Schein (1992), author of *Organisational Culture and Leadership*, defines culture as having three components:

➤ basic assumptions
➤ values
➤ and artefacts.

In developing effective change communication programs, understanding the corporate culture is a vital step in the process. Without understanding how things are done in the workplace, change communication practitioners will have difficulty identifying the key drivers that will engage employees to embrace the change.

Espoused values are the 'articulated, publicly announced principles and values that the group claims to be trying to achieve' (Schein 1992: 9) while basic assumptions are similar to 'theories in use' or values in use (Argyris & Schön 1996). Basic assumptions refer to tacit knowledge or things we know but are usually unspoken, such as how we address the CEO. Artefacts refer to physical and articulated elements in the organisation, such as the company's logo, office layout, corporate colours, and slogans.

Geert Hofstede (1980) is another important scholar in the area of organisational culture. His research on national and regional cultures is important in understanding public relations practice in global and international settings. While some scholars have criticised his work for being too simplistic, it is useful to know the five dimensions Hofstede suggests as a basis for understanding cultural differences between countries. These five dimensions are:

1 *power distance*: the extent to which the less powerful members accept and expect that power is unequally distributed
2 *uncertainty avoidance*: the extent to which members are able to cope with anxiety by reducing uncertainty
3 *individualism vs collectivism*: the extent to which people are able to stand for themselves or are likely to act as part of a group
4 *masculinity vs feminism*: the extent to which cultures place value on such matters as competitiveness, assertiveness, and ambition, and focus on material possession (masculine) or relationships and quality of life (feminine)
5 *long- vs short-term orientation*: the importance placed on the future as against a focus on the past and the present.

Hofstede has developed a comparative mapping of cultures in relation to these dimensions, which helps to explain why people of different cultures may interact differently. If an organisation's workforce or audience are culturally diverse the cultural influences are worth knowing about because they will assist in the communication process.

REFLECT AND DISCUSS

> ➤ Imagine you were working as a public relations officer for an Australian company based in Beijing, such as ANZ or Foster's. How would you use your Australian education to prepare for practice in Asia? Would your current knowledge be sufficient? If not, what other areas do you need to learn?
>
> ➤ Likewise, if you are an Asian person working in Australia, what areas of culture would you need to adapt to?

Marianne D Sison

Critical perspectives

Critical theory is a wide and expansive field and its origins can be traced to the ideas of Karl Marx's critique of the political economy, Habermas' theory of communicative action, and Michel Foucault's writings on sites of power (Mumby 2001; Littlejohn 1999). Its contribution to public relations scholarship is summarised by L'Etang (2005: 522): 'Critical theory encourages us to be self-aware and transparent in the way we think, write and teach'.

Challenges to the public relations role from critical theory are typified by Trujillo and Toth (1987: 218) who see political and radical change implications of public relations activity. The political approach assumes that an organisation's internal and external publics have conflicting interests. On the one hand, public relations is seen as a powerful resource used by corporations and governments to promote their causes (Beder 2000; Ewen 1996). On the other hand, public relations insiders still perceive that they have limited influence and power because of their non-membership in the dominant coalition (Berger & Reber 2006). The other view is that practitioners could use power to represent other publics and to influence the organisation to behave in an ethical and socially responsible manner. This latter view is reflective of the radical change approach.

In particular, applications of the critical approach to organisational communication (Mumby 2000) and to public relations (Motion & Weaver 2005; Roper 2005; L'Etang 1996; Berger & Reber 2006) suggest that we should explore:

➤ notions of voice and who has voice in an organisation
➤ diversity with a strong consciousness against hegemony or power imbalance
➤ the assumed acceptance of dominant ideas.

Difference and dissensus are critical for dialogue and dialogue includes a dialectical process in which people from various sides challenge and oppose each other (Mumby 2000: 86). Dialectic is defined as the 'art of investigating the truth of opinions; the testing of truth by discussion' (*Australian Concise Oxford Dictionary* 2004: 384). These dialectical processes are part of everyday practice as differences and dissention are part of the normative mode of public relations where relationships move through constant reframing and change (Chia 2008).

The current fixation on public relations' membership in the dominant coalition underrates the real power and influence that practitioners might exercise from within. O'Neil's (2003) study found that practitioners' ability to effectively engage in persuasive communication towards a supervisor, which is called 'upward influence', are explained by the amount and type of the practitioner's organisational power—formal and informal—and not by gender. Berger (2005) proposed the notions of 'power over' (dominance), 'power with' (collaboration and negotiation) and 'power to' (resistance) in exploring the power relations with the dominant coalition. This presents real and complex tensions for the public relations practitioner who might wish to capitalise on the opportunity to position communication and relational management so that organisations appreciate the value of the profession, while at the same time holding true to the values and ethics inherent to transparency, shared meaning, and decision making.

REFLECT AND DISCUSS

> ➤ Whom do practitioners serve? Their own career interests? The organisation? The profession? The interests of others in the margins? The larger society?
>
> ➤ Who is defining that service (Rakow 1989)? Is it the practitioner? The professional association? The CEO or other top manager? A journalist or community official outside the organisation? (Berger 2005:23)

Have you climbed all the rungs of the ladder?

Development of theoretical frameworks will continue as public relations scholars and practitioners constantly find new ways to think about and implement public relations practice so that it has value and is valued by the community, the public and the organisations they work for.

While systems theory, which focuses on control and stability, and critical theory, which focuses on power relations and control, may seem to be diametrically opposed, they may not necessarily be so (Mumby 1997, cited in Littlejohn 1999: 226–7). In applying these concepts to organisational communication, unobtrusive control within organisations is related to the concept of hegemony, which refers to the 'process of domination, in which one set of ideas subverts or co-opts another' (Littlejohn 1999: 229). Concepts such as dissensus and dialectics, often mentioned in critical studies, share some commonalities with concepts of pluralism and requisite variety, which characterise open systems. These commonalities refer to the value given to a multiplicity of voices, viewpoints and perspectives.

CASE STUDY SUPPORTING ORGANISATIONAL CHANGE

THE SITUATION

The Victorian Managed Insurance Authority (VMIA) is a statutory authority providing insurance for state assets and risk management services to state departments and agencies. In 2006–7, VMIA engaged consultancy Scaffidi Hugh-Jones (SHJ) to develop a communication strategy that would help smooth the path of a major reorganisation.

Marianne D Sison

The reorganisation had four objectives:

➤ client impact—tailored solutions and segmented offerings
➤ product and service development
➤ increased career paths and professional development opportunities
➤ enhanced internal and external communication.

Other aspects of the change included the relocation of selected staff to new office accommodation, changes to business information systems, communication with and management of stakeholders (internal and external), the recruitment of new personnel, and the development of a 360 degree performance management system.

SHJ analysed the risks associated with the change to determine the best model to communicate the effects of change and to assist and support managers through the change process.

SHJ drew particularly upon the work of Claes Janssen's *Four Room Apartment* model (1982) chosen for its accurate reflection of the human change process.

THE MODEL

Claes Janssen is the originator of the Four Room Apartment model of change, which was further developed by Marvin Weisbord. The model was developed from Dr Elisabeth Kubler-Ross' work on the psychological acceptance of the process of death.

The four rooms of change are the Contentment Room, the Denial Room, the Confusion Room, and the Renewal Room.

The Four Room Apartment correlates exactly with the change states documented by Dr Clare W Graves (cf. Beck & Cowan 1996), who uncovered spiralling value systems in mature adults as they respond to changes in their life conditions. Thus the progression through change can be simply represented as:

Stability > Stress > Crisis > Breakout > Stability

The Four Room model correlates to this progression as indicated below.

Change state	Room
Alpha state—Stability	The Contentment Room
Beta state—Stress	The Denial Room
Gamma state—Crisis	The Confusion Room
Delta state—Breakout	The Renewal Room

The model brings a depth of understanding of the human experience at each stage of the change process in terms of thinking, feelings, and behaviours. It is often presented in cartoon fashion as a discussion piece (see next page).

FIGURE **3.4** \ Claes Janssen's Four Room Apartment model

Source: Jock Macneish

The Four Room Apartment helps people to understand and open up to the emotions connected with the various states of change. It conveys the message that these emotions are a normal part of the change process, and encourages people to accept rather than struggle against their change experience.

VMIA AND THE MODEL

Since all change involves periods of uncertainty, VMIA took positive steps to ensure that this was kept to a minimum and that everyone felt supported throughout the process.

With the assistance of SHJ, the VMIA developed a package of communication including:

➤ a CEO briefing to employees
➤ information and discussion workshops for everyone, to talk about the nature of change in general and also to seek feedback on where the company is now, how employees

felt about the changes and what support they thought was needed during the change process

➤ detailed plans for the change process.

In addition, VMIA and SHJ developed the Change Support Pack that drew heavily on the Four Rooms model. It used the model to identify, analyse, and address employee issues. The pack contained information on the process of change and the support available to employees. It offered managers a chance to record their own thoughts.

A key element was an explanation of the Four Rooms model, designed to alert managers to the stages of change through which they and their staff could go. To further the communication process, SHJ developed behavioural and communication guidelines for each of the four rooms. These included the following:

CONTENTMENT ROOM

➤ When things are stable, let people get on with their job as much as you can.

➤ This can also be a good time for foundation building or make and mend type work, such as making plans, revising and improving procedures, learning and development, team building, etc.

DENIAL ROOM

➤ When things are stressful and people are in denial, remember not to give advice (they will not listen anyway).

➤ Instead, ask questions to raise awareness and help people see what is going on.

➤ Offer support.

➤ Remain flexible and open; adjust plans to reduce stress.

➤ Remember that the state is temporary and a sign that something needs to change.

CONFUSION ROOM

➤ During a crisis reassure people that it is normal and all right to be confused.

➤ Be positive.

➤ Focus on the future and what is possible.

➤ Structure and prioritise tasks. Be flexible.

➤ Get people together.

➤ Remember that we look to a leader during times of crisis.

RENEWAL ROOM

➤ Share the excitement of renewal.

➤ Capture all those great ideas.

➤ Offer help to make them happen.

➤ Channel the enthusiasm into structured plans.

➤ Celebrate success and reward effort.

➤ Draw connections between the change journey and your success.

The checklists were designed to inform the change process and complement the actions and behaviours seen throughout the organisation.

IMPACT AND RESULTS

The model supported the communication strategy, explaining how the scope of the change might impact on stakeholders, together with an appreciation of what it feels like to navigate the change journey.

REFLECT AND **DISCUSS**

Using the principles discussed in the case study, develop a plan for your local charity organisation, which is about to change its structure by employing more paid management staff to supervise its volunteer staff.

➤ Identify the stakeholders requiring communication.

➤ Analyse how each stakeholder group might think and feel, and how they are likely to behave.

➤ Develop a communication strategy for each stakeholder group.

➤ Discuss ways of evaluating your communication change plan.

CHAPTER **SUMMARY**

➤ There are a number of key theories underpinning public relations scholarship and a multiple perspectives approach is necessary to respond to the changing demands of the public relations environment.

➤ Public relations scholarship is influenced by theoretical perspectives in social science, organisational theory, and communication.

➤ Systems theory allows practitioners to understand how their practice could impact on other elements, and that feedback is important in making sense of systems

➤ Communication theory provides valuable guidelines for how to construct and communicate a message.

➤ Public relations theory draws from the four models of public relations developed by Grunig and Hunt and from subsequent refinements, including the mixed motive and personal influence models.

➤ Rhetorical and interpretive approaches to public relations practice need to be recognised when constructing organisational messages, images, and activities to expect the variety of meanings possible among its stakeholders.

➤ Cultural theory reminds us of the influence of culture and cultural environments in setting context for public relations activity.

➤ Critical perspectives need to be considered by practitioners to understand how power may be used for socially responsible practice.

FURTHER READING

Botan, C & Hazleton, V 2006, *Public Relations Theory II*, Lawrence Erlbaum, Mahwah.

Cheney, G & Christensen, L 2006, 'What Should Public Relations Theory Do, Practically Speaking?', *Journal of Communication Management*, 10(1): 100–2.

WEB RESOURCES

PRIA Golden Target Awards, at www.lib.uts.edu.au/gta/show.php?id=548.

QUIT Campaign, at www.quit.org.au/browse.asp?ContainerID=1634.

REFERENCES

Aldoory, L & Sha, B L 2006, 'Situation Theory of Publics', in E Toth (ed.), *The Future of Excellence in Public Relations and Communication Management*, Lawrence Erlbaum, Mahwah.

Argyris, C & Schön, D 1996, *Organizational Learning II: Theory, Method and Practice*, Addison-Wesley, Reading.

Barney, R D & Black, J 1994, 'Ethics and Professional Persuasive Communications', *Public Relations Review*, 20(3), 233–48.

Beck, D & Cowan, C 1996, *Spiral Dynamics: Mastering Values, Leadership and Change*, Blackwell, Malden.

Beder, S 2000, *Global Spin: The Corporate Assault On Environmentalism*, Scribe, Melbourne.

Berger, B 2005, 'Power Over, Power With, and Power to Relations: Critical Reflections on Public Relations, the Dominant Coalition, and Activism', *Journal of Public Relations Research*, 17(1): 5–28.

Berger, B & Reber, B 2006, *Gaining Influence in Public Relations: The Role of Resistance in Practice*, Lawrence Erlbaum, Mahwah.

Botan, C & Taylor, M 2004, 'Public Relations State of the Field', *Journal of Communication*, 54: 645–61.

Botan, C H & Hazleton, V (eds) 1989, *Public Relations*, Lawrence Erlbaum, Mahwah.

Botan, C H & Hazleton, V (eds) 2006, *Public Relations Theory II*, Lawrence Erlbaum, Mahwah.

Bruning, S D & Ledingham, J A 2000, 'Perception of Relationships and Evaluations of Satisfaction: An Exploration of Interaction', *Public Relations Review*, 26(1): 85–95.

Burrell, G & Morgan, G 1979, *Sociological Paradigms and Organisational Dynamics: Elements of the Sociology of Corporate Life*, Heinemann, London.

Cheney, G 2000, 'Interpreting Interpretive Research: Toward Perspectivism Without Relativism', in S Corman & M Poole (eds), *Perspectives in Organizational Communication: Finding Common Ground*, Guilford Press, New York.

Cheney, G & Christensen, L 2001, 'Public Relations as Contested Terrain: A Critical Response', in R Heath (ed.), *Handbook of Public Relations*, Sage, Thousand Oaks.

Cheney, G 2006, 'What Should Public Relations Theory Do, Practically Speaking?', *Journal of Communication Management*, 10(1): 100–2.

Cheney, G, Zorn Jr, T E & Ganesh, S 2004, *Organizational Communication in an Age of Globalization: Issues, Reflections, Practices*, Waveland Press, Prospect Heights.

Chia, J 2008, 'Managing Complexity as Relational Opportunity', paper presented at the International Communication Association Conference, Montreal, 21–26 May.

Chia, J & Peters, M 2008, 'Employee Engagement in Organisations' Social Capital. Does Public Relations Have a Role?', *Asia Pacific Public Relations Journal*, 9: 103–20.

Chia, J 2005, 'Is Trust a Necessary Component of Relationship Management?', *Journal of Communication Management*, 9(3): 277–95.

Conrad, C & Poole, M 2002, *Strategic Organizational Communication*, 5th edn, Harcourt College Publishers, Fort Worth.

Cowan, C & Todorovic, N 2005, *The Never Ending Quest: Clare W Graves Explores Human Nature*, ECLET Publishing, Santa Barbara.

Creedon, P 1993, 'Acknowledging the Infrasystem: A Critical Feminist Analysis of Systems Theory', *Public Relations Review*, 19: 157–66.

Cunningham, S & Turner, G 2005, *Media and Communications in Australia*, 2nd edn, Allen & Unwin, Sydney.

Cutlip, S, Center, A & Broom, G 2000, *Effective Public Relations*, 8th edn, Prentice Hall, Upper Saddle River.

Dayrit Sison, M 2007, *Exploring the Roles of Australian Communication Practitioners in Organisational Value Setting: Agents of Conscience, Control and/or Compliance?*, unpublished PhD thesis, RMIT University, Melbourne.

Deetz, S 2001, 'Conceptual Foundations', in F Jablin & L Putnam (eds), *The New Handbook of Organizational Communication: Advances in Theory, Research, and Methods*, Sage, Thousand Oaks.

Dozier, D, Grunig, L & Grunig, J 1995, *Manager's Guide to Excellence in Public Relations and Communication Management*, Lawrence Erlbaum, Mahwah.

Ewen, S 1996, *A Social History of Spin*, Basic Books, New York.

Grunig, J E, Grunig, L A & Dozier, D 2006, 'The Excellence Theory', in C Botan & V Hazleton (eds), *Public Relations Theory II*, Lawrence Erlbaum, Mahwah.

Grunig, J E, Grunig, L A, Sriramesh, K & Lyra, A 1995, 'Models of Public Relations in an International Setting', *Journal of Public Relations Research*, 7(3): 163–86.

Grunig, J E & Hunt, T 1984, *Managing Public Relations*, Holt, Rinehart and Winston, New York.

Hallahan, K 1999, 'Seven Models of Framing: Implications for Public Relations', *Journal of Public Relations Research*, 11(3): 205–42.

Heath, R 1992, 'The Wrangle in the Marketplace: A Rhetorical Perspective of Public Relations', in E Toth & R Heath (eds), *Rhetorical and Critical Approaches to Public Relations*, Lawrence Erlbaum, Hillsdale.

Heath, R 2001, 'Shifting Foundations: Public Relations as Relationship Building', in R Heath (ed.), *Handbook of Public Relations*, Sage, Thousand Oaks.

Hofstede, G 1980, *Culture's Consequences: International Differences In Work-related Values*, Sage, Los Angeles.

Katz, D & Kahn, R 1966, *The Social Psychology of Organizations*, John Wiley & Sons, New York.

L'Etang, J 2005, 'Critical Public Relations: Some Reflections', *Public Relations Review*, 31(4): 521–6.

L'Etang, J & Pieczka, M 1996, *Critical Perspectives in Public Relations*, International Thomson Business Press, London.

Ledingham, J A 2006, 'Relationships Management: A General Theory of Public Relations', in C H Botan & V Hazleton (eds), *Public Relations Theory II*, Lawrence Erlbaum, Mahwah.

Ledingham, J A & Bruning, S D 1998, 'Relationship Management and Public Relations: Dimensions of an Organization–Public Relationship', *Public Relations Review*, 24(1): 55–65.

Ledingham, J A & Bruning, S D (eds) 2000, *Public Relations as Relationship Management: A Relational Approach to the Study and Practice of Public Relations*, Lawrence Erlbaum, Mahwah.

Lewin, K, http://psychology.about.com.

Littlejohn, S W 1999, *Theories of Human Communication*, 6th edn, Wadsworth Publishing Company, Wadsworth.

Littlejohn, S W & Foss, K A 2008, *Theories of Human Communication*, 9th edn, Thomson Wadsworth, Belmont.

Marsh, C 2003, 'Antecedents of Two-way Symmetry in Classical Greek Rhetoric: The Rhetoric of Isocrates', *Public Relations Review*, 29(3): 351–67.

May, S & Mumby, D K 2005, *Engaging Organizational Communication Theory and Research: Multiple Perspectives*, Sage, Thousand Oaks.

McKie, D & Munshi, D 2007, *Reconfiguring Public Relations: Equity, Ecology and Enterprise*, Routledge, London.

McLeod, J M & Chaffee, S H 1973, 'Interpersonal Approaches to Communications Research', *American Behavioral Scientist*, 16: 469–500.

MacNeish, J & Richardson, T 2000, *The Choice: Either Change the System or Polish the Fruit*, 4th edn, Don't Press, Melbourne.

Miles, R 1980, *Macro Organizational Behavior*, Scott Foresman and Company, Glenview.

Motion, J & Weaver, C 2005, 'A Discourse Perspective for Critical Public Relations Research: Life Sciences Network and the Battle for Truth', *Journal of Public Relations Research*, 17(1): 49–67.

Mumby, D K 2000, 'Common Ground from the Critical Perspective: Overcoming Binary Oppositions', in S Corman & M Poole (eds), *Perspectives on Organizational Communication: Finding Common Ground*, Guilford Press, New York.

Murphy, P 1991, 'The Limits of Symmetry: A Game Theory Approach to Symmetric and Asymmetric Public Relations', in J E Grunig & L A Grunig (eds), *Public Relations Research Annual*, vol. 3, Lawrence Erlbaum, Hillsdale.

O'Neil, J 2003, 'An Investigation of the Sources of Influences of Corporate Public Relations Practitioners', *Public Relations Review*, 29(2): 159–69.

Pfau, M & Wan, H-H 2006, 'Persuasion: An Intrinsic Function of Public Relations', in C Botan & V Hazleton (eds), *Public Relations Theory II*, Lawrence Erlbaum, Mahwah.

Putnam, L & Fairhurst, G 2001, 'Discourse Analysis in Organizations: Issues and Concerns', in F Jablin & L Putnam (eds), *The New Handbook of Organizational Communication: Advances in Theory, Research, and Methods*, Sage, Thousand Oaks.

Roper, J 2005, 'Symmetrical Communication: Excellent Public Relations or a Strategy for Hegemony?', *Journal of Public Relations Research*, 17(1): 69–86.

Sallot, L M, Lyon, L J, Acosta-Alzuru, C & Jones, K O 2008, 'From Aardvark to Zebra Redux: An Analysis of Theory Development in Public Relations Academic Journals into the Twenty-first Century', in T L Hansen-Horn & B Dostal Neff (eds), *Public Relations: From Theory to Practice*, Pearson Education, Boston.

Schein, E 1992, *Organizational Culture and Leadership*, Jossey-Bass, San Francisco.

Severin, W J & Tankard, J W 1992, *Communication Theories: Origins, Methods, and Uses in the Mass Media*, Longman, New York.

Skerlep, A 2001, 'Re-evaluating the Role of Rhetoric in Public Relations Theory and in Strategies of Corporate Discourse', *Journal of Communication Management*, 6(2): 176–87.

Toth, E & Heath, R (eds) 1992, *Rhetorical and Critical Approaches to Public Relations*, Lawrence Erlbaum, Hillsdale.

Trujillo, N & Toth, E 1987, 'Organizational Perspectives for Public Relations Research and Practice', *Management Communication Quarterly*, 1(2): 199–231.

Van Leuven, J 1989, 'Theoretical Models for Public Relations Campaigns', in C H Botan (ed.), *Public Relations Theory*, Lawrence Erlbaum, Mahwah.

QUIT Victoria 2005, *Smoking Rates*, retrieved from www.quit.org.au/browse.asp?ContainerID=1634, 20 January 2008.

Wilber, K 2000, *Integral Psychology*, Shambhala, Boston.

Zorn, T E, Page, D J & Cheney, G 2000, 'Nuts About Change: Multiple Perspectives on Change-oriented Communication in a Public Sector Organization', *Management Communication Quarterly*, 13(4): 515–66.

Chapter **4**

PUBLIC RELATIONS ETHICS

Elspeth Tilley

PRACTITIONER PROFILE \ FIONA CASSIDY

Fiona Cassidy, the 2007–8 president of the Public Relations Institute of New Zealand, believes that working on projects you believe in is one of the most important contributions a public relations practitioner can make to the ethics of the profession. Her advice to new graduates is to 'Work with people whose values you admire, and get experience by volunteering for causes you believe in'. After fifteen years' experience at a strategic communications level developing, implementing, monitoring, and evaluating campaigns and initiatives in all areas of communication from government to marketing to crisis work, Fiona's own reputation for competence, integrity, and professionalism means that she can pick and choose the projects she is passionate about, such as health communication and Indigenous issues, and especially work where these interests combine. She has worked on a wide range of projects including the incorporation of Māori language into New Zealand schools, to encourage immunisation uptake, to reduce smoking, and to prepare for an influenza pandemic, among others.

Fiona also believes in the importance of life-long learning and formal qualifications: she has two Masters degrees, and continues to update her skills with, for example, a certificate in Māori language proficiency in 2007. She's also planning another postgraduate qualification in public relations research.

> It is part of our PRINZ code of ethics that practitioners constantly advance the profession through continued professional development, research, and education, but aside from that, I just enjoy it—and there is always more that's interesting and useful to learn.

CHAPTER **AIMS**

By the end of this chapter, you should be able to:

➤ understand the fundamental importance of ethics to the study and application of professional public relations

➤ be familiar with the main theoretical approaches to ethical reasoning

➤ apply a range of practical ethics tools so that you feel confident to try different ethics approaches and tools when planning public relations activity or facing ethical dilemmas

➤ confidently present the need for a systematic approach to ethics within the organisation you work with.

Introduction

By now you have probably noticed that the word 'ethics' appears frequently in the chapters of this book. As public relations evolves from an image-building function to a reputation and relationship management role in organisations, ethics becomes increasingly central to the philosophy and the practice of public relations.

When Ivy Ledbetter Lee first proposed, in the early twentieth century, that public relations should provide an organisation's 'conscience' (Ryan & Martinson 1983; Grunig & Hunt 1984; Bowen 2002), his ideas were new and unique. By 'conscience' he meant that public relations should help organisations be responsible for their effects on the social and physical environments—or, in Lee's own words, to remember that 'A purely selfish policy is not a good policy' (Lee 1925: 54). Lee wrote a *Declaration of Principles* for public relations in 1904, a document that, at the time, was groundbreaking in proposing accuracy and transparency as the cornerstones of public relations activity (Morse 1906: 460).

REFLECT AND DISCUSS

➤ Ivy Lee's own clients' actions have not always matched his declared principles—can you locate any information online about Lee's public relations clients, one of whom was John D Rockefeller?

➤ What information can you find, for example, about the Ludlow Massacre?

➤ Can you suggest any reasons why Lee found it difficult to practice what he preached?

Since Lee's time, definitions of the profession have shifted to become almost entirely about ethics, reflecting his emphases on unselfish and truthful communication. As James Grunig (2006: 165) states:

> If the role of public relations in strategic management is to bring the voices of publics into the decision-making process, public relations should be able to improve the ethics and social responsibility of organizational behaviors.

Quotes such as Grunig's, and the rise of social responsibility programs as a formal part of the public relations role, signal that ethics is now absolutely central to contemporary understandings of what public relations is about.

Social responsibility refers to the idea that all organisations and individuals have a duty to protect and benefit the whole planet and all the people on it when they act, not just serve their own short-term interests. In the corporate world, measures of social responsibility include balanced reporting systems such as the 'triple bottom line' (Elkington 1994), which measures the impact on 'Earth' and 'Earthlings' alongside the traditional financial measure of 'Earnings'.

Yet surprisingly, for a concept that is so often considered fundamental to the professional evolution of public relations, ethics is seldom explicitly defined. So what exactly is ethics?

What is ethics?

Ethics is about standards of behaviour, specifically, concern for 'good' behaviour and consideration of how our behaviour, as an individual or an organisation, affects the wellbeing of others or society as a whole. Ethics involves morals (our sense of what is just or unjust, often called our conscience) and values (the principles, standards, or qualities we consider worthwhile or valuable in ourselves and others, such as truthfulness or dependability). If we are making an effort to behave ethically, we will consider the morals and values involved in our actions before we act.

Some values are thought to be fairly widespread. Michael Josephson, for example, argues (in Seib & Fitzpatrick 1995) the following ten values to be universal, that is, equally important in all cultures and time periods:

1 honesty
2 integrity
3 keeping promises
4 fidelity
5 fairness

6 caring for others
7 respect for others
8 responsible citizenship
9 pursuit of excellence
10 accountability.

REFLECT AND DISCUSS

> ➤ What does each of the values above mean to you? Write a definition for each in your own words, then compare your definition with someone else's. How do you differ, and how are you similar?
>
> ➤ What is the relevance of each of these values for the practice of public relations? Write a few words for each suggesting how they fit into the communication process.
>
> ➤ Do you agree with Josephson that these values are universal? Do you think that 'responsible citizenship', for example, means the same thing now as it did for, say, your grandparents' generation? Likewise, do you think that all cultures have the same ideas about what is fair, with respect to, say, attitudes towards older members of society or gender roles? Write a few sentences arguing for or against the idea that ethics can be universal.

Is it easy to be ethical?

If we have a simple ten step list for ethical values, does that make it easy to be ethical? Those who subscribe to the universal standards view of ethics sometimes argue that what is ethical is obvious and natural, and that choosing the most ethical behaviour should therefore just be 'as normal and as unconscious as shaking hands' (Howard & Mathews 1988: 96). At a public relations conference in New Zealand in 2005, a senior practitioner in the audience echoed this sentiment when he said, 'We know exactly how to be ethical, we're good people. We just need to stop talking about it and get on with it' (PRINZ conference audience member, personal communication, 27 July 2005).

Surveys typically indicate that the majority of public relations professionals believe they are highly ethical (see, for example, Young 2004). Nonetheless, the profession continues to produce damaging examples of questionable practice. There are so many of these examples in the media that 'the consumer of mass culture stereotypes is ... likely to think of PR ethics as an oxymoron' (Brown 2003: 497). In New Zealand, for example, media headlines about public relations spin abounded when a government department media log, obtained under freedom of information law, recorded that public relations staff 'agreed to lie in unison' (Fountaine 2005: 29).

So why does the discrepancy between practitioners' views of themselves and others' view of their practice arise? Actually being ethical may not be as simple as thinking of oneself as a good person or knowing a list of values, as Ivy Lee's professional history illustrates. Understanding what is considered unethical can help us to work towards understanding what is ethical.

What does it mean to be unethical?

The online environment provides some useful illustrations of public relations actions that have been labelled as unethical by people outside the profession. High-profile examples include the following:

➤ WalMarting Across America, in which Richard Edelman, president and CEO of multinational public relations firm Edelman, publicly apologised on his blog after two people who appeared to be disinterested parties taking a fun road trip from one WalMart carpark to the next were revealed to be sponsored by Edelman on behalf of WalMart (Taylor 2006).

➤ The Zero Movement, which led to the Coca-Cola Company being ridiculed by blogger groups and critiqued in mainstream media after what looked like an unaffiliated grassroots webpage and discussion board were revealed to be brand-building for Coke Zero (Hearn 2006).

➤ Al Gore's Penguin Army, an apparently amateur YouTube video lampooning Al Gore's movie *An Inconvenient Truth*, which the *Wall Street Journal* discovered may have originated in a public relations company with links to the Republican Party and oil companies (Regalado & Searcey 2006).

REFLECT AND DISCUSS

➤ What do you think the main criticisms may have been of each company involved in the above incidents?

➤ If you were the public relations professional for each company in the above examples, what would you have done differently?

➤ What is a front group? Can you find any examples of front groups created by influential figures in public relations' history, such as Edward Bernays? (For one example, see Haugland 2000.)

➤ Would you call any of the online activity described above as being conducted by a front group? Why?

None of the firms involved in these cases was criticised for creating online materials, but all were faulted by key publics for failing to clearly identify such materials as commercial output. By contrast, the movie studio Paramount was praised by internet users for conspicuously labelling its YouTube video promoting Gore's film as produced by Paramount (Regalado & Searcey 2006).

These and other cases suggest that many public relations practitioners continue to get it wrong when assessing whether their actions will align with their publics' expectations for ethical behaviour. A poor decision on ethical matters, however, does not necessarily mean the perpetrator is intentionally a 'bad person'. Often, the cause of unethical practice is a result of ignorance of what is required for ethical behaviour, or lack of a practical framework for ethical decision making rather than deliberate wrongdoing. A useful fictional example occurs in the Jim Carrey movie *Fun With Dick and Jane* (Parisot 2005), which was loosely inspired by the Enron and WorldCom scandals in the USA. Carrey plays Dick Harper, a gullible public relations executive who fails to check information supplied to him by senior managers before announcing it on television, then finds himself charged with criminally misleading the public. Harper is a likeable, well intentioned, trusting, and essentially decent person, but as the movie unfolds there is no escaping the fact that his initial failure to follow basic good procedure leads to increasingly unethical behaviour.

REFLECT AND DISCUSS

> ➤ In the movie *Fun With Dick and Jane* Dick Harper's dilemma highlights some key issues in public relations ethics. Answer the following questions, then, if you can get a copy, watch the movie and answer them again. Have your answers changed?
>
> ➤ Where does an employee's first duty lie? Is it to obey an employer's directives, or to consider wider public interest?
>
> ➤ Can public relations operate ethically if it is not given access to all of an organisation's operational information? Write a short paragraph arguing for the ethical importance of public relations staff occupying a seat at the boardroom table and being directly involved in key business decisions.
>
> ➤ Imagine that you work for a company that you love, in a public relations job that you adore. Your boss asks you to do something that you consider is not in the public interest. You have been told you will lose your job if you refuse a direct instruction. How would you respond?

In practice, then, ethics is never as simple as just good intent. What we know to be good in any given situation is highly individual and may not fit with broader social norms or the expectations of specific publics. Morals and values are a result of upbringing, family, education, culture, reference groups, previous experiences, age, religious affiliation, and a host of other influences. It is likely that no two people, let alone two cultures, have exactly the same morals and values or place the same degree of importance on them. It is inevitable then, that when multiple viewpoints are involved, as they are by definition when an organisation communicates with its publics and audiences, ethics is not normal, unconscious, or straightforward. On the contrary, ethics needs careful, proactive consideration, and public relations practitioners need thorough ethical learning, and the ability to use systematic methods to encompass, respect, and balance multiple viewpoints, before arriving at a decision as to what is the best course of action.

Being mindful of ethics in every situation

Cross-cultural communication theorist William Gudykunst (2005) uses mindfulness—originally a Buddhist term meaning alertness or awareness—to describe a three-part approach to communication competence involving constant mental attention to willingness, knowledge, and skill. We can adapt this idea for public relations to suggest that the most ethically competent practitioner will be the one who is always:

➤ willing to see ethics as important
➤ aware of ethics as a challenging (not simple) area and therefore constantly increasing their knowledge
➤ continually assessing and improving their own ethical skill.

The moment we become unconscious or mindless of ethical considerations in any given situation is the moment we become a Dick Harper: likeable enough but utterly ethically incompetent.

Willingness: the first step towards mindfulness

Some of the most fundamental steps in making ethics a mindful quality for the public relations practitioner are also very easy and achievable. Simply make ethics a noticeable topic in your workplace so that people are willing to see it as important. You could, for example, put large colourful copies of your association's code of ethics and your organisation's code of conduct on the wall in a prominent place. (When I visit public relations workplaces, I always ask where their code of ethics is kept. Some do not know, others find it in a bottom drawer after a search, and just a handful can point to it on display. All except the last group are visibly embarrassed by the question.) Some other suggestions are in Box 4.1 on page 97.

BOX **4.1** \ MAKING ETHICS VISIBLE

➤ Appoint an ethics officer for your public relations team (and one for the organisation as a whole if it does not have one already) who is responsible for creating awareness of the importance of ethics and helping people with ethical queries.

➤ Start an ethics column in the internal newsletter, with cartoons or jokes to illustrate hypothetical situations. Ask different staff members or groups of people to contribute their thoughts.

➤ Provide a library of ethics-related reading material in the workplace.

➤ Invite interesting speakers to the workplace to talk about their ethics experiences in public relations and to offer anecdotes and advice.

➤ Schedule regular informal ethics group discussions where team members can reflect on challenges and practices.

➤ Schedule five minutes for a personal ethical reflection time each morning during which you think about what values you want to follow for the day, and again each afternoon when you reflect on how difficult or easy it was to maintain those values.

In short, make ethics a real life, relevant, non-frightening topic that is regularly talked about in a non-threatening way, so that people are happy to discuss and share ideas on it without feeling judged or embarrassed. All of these things will signal and foster a culture of willingness to make ethics mindfully central to the daily routine of public relations work.

REFLECT AND **DISCUSS**

➤ Suggest three other ways that you could make ethics visible in your workplace.

Knowledge: the second step to ethical mindfulness

The knowledge aspect of mindfulness can be fostered by reading, then thinking critically about and discussing what various people have written on ethics, not only in books and academic articles but also in blogs and online forums where professionals gather to examine and debate their work. There is plenty of scope for debate: theoretical work on public relations ethics offers diverse and competing frameworks, as is the nature of robust scholarship (see Further reading, on pages 118–19).

Academic literature cannot offer a single magic solution for ethical dilemmas but it can stimulate you to think independently and build the knowledge and capacities for

Elspeth Tilley

evaluation and analysis that are crucial to ethical reasoning. An overview of schools of thought in the field, as provided later in this chapter, cannot substitute for wide, eclectic, and frequent reading in public relations ethics and regular analysis of what is read, but it can at least provide an orientation point for starting the journey into the fascinating world of ethical reasoning and theory.

REFLECT AND DISCUSS

> ➤ Academic literature (as a whole) debates ethics rather than providing agreed answers. Why do you think this is?
> ➤ Find two academic articles that provide conflicting or alternative perspectives on public relations ethics. (You may find a citation index useful in identifying who has cited whom, which can alert you to situations where one academic has criticised or argued with something published earlier. Ask your librarian for help.)
> ➤ Summarise each article's perspective. Which aspects of each argument, if any, do you find convincing? Why?

Skill: the third step in ethical mindfulness

Achieving knowledge of a range of ethical systems is part of mindfulness: the final step is to become skilful in using them, which means discussing, practising, combining, selecting, and applying them every day as part of regular public relations activity. The section below outlines some approaches to ethics, including some practical tools for highlighting the ethical aspects of a situation. To become skilful, these approaches should not only be read about, but actively engaged with. Try applying them to case studies or real life situations as you read, and assess whether they are useful.

Ethics schools of thought

There are several theoretical schools of thought on ethics (and debate between them as to where their boundaries lie), and each has advantages and disadvantages when applied to public relations. For simplicity, we will use the convention of dividing ethics theory into the three schools of virtue, deontology, and consequentialism. Larry Temkin (2004: 354) provides a useful summary of the focus of each field:

> ➤ Virtue theorists ask the question: 'What kind of person ought I to be?'
> ➤ Deontologists ask the question: 'What are my duties?'
> ➤ Consequentialists ask the question: 'How ought the world to be?'

As you will see below, the most comprehensive approach is one that can incorporate multiple ethical aspects from each of the three schools, prompting practitioners to think about virtues as well as setting some reasonable prohibitions or limits on behaviour, and consider the overall goals of any given campaign. All three schools will be looked at before suggesting a way to combine them in daily public relations practice.

Virtue ethics: what kind of person ought I be?

Virtue ethics is about the importance of developing a strong sense of personal values, or good character, to guide ethical behaviour. Its best known proponent is the Greek philosopher Aristotle (384–22 BC), who developed the idea of the 'golden mean' (1985: 42–52). Aristotle uses 'mean' in the mathematical sense of the midpoint in any series of numbers to refer to what a 'reasonable' person would do in the circumstances.

BOX **4.2** \ ARISTOTLE AND THE INTERMEDIATE APPROACH

For Aristotle being reasonable meant finding an intermediate approach between the most inappropriate or extreme responses in any situation. He used the example of bravery (1985: 46) to illustrate the virtuous mean between too much confidence (insufficient fear, or rashness) and too little confidence (excess fear, or cowardice). To apply this idea to public relations, if, for example, you needed to counsel management that the organisation had made a public blunder, a golden mean approach would contain neither too much nor too little criticism. You would not trivialise or ignore the mistake, because the organisation's leaders would not learn from that, but neither would you criticise excessively, so that they became defensive and unable to listen.

In public relations theory, James Grunig's mixed motives approach (2001) (see Chapters 2 and 3) is similar to the golden mean approach: the organisation must listen to publics and meet their needs where possible but it cannot accommodate them absolutely, so that the organisation's own interests are forgotten. Rather, a middle ground approach to organisation–public relationships is taken, which tries to balance all parties' needs over time.

To practise virtue ethics, you need to care about what kind of person you want to be and behave in ways that are true to that ideal. Asking self-reflexive questions is an important first step:

➤ Harrison (2004: 2) recommends public relations practitioners ask, 'How ought a person of good character, a person of integrity, feel and act in this situation?'
➤ Harrison and Galloway (2005: 2) recommend asking, 'What is it that public relations practitioners do of which we can be (or are) proud?'

Elspeth Tilley

REFLECT AND DISCUSS

> ➤ From your knowledge of public relations and your sense of your own values, what is it that public relations practitioners do that would make you personally feel proud?

Advantages of virtue ethics

A key benefit of virtue ethics is that it encourages practitioners to consciously consider their ethical beliefs and define a personal moral bottom line. David Martinson (2000: 19) suggests virtue ethics is most helpful to public relations practitioners when it 'stimulat[es] the moral imagination … to recognize ethical issues'.

Disadvantages of virtue ethics

Virtue ethics is very individualistic, with little or no acknowledgment that what is considered reasonable may differ by gender, age, culture, and other factors, may change in different circumstances, and may even change over the course of a person's life. Kim and Choi (2003) found that age was a factor, while Lois Boynton (2003) found that public relations practitioners' personality type had a strong effect on their determinations of ethical reasonableness. Moral reckoning processes were very different for:

> ➤ absolutists (people who live by firm principles)
> ➤ debaters (people who like to argue through the differing perspectives of a situation)
> ➤ loyalists (people who prioritise relationships)
> ➤ avoiders (people who dislike conflict).

REFLECT AND DISCUSS

> ➤ Which of the above categories do you think describes you? Why?
> ➤ Imagine you are in a four-person team working on a public relations project. There is one type of each of the above four in the team. An ethical issue has arisen and a decision must be made. Write four sentences, each sentence describing something positive that each of the four team members can offer to the team's problem-solving approach.

People are different, therefore what they think is ethical will differ. Yet if virtue ethics is the only yardstick, each person may be convinced that their viewpoint is virtuous. One fierce critic of virtue ethics (McElreath 1997: 56) says that, because it instructs individuals to rely upon their personal, instinctive moral reasoning style, virtue ethics 'invites moral anarchy' and encourages blinkered self-righteousness in which every person thinks their own way of seeing things is the reasonable one. Such a position—we might call it ethical imperialism— could be particularly problematic in cross-cultural or intercultural public relations. Nancy Roth, Todd Hunt, Maria Stavropoulos and Karen Babik (1996: 151) note substantial differences in understanding 'what counts as ethical practice' across cultures (see also Davis, Johnson & Ohmer 1998), while Shuter argues that individualistic and collectivist cultures may have ethical expectations so different as to be 'culturally incompatible' (2003: 450).

BOX **4.3** \ ETHICAL CONTEXT

Much communication theory, including that used in public relations, privileges Western ethical worldviews (Fitch & Surma 2006; Shuter 2003). Chapters 1, 2 and 3 have pointed to the need to widen theoretical perspectives so that intercultural and international viewpoints are considered. Students are also directed to Chapter 13 of this book, which specifically focuses on public relations in Asia so that they are conversant with other points of view. Public relations practitioners communicating across cultures must be conscious of underpinning differences in order not to impose their own ethical expectations on publics.

➤ Individualistic cultures tend to value 'reason, logic, evidence, and truthfulness' (Shuter: 451) but 'these standards would be considered morally insufficient' in collectivist cultures.
➤ Collectivist cultures place the wellbeing of the group before that of individuals. Confucian ethics, for example, 'is grounded in community or family obligations and duties' (452).

Shuter identifies similarly fundamental differences in ethical logic between the US and Islamic cultures, which mean that, in a conflict, each can be convinced its actions are the only possible ethical ones.

While virtue ethics is a useful starting point, in many, if not most, ethical dilemmas faced during the complex exchanges of multiple viewpoints involved in public relations, more guidance will be needed than a sense of personal good character. Furthermore, not everybody is sure about their own personal sense of values and identity. If, especially, you are starting out in public relations and are as yet insecure in your own value system or uncertain what is reasonable, it can be helpful to use some third party virtue tests such as:

➤ the front page or publicity test (Would you feel comfortable with the decisions you are making being on the front page of the newspaper?)
➤ the 'significant other' test (Would you feel comfortable that any significant person whose values you admire and whose approval you desire, such as a loved relative, would applaud your planned behaviour in this campaign?).

Elspeth Tilley

These questions help to expand the test of what is reasonable beyond just the individual to encompass broader social norms.

Other ways to compensate for the individualistic bias of virtue ethics include discussion or research to uncover the values of all parties to a communication process, such as client, employer, publics, and team members. Once uncovered, such values can be turned into concrete measures of ethical performance by stating them as objectives and evaluating them at the end of a public relations campaign (Tilley 2005b; see also more on this later in the chapter). A single public relations campaign may not be successful in meeting all diverse ethical expectations from a range of publics, but explicit research to track and evaluate ethics objectives will at least give a clear picture of which values the overall campaign favoured.

Another way to compensate for the individualistic bias of virtue ethics is to refer to some guidelines that give a broader picture of what is considered acceptable to a group, rather than to individuals. This is the deontological approach.

Deontology: what are my duties?

Deontological ethics evolved largely from the writings of German philosopher Immanuel Kant (1724–1804), and involves following a prescribed set of duties or obligations, for example, religious rules such as the Ten Commandments. There are many aspects to Kant's theory but his central belief was in the existence of absolute moral principles, that is, that there are rules (categorical imperatives) for good behaviour that will hold true no matter the situation (1956). Public relations practitioners can follow deontology in its simplest sense by checking that their actions meet such rule-based prescriptions as:

> ➤ the law
> ➤ codes of conduct or ethics (clients', employers', or professional associations')
> ➤ agreed principles or regulations for activities in certain contexts, such as the (largely unwritten) norms of netiquette that govern online behaviour.

Two deontologically influenced positions in public relations theory are advocacy and the rhetorical position. Both argue that, provided practitioners' specific behaviours are ethical against agreed standards such as professional ethics codes, the primary ethical duty of public relations is to articulate the client's position so that it can be publicly considered in a competitive 'market-place of ideas' (an idea with antecedents in the work of Aristotle, Socrates, John Stuart Mill, and others; see Hofstadter & Metzger 1955).

Advocacy

The advocacy approach is usually associated with Bernays (1928, 1955), and still has followers today. Martinson, for example, argues that 'the public relations practitioner representing a particular political cause … can ethically attempt to persuade outside publics of the "correctness" of the viewpoint he/she is espousing' (2004: n.p.), provided they do not lie or mislead in the process.

REFLECT AND DISCUSS

> ➤ Do you think that all clients can be represented ethically if no lying is involved?
> ➤ Watch a copy of the movie *Thank You for Smoking* (Reitman 2006). Fictional public relations practitioner Nick Naylor represents the tobacco industry. He never actually lies, but do you think he is ethical? Why?

Rhetorical approach

Heath (2008) is the best-known proponent of the rhetorical position, arguing that 'public relations practitioners can learn from the past and build their practice on a rich rhetorical heritage' (223). The best rhetoric, Heath argues, is of itself ethical by nature. It 'puts information and thoughtful interpretations before audiences for their consideration' and requires the communicator 'to prove any point he or she asserts' (212). It is also conducted within a broader commitment to total organisational ethics, so that rhetoric matches behaviour:

> Any organization that does not aspire to the highest levels of corporate responsibility is likely to find that its actions discredit its statements. Actions speak, and they speak louder than words (2008: 212).

REFLECT AND DISCUSS

> ➤ What does Heath mean by 'actions speak louder than words'? Explain this in your own words with reference to public relations cases you have studied.
> ➤ Find an example in the media of an organisation that has recently had its statements discredited by its behaviour. What happened, and why?

Rules for deontology

The law

Deontology involves following rules or standards. Legal compliance is usually considered to be the absolute minimum deontological standard, and often inadequate for truly ethical behaviour. As Shannon Bowen observes, laws set a limit for 'what can be done' without attracting censure or penalty, while ethics refers to 'what should be done' (2008: 162–3). There is nothing illegal about, say, creating a .org domain discussion board or website without revealing a commercial interest behind it, but the unspoken assumption of such forums is that they are an outlet for non-commercial activity. In the preceding Edelman case, for example, Edelman might have predicted that it would attract criticism for its WalMarting Across America site if it tested for ethics above legality. One such test that, if applied, may have sounded an alarm bell as to the site's reception by the online community, is the Word of Mouth Marketing Association (WOMMA) Code of Ethics (2007). The next section discusses when and how such codes may be useful.

REFLECT AND DISCUSS

> ➤ The WOMMA code states that members will 'practise openness about the relationship between consumers, advocates, and marketers' (WOMMA 2007).
> ➤ Do you think that the WalMarting Across America site complied with this principle? How might this code principle be useful internally when planning website content?

Ethics codes

Ethics codes are probably the most commonly used and practical deontological tool, although because stating rules too precisely can make codes inflexible, there is a growing trend to design them using 'values rather than prohibitions' (Harrison 2004: 3), that is, to orient them more towards virtue than deontology. One such code is the National Communication Association's Credo for Ethical Communication, which is mainly a statement of values rather than a set of explicit rules, but it is simple, clear, broad enough to be applicable to many different situations, and makes a useful aspirational guideline for printing out and displaying on a workplace wall for constant reference.

BOX 4.4 \ *NCA CREDO FOR ETHICAL COMMUNICATION*

Questions of right and wrong arise whenever people communicate. Ethical communication is fundamental to responsible thinking, decision making, and the development of relationships and communities within and across contexts, cultures, channels, and media. Moreover, ethical communication enhances human worth and dignity by fostering truthfulness, fairness, responsibility, personal integrity, and respect for self and others. We believe that unethical communication threatens the quality of all communication and consequently the well-being of individuals and the society in which we live. Therefore we, the members of the National Communication Association, endorse and are committed to practising the following principles of ethical communication.

1 We advocate truthfulness, accuracy, honesty, and reason as essential to the integrity of communication.

2 We endorse freedom of expression, diversity of perspective, and tolerance of dissent to achieve the informed and responsible decision making fundamental to a civil society.

3 We strive to understand and respect other communicators before evaluating and responding to their messages.

4 We promote access to communication resources and opportunities as necessary to fulfil human potential and contribute to the well-being of families, communities, and society.

5 We promote communication climates of caring and mutual understanding that respect the unique needs and characteristics of individual communicators.

6 We condemn communication that degrades individuals and humanity through distortion, intimidation, coercion, and violence, and through the expression of intolerance and hatred.

7 We are committed to the courageous expression of personal convictions in pursuit of fairness and justice.

8 We advocate sharing information, opinions, and feelings when facing significant choices while also respecting privacy and confidentiality.

9 We accept responsibility for the short- and long-term consequences for our own communication and expect the same of others.

Source: National Communication Association 1999

REFLECT AND DISCUSS

➤ Which of the NCA principles do you expect might be most relevant or helpful for public relations? Why?

Another useful code is the Public Relations Institute of New Zealand's ethics code, which has two sections (on the following pages; used with permission). First, it has a statement of values, designed to reflect some consensus as to what members think constitutes professional and ethical conduct, then an applied section, designed to cover the daily working needs of its members. This second part of the code includes specific challenges likely to arise in the course of public relations practice, for example tensions between openness and privacy. Again, this code is worth printing and having on hand even if you are not based in New Zealand, as it complements the NCA's code, which is more about general principles of communication, by providing some process guidelines specific to public relations.

Elspeth Tilley

BOX **4.5** \ PUBLIC RELATIONS INSTITUTE OF NEW ZEALAND

Public relations professionals use communications to develop or maintain trusting, productive relationships between our clients or employers and their stakeholders. We promote the views of those we represent to contribute to public debate and informed decision making in a democratic society.

We balance our role as advocates for individuals or groups with the public interest. We must also balance a commitment to promote open communication with the privacy rights of individuals and organisations.

VALUES

These values provide the foundation for the Public Relations Institute of New Zealand Code of Ethics and set the industry standard for the professional practice of public relations. They are the fundamental beliefs that guide our behaviour and decision-making processes.

ADVOCACY

We serve the public interest by acting as responsible advocates for those we represent.

We provide a voice for the ideas, facts and viewpoints of those we represent to aid informed public debate.

HONESTY

We are accurate and truthful in advancing the interests of those we represent and in communicating with the public.

EXPERTISE

We acquire and responsibly use specialised knowledge and experience.

We advance the profession through continued professional development, research and education.

We build mutual understanding, credibility and relationships among an array of institutions and audiences.

INDEPENDENCE

We provide objective counsel to those we represent.

We are accountable for our actions.

LOYALTY

We are faithful to those we represent, while honouring our obligations to serve the public interest.

We safeguard the confidences of former or present employers and clients.

FAIRNESS

We deal fairly with clients, employers, competitors, peers, suppliers, the media and the society.

We respect all opinions and support the right of free expression.

PRINZ CODE OF ETHICS

The primary obligation of membership of the Public Relations Institute of New Zealand is the ethical practice of public relations. This Code sets out the principles and standards that guide our decisions and actions.

1 Advocacy and Honesty

A member shall:

i   Provide independent, objective counsel for clients or employers

ii   Promote the ethical, well-founded views of clients or employers

iii Be honest and accurate in all communications—and act promptly to correct erroneous communications

iv   Avoid deceptive practices.

2 Balancing Openness and Privacy

A member shall:

i   Promote open communication in the public interest wherever possible

ii   Respect the rights of others to have their say

iii Be prepared to name clients or employers represented and the sponsors for causes and interests represented

iv   Safeguard the confidences and privacy rights of present, former and prospective clients and employers.

3 Conflicts of Interest

A member shall:

i   Disclose promptly any existing or potential conflict of interest to affected clients or organisations

ii   Disclose any client or business interest in published or broadcast editorial work.

4 Law Abiding

A member shall:

i   Abide by the laws affecting the practice of public relations and the laws and regulations affecting the client.

5 Professionalism

A member shall:

i   Actively pursue personal professional development

ii   Explain realistically what public relations activities can accomplish

iii Counsel colleagues on ethical decision making

iv   Decline representation of clients or organisations that urge or require actions contrary to this code

v   Not engage in irrelevant or unsubstantiated personal criticism.

No code is perfect but if used proactively to guide practice rather than reactively to solve problems they can provide a solid introduction to and constant reminder about the general principles of thinking ethically.

REFLECT AND DISCUSS

➤ How can an ethics code be used proactively instead of reactively in public relations planning? List three or more suggested ways.

Codes can be used as benchmarks for choosing and setting ethical objectives in a campaign. An obvious (and therefore rarely explicitly stated or tested) objective for all campaigns is for each specific campaign activity at every stage to fully adhere to relevant professional codes. Like virtue ethics, deontology can be incorporated into a campaign's planning and evaluation procedures by setting specific objectives such as 'We will adhere to the ethics code in everything we do' and checking back to determine whether such objectives have actually been attained (see the section on proactive ethics).

Advantages of deontology

One of the advantages of deontology is that by directing practitioners to codes, rules, and agreed standards it can provide clear directives and a bottom line. It is less muddy or personal than virtue-based approaches, and often has some built-in accountability. Many codes have sanctions for breaches, so there is some professional enforcement of their principles. The Public Relations Institute of Australia, for example, circulated an email to members naming a member who had been found to have breached the code by exaggerating their qualifications and experience when presenting themselves to prospective clients. Many other codes do not have sanctions: the WOMMA code referred to, for example, is voluntary, and ironically, Edelman was one of the instigators of its design.

Disadvantages of deontology

The key disadvantage of a deontological approach to ethics is its inflexibility. Codes and rules cannot possibly cover every situation—and sometimes rules can be followed to the letter yet ethical intention is still absent. A particular set of accounting 'rules' was carefully followed by Enron, for example, but the attention paid to them tended to obscure rather than surface ethical considerations (McLean 2007).

REFLECT AND DISCUSS

> ➤ What was Enron and what happened to it? Why was Enron unethical?

Sometimes, breaking a rule may be an ethical choice. Conservationists, for example, may choose to deliberately break laws as part of their protest action. In Tasmania, a woman was charged with creating a nuisance and disobeying police orders after she dressed as an angel and chained herself to a tripod to draw public attention to logging (Cordingley 2007). The community was divided as to the ethics of her action: deontological judgments about her law-breaking conflicted with assessments made using a consequentialist approach (defined below) in which actions are judged by their outcomes rather than by some rightness inherent in acts themselves.

These cases suggest that there is usually more to thinking through the ethics of an action than unfailingly following laws or rules. Again the idea of mindfulness is useful: duties and rules can be helpful when followed with mindfulness of their consequences, but may still be unethical if followed unthinkingly. Consequentialism offers a third way of thinking about ethics.

Consequentialism: how ought the world be?

Consequentialists judge actions by their outcomes. The best-known technique is utilitarianism, derived primarily from the work of eighteenth century English philosopher Jeremy Bentham, in which an assessment is made of who is affected by an action, and in what ways; the right action is deemed to be that which creates maximum total benefit. It is of course difficult to define precisely what is a 'benefit' and in what timeframe it should be calculated (is, for example, maintaining jobs for loggers likely to be more or less beneficial, and to whom, than long-term forest preservation?), but for everyday public relations, a practical utilitarian method is the overall benefit–harm assessment, in which a judgment is made as to how total benefits to all publics from a public relations activity can be maximised and harm minimised.

BOX 4.6 \ BENEFIT AND HARM

It is useful, when assessing benefit and harm, to test:

➤ reversibility (would you be happy for the outcome to affect you in the same way it will your publics?)

➤ universalisability (would the outcome for society be acceptable if everyone behaved this way?).

To apply reversibility to public relations, the twentieth century US philosopher John Rawls' concept of a 'veil of ignorance' (1971) is especially helpful. Pretend that you do not know whether you might yourself be a member of one of the publics affected by your intended actions, and then see whether you still think the actions would be acceptable if the veil of ignorance were removed and you discovered that you were the one affected by your actions.

To apply universalisability, ask yourself whether you would be happy for every public relations practitioner, including consultancies that compete with you for clients, to use the methods you are about to employ.

Rawls' concept of the original position is also an important perspective on consequentialist ethics, and one that stands behind many modern affirmative action programs such as those to correct workplace gender and diversity imbalances. In this concept, the more ethical outcome is seen to be that in which prior deficits are taken into account in distribution of benefits, not just future benefit and harm from this point on. Rawls asks us to imagine that once there was a world of perfect equality (the original position). The right action is the one that takes us closer to that position, not further away.

REFLECT AND DISCUSS

> ➤ If a classical utilitarian were dividing a chocolate bar among six people they would probably cut it into six equal portions to create maximum happiness; if Rawls was dividing a chocolate bar he'd probably check to see who already had a chocolate bar in their bag and leave them out of the division. Which do you think is fairer? Why? Explain and justify your thinking.

Advantages of consequentialism

Like any other ethics system, considering consequences cannot magically provide right answers as to what is ethical, but reflection on the different impacts from different actions builds our awareness of our own moral and cultural assumptions as to what is right.

This latter, awareness–building, is in fact the aim of most ethics systems: you should not expect any single system to 'guarantee an ethical decision. They are mainly useful to ensure that the ethical components of the situation will be surfaced so that they might be considered' (Seib & Fitzpatrick 1995: 37).

BOX **4.7** \ SOCS

One practical consequentialist tool that I use frequently to surface ethical issues in public relations is a brainstorming technique I call SOCS, which stands for **s**takeholders, **o**ptions, **c**onsequences, and **s**trategy. To use it, follow these steps.

1   Brainstorm a list of all **s**takeholders or affected parties in the given situation and write them in a cluster at the centre of a large sheet of paper.
2   Brainstorm all possible **o**ptions for acting in the given situation and write them around the outside of the paper (mind-mapping software is useful for this).
3   Connect each stakeholder to each possible option, and along the connecting line write the risks, costs, and benefits to them from each different course of action (**c**onsequences).

You should end up with a large spider design that makes visible the consequences of each option for each party.

4   Finally, analyse the visual information using ethical considerations such as reasonableness, publicity test, laws and codes, original position, and veil of ignorance.

This process can help you to **s**trategise, that is, to prioritise risks, costs, and benefits, identify what course of action maximises preferable benefits for all groups, considers their current needs and capacities, does nothing unacceptable, and minimises risk of harm.

SOCS is not a perfect system but it puts publics at the centre of the decision-making process, and makes ethical reasoning more systematic, less intuitive, and less loaded with personal values, than going with gut instinct as to what is right or wrong.

Disadvantages of consequentialism

While outcome assessments are clearly a crucial component of public relations ethics, on their own, strictly consequentialist approaches may be insufficient. Predicting outcomes is foretelling the future, and anticipated results will not always follow from chosen actions. Furthermore, a focus on outcomes can sometimes obscure the ethics of the means used. Thus, for example, a pure consequentialist may endorse a lie and perhaps even a murder if it ultimately resulted in widespread benefit. The most comprehensive ethical consideration occurs when both ends and means are tested for virtue, duty, and impact on real people. The next section outlines a system for doing this proactively, that is, for trying to consider ethics and take steps to act ethically before ethical problems arise.

Proactive and inclusive public relations ethics

Much of the recent public relations theory presented in Chapter 3 discussed a move towards using dialogue (two-way communication) instead of propaganda (one-way communication). Practical discussions on this shift are provided in Chapter 6. Botan argues that:

> Dialogical communicators assume that their publics have as varied and valid interpretations of the world as do their clients. They assume that the goal of public relations is not reducing publics to the service of clients but joining with publics in the process of interpreting the world together (1993: 71).

Grunig's point (2006: 165) about 'bring[ing] the voices of publics into the decision-making process' is similar. Both are describing what we might call an ethics of inclusion.

Ethics of inclusion

Ghassan Hage defines an ethics of inclusion as dealing with 'the question of how to sustain the human viability of the other' (2003: 75). He illustrates this with a motto from his first language, Lebanese: '*Khidna b helmak!*' The phrase 'literally means "Hey, include me in your dreams" ' (75) and is used to remind a communicator to recognise the views and interests of others when communicating.

Hage argues that:

> Such a recognition not only involves the recognition of the mere existence of the other, it fundamentally involves a recognition of their humanity. This is why, when the Lebanese exclaim '*Khidna b helmak*', they often add, 'Are you mistaking me for a chair?' or 'Are you mistaking me for an electric pole?', meaning: have you missed the subtle fact that I should be a human being for you and not just an object? (2003: 75).

In practical terms, an ethics of inclusion means that it is no longer considered sufficient for a practitioner to impose their own interpretation of what is ethical upon a situation. Ethics, like many other parts of the public relations process, is becoming more dialogic and consultative, that is, publics need to be intentionally involved from the outset. A typical process for doing this might follow these steps:

1 When you research publics as part of typical preparatory campaign activity, research their ethical values as a benchmark. What virtues are important to them? What rules do they follow? What outcomes do they expect?

2   When you set campaign objectives, consult with publics to reach consensus objectives for the ethics of the campaign. What outcomes can you agree to aim for, and what communication behaviours, messages, and tactics will the publics consider ethical?

3   When you plan campaigning, build in ethics checks for every tactic or communication channel. When you pre-test for readability, pre-test for ethical acceptability too.

4   When you evaluate, go back to publics to find out how they think you fared in terms of overall ethical performance. Did you achieve the virtues, duties, and outcomes that you had promised or is there, in the eyes of your publics an area you need to work on?

The ethics pyramid (Tilley 2005) provides one possible tool for managing this process. You may find it helpful to follow the pyramid graphic below as a prompt (start from the bottom and work up).

FIGURE **4.1** \ The ethics pyramid

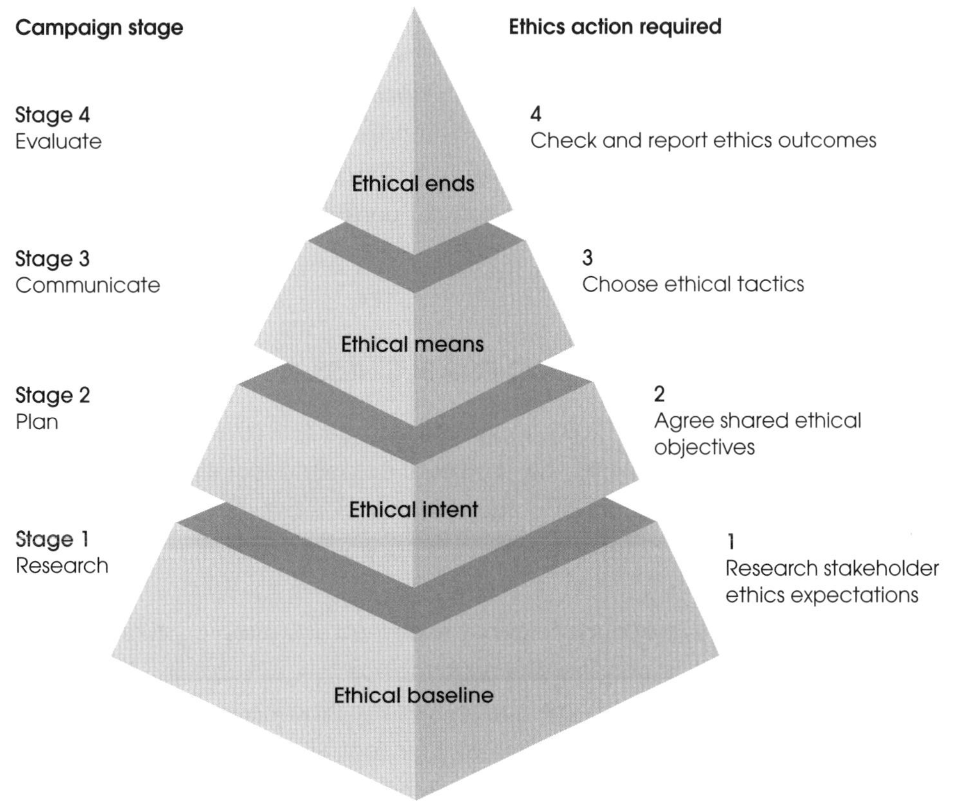

Source: Tilley 2005

Elspeth Tilley

Again, obtaining data from others as to your ethical performance cannot provide right answers or encompass all the possible complexities of multiple relationships, but using a proactive and inclusive system such as the pyramid is another way of taking some of the 'I must be doing right because I think I'm an all right person' trap out of ethics. It also turns ethics into something concrete that clients and employers can recognise as having actual value to their business rather than just being an optional philanthropic virtue. Tracking improvements in ethical performance can provide data that enhance reputation by showing evidence that the organisation actually cares what publics think of its ethics and is responding directly to their expectations.

Spearheading proactive ethics: internal persuasion

If public relations is to fulfil a role as organisational conscience, and proactively consult with publics about ethics as part of that role, perhaps the most crucial skill for the job is to be highly persuasive—not in convincing external publics that your organisation is already behaving ethically, but in convincing your organisation to invest in behaving ethically. Fortunately, in addition to the moral argument for behaving ethically, there is also a business argument. Public relations practitioners now have ample research and evidence at their disposal to make a strong case to management that good ethics equates with good financial performance. Numerous studies show a relationship between corporate social responsibility—responsible behaviour, including environmental considerations, equitable staffing practices, and a whole range of other ethically focused behaviours—and good financial performance (see Chapter 9 for case studies).

BOX **4.8** \ GOOD ETHICS IS GOOD FOR BUSINESS

➤ Orlitzky, Schmidt, and Rynes (2003: 403) used meta-analysis (overview and collation of existing data) to examine fifty-two studies of corporate social responsibility that span thirty years. They found that 'corporate virtue ... is likely to pay off', and identify a correlation between good corporate social performance and good financial performance.

➤ The United Kingdom Environment Agency examined sixty research studies of environmental practice and financial performance over six years and found that 'companies with sound environmental policies and practices are highly likely to see improved financial performance' (Kelly 2005). In fact, 85 per cent 'showed a positive correlation between environmental management and financial performance'.

Conversely, Cialdini, Petrova, and Goldstein (2004) found that unethical behaviour not only devalues an organisation's external reputation, but also has costly internal consequences. Productivity is reduced and staff turnover soars because of loss of trust, morale, and cooperativeness among employees, and surveillance and compliance costs rise because incidences of individual theft and other dishonesty in the workplace increase as employees match their own values with those they perceive to be operating for the organisation as a whole.

REFLECT AND DISCUSS

> ➤ Why do you think unethical leadership correlates with high staff turnover?
> ➤ If you worked for an organisation that was experiencing high levels of internal pilfering, what would you do about it and why?

Citing the studies above (and others from your own research) may be one way to convince management to invest in ethics training and resources for all staff. This kind of research provides compelling return on investment (ROI) reasons for spending time and money to consider ethics and develop a proactive ethics compliance plan to support staff efforts to become ethically mindful.

Another way to convince management about the benefits of ethics is to show them case studies of good ethics in action as models to follow. Most case studies in this scholarly text include models of best practice but some cases also provide insight into the outcomes of poorly managed campaigns and half hearted responses to community engagement; in this way reality and understanding of practice is constructed.

CASE STUDY KAPITI COAST COMMUNITY VISIONING

Below you will find a case study relating to public relations ethics. Although public relations case studies that explicitly refer to ethics or describe ethical reasoning processes are relatively rare, perhaps because of the prevalence of the unconscious approach referred to above, this case provides an exemplar because it demonstrates:

➤ the ever-increasing role of public relations in providing an ethics of inclusion
➤ simple how-to steps for inclusion.

This case study illustrates how public relations was used to give recognition to the humanity of publics, to facilitate and enact their dreams via an ethics of inclusion, not just

Elspeth Tilley

to use them as a means towards a predetermined end. This approach built long-term relationship value for the council involved, even though it was more costly and time-consuming in the short term than other options.

SYNOPSIS

Seeking to transform consultation from an ideal to a reality, Kapiti Coast District Council took a blank page to the community and asked for ideas about the region's future. All ideas were captured and are now in a plan that truly represents the people's vision.

BACKGROUND

The New Zealand Local Government Act requires local authorities to develop a Long Term Council Community Plan (LTCCP). Councils can choose from three possible approaches. The first is to revise existing plans and prepare short-term interim versions that have to be completely revised within three years. Consultation is required but not to a high level. The second is to conduct a largely inhouse planning exercise involving staff and politicians and then seek community submissions on it. This is advantageous to the bodies involved in that it takes minimal time and resources. The third and most challenging approach is to start with the community and ask them to initiate ideas about what they want. This was the option chosen by Kapiti Coast District Council (KCDC).

GOAL AND STRATEGY

Planned consultation generally involves a few poorly-attended evening meetings. On the Kapiti Coast, even crucial issues such as the long-term water strategy attracted few public submissions. KCDC wanted to change this, to attract the widest possible community awareness, involvement, and engagement with the plan. The strategy involved a large travelling roadshow of displays and information at school halls. Workshops titled 'Your chance to dream' were open 9.00 a.m. to 9.00 p.m. every day, and were promoted in direct mail letters from the mayor to all residents, and in radio and newspaper advertising.

MESSAGES

The mayor's message was that people needed to take this chance to influence the district's future. The consistent message of the later *Reportback* publications was that every idea was appreciated and kept. Advertising contained a 'Your Chance to Dream' message, which was backed up with evidence that those dreams were valued.

TACTICS TO ENGAGE THE COMMUNITY

Direct mail to all residents that explained the aims, timeline, and meetings was supported with *Reportbacks* via:

* Advertisements in the *Kapiti Observer*, which circulates to 95 per cent of the district * Community newsletter * News and feature coverage * Radio advertising and radio interview support * Website * Talkback on issues * Fact sheets/stories for school students and school newsletters * Information/speech notes for Mayor, elected members/ staff for Rotary, Lions, Probus clubs * Fact sheets/brochure for website and general use including handing out to commuters on stations/bus stops * Signs/displays and addresses for information in libraries and council service centres * Displays and noticeboard support * Promote overall program of meetings * Promote individual meetings in media/areas/noticeboards * Photographic stock for displays, the website and follow-up publications * Displays used at meetings * Shop space in mall for display and workshops * Sign-write council vehicles used to carry workshop display gear * Train workshop staff in facilitation and problem solving.

PROCESS

Using aerial photographs of each area proved to be the key to unlocking people's ideas and concerns. People were asked where they lived and then taken to the appropriate picture to identify their house, street, and area. From initial concerns over issues such as a hole in the footpath, people started to look at their neighbourhood as a whole, then to the larger area and to district-wide concerns. Every idea was recorded on Post-it notes and transcribed onto a consultation database. These data were analysed for themes, and mind maps were used to show patterns and link ideas to strategies. The Post-it note ideas became the basis for reportbacks to the community.

RESULTS

The first venue received more than 100 visits on its first day. On the second day, the number of visits to the first venue dropped to ten. Subsequent venues for the first week had varying levels of attendance. KCDC staff worried that the approach was wrong. But then the reportbacks to the community began. The response was almost immediate. The reportbacks showed that ideas were recorded and not judged. Input was wanted and valued. People responded. By the end of the workshop sessions, 4500 people, more than 10 per cent of the district's population, had attended and provided input. Prior experience of low interest in consultation was proved wrong.

Source: Tony Cronin 2008

Elspeth Tilley

REFLECT AND DISCUSS

➤ What things do you think this project did well? Why?

➤ What things do you think could have been improved? Why?

➤ Compare the actions in this case to Josephson's ten ethical values on page 93. Does it embody every value? How, or why not?

CHAPTER SUMMARY

➤ Attention to ethics is essential to public relations' evolution from technical process to managerial function.

➤ Most public relations people are good people, but good intent is not enough to guarantee ethical outcomes.

➤ Ethics is not necessarily natural or instinctual, and if you leave it to chance you put yourself and your organisation at risk of unconscious incompetence. Make ethics a proactive, deliberate, planned, and sustained component of your everyday public relations activity.

➤ Ethics does not mean the same thing to everybody: ethics has some broad components, such as the laws under which we must operate, but it is also very personal. To respect others' values, create an open system whereby publics and audiences can have a say as to what they believe is ethical.

➤ There are not necessarily any single right answers to ethical questions. Different ethical systems give different assessments of the ethics of an action. Aim to bring ethical considerations to the surface, assess and weigh your activities in terms of character virtue, relevant rules, and outcomes, and be able to demonstrate to others that your actions were undertaken in a considered, responsible, inclusive, and accountable way, with reference to credible guidelines.

FURTHER READING

Baker, S 1997, 'Applying Kidder's Ethical Decision-making Checklist to Media Ethics', *Journal of Mass Media Ethics*, 12(4): 197–210.

Baker, S 2002, 'The Theoretical Ground for Public Relations Practice and Ethics: A Koehnian Analysis', *Journal of Business Ethics*, 35(3): 191–205.

Baker, S & Martinson, D L 2001, 'The TARES Test: Five Principles for Ethical Persuasion', *Journal of Mass Media Ethics*, 16(2 & 3): 148–75.

Barney, R D & Black, J 1994, 'Ethics and Professional Persuasive Communications', *Public Relations Review*, 20(3): 233–48.

Bowen, S A 2004, 'Expansion of Ethics as the Tenth Generic Principle of Public Relations Excellence: A Kantian Theory and Model for Managing Ethical Issues', *Journal of Public Relations Research*, 16(1): 65–92.

Edgett, R 2002, 'Toward an Ethical Framework for Advocacy in Public Relations', *Journal of Public Relations Research*, 14(1): 1–26.

Fitzpatrick, K & Gauthier, C 2001, 'Toward a Professional Responsibility Theory of Public Relations Ethics', *Journal of Mass Media Ethics*, 16 (2 & 3): 193–212.

Grunig, L, Toth, E & Childers Hon, L 2000, 'Feminist Values in Public Relations', *Journal of Public Relations Research*, 12(1): 49–68.

Harrison, K & Galloway, C 2005, 'Public Relations Ethics: A Simpler (but not Simplistic) Approach to the Complexities', *PRism* 3, retrieved from http://praxis.massey.ac.nz/fileadmin/Praxis/Files/Journal_Files/Issue3/Harrison_Galloway.pdf, 2 January 2008.

Leeper, K A 1996, 'Public Relations Ethics and Communitarianism: A Preliminary Investigation', *Public Relations Review*, 22(2): 163–79.

Leeper, R V 1996, 'Moral Objectivity, Jurgen Habermas's Discourse Ethics, and Public Relations', *Public Relations Review*, 22(2): 133–50.

Marsh, C W 2001, 'Public Relations Ethics: Contrasting Models from the Rhetorics of Plato, Aristotle, and Isocrates', *Journal of Mass Media Ethics*, 16(2 & 3): 78–98.

Pearson, R 1989, 'Albert J Sullivan's Theory of Public Relations Ethics', *Public Relations Review*, 15(2): 52–62.

Pratt, C, Im, S H & Montague, S 1994, 'Investigating the Application of Deontology Among U.S. Public Relations Practitioners', *Journal of Public Relations Research*, 6(4): 241–66.

Tilley, E 2005, 'Responding to Terrorism Using Ethical Means; The Propaganda Index', *Communication Research Reports*, 22(1), 69–77.

WEB RESOURCES

'Al Gore's Penguin Army' 2006, at www.youtube.com/comment_servlet?all_comments&v=IZSqXUSwHRI&fromurl=/watch%3Fv%3DIZSqXUSwHRI%26mode%3Drelated%26search%3D.

Ethics Resource Center, at www.ethics.org.

Global Alliance for Public Relations and Communication Management Benchmarking of codes of ethics in Public Relations, at www.globalpr.org/knowledge/ethics.asp.

Holt, A, PR Ethics Resource Centre, at http://iml.jou.ufl.edu/projects/Spring02/Holt.

Institute of Communication Ethics, at www.communication-ethics.org.uk.

International Business Ethics Network, at www.business-ethics.org/index.asp.

Josephson Institute of Ethics, at www.josephsoninstitute.org.

All About Public Relations with Steven R Van Hook, at www.aboutpublicrelations.net/ethics.htm.

Miyamoto, C, *Challenges We Just Can't Ignore*, at www.geocities.com/wallstreet/8925/ethics.htm.

PRSA, *Public Relations: Ethics Decision Making*, at www.prsa.org/_Chapters/resources/ethicspdf/
  decisionguide.pdf.

PRSA, *Ethics Resources*, at www.prsa.org/_About/ethics.

PRSA, *Ethics Case Study*, at www.prsa.org/_Chapters/resources/ethicspdf/CS3A.pdf.

Public Relations Resource Centre, a useful gateway to a number of ethics articles and online
  resources, at http://praxis.massey.ac.nz/ethics.html.

St James Ethics Centre, Australia, at www.ethics.org.au.

University of Sydney Ethics Research Network, at www.arts.usyd.edu.au/research_projects/
  ethicsproject/index.shtml.

REFERENCES

Aristotle 1985, *Nicomachean Ethics*, trans. T Irwin, Hackett Publishing, Indianapolis.

Bernays, E L 1928, *Propaganda*, Liveright, New York.

Bernays, E L 1955, *The Engineering of Consent*, University of Oklahoma Press, Norman.

Botan, C 1993, 'A Human Nature Approach to Image and Ethics in International Public Relations', *Journal of
  Public Relations Research*, 5(2) (April): 71–81.

Bowen, S A 2008, 'Foundations in Moral Philosophy for Public Relations Ethics', in T L Hansen-Horn & B Dostal Neff
  (eds), *Public Relations: From Theory to Practice*, Pearson, Boston.

Bowen, S A 2002, 'Elite Executives in Issues Management: The Role of Ethical Paradigms in Decision Making',
  Journal of Public Affairs, 2(4): 270–83.

Boynton, L 2003, 'The Gray Areas of Ethical Decision-Making: The Emergence of an Ethical Action Continuum
  Among Public Relations Practitioners', paper presented to the Public Relations Division for the AEJMC
  conference, August 2003, retrieved from http://list.msu.edu/cgi bin/wa?A2=ind0309d&L=aejmc&F=&S=&P
  =17191, 2 February 2005.

Brown, R E 2003, review of *Public Relations Ethics: Some Foundations, Public Relations Review*, 29(4): 496–8.

Cialdini, R, Petrova, P & Goldstein, N 2004, 'The Hidden Costs of Organizational Dishonesty', *MIT Sloan
  Management Review*, 45(3), Spring: 67–73.

Cordingley, G 2007, 'Forestry to Pursue Angel Claim', *Hobart Mercury*, 3 October, retrieved from www.news.
  com.au/mercury/story/0,22884,22523829-3462,00.html, 3 January 2008.

Davis, M A, Johnson, N B & Ohmer, D G 1998, 'Issue-contingent Effects on Ethical Decision Making: A Cross
  Cultural Comparison', *Journal of Business Ethics*, 17: 373–89.

Elkington, J 1994, 'Towards the Sustainable Corporation: Win–Win–Win Business Strategies for Sustainable
  Development', *California Management Review*, 36(2): 90–100.

Fitch, K & Surma, A 2006, 'The Challenges of International Education: Developing a Public Relations Unit for the
  Asian Region', *Journal of University Teaching and Learning Practice 3*, retrieved from http://jutlp.uow.edu.
  au/2006_v03_i02/pdf/fitch_008.pdf, 4 January 2008.

Grunig, J & Hunt, T 2001, 'Two-way Symmetrical Public Relations: Past, Present, and Future', in R Heath & G Vasquez (eds), *Handbook of Public Relations*, Sage, Thousand Oaks.

Grunig, J & Hunt, T 2006, 'Furnishing the Edifice: Ongoing Research on Public Relations as a Strategic Management Function', *Journal of Public Relations Research*, 18(2): 151–76.

Gudykunst, W B 2005, *Theorizing About Intercultural Communication*, Sage, Thousand Oaks.

Haugland, A 2000, 'Book Propaganda: Edward L Bernays' 1930 Campaign Against Dollar Books', *Book History*, 3: 231–52.

Hage, G 2003, 'A Viable Ethics: Journalists and the "Ethnic Question" ', in C Lumby & E Probyn (eds), *Remote Control: New Media, New Ethics*, Cambridge University Press, Cambridge, 74–86.

Harrison, J 2004, 'Conflicts of Duty and the Virtues of Aristotle in Public Relations Ethics: Continuing the Conversation Commenced by Monica Walle', *PRism*, 2(1), retrieved from http://praxis.massey.ac.nz/fileadmin/Praxis/Files/Journal_Files/Issue2/Harrison.pdf, 2 September 2004.

Heath, R L 2008, 'Rhetorical Theory, Public Relations, and Meaning: Giving Voice to Ideas', in T L Hansen-Horn & B Dostal Neff (eds), *Public Relations: From Theory to Practice*, Pearson, Boston.

Hofstadter, R & Metzger, W 1955, *The Development of Academic Freedom in the United States*, Columbia University Press, New York.

Hunt, T & Grunig, J 1984, *Managing Public Relations*, Holt, Rinehart and Winston, New York.

Kant, I 1956, *Groundwork of the Metaphysic of Morals,* trans. H J Paton, Harper & Row, New York.

Kelly, M 2005, 'Holy Grail Found: Absolute, Definitive Proof that Responsible Companies Perform Better Financially', *Business Ethics: Corporate Social Responsibility Report*, Winter, retrieved from www.business-ethics.com/current_issue/winter_2005_holy_grail_article.html, 16 February 2009.

Kim, Y W & Choi, Y J 2003, 'Ethical Standards Appear to Change with Age and Ideology: A Survey of Practitioners', *Public Relations Review*, 29(1): 79–89.

Lee, I L 1925, *Publicity: Some of the Things it is and is Not*, Industries Publishing, New York.

Martinson, D L 2000, 'Ethical Decision Making in Public Relations: What Would Aristotle Say?', *Public Relations Quarterly*, 45(3): 18–21.

Martinson, D L 2004, 'An Essential Component in Teaching Public Relations Ethics', *TPR: Teaching Public Relations*, 64, Summer: n.p., retrieved from: http://lamar.colostate.edu/~aejmcpr/64martinson.pdf, 4 September 2004.

McElreath, M P 1997, *Managing Strategic and Ethical Public Relations Campaigns*, 2nd edn, Brown & Benchmark, Dubuque.

McLean, B 2007, 'The Smartest Guys in the Room: The Enron Saga', keynote address to 2007 Journalism Educators' Association of New Zealand conference, 10–12 December, Massey University, Wellington.

Morse, S 1906, 'An Awakening in Wall Street: How the Trusts, After Years of Silence, Now Speak Though Authorized and Acknowledged Press Agents', *American Magazine*, 62 (September): 457–63.

National Communication Association 1999, 'National Communication Association Credo for Ethical Communication', retrieved from www.natcom.org/nca/Template2.asp?bid=514, 3 January 2008.

Orlitzky, M, Schmidt, F L & Rynes, S L 2003, 'Corporate Social and Financial Performance: A Meta-analysis', *Organization Studies*, 24(3): 403–41.

Parisot, D (director) 2005, *Fun With Dick and Jane*, produced by J Carrey & B Grazer, from the novel of the same name by G Gaiser.

Rawls, J 1971, *A Theory of Justice*, Belknap, with Harvard University Press, Cambridge, MA.

Reitman, J (director) 2006, *Thank You for Smoking*, produced by Room 9 Entertainment, distributed by Twentieth Century Fox Film Corporation.

Regalado, A & Searcey, D 2006, 'Where Did That Video Spoofing Gore's Film Come From?', *Wall Street Journal*, 3 August, retrieved from http://online.wsj.com/public/article/SB115457177198425388-0TpYE6bU6EGvfSqtP8_hHjJJ77l_20060810.html?mod=blogs, 2 January 2008.

Roth, N L, Hunt, T, Stavropoulos, M & Babik, K 1996, 'Can't We All Just Get Along?: Cultural Variables in Codes of Ethics', *Public Relations Review*, 22(2): 151–61.

Ryan, M & Martinson, D L 1983, 'The PR Officer as Corporate Conscience', *Public Relations Quarterly*, 28(2): 20–3.

Seib, P M & Fitzpatrick, K 1995, *Public Relations Ethics*, Harcourt Brace, Fort Worth.

Taylor, D 2006, 'Edelman Screws Up with Duplicitous WalMart Blog, But it's OK?', retrieved from www.intuitive.com/blog/edelman_screws_up_with_duplicitious_walmart_blog.html, 28 September 2007.

Tilley, E 2005, 'The Ethics Pyramid: Making Ethics Unavoidable in the Public Relations Process', *Journal of Mass Media Ethics*, 20(4): 305–20.

Temkin, L S 2004, 'Thinking About the Needy, Justice, and International Organizations', *Journal of Ethics*, 8: 349–95.

WOMMA 2007, *The WOMMA Ethics Code*, retrieved from www.womma.org/ethics/code/read, 1 January 2008.

Young, P 2004, 'Are Ethics Good Business?', Global PR Blog, retrieved from www.globalprblogweek.com/archives/are_ethics_good_busi.php, 28 December 2007.

Part **2**

THEORY AND PRACTICE ON THE JOB

Chapter **5**

PUBLIC RELATIONS RESEARCH

Gae Synnott

PRACTITIONER PROFILE \ RON KAWALILAK

'One of my key beliefs in public relations is that it's pardonable to be defeated, but not to be surprised,' says Ron Kawalilak, director of Strategic Development and Corporate Affairs with the Department of Environment and Conservation (DEC) in Western Australia. 'Not every strategy or public relations program you're going to develop is going to succeed fully. But if you fail because of a lack of research or evaluation, that's unacceptable and avoidable.'

Working primarily as an inhouse practitioner in the natural resources and environment fields, Ron has worked in public relations in Canada and Australia since 1976. 'I prefer the inhouse role because you are there at the outset of things, you can see an issue or opportunity through to the end, and then you get to live with the ongoing consequences of the choices you helped make,' he says. 'That tends to keep you focused and sharp.'

Central to the communications planning that is done by DEC is, according to Ron, 'the process of identifying issues and needs in a logical progression so that a solution does not appear before the problem or opportunity is clear. Good insights, developed through research, are essential.

'It's a myth that research costs too much and takes a lot of time,' he says. Ron advocates low cost options such as ongoing environmental scanning or monitoring, media content analysis, the use of secondary analysis of existing survey research that is available on the internet, in periodicals, and other sources, and other forms of research that can be done inhouse.

'We use specialist researchers and techniques when it's appropriate and when it adds value to our public relations or communications program,' he says.

CHAPTER **AIMS**

By the end of this chapter you should be able to:

➤ understand the role of research in effective public relations practice
➤ clearly demonstrate the rationale for undertaking research
➤ examine research at different stages in the public relations process and the contributions it can make at each stage
➤ plan research to understand and measure public opinion
➤ understand and discuss some of the realities and challenges of public relations research.

Introduction

Research is an important tool for public relations practitioners. Almost every communication problem or project calls for varying degrees of research: fact finding, opinion assessment, message testing, planning, execution, and evaluation. If done at the start of a program, it enables us to create programs based on a better understanding of issues and with a better appreciation of context, which in turn gives us confidence in the recommended communication solution. Research carried out during a program to monitor progress allows us to fine tune the activity to ensure that the desired outcomes are achieved. Research at the conclusion of a program enables us to test whether the desired results were achieved and to report them to management. Remember that the reason for public relations activity is to contribute to organisational reputation and relationship management: ultimately, all public relations programs should be linked to their impact on reputation and relationships.

Research is central to how public relations practitioners approach their work. Wilcox et al. (2006: 153) liken planning to putting together a jigsaw puzzle, with research providing the clues about where to place the individual pieces. Practitioners constantly ask questions in their quest to fully scope a problem, issue, or opportunity before they start to develop strategies to deal with the situation. Research is the process of asking questions and finding the answers that provide useful information relevant to the project at hand. Research helps to build the base of professionalism and public relations knowledge. Armed with research and analysis practitioners can present and justify plans supported by evidence and theory. Without research and analysis, practitioners can only guess or make assumptions about the problem, issue, or opportunity, and about the solution. As Glen Broom and David Dozier (1990: xiii) state, 'Using research in public relations is better than not using research in public relations'.

Whether performing research themselves or working with professional research firms, public relations practitioners must understand the rationale and the tools of the research approach to solving business problems and developing effective communication solutions.

Much of what will be talked about in this chapter is program-based research undertaken by or for practitioners. In fact, it has been written from the perspective of the public relations practitioner who is given a job to do and who needs to know how to do research to help them tackle the job. However, there is also the need for broader research into public relations itself and the application of theory to the practice of public relations. Much of the advances in theory are coming from research being undertaken in academia, and it is a constant challenge for the profession to find ways of linking in to the good work being done by academics, much of which has the potential to assist practitioners.

Getting into the research mindset

A working definition of research is the process of systematically gathering information that will provide the basis to establish an understanding of situations and issues and make sense of them. Research is always designed for a purpose. There is always a reason for doing the research and the researcher has to be both clear about how the information will be used and sure that the research process will contribute in some way to the job at hand. The potentially alarming situation of, for example, the increasing incidence of deafness among 20–30 year olds seems to be related to extensive iPod use and listening to loud music. Sense needs to be made of what is happening. Is this generation aware of what is happening? Do they know that deafness cannot be cured? Is there a safe level of iPod use and how do we communicate this? Deafness is often associated with the elderly but it seems to be becoming a problem for the young. Communication about it can only be effective if people understand what it is.

In simple terms, research is the process of posing questions and finding the answers. Knowing which questions to ask and how to get hold of the answers is a skill to be developed. In Table 5.1 (on page 128) there are three quick steps to get you to start to think like a public relations professional. Imagine you have been given the job of creating a public relations program to raise awareness about the issue of premature deafness.

Gae Synnott

TABLE **5.1** \ **Three quick steps towards thinking like a public relations professional**

Step 1	You ask
Understanding the problem, issue or opportunity Premature deafness in 20–30 year olds and what that means	• What's the overall context? • What type of extra information would help me to develop a good program?
Step 2	**You ask**
Framing the research questions	• What do I need to find out? • What's my research objective? • What questions will elicit the information I need? • How do I frame the questions to get useful material and data?
Step 3	**You ask**
Designing the research activity	• Where, or from whom, will I find the information and answers I need? • What do I do to get the information? • What will I be able to do with the information once I have it?

Source: Gae Synott 2008

Research theory as a basis for practice

The hierarchy of effects model

One useful tool to help in developing objectives is the hierarchy of effects model, originally developed by the advertising profession to identify the different steps in the thought process that leads people from knowing nothing about a product to becoming a customer. It is, in essence, a learning hierarchy. In its adaptation to public relations (McElreath 1993: 79; Pavlik 1987: 74), it is used to identify the different effects that can be aimed for in communication; and incorporates the practitioner tasks to be undertaken.

TABLE **5.2** \ **The hierarchy of effects model**

6	Changing/reinforcing behaviours
5	Changing/reinforcing attitudes/opinions
4	Comprehending the message/campaign/program
3	Receiving the message/campaign/program
2	Disseminating the message/campaign/program
1	Formulating the message/campaign/program

Source: McElreath 1993: 79

If, for example, you are starting from a position where your audience has no awareness of the problem, in this discussion premature deafness through continual iPod use, and no knowledge about the problem, issue, or opportunity, then your steps will need to include:

➤ building awareness of the issue
➤ progressively building interest and knowledge to the point where the audience starts to develop an attitude
➤ providing good reasons for taking action and support the audience in taking that step
➤ reinforcing the action.

Your objective in this case might be to raise awareness, and your program will be designed to achieve an increase in awareness. Once you have achieved the desired level of awareness among the audience your objective will be revised to move the target audience to the next level. The 20–30 year olds who find out through this program about the dangers of continuous exposure to loud music will now want to understand what they can do about the potential problem.

Research will help to establish the current level of awareness with your audience, which then enables a realistic target to be set for increased awareness. At the end of the program of communication activity, you would use research to measure whether the level of awareness has changed, by how much, and what the audience now knows about the problem, issue, or opportunity as a result of the communication program.

The links between attitudes, opinions, and behaviour

Attitude is described as having three main components: cognitive (thinking), affective (feeling), and behavioural (doing). To achieve attitude change, one must understand the facts of the case in a rational manner, and feel and believe before one changes his or her behaviour. This suggests that there is a causal link between providing information and achieving attitude and behaviour change, and many public relations campaigns are based on this thesis.

But behaviour can be influenced by other factors, such as situation, motivation, constraints, and the factors outlined in Grunig and Hunt's situational theory (1994); in fact, behaviour may come first, followed by attitude change to justify the action.

Public opinion formation

Public opinion is an important concept that refers to expressions of the public's attitudes and their evaluation of what is happening in society (Seitel 2007: 66). Public opinion is what most people in a particular target audience think about an issue (Seitel 2007). It is based on perceptions and evaluations rather than fact, and is subject to change while it is forming. Practitioners who are monitoring an emerging issue, such as increasing incidence of the ugly parent syndrome (loud and abusive parents being out of control at their children's sports venues), tend to watch closely for signs that an issue is growing in strength and firming up, as people tend to take their cue on how they feel about an issue by what others are saying. This is a type of herd mentality, one in which people follow others in making up their mind on an issue and the media contribute to this by setting the agenda for the issue.

Public relations practitioners may be interested in public opinion about anything from a localised development proposal, to changes at the local school, through to broader social issues such as capital punishment or crime prevention. Research on public opinion helps us to develop campaigns on those issues.

The Wisdom of Crowds

This book by James Surowiecki (2004) suggests that when it comes to making a decision or solving a problem, large groups of ordinary people are smarter than a handful of experts. In his book, he gives many examples that show how the collective wisdom of a group of diverse, independent people produces an accuracy and insight that the experts often fail to match. This is public opinion in action, and this phenomenon may help to explain publics, audiences and behaviours.

The influence of crowds is important, even more so because of the use of technology that links people and spreads ideas. Marie Howarth, of Creative Nature Communications in Western Australia, summarised it this way in a recent presentation:

> The heady influx of techno toys and digital devices is helping us to connect with each other like never before, regardless of physical barriers such as time and location, or inequalities in financial influence, political position—even social skills and appearance (personal communication, April 2008).

When and how public relations practitioners use research

Defining qualitative and quantitative research

Research can be qualitative or quantitative, and both forms of research are useful to public relations practitioners. Qualitative research provides an indepth understanding of issues, whereas quantitative research provides statistics and trends. Qualitative research is primarily descriptive, whereas quantitative research is predictive. As described by Newsom, Turk & Kruckeberg (2007), '*quantitative* is the *what* and *qualitative* is the *why*' (66).

Qualitative research is used to:

➤ identify a range of opinions on a topic
➤ get a general sense of how things are going
➤ understand stakeholders and issues better
➤ test stakeholder responses.

Qualitative methods include one-to-one contact, such as interviews with community leaders or topic experts, focus groups, open-ended surveys and communication audits.

Quantitative research provides information about:

➤ the proportion of people who think or act a certain way on the subject in question
➤ attitudes—positive, negative, or neutral
➤ awareness levels
➤ behaviour or intended behaviour
➤ level and type of media coverage.

Quantitative methods include surveys with closed questions (administered by phone, mail, face to face or web-based) and media content analysis.

Both can be used in one program in which you might use separate qualitative and quantitative techniques for different parts of the program. Focus groups (a qualitative technique) could help gather information to be used in planning the program, and then in evaluating after the program has been completed, to understand why parents are becoming angry at sporting events and lashing out at umpires, players, and other spectators. The first discussion might focus on investigating the current situation, issues, possible solutions, how different solutions might be received and perceived by the target audience, and how best to get the ideas across. The second discussion, after the program, might focus on whether the situation has improved, what is now different, how people feel about it, what more could be done, and what worked well and what did not.

In the same program, quantitative research could assist to segment publics and audiences, establish difference between publics and audiences, establish benchmarks (what is the current level of awareness or knowledge and what is the current attitude?), and test impacts at the end of the program. Surveys could be undertaken with sports umpires to see how many have observed parental violence or outrage and when and where it has happened to gain a better understanding of the extent of the problem. The multiple perspectives contributed by the different research techniques can add significant information for the public relations practitioner to work with.

Remember that listening in research is important. Wait for and hear what is being said, felt, and understood—it is part of meaning making and sense making (Kreps 2008).

When we use research

Research is relevant at all stages of public relations planning and implementation (IPRA, 1994):

➤ *Before*—The input or preparation stage, in which planning is undertaken, objectives are set, where as much as there is to know about the issue, the context, and the target audience is learnt, and where the communication tools to be used during the program are produced.
➤ *During*—The output or implementation stage, in which the process is monitored, the practitioner checks that what they said they would do is being done, and where early signs of success or any need to fine tune or redirect the program are looked for.

➤ *After*—The outcome stage, in which the impact occurs and evaluation is conducted to find out whether the objectives that were set have been achieved.

Before we come to the uses of research as part of the planning process, we need to consider the range of environmental scanning that all public relations practitioners should do on a regular basis to stay informed about current events and key issues.

Keeping up to date

Every public relations practitioner needs to have a process in place for a fairly wide ongoing scan of current events, key issues, and trends. This provides a solid foundation that helps to pull together and connect the threads of information into a meaningful picture.

If a public relations practitioner were about to start a new business, the environmental scan that the practitioner would do would cover broad trends within:

➤ politics, including legislative and regulatory changes
➤ economics, including economic trends
➤ social issues
➤ technology
➤ industrial developments
➤ environmental trends and issues.

In addition to these areas, the public relations practitioner also needs to keep up to date with professional trends, news related to the organisation or client set, case studies, and new communication methods. Advice from senior Western Australian government practitioner Sheryl Fewster is that public relations practitioners need to:

> Google widely to gather case studies and different approaches, which will help you in thinking about the communication problems you're facing. Recent work or research in the human resources area might be useful in the employee communication program you're developing (personal communication, February 2008).

Knowing where to find current information is more important than keeping outdated information. This means that it is both critical and helpful to know your way around the internet and to bookmark sites of interest that you can get back to quickly.

REFLECT AND DISCUSS

➤ Where would you source information about the latest tourism statistics?
➤ If you worked for a large multinational oil company, what web pages or blog sites would you visit on a regular basis to monitor environmental trends and issues? What professional networks should you tap into?

Research at the before or input stage

When developing the public relations program or plan there are a number of aspects to focus on, and research can help with many of them. Here are some of the questions you might ask:

➤ Identifying the problem, issue or opportunity (the project):
  • What do we know about the project?
  • What is its history and how has it evolved?
  • What more do we need to know about it so we can fully understand its potential importance and scope?
  • How is the organisation currently perceived?

➤ Identifying the audience or public:
  • Who are they?
  • Are there a number of discrete or different audiences, publics?
  • How do we define or describe them?

➤ Understanding the audience or public:
  • What brings them into this project?
  • What's their interest or issue?
  • Are they supportive, neutral, or opposed?
  • Are they active, aware, or passive?
  • How are they organised?
  • What's the best way to reach them?
  • What level of contact has been had with them before now?

➤ Establishing the ethical considerations (see Chapter 4):
  • What are the ethical values of our primary publics?
  • What virtues are important to them?
  • What rules do they follow?
  • What outcomes do they expect?

➤ Understanding and measuring public opinion:
  • What is the level of awareness, attitude, and behaviour in relation to this project?
  • What is the recent history in terms of this project?

➤ Setting objectives and establishing targets for what the program will achieve:
  • What do we specifically want to achieve with this program?
  • What do we want to achieve in terms of outputs and process?
  • What do we want to achieve in terms of outcomes or impacts?
  • Given our starting point or benchmark, what is feasible as a target? If, say, there is a low level of awareness, the program should aim to build awareness before targeting behavioural change.

- Do we want to achieve different things with different audiences and publics?
- From the ethical viewpoint, is there an opportunity to consult with publics to reach consensus objectives for the ethics of the campaign? What outcomes can we agree to aim for?

➤ Establishing benchmarks:
  - What is the starting point on this project?
  - What can it be measured against later?

➤ Determining strategy, tactics, messages, and communication channels:
  - What kind of campaign will be needed?
  - What strategies will be most effective with each target audience?
  - Which channels will be most effective with each target audience?
  - What do they already know?
  - What can I learn from case studies and other situations that might be effective in this project?
  - What communication behaviours, messages, and tactics will the publics consider ethical?
  - What pre-testing needs to be done?

The public relations plan is the practitioner's working theory of what has to be done to achieve a desired outcome. Research at the start not only provides good information to build an effective program, but it also enables you to set specific and measurable objectives that you will be able to evaluate against later in the program.

This is where you would utilise the hierarchy of effects framework to set realistic objectives. If, for example, you are starting from a position where your audience or publics have no awareness and no knowledge about the problem, issue, or opportunity, then you need to first invest effort in making them aware, then progressively build their interest and knowledge to the point where they start to develop an attitude that may ultimately result in them taking action. The public relations practitioner's objective in this case might be to raise awareness, with a program designed to achieve this increase in awareness. If the target audience already knows something about the problem, the campaign may focus on what they can do to ameliorate the effects or how to minimise further damage in future.

Research will help to establish the current level of awareness with your audience or publics, which then enables a realistic target to be set for increased awareness. At the end of the program of communication activity, research would be used to measure whether the level of awareness has changed, by how much, and what the target audience now knows about the problem, issue, or opportunity as a result of the communication program.

Research at the input stage provides the framework for evaluation at the end of the program because evaluation later measures change against the situation at the start of the program.

A second useful tool to help in developing objectives is to make a distinction between process objectives and outcome objectives. Process objectives detail what actions will be taken in the program (for example, the production of newsletters, events held). Outcome objectives detail what outcomes will be achieved as a result of the program as per the hierarchy of effects described above. Both types of objectives are relevant to public relations programming, and both types of objectives can be measured through research activity.

REFLECT AND DISCUSS

Think about a proposed community development where you live—real or imagined. If you were planning the campaign to achieve a high level of community input and discussion about the proposed development, how would you find out about the following:

➤ Who is likely to be interested in providing input?
➤ Whose input is critical to the process and how to achieve it?
➤ What channels of communication are likely to work best in this community?
➤ What level of information do people already have?
➤ What key questions are people likely to have about the proposal?

As a community resident, what objectives would you set for the way in which you want to be consulted, and the way in which your comments will be used in the planning process?

Everyone has a network that they tap into to build a picture about what is being dealt with. Research is likely to be a combination of formal research and informal means that include internet searches and personal discussions.

Research at the output or implementation stage

This is the action stage of the public relations program in which the plan is being implemented and things are being made to happen. Research at this stage focuses on monitoring the action and implementation of the plan to check that we are doing what we said we would, and to look for early signs of success or any need to fine tune or redirect the program. It is the process objectives that are focused on at this stage.

If our task is to promote a forthcoming conference, some of the following tools and tactics might be included.

Gae Synnott

TABLE **5.3** \ **Tools and tactics for promoting a forthcoming conference**

Tools and tactics prior to conference	The monitoring points	Monitoring methodologies
Set up a website and web links for the conference	• Has the website been developed? • Is it live and easy to use?	• Action completed • Feedback from users
	• How many hits are we getting? • Do we need to promote the site more?	• Hit rates
Develop background material on key speakers and topics in electronic and hard copy form	• Has background material been developed? • Have we produced it in hard copy and electronic form? • Is it complete? • Is it useful?	• Action completed • Feedback from users
Alert specialist media to the conference and provide background material and web links	• Is our list of specialist media up to date? • Have we made contact with all specialist media?	• Action completed
	• What level of interest has there been?	• Enquiry or response rates • Web hits
Liaise with specialist media to organise preconference publicity	• What publicity are we trying to achieve? • How many interviews have we been able to organise? • What media coverage have we achieved to date? • Are the media picking up the right messages? • Do we need to push this more actively? • Are there other angles we could use to generate interest? • Do we need to get more staff involved in this project?	• Media monitoring of coverage • Media content analysis (is coverage positive, neutral, or negative?)

Source: Gae Synnott 2008

REFLECT AND **DISCUSS**

Think about the above scenario and what more you could do if your monitoring activity reveals a total lack of media interest and coverage of the conference. With two more weeks to go before the conference starts, what communication activities could you undertake to promote the conference and ensure that it reaches the target number of people you want to attend?

One of the benefits of doing monitoring research at this stage is that it enables you to check progress against your objectives and action plans. In addition to exploring and checking whether the program is rolling out as planned, you are also looking to see whether any adjustments to the plan are required, whether you need to boost your efforts, or focus more closely on a particular aspect of the program. Adjustments or increased effort at this point may have a significant effect on whether the desired results are achieved.

If your program has a long implementation phase, you will need to continually review and check that it is on track.

Research at the impact or outcome stage

At the end of the program we want to know whether it worked. The impact or outcome stage is where the impact becomes visible and can be assessed, and where it is evaluated to find out whether the objectives that were set were achieved. Remember that at the start of the program objectives were set for the program, and targets established for what would be achieved. At that stage the importance of understanding what the situation is at the start of the program was emphasised, because this enables the measurement of any differences at the end, such as an increase in awareness, an increased level of support, or increased attendance at an event.

At the end of the program we want to know not only what was done, but also whether the program had the desired impact on the problem, issue, or opportunity. A decision must be made as to whether sufficient effort has been put into the project and the problem resolved, or whether more time and effort need to be invested in it. It may be that the program was designed to move only part of the way towards a particular goal, for example, increased awareness, and because the target audience and publics are now more aware you can now move into the next phase of activity to build knowledge and build positive attitudes towards the problem, issue, or opportunity.

The Perth International Arts Festival runs the Perth Festival every year, and every year it offers a program with a different mix of artists and entertainment. Every year the Perth Festival undertakes research to find out audience response to the mix provided, which helps them to make improvements to the program for the following year. This is a cycle of listening, acting, listening, and acting on the information received (see case study at the end of this chapter).

Management and clients will want to know whether the investment of time and effort has been worthwhile. Organisational leaders look for results and often require results to be quantified, certainly measurable. Gael Walker's 1993 findings from an Australian national survey into public relations research and evaluation found support for the notion of evidence-based practice, noting that those who could demonstrate their effectiveness were more likely to win a share of scarce resources (1997) but only 55 per cent of practitioners reported very frequently or occasionally evaluating the impact of their programs.

A more recent Australian study (Simmons & Watson, 2006) found that practitioners still focus on measuring outputs such as media coverage rather than outcomes as a way of demonstrating performance.

Public relations practitioners will want to assess the lessons learnt from each project—What worked well? What did not? What would we do differently next time?

The research questions that are addressed at this stage include the following:

➤ Did our audience and publics understand the message?
➤ Did they change their opinion?
➤ Did they change attitudes?
➤ Did they do what we wanted?
➤ Did they repeat the behaviour?
➤ Did we achieve social or cultural change?
➤ Has the problem been solved?
➤ Was the program conducted responsibly and ethically?
➤ Have we developed a model that we would be happy to use again?

In the example below, the waste authority wants to evaluate the effectiveness of a program to train people in practical ways to minimise waste or use it as a resource.

TABLE **5.4** | **How to evaluate the effectiveness of a program established to train people**

Outcome objectives	Evaluation measures to test achievement
To achieve attitudinal, awareness, and behavioural changes in domestic waste practices among the wider community.	Annual survey re: waste attitudes and behaviour.
To demonstrate that the training program is having an impact on the waste stream.	Council random waste audits of household bins and monitor number of compost bins and worm farm kits purchased through councils.

Source: Mindarie Regional Council 2008

Presenting research findings

An important part of the research process is the presentation of results. This is where the story about what the research shows is told. It is not just a presentation of the data, but it is also your interpretation of the data so the results are clear and able to be acted on. Lisa Lough, managing director of CATALYSE®, presents the results of research projects undertaken by her firm in PowerPoint format, supplemented by a written report, and she ensures that strong visual components support the key points to be gleaned from the results. Lisa's tips for how to present effectively are these:

1   Make sure the information presented is relevant and applicable to avoid the 'So what?' factor.

2 Present the results so they can be understood by someone who has not been as intimately involved in the project as you have.

3 Take out what is not needed. Only include what is important to telling the story; avoid information overload, which means taking out the clutter and reducing the number of words.

4 Design each slide to take the eye to the most important points, and then to follow through the sequence of ideas presented.

5 The results do not have to be presented in the order that the questions were asked in the research. Identify which are the most important findings and discuss them first, then move into the supplementary findings.

6 All the detail uncovered by the research does not have to be presented because the full information is provided in the written report. For presentation, make a judgment about the information that is relevant to talk about.

7 Make sure you understand what you are reporting. It is important to be clear about whether you are reporting that a percentage of respondents said or a percentage of responses indicated, and to know whether the findings of interest can be extrapolated to the total population.

8 Understand whether a variance is statistically significant. What looks like a significant difference may be explained by the margins of error in the research design. It is the public relations practitioner's job to help the audience draw accurate conclusions.

9 Be consistent in how the data are presented. Put short quotes in apostrophes and set larger quotes in narrower margins and smaller type, and then the data can be readily differentiated from your interpretation.

Below is a page from a research report that shows how information can be presented.

FIGURE **5.1** \ Target audience for music concerts

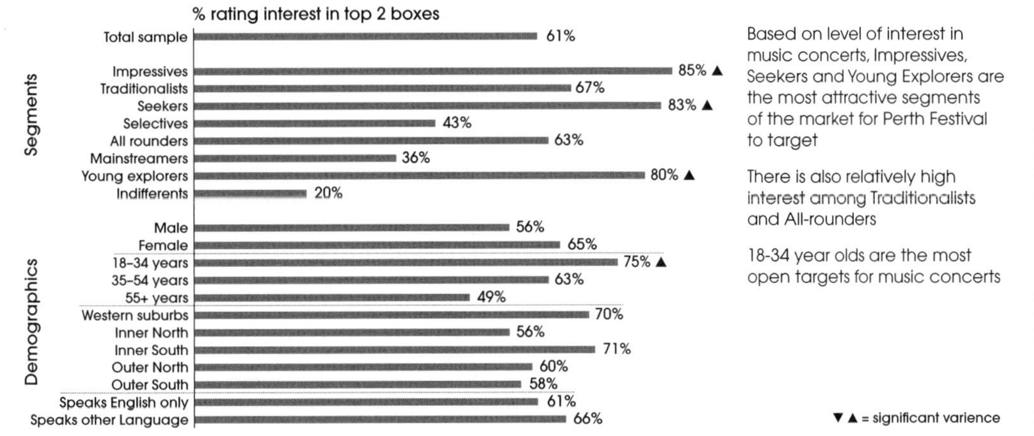

Q. I'm going to read out a list of activities that people may get involved with over summer. Please let me know how interested you are in each activity by giving it a rating of 5. A score of 1 means that you are not at all interested and a score of 5 means that you are extrememly interested. Base: General community, excludes don't know and refused (n=400)
* small sample size (n<30)

Gae Synnott

Some of the lessons to learn as a junior practitioner coming in to this field relate to knowing which information to include in the presentation and which to leave out. A lot of judgment is also involved in knowing the order in which to present.

Research applications

In addition to undertaking research to help with the planning process, research is used in public relations to help determine specific things that might be happening. An issue might be followed over a period of time, so it will need to be monitored to see whether action needs to be taken, or a look might need to be taken at what seems to be a spike of interest in an issue to determine whether it has significance.

Understanding and working with public opinion

Public opinion is what most people in a particular target public think about an issue. Public opinion is based on perceptions and evaluations rather than fact, and is subject to change while it is forming. Practitioners who are monitoring an emerging issue as part of an issues management program tend to watch closely for signs that an issue is growing in strength and firming up as people tend to take their cue on how they feel about an issue from what others are saying (Heath & Coombs 2006).

Because public opinion can change markedly and rapidly, the role of research is to understand what the opinion is at a particular point in time, knowing that further measurements will need to be taken to test whether it is still the same or whether it has changed. Keith Patterson from Patterson Market Research in Western Australia, describes this as 'trying to find out what the world at large thinks or does' in relation to the issue, or very simply measuring what is. The practitioner will listen to what is being said, respond through distribution of messages, and monitor again to assess whether specific messages or sources are having an impact on the formation of public opinion. This is likely to be an ongoing cycle.

The relevant target public or audience for an issue can be large or small, and there may be a number of specific target publics who are involved in the one issue. Even though different publics and audiences may have the same opinion, their opinion may be based on a different set of perceptions or values; it is useful to understand and monitor them separately, with a separate communication program for each. As Patterson explains, a public opinion poll will be audited so the researcher needs to be very confident in the procedures being used, specifically, the sampling distributions. This means creating the best possible subset of the population of interest to ensure that the sample is representative and that the sample can be replicated. If, for example, the poll is being undertaken by the major political parties to understand whether people will vote

Labor or Liberal at the next election, the parameters of age, gender, and location must be accurate. Socioeconomic factors that might lead to voting allegiance patterns must also be factored in to the sampling distributions. As a first step in accurate sampling, information from the Australian census is critical in helping to understand electorates.

The more interested you are in measuring change, the more important it is to have representative samples that can be replicated. The first survey sets the benchmark; subsequent surveys test change.

Some additional issues in public opinion research include the following:

➤ The question of the extent to which the measurement process may influence the result. The publishing of information or survey results has an effect on public opinion, as can be seen in the fluctuations in voting preferences tracked during the lead-up to an election.

➤ The frequency of testing. There is no point testing something unless there is a chance that it has changed. Likewise, there is no point testing if there is no ability to change your actions as a result of the research.

➤ The measuring instrument must be able to remove all the non-relevant variables and test the change that results from the specific variables the practitioner is interested in.

REFLECT AND DISCUSS

> ➤ Choose an issue that is emerging in your community and that is likely to attract some extensive media coverage, for example, uranium mining, increased smoking bans, mandatory reporting of child abuse. Watch the issue over a two-week period and track who is speaking out on the issue and how long it takes for clear positions (for and against) to emerge.
>
> ➤ Then speculate what might happen with the issue if survey results were published that showed that 66 per cent of the community is overwhelmingly in support of or against the issue, for example, uranium mining.

Research for issues management

Issues management, addressed in Chapter 10, is the constant awareness of, and sensitivity to, the views of publics and audiences and growth of public opinion. Dealing with multiple publics and audiences who may support or contest the organisation's mission means that actions and attitudes are constantly on the move.

If communication breaks down, or a particular idea takes hold, issues can escalate and, if not managed, can grow into crises.

A key idea then is to identify issues early in their development and think about what you will need to monitor to determine if the issue is growing and when it could require intervention. Heath (1997: 81) explains the process this way:

> Often, one or more members of the organisation recognise the nature and seriousness of an issue and sell it to management. As management comes to share the sense of opportunity or harm that can result from the issue, they move to name it, collect information about it, discuss it, and assign individuals to the issue.

The first phase of research for issues management is called 'issues scanning', which involves scanning the environment to:

- ➤ see what issues are emerging
- ➤ assess their substance
- ➤ identify why they are staying alive and who is keeping them alive
- ➤ learn from the analysis (Heath 1997: 83).

The second phase of research for issues management is called 'issues monitoring', which involves watching the issue to see how it develops. The organisation is likely to be particularly interested in issues that have the potential to impact on reputation and relationships.

A good way to start is to conduct a review of online material that will uncover media and other coverage of a particular issue. Some specific questions to ask include:

- ➤ What questions does this raise?
- ➤ What is needed to keep a close watch on this issue as this develops?

Research as part of community engagement

Community engagement is a growing specialisation within public relations practice. Essentially, it comes from recognition that organisations are part of communities and that there is an interdependence between all parties within a community in that the actions of one will affect others. From this acknowledgment of interdependency, the next step is to embrace the principles of community democracy, which suggests that people who are going to be affected by a decision should have some input into that decision. By extension, if people in a community are to be affected by the actions of an organisation, then they should have some input into decisions that will affect them.

The International Association of Public Participation (IAP2) has developed a public participation spectrum that sets out the range of ways in which the community can become involved in discussions with organisations, with community involvement in decision making increasing as participants move along the spectrum. Many community relations practitioners use the IAP2 Public Participation Spectrum as a guide for how to involve communities more effectively. Research is an essential element of this thinking because closer interaction and dialogue enable greater ability to understand the perspectives of others. Community engagement is a tool that provides good information that organisations can use in planning.

The steps in the IAP2 Public Participation Spectrum are shown in the first row. The research contribution is explored in the row below.

TABLE **5.5** \ **Steps in the IAP2 Public Participation Spectrum and the contribution of research**

Education	Consultation	Joint planning	Joint decision making	Empowerment
The promise to the public				
We will keep you informed.	We will keep you informed, listen to and acknowledge concerns and provide feedback on how public input influenced the decision.	We will work with you to ensure that your concerns and aspirations are directly reflected in the alternatives developed and provide feedback on how public input influenced the decision.	We will look to you for direct advice and innovation in formulating solutions and incorporate your advice and recommendations into the decisions to the maximum extent possible.	We will implement what you decide.
The research component				
Traditional research used to find out what people know about a project. Communication is undertaken to build awareness and knowledge.	Through a process of consultation, organisations present proposals and seek comment and feedback on the proposals presented.	Through a process of dialogue, all parties generate the options and have input into how the project takes shape.	Through a process of dialogue, all those affected by a decision have input into the decision. Good opportunity for discussion and consideration of ideas and viewpoints.	The community is empowered to make the decision. The organisation acknowledges the expertise of those affected by the decision.

Source: 'The promise', International Association for Public Participation; 'The research', Gae Synnott

While many factors will contribute to an organisation's decision about which level to operate from on the spectrum, the process of building dialogue and improving understanding of issues is central to the community engagement approach. This is research in action.

Among the tools of community engagement research are some useful methodologies for gathering community views and monitoring views, values, and attitudes over time. These include:

➤ community panels and advisory groups
➤ town hall meetings

➤ community dialogues
➤ community planning workshops
➤ multicriteria analysis.

MINI-CASE STUDY \ A PUBLIC HEALTH CONSULTATION FRAMEWORK

The Department of Health in Western Australia has developed a framework for consultation that ensures that the public health components of a proposal are fully investigated and agreed to, and that issues of importance to communities are identified and understood prior to finalisation of the plans. While community consultation and engagement are designed to enable proponents to understand issues related to a proposal, public health impacts tend not to be specifically addressed although they may come out as part of environmental and social impacts. The public health consultation framework provides a framework for discussion during the engagement process so that factors that could result in positive or negatives outcomes are proactively identified.

The framework identifies eight areas for discussion. These are presented on a poster as a wheel with eight spokes:

➤ people and community wellbeing
➤ the natural environment
➤ transport
➤ economic environment
➤ community services
➤ social environment
➤ sustainability
➤ lifestyle.

Within each spoke is a list of factors. People and Community Wellbeing, for example, includes these factors:

➤ community structure
➤ social contacts
➤ community participation
➤ crime and antisocial behaviour
➤ discrimination
➤ safe environments
➤ social networks
➤ feelings of trust
➤ feelings of power and control over life decisions.

Using the framework, there is a set of questions to prompt discussion:

➤ For you or your family, could the proposal result in changes in any of these factors?
➤ For your community, could the proposal result in changes in any of these factors?
➤ Which of these factors are most important to you?
➤ What outcomes would you like to see?
➤ What outcomes would you not like to see?

The framework is useful because it helps to research areas of importance to a proposal that might not otherwise emerge.

Research for behavioural change programs

When you are planning a behavioural change program, the research undertaken at the start of the program is especially important. Not only are you interested in establishing what the current behaviour is, but you also want to understand the best way to change the behaviour. This is an area of practice that has developed strongly in recent years; a good reference for public relations practitioners is the Community-Based Social Marketing (CBSM) literature and listserve (McKenzie-Mohr & Smith, 1999). While the CBSM website is designed for people involved in sustainability projects, such as initiatives to reduce waste and pollution, and to increase water and energy efficiency, the information will be useful to anyone who needs to develop a behavioural change program.

Doug McKenzie-Mohr and William Smith recommend a series of CBSM steps to follow, which are mainly research-based. They include:

➤ identify the behaviour to be changed
➤ understand the perceived barriers to the desired behaviour and the perceived benefits of current behaviour (that is, why are they following certain practices and not others)
➤ investigate the various actions that could be taken to remove the barriers and make it easier for people to follow the desired behaviours, while at the same time making the current behaviour less attractive
➤ put one or two of these actions or programs to the test through a pilot program.

REFLECT AND DISCUSS

➤ Log on to the CBSM website www.cbsm.com (you will need to complete a free registration) and pick a topic you are interested in.
➤ List five things you have picked up from the website that would help you to plan a behavioural change program. What are the first steps you need to put in place as you develop the program?

How do we obtain reliable and relevant knowledge?

How accurate does it need to be?

All kinds of information is used in public relations. Sometimes the information needs to be based on statistics and accurate data, sometimes it can be indicative. Practitioners need to identify not only what information is needed to help make a decision, but also to confirm what level of rigour the information needs to have. In recognising that survey accuracy costs money, Patterson (personal communication, April 2008) made a case for the level of accuracy to be determined by the basis upon which decisions are to be made. He says that there's not much point creating a survey that is accurate to within 5 per cent if a reaction will only be warranted if a much greater shift in attitude is determined. When considering the requirement for survey accuracy, he asks, 'At what level of difference in the results would you want to take some corrective action?' Having said that, it can be important to pick up a shift in attitude before it has a chance to gather real momentum. It can be very important to pick up a movement in community attitudes of as little as 5 or 10 per cent in order to take corrective action before a real groundswell develops.

In a different public relations program, a picture might be gradually built up about something that cannot be directly tested through formal research. Like detective work, it might involve talking to a range of people or accessing a number of websites to gradually build some clarity about the topic of interest. Both types of research are valuable in public relations.

Primary or secondary

Research can be primary or secondary (see Guth & Marsh 2009). Primary research is research data generated by the practitioner; secondary research data have been gathered by someone else. As a result, secondary research data are unlikely to be tailored specifically to the project the practitioner is dealing with, but will provide useful background and contextual material.

Practitioners generally start with secondary data collection. Secondary research data include reports, statistical reports such as those generated by the Australian Bureau of Statistics, media clippings, case studies, journal articles, and online databases. If these sources do not generate sufficient information, sources should be expanded to include annual reports and stock exchange libraries, published reports from official government inquiries, PhD theses, conference papers, and parliamentary Bills and papers. Online databases are now the most frequently used way to gather information.

A common task at the start of a public relations program is to undertake a literature review to find out relevant information that will be useful in understanding the project and developing a communication solution. This may reveal previous work that can be adapted and applied. A literature review often involves searches of media clippings to see how the media have portrayed the project and the organisation. A search on the internet is usually the first step.

REFLECT AND DISCUSS

> What five secondary data sources could you access to obtain information to help you to establish an annual community event such as a walkathon to raise money for a not-for-profit organisation?

Primary data can be split into two categories: field research, in which the practitioner talks to people who know something about the topic, and formal research, which is the more highly structured quantitative and qualitative research. Field research can be done with:

➤ industry experts, who include people from professional and industry associations, public relations officers, and other knowledgeable people within an organisation
➤ trade press and industry commentators, people who write about or otherwise cover that particular industry
➤ those directly involved with an issue, which includes unions and government representatives.

Formal or informal

Some of the research we talk about in public relations practice is formal, such as focus groups and surveys, where the design of the research instrument is critical to its ability to produce valid, reliable, and statistically significant results in which you can have total confidence. In these research projects bias must be avoided, as must leading questions, to design the sampling strategy to ensure that the research results can be extrapolated to the total population of interest.

There will be other times when the research does not need to be this precise, where indicative and exploratory results will be satisfactory. This research can be done by the public relations practitioner. Internet research of case studies falls into this category, as do one-on-one discussions with stakeholders and the quick ring around of contacts to get some relevant market information before attending a client meeting. Different research, different objectives.

New research tools

The traditional tools of surveys and focus groups are still very much in use, but technology has provided a range of new tools. Often these new technologies enable much public relations research to be conducted faster and at a lower cost than in the past.

These include:

➤ online surveys—often a good way to get a quick response and can be done at any time; if the results need to be representative, online surveys can ask for relevant demographics and samples can be supplemented with phone surveys to ensure the representativeness of the sample
➤ hotline on a specific issue
➤ blogs as a qualitative research tool
➤ online databases.

Marie Howarth offers these thoughts about the influence of the new media:

If you want to attract attention find a blogger with clout. If you want to build a following, establish your own online community. If you want to set new trends, seek out the connectors, mavens and influencers who help shape opinion online (personal communication, April 2008).

REFLECT AND DISCUSS

➤ How do you respond to Howarth's comments? Choose an organisation and find five blogs that would be of specific interest to that organisation.
➤ Participate in an online survey. What do you notice about it in terms of number of questions asked, how easy it was to answer, and the length of time it took you to complete?
➤ Look at Telstra's alternative website, www.nowwearetalking.com.au (profiled further in Chapter 12), and identify a further five issues you would need to work on if you were part of the Telstra public relations team.

One of the limitations with traditional surveys is that potential research participants are often busy people so many reject the offer to participate. Rejection may also be caused by 'survey fatigue', that is by the same people being asked many times to participate. Most research projects build in an expectation of a certain percentage of knockbacks when they try to recruit people to answer a survey, so the extra effort involved to recruit participants does have a cost impact. The development of web-based surveys, in which people participate at a time to suit them, means that people self-select whether to get involved. A common research design is to offer the web-based survey as a first option, and then follow it up with phone surveys to achieve the required sample size and representativeness.

When do you need professional assistance?

You have three options, the first of which is to conduct the research yourself.

The second option is to use professional assistance for part of the research project including:

➤ identification of target audience and sample
➤ composing or evaluating the questions on your research instrument (survey or focus group script)
➤ analysing or interpreting the statistics you generate
➤ making projections based on your data.

The third option is to turn your whole project over to the professionals. In addition to doing the research they can provide:

➤ interviewer training and monitoring
➤ large capacity computer processing
➤ focus group facilities with video cameras and observation booths
➤ phone interview facilities with many lines
➤ computer-assisted phone interviewing technology
➤ graphic design assistance for presenting research results and reports
➤ statistical analysis skills.

Issues with public relations research

Budgets

Budgets for public relations research can be an issue. While practitioners see research as an investment that leads to a more effective program, there is sometimes pressure to spend the money on program activities rather than research.

Some ways to minimise the research cost and ensure that it provides value for money include the following:

➤ Make sure the findings will be of value. This means, always be clear about why you are doing the research, how you will use the information collected, and what this will add to your ability to produce an effective plan.
➤ Try secondary research sources first. Gathering relevant information from existing reports and databases may provide sufficient information for your needs, and is generally less expensive than primary research activity.
➤ Piggyback on omnibus surveys. This is where you may be able to add one or two questions onto a survey that is done regularly and involves a number of companies. In this case you pay only a proportion of the research cost.

➤ Use students studying market research as a resource, particularly for field-based survey work. Often this is organised by the university and represents a component of assessable work for the student.

➤ Use the internet to find out as much information as you can. Again, this is a secondary research technique.

➤ Work with smaller samples. The relevant sample size depends on the level of confidence you want to be able to have in the results. A smaller sample size will reduce the level of confidence of the results but may make a significant difference to the budget. You will have to consider whether the trade-off is appropriate.

➤ Do the research yourself. There may be some research that you can do yourself rather than involving others or using the professional services of a market research firm. Whether this is an option depends on the research task and your research objectives. You will not want to compromise the quality when your research needs to define benchmarks and produce quantitative results that will be used as a basis for subsequent evaluation. You need to be careful of design issues such as bias and the use of leading questions that will skew your results. There are times when professional assistance to design and implement the research program is important.

Survey fatigue has an impact on budgets for public relations research because more calls may be needed before the targeted respondent can actually be contacted. The refusal rate of people declining to participate will determine the number of calls that need to be made to achieve the desired sample size. Both of these factors add to the cost of research programs, and both are beyond the control of the public relations practitioner and the research company.

Doing the research only once

Sometimes the response to a limited budget is to do the research once, report the current status, and be satisfied with that. The reality is that things change, blips grow, and without a second or ongoing look at the issue, an important development can be missed. If your interest is to use research to improve your programs and achieve better results, you will need to do it more than once so you have reliable and up-to-date information.

Research as a low priority

Sometimes the research budget is cut because the research is seen as nice to have but not essential, and not contributing to results and effectiveness, which may mean that the practitioner has not argued the case for good research well enough.

Research must be linked to specific actions. General research without a specific focus is a waste of time and money. Mounting a good rationale for research requires the public relations professional to be sufficiently aware of the research options to be able to present the compelling business case.

Other barriers to investing in research, identified in the Simmons & Watson (2006) study include time as the greatest barrier for government sector practitioners, while consultants tend to perceive greater budgetary, training, and client acceptance barriers.

Speed of activity and the pressure to move on to the next project

Sometimes we just do not get around to doing something because we do not have enough time. Sometimes we think we have enough knowledge to develop a program without additional research. Sometimes we use our intuitive sense to feel whether something has worked. None of these are professional approaches to public relations practice.

The best approach to research is to recognise its contribution and allocate time and budget for it as a standard part of your project management.

Make sure you understand about sampling

As Lough and Patterson (personal communication, April 2008) pointed out, sampling is a critical issue with research. If a public relations practitioner wants to be able to say with certainty that X per cent of the population supports this proposal, you need to make sure the sample is representative of the total population. A key decision is to determine the sample for the research—whose views you want to test. A second key decision is to determine the size of the sample. This is a trade-off between the cost of the survey and the confidence you want to have in the results. If you need to be able to extrapolate the findings, professional assistance with the sampling will be needed.

Samples and sample size

The target or audience may be the residents of a large town, population 100 000. You might want to know their views about the development of a new recreation facility, the proposed features of the facility, and its potential usage. Rather than surveying the entire population, you can survey a representative sample to determine what everyone thinks. If the sample is representative of the total population you will be able to extrapolate the findings, which means you will be able to say with certainty that X per cent of the population supports this proposal.

A representative sample of, say, 400 has an approximate 5 per cent margin for error. This means that the result will be within plus or minus 5 per cent of the way the total population would have responded. A smaller sample increases the margin for error and a larger sample reduces it. For most purposes a 5 per cent margin for error is considered acceptable.

Types of sampling: random or probability

For a public relations practitioner to be able to extrapolate the survey results to the total population, the sample must be randomly drawn. This means the sample must be selected in a way that gives everyone an equal chance of being selected. This is called a random sample and it generally means that the sample selection is free of bias.

There are three additional and valid ways of drawing samples: convenience, purposive or expert, and quota.

Convenience sampling

Rather than drawing your sample from the total population you might decide to select your sample from a shopping centre. You decide to approach every fifth person, regardless of factors such as gender and age. In one sense this is random sampling but there is no guarantee that those sampled will be representative of the total population.

Purposive or expert sampling

Alternatively, you might draw your sample from people with a particular background or expertise, such as members of the existing recreation facility or health professionals who work at the existing facility. The information that you get from this sample will draw on their expertise, and their input may be very useful in planning the new facility.

Quota sampling

This sampling method is used to try to match the sample with characteristics of the total population in terms of age, gender, residential location, and income.

Academic research

While public relations practitioners use research to plan, implement, and evaluate public relations programs, there is another level of research that needs to continue to build the body of knowledge on which practice is based. This research is undertaken largely in academic institutions by staff and students at Masters and Doctoral level who are researching the application of social sciences and other disciplines to the practice of public relations.

Academic research has contributed to public relations practice in a number of areas. As practitioners, a number of the frameworks we use to plan activity comes from research that has shown the right way to structure our activity. Thus, from the application of social psychology we understand about motivation and why people behave as they do, which allows us to construct messages with some knowledge of motivation.

Research into the influence of the media and their agenda-setting role has helped us plan communication campaigns with a strong media component.

Research into interpersonal communication in the workplace enables us to plan communication campaigns in which the most credible people—supervisors—are a central component in the plan.

A number of international academic journals, including the *Journal of Public Relations Research* and *Public Relations Review*, publish research papers. In our region there are a number of publications and forums for research to be shared. They include the following:

➤ The *Asia Pacific Public Relations Journal*, which is published in Australia and focuses on current Australian research. The Public Relations Institute of Australia (PRIA) values scholarly contributions and supports the journal.

➤ *PRism Online Public Relations Journal*, moderated by Elspeth Tilley through Massey University, New Zealand.

➤ Public relations educators in Australia present their research at an annual forum that is part of the National Conference of the Public Relations Institute of Australia, and at the annual ANZCA (Australia New Zealand Communication Association) conference, and these refereed papers are published in journals.

➤ Public relations scholars are presenting their research to the European Research conference, the International Communication Association conference, and others on the international stage where the exchange of ideas is directed by up-to-date public relations research.

CASE STUDY | PERTH INTERNATIONAL ARTS FESTIVAL

The Perth International Arts Festival is the oldest annual international multi-arts festival in the southern hemisphere. The three-week long festival, held annually in February, attracts more than 300 000 patrons to events in Perth and well as in the Great Southern region. It has grown in the past fifty-five years to become a festival of major international standing with an enviable worldwide reputation and an astonishing breadth of work.

Coralie Stupart, marketing and audience development manager with the Perth Festival, works closely with Lisa Lough from CATALYSE® to design the annual research program, the results of which are a key strategic resource for the organisation. Since the first market segmentation research in 2005, Coralie and Lisa have worked closely to develop a research tool that provides actionable information and to develop an organisational culture that embraces the research and uses it as a basis for constructive analysis and continual improvement.

The 2005 market segmentation research identified eight community segments, four of which are festival supporters to varying degrees, and four of which present an opportunity to build involvement with the festival. Details about each segment covers demographic data, who comes to what performances, what attracts them to attend, and much more that assists in the marketing process. Having these market segments changed the way the festival operated from that point, the segments being used as a basis for programming and marketing decisions with the aim of continually increasing the paid audience at each festival. The market segments are now part of the organisational language, with everyone in the organisation aware of the segments and constantly thinking about what would appeal to each segment as a way of meeting their needs, boosting their festival experience, and constantly improving what is on offer.

During the festival, research on patron experiences is done onsite at selected events to monitor the segments, which leads to decisions about how to increase commitment, build a larger percentage of people who are diehard festival fans, and what programming might bring new people into events. The patron experience research tests the extent to which people know it is a festival event and their commitment to the festival, and also rates the event experience by looking at such factors as venue, ambience, performers, value for money, quality of sound and vision, seating, customer service, and a range of other factors. The research data and analysis enable proactive decisions to be made so as to better service patrons, to remove barriers to their participation, and to improve style, tone, and content of messages.

A brand perceptions study is also undertaken each year to determine how the community feels about the festival and the festival brand. This is a phone survey, that has a sample of 400 and a more strategic focus.

Results of the research are eagerly anticipated, and are scrutinised and discussed at length by the whole organisation. The value of the research findings include:

➤ the board looks for information about the health of the brand and for strategic insights
➤ the general manager and artistic director use the information in setting strategic direction; with a new artistic director appointed every four years the research results are a good source of background information
➤ programming and production staff look for evaluations of programming decisions, event experience, venue favourability, and whatever will be helpful in planning for the following year
➤ ticketing and operations staff look at ticketing preferences, customer service issues, human resources and brand management issues, and points to focus on during inductions
➤ the sponsorship team looks for patron profiles to match with sponsor requests
➤ the marketing staff looks at audience development and brand management, information which feeds into decisions about marketing planning and how to build more engagement with the arts
➤ the public relations team works closely with the marketing and audience development team to develop key messages and to constantly improve the process of building relationships with the audience segments.

Coralie Stupart is working to an objective to double the paid audience over a five-year period. From her perspective, research is a critical input to this objective.

CHAPTER **SUMMARY**

- ➤ Research is an important tool for public relations practitioners.
- ➤ Almost every communication problem or project calls for varying degrees of research: fact finding, opinion assessment, message testing, planning, execution and evaluation.
- ➤ Research can make a real difference to the effectiveness of public relations because it provides information that helps to plan, implement, and evaluate.
- ➤ Research must be relevant and should lead to further action.
- ➤ At the start of a program, research enables the creation of programs based on a better understanding of the issues and with a better appreciation of context.
- ➤ Research done during a program to monitor progress allows the activity to be fine tuned to ensure that the desired outcomes are achieved.
- ➤ Research at the conclusion of a program allows us to test whether the desired results were achieved and to report these to management.
- ➤ Many different research methodologies are available: the most appropriate for what needs to be found out must be used.
- ➤ Sufficient time and budget need to be allocated for research.
- ➤ Armed with research and analysis, practitioners can present and justify public relations plans that are supported by evidence and theory.
- ➤ Without research and analysis, practitioners are guessing or making assumptions about the problem, issue, or opportunity, as well as about the solution.

FURTHER READING

Brody, E W & Stone, G C 1989, *Public Relations Research*, Praeger, New York.

Cutlip, S, Center, A & Broom, G 2006, *Effective Public Relations*, 9th edn, Prentice Hall, Englewood Cliffs.

Daymon, C & Holloway, I 2002, *Qualitative Research Methods in Public Relations and Marketing Communications*, Routledge, London.

Grunig, J E & Grunig, L A 1989, *Public Relations Research Annual,* vol. 1, Lawrence Erlbaum, Englewood Cliffs.

Grunig, J E & Grunig, L A 1990, *Public Relations Research Annual,* vol. 2, Lawrence Erlbaum, Englewood Cliffs.

Stacks, D W 2002, *Primer of Public Relations Research*, Guildford Press, New York.

Watson, T & Noble, P 2007, *Evaluating Public Relations: A Best Practice Guide to Public Relations Planning, Research and Evaluation*, 2nd edn, Kogan Page, London.

WEB RESOURCES

Asia Pacific Public Relations Journal, at www.deakin.edu.au/arts-ed/apprj.

Community-Based Social Marketing principles and discussion forums, at www.cbsm.com.

IAP2's Public Participation Spectrum, at www.iap2.org.au.

Western Australian Department of Health's framework (full copy), at www.health.wa.gov.au.

REFERENCES

Broom, G M & Dozier, D M 1990, *Using Research in Public Relations: Applications to Program Management*, Prentice Hall, Englewood Cliffs.

Grunig, J & Hunt, T 1994, *Managing Public Relations*, Harcourt Brace, Fort Worth.

Guth, D & Marsh, C 2009, *Public Relations. A Values-Driven Approach*, 4th edn, Allyn & Bacon, Boston.

Heath, R 1997, *Strategic Issues Management: Organizations and Public Policy Changes*, Sage, Thousand Oaks and London.

Heath, R & Coombs, T 2006, *Today's Public Relations. An Introduction*, Sage, Thousand Oaks.

International Public Relations Association (IPRA) 1994, *Public Relations Evaluation: Professional Accountability*, Gold Paper 11.

Kreps, G 2008, 'A Weickian Approach to Public Relations and Crisis Management', in T Hansen-Horn & B Neff, *Public Relations: From Theory to Practice*, Allyn & Bacon, Boston.

McElreath, M 1993, *Managing Systematic and Ethical Public Relations*, Brown & Benchmark, Dubuque.

McKenzie-Mohr, D & Smith, W 1999, *Fostering Sustainable Behaviour: An Introduction to Community-Based Social Marketing*, New Society Publishers, Gabriola Island.

Pavlik, J 1987, *Public Relations: What Research Tells Us*, Sage, Newbury Park.

Seitel, F (ed.) 2007, *The Practice of Public Relations*, Prentice Hall, Upper Saddle River.

Simmons, P & Watson, T 2005, 'Public Relations Evaluation in Australia: Practices and Attitudes Across Sectors and Employment Status', *Asia Pacific Public Relations Journal*, 6(2): 1–14, accessed at www.deakin.edu.au/arts-ed/apprj/vol6no2.php, 14 February 2009.

Surowiecki, J 2004, *The Wisdom of Crowds*, Random House, New York.

Walker, G 1997, 'Public relations practitioners' use of research, measurement and evaluation', *Australian Journal of Communication*, 24(2): 97–113.

Wilcox, D, Cameron, G, Ault, P & Agee, W K 2006, *Public Relations: Strategies and Tactics*, 8th edn, Allyn & Bacon, Boston.

Chapter **6**

PUBLIC RELATIONS PRACTICE

Gae Synnott

PRACTITIONER PROFILE | LELDE MCCOY

How the rules have changed in public relations from twenty years ago when the practice was based more on positive image creation rather than the building of substantive relationships between organisations and their stakeholders.

As the managing director of the Reputation Group, Lelde McCoy specialises in projects that build and defend the reputations of organisations and their brands.

The building of an organisation's reputational value has become an important part of corporate strategy. Corporate reputations are formed not only by all the messages and images stakeholders receive about an organisation but also by their personal experiences of its performance.

McCoy believes that public relations today is about reputation-enhancing behaviours.

To many people reputation management refers more to protecting a company's name through issues management rather than a planned program of actions to grow a company's profile and respect for it. The reputation work I do aligns corporate branding, corporate responsibility and stakeholder relations with corporate strategy to create competitive advantage.

After graduating in economics and journalism Lelde McCoy worked inhouse in communications departments in the packaging, brewing, and gas industries. Most of her professional life has been spent in consulting. To keep abreast of the latest practices in strategic communications management, she has also studied at Masters level at the S I Newhouse School of Public Communication at Syracuse University in the USA.

A former national president of the Public Relations Institute of Australia McCoy's advice to new practitioners is to learn how to be strategic, a skill that takes time and further professional development.

Our value as public relations practitioners is enhanced when we influence outcomes and affect results. We can no longer be just mechanics but need to be designers of the future and catalysts for change. Being strategic means not seeing yourself as an adjunct to the business strategy, but as an integral part of the process.

CHAPTER **AIMS**

By the end of this chapter you should be able to:

➤ outline differences and similarities between public relations practice in different environments
➤ understand the common elements in effective public relations practice, regardless of operating environment
➤ identify what is involved in the public relations role
➤ examine the growing role of community relations and the interdependent nature of relationships between organisations and their communities
➤ recognise some of the realities and challenges of professional public relations practice.

Introduction

The contemporary public relations practitioner is a multiskilled person with a values-based approach to the job.

Far from being the paid mouthpiece of an organisation, today's practitioner is driven by the outcome that needs to be achieved in terms of organisational reputation and relationship management.

The role requires strategic and technical competences such as:

➤ an understanding of the big picture and why an issue or a public is relevant for an organisation
➤ the ability to see an issue from a range of perspectives
➤ the ability to uncover the real issues or problems to be resolved and the outcomes to be addressed
➤ an understanding of the importance of relationships and the skills to build and strengthen relationships and dialogue
➤ confidence in the communication solutions being recommended, based on relevant theoretical frameworks and a comprehensive appreciation of all aspects
➤ the skill set to create and implement the communication solutions.

Public relations is one of the critical strategic tools used by an organisation to help it achieve its objectives. As systems theory tells us, organisations continually adapt and adjust to outside conditions and pressures in their operating environment as they strive to achieve organisational goals. The public relations practitioner, who is part of this problem-solving and change process, draws on communication skills across a broad spectrum to help organisations solve problems, assist change, build relationships with key publics and audiences, communicate ideas, create dialogue, improve how the organisation is perceived, manage issues, and improve understanding and awareness. Through the strategic, ethical, and appropriate use of communication, the public relations practitioner works to achieve specific outcomes helpful to the organisation, which can involve change in the organisation, in the operating environment, or in both. The range of situations that an organisation might face is very broad, so public relations thinking focuses on how best to use communication to achieve a specific result in a given situation.

Increasingly, public relations practitioners look to achieve mutually beneficial results rather than to work for the one-sided interest of an organisation. In this sense, public relations has a strong role in ensuring socially responsible action.

At its crux, the public relations practitioner is a solver of problems and situations. The acts of finding out crucial information, asking 'What if …?', linking ideas, building concepts, and testing approaches are as relevant to public relations practice as the more commonly-acknowledged writing and media skills.

Public relations thinking is documented as a plan or a program, and without a plan things rarely happen. The act of planning leads to action, which leads to results. The plan is the practitioner's working theory of what has to be done to achieve a desired outcome. Public relations is an active profession that benefits from clear thinking, specific targets, and a good understanding of the operating context and the critical success factors at play for an organisation.

Gae Synnott

Planning enables us to:

➤ help create the desired future for the organisation
➤ make something happen or prevent it from happening
➤ pre-empt organisational, stakeholder, media, and community needs and to be one step ahead
➤ establish relevant objectives that have long-term positive outcomes, and then implement strategies that move you in tangible steps towards those goals
➤ commit resources to where they are most useful
➤ build increased management participation and support
➤ achieve productive relationships with those important to the organisation
➤ ensure a positive rather than defensive program approach.

This translates into tangible activities such as:

➤ promoting a product or service to build awareness and stimulate sales
➤ opening a new facility
➤ holding an event to celebrate achievements
➤ researching and understanding a particular set of publics' or audience needs so these needs can be accommodated in the public relations program
➤ reporting on corporate sustainability performance
➤ working with the community to plan a new community development
➤ building support for a cause or an idea.

The common elements

Because public relations is a diverse profession in which practitioners deal with a range of issues for a range of organisations, it is sometimes difficult to see and appreciate the common elements. Yet the commonality exists.

➤ Codes of practice (see Chapter 4) clarify the standards that must be met in how the job is done so that public relations can be seen as a profession.
➤ Theories (see Chapter 3) provide common understanding as a basis for conceptualising problems and potential solutions, and this body of knowledge is growing all the time.
➤ Communication tools such as websites, newsletters, and community forums provide a repertoire to be drawn from according to the needs of the situation.
➤ Practitioners focus their activity around target publics or audiences—one, a few, or many—and what is to be achieved in relation to that audience.
➤ Practitioners operate in environments where their efforts are constantly being assessed to determine contribution and effectiveness.
➤ Practitioners work on matters of importance to the organisations they work for.

Beyond these visible areas of commonality, there are some fundamental elements that bind us.

A common view of effective public relations practice

At this stage of your career in public relations, you may not have seen many public relations practitioners in action, and if you were asked to identify the attributes of your public relations role model it might be difficult to do. The values and attributes of the role model in public relations shown in Table 6.1 below came from a research project with a sample of public relations practitioners in Malaysia in the late 1990s (Synnott 2002). They identified eight categories of public relations effectiveness, and within each category identified a list of constructs which typified role model performance, a sample of which are shown below.

TABLE **6.1** \ **The eight categories of public relations effectiveness**

Category	Constructs
1 Work practices and approach	• Takes responsibility for their work • Takes a win–win approach • Committed to getting the job done • Provides a value-added service • Gives and shares advice; seeks advice • Adopts high standards in approach to public relations • Works on building relationships • Looks at all sides
2 Skills, abilities and knowledge	• Can give advice to management • Good grasp of issues important to the company and the profession • Uses public relations knowledge to optimise company's image • Understands what is required; knows the job • High level of technical ability • Capable of strategy and execution • Deals with difficult issues • Good understanding of public relations and media requirements
3 Experience and background	• Solid experience • Long and broad public relations exposure • Track record • Sound journalism experience • Has government public relations experience
4 Personal attributes	• High degree of professionalism • People oriented • Genuine • Creative • Works to build own knowledge and expand professional capabilities • Shares knowledge with others • Has good corporate citizen values • Puts in heart and soul, passionate; strong personal commitment shows through in work

Continued …

Gae Synnott

Category	Constructs
5 Judgment and ethics	• Honest • Ethical • Has integrity and will do what they feel is right • Aware of implications
6 Relationship with management	• Seen by management as contributing to organisational goals • Accepted by management • Management sees them as equals
7 Image and reputation	• Highly regarded by industry • Good reputation in industry and the profession • High credibility and acceptance • Well known in public relations profession • Very established in profession • Inspires confidence in their public relations advice
8 Works for the profession	• Builds the profession • Protects the image and reputation of the profession • Gives time to develop the profession • Committed to the profession • Sets standards in making public relations a management tool • Builds image and importance of public relations to company

Source: Synnott 2001: 430–1

Our actions are guided by our values

In recent years, there has been an emerging focus on values in the public relations profession, with identification by various scholars (Toth & Pavlik, 2000; Grunig, Toth & Hon, 2000) of the values underwriting the practice of public relations. If it is possible to identify shared values across the profession, across regional and organisational boundaries, then we might be able to surmise that values are a contributor to commonality in public relations practice.

Let us consider how people construct meaning about the world and what goes on around them. People are engaged in an ongoing process of observation, interpretation, prediction, and control of their external environment (Featherston 1995). In the process of actively making sense of the world we draw on underlying assumptions and values, and construct a mental map of how things work. We create constructs to explain what happens and use these personal constructs to understand life events and make sense of our experiences.

We make judgments within the context of these constructs, and these constructs guide our actions (Kelly's personal construct theory 1955). We see ourselves, and others see us, by the standards that guide our actions. Core personal constructs, or values, are involved in the day-to-day processes of maintaining identity and continued existence. These personal values or constructs are established through community and family, through schooling and occupational training, and are largely established before practitioners come into a workplace.

Each of us operates within a number of cultural realms or levels—national, organisational, professional, and individual. One study (Grunig, Grunig & Vércîc 1997) identified six potential differences between countries that are likely to create different operating conditions for public relations practitioners in different countries:

1   level of economic development in a country
2   the political environment in which public relations is practised
3   the cultural environment
4   language differences
5   the potential for activism
6   the role of the mass media.

In cultural terms, public relations practices often appear to be correlated with the culture of the country involved (see Sriramesh & White 1992; Hazleton & Cutbirth 1993; Coombes, Holladay, Hasenauer & Signitzer 1994). In some parts of Asia, for example, public relations is more often influenced by Eastern theology and hierarchical principles (Taylor & Kent 1999; see also Chapter 13), whereas the personal influence model appears to be relevant in India, South Korea, Japan, Taiwan, and Greece. Hofstede stated that national culture holds fundamental invisible values, while organisational cultures reside mainly in the visible practices of an organisation (Hofstede et al. 1990).

At a professional level, each model of public relations practice—symmetrical/systems, rhetorical/critical, feminist, social scientific, and the dominant applied model based on a journalistic heritage and business orientation (Botan 1993)—contains assumptions and values. Values are at the core of professionalism (J Grunig 2000: 26) because they explain how practitioners make strategic choices for their professions and the organisations for which they work and they form the basis of professional ethics because they create guidelines and beliefs about the practice. Are these values adopted professional values or core personal values, and which is more relevant in the practice of public relations?

The reality is that we have a number of frameworks that guide our thinking about the job. While still to be explored fully, our values may be part of what brings us into the profession, as well as helping to define professional public relations practice and how we do what we do.

REFLECT AND DISCUSS

> ➤ Think about the values that are important to you.
> ➤ Would these values influence you in the type of organisation you might choose to work for? In what way?
> ➤ Can you think of an organisation that appears to have values you might find difficult to accept?

Gae Synnott

The public relations role in different types of organisations

Practitioners have a range of skills, qualifications, and experience that they apply to achieve the desired results. The starting point, or context, for the practitioner's work is the organisation's objectives because these are the measure of what is important to the organisation. The practitioner looks at the organisation's strategic plan, finds out the organisational objectives, thinks about which relationships are important, thinks about how communication can be effectively used to build the relationships that will help in the achievement of those objectives, and then designs and implements the process to deliver the desired results.

REFLECT AND DISCUSS

> ➤ Find a strategic plan for an organisation (Hint: public companies generally provide copies of their strategic plan to the Stock Exchange, or report on the strategic plan in their annual report).
> ➤ Can you find a statement of organisational objectives?
> ➤ If the communication objectives are not specified, write down your thoughts about how you believe communication could help that organisation to achieve its objectives.

The underlying reason for doing public relations activity—support of organisational goals—is the same, regardless of organisation. The strategies and activities used are likely to differ, depending on what is most relevant to the organisation's situation, its stakeholders, and the issues it is facing. The structure of the communications function will differ depending on the size, focus, and complexity of the organisation. In more complex organisations, diverse teams undertake a range of communication management activities or organisations might outsource elements of community activity. The publics and audiences will be different for each organisation, depending on the organisational objectives and priorities. While the categories of publics and audiences are generic and include media, employees, neighbours, communities, investors, government, regulators, special interest groups, and customers, the selection of which publics and audiences to engage with, the purpose and desired outcome, and therefore the planned activities to undertake will all be different.

Public relations practitioners make a choice about where they would like to work. Here some of the options are discussed in more detail.

The not-for-profit sector

The not-for-profit (NFP) sector is huge and growing, with great diversity in size and scope of organisations. The larger organisations, such as International Red Cross, Oxfam, and World Vision, are corporate in nature. In some traditional NFP sectors, such as retirement villages and aged care, for example, private companies are now moving into service provision and bringing sophisticated management systems with them. At the same time, there are still many smaller NFPs—smaller in size and scope—that operate with less sophisticated organisational structures, providing a specific service.

A public relations person in the NFP sector needs to be multiskilled and a jack or a jill of all trades. The roles of public relations, marketing, and fundraising often overlap, and are roles that are usually evaluated in terms of the amount of dollars that publicity, events, and fundraising programs bring to the organisation.

Two big issues for the NFP sector are governance and accountability. There are some notable cases in which concerns have been raised about the lack of good governance and accountability in NFPs. One such case was the Bali Fund, established by the Australian Red Cross after the 12 October 2002 bombing attack in Bali, to which Australians donated $14.3 million to help victims of the attack. But concerns were raised, as they have been by other communities and donors to other NFPs, when funds raised from a community are used for administrative purposes rather than being passed on to the people that the fundraising and the donors seek to help.

Key challenges are to understand how best to be accountable for the funds raised, and to determine how best practice in management can be demonstrated. Public relations and its capabilities in reputation management are often less recognised or utilised in this sector.

The NFP sector is often seen as a good training ground for public relations practitioners. It is a safe environment to learn in because:

➤ it offers good opportunities to be creative, particularly in terms of creative ways to achieve big results with small budgets
➤ it offers good opportunities to try new approaches and new ways of doing things
➤ it can be a very sociable environment, with lots of events and activities related to the promotional and fundraising components
➤ it develops very good people skills because of the need to involve and manage volunteer help
➤ it is generally cause-based, which means that the values driving the organisation are very clear and you can align yourself strongly with the organisation
➤ everyone tends to pitch in and help where the help is needed, which means that you learn a lot from others and you learn about other aspects of the business in addition to public relations
➤ the experience that you gain in a community-based NFP organisation helps you to understand how community organisations work, how communication works, and the importance of target audiences; this indepth knowledge will be invaluable in any sector you work in.

Gae Synnott

Some of the challenges of the NFP sector are:

➤ the fact that there is little money to work with
➤ that organisations are often hierarchical and it may be difficult for the public relations professional person to liaise directly or closely with the decision makers
➤ people high up in the hierarchy, who may have been with the organisation for some time, may be emotionally attached to the cause, which may have an influence on effective decision making
➤ the need for patience, as it sometimes takes a number of attempts to see things happen
➤ dealing with volunteers; as mentioned above, dealing with volunteers helps to develop strong skills in diplomacy, and the public relations professional needs to understand what motivates the volunteers and how to continually engage them in the work to be done.

Graham Lovelock, a Perth-based practitioner who has worked in both the NFP and corporate environments, sees the following differences between the two working environments:

➤ In the corporate sector, it may be easier to see the results and determine the role of public relations in achieving those results, whereas in the NFP sector there may be a number of factors that influence the result of fundraising dollars coming in the door, and the contribution of the public relations effort may not be as easy to delineate.
➤ The corporate sector has a highly developed approach to risk analysis and risk management that translates into risk management plans and strategic initiatives to manage issues proactively. In the NFP sector, risk analysis and risk management tend to be focused on issues of governance and accountability.
➤ In the corporate sector, the timeframes tend to be longer, with a continual input from public relations to progress incrementally towards achievement of corporate goals. In the NFP sector, the timeframe tends to be condensed because of the immediacy of the need for funds. It generally takes three years for a fundraising event to get a profile and a following and to be effective in terms of fundraising, yet decisions about promotional strategies may be made before an idea is fully allowed to prove itself because of the necessity to try another strategy that may get money in quicker.
➤ In the corporate sector, more research can be done at the start of a program to test the concept because of the availability of budgets; in the NFP sector budgets for research are less likely to be available.

An emerging area of opportunity in the NFP sector, and a potential solution to the need to attract funds, can be found in partnerships with the corporate sector as part of their corporate social responsibility and/or cause-related marketing programs (CRM). For example, Alcoa Australia's support of Greening Australia. Corporations are looking to partner with NFPs that have good visibility. This will provide opportunities for the public relations practitioner to build the NFP profile and to research organisations with whom they would have a good match. It is one area in which the NFP practitioner could cement their position at a more strategic level. The partnering of the corporate sector with the NFP sector as part of community corporate investment adds to the understanding of public relations activity and management across the sectors. As Sir Dominic Cadbury says in the foreword to a book on CRM (Adkins, 1999); 'Get it right and everyone benefits' (viii). The delineation between corporate and NFP public relations is no longer as evident, as community partnerships bring these sectors together (Tracey, Phillips & Haugh, 2005). The public relations practitioner plays a key role in negotiation and in working out projects that benefit all parties and demonstrate good corporate citizenship by contributing to society.

REFLECT AND DISCUSS

Identify three innovative partnerships between the not-for-profit sector and corporate sponsorship. For each one think about:

➤ why it is innovative

➤ what benefits each party achieves by being involved.

The corporate sector

Corporations exist to provide returns to shareholders, and their focus is on improving and building the business to ensure future viability and ongoing profitability. Corporations protect their competitive advantage and their reputation. The public relations role is to facilitate the business through relationship management, to support the achievement of corporate goals, and to contribute to enhancement of the corporate reputation. The guidelines are known, the priorities and expectations are clear.

Organisations differentiate between line and staff functions: line functions are directly involved in producing the product or service that generates profits when sold, the staff functions provide a service to the line functions. In a resource company, for example, the production and engineering departments are classified as line functions because their efforts are directly involved in mining and refining the company's product. Human resources, accounting, legal services, information technology, and public relations are all classified as staff functions, important because of the services they provide that facilitate the work of the business.

Depending on the type of organisation, the public relations officer might report to two bosses—their functional manager (the public relations manager) and their line manager. A community relations officer on a minesite, say, will report to the public

manager on communications programs, and to the minesite line manager on
programs relevant to the site. The line manager will determine the projects that
communication assistance while the functional manager will establish communication
communication tools, and company-wide communication projects.

Further up the organisation, at the senior practitioner level, the corporate public
relations manager is likely to be part of the senior management team, in close contact
with the chief executive officer, and able to discuss communications issues at a strategic
level. If risk analysis and risk management are part of the organisation's approach to
business, public relations and the communications expertise it contributes are critical parts
of decision making.

Within the public relations function, the manager generally has a team of
practitioners, each with well-defined roles, working in different communication streams.
Ideally, all activity should be proactive; none should be reactive.

At the entry level, the corporate sector is looking for a formal qualification in public
relations, good written and verbal interpersonal communication skills, graphic design, and
computer literacy, including the ability to produce PowerPoint presentations.

The career progression might then be into a specialist public relations position with
some management responsibility in that specific area. The person in this position needs to
demonstrate that they can produce annual activity plans and achieve successful outcomes
in line with those plans. This person would also have a helicopter view that enables them
to understand the context and operating environment.

At the management level, the position scope includes the following skills:

➤ *Media relations*—maintenance of strong relationships with national, state, and local
   media, daily involvement in preparing media releases, background briefings, media
   training for executives, determining interview, and photo opportunities.
➤ *Government relations*—maintenance of strong relationships with federal, state, territory,
   and local politicians and bureaucrats; needs to understand government, political, and
   parliamentary processes
➤ *Shareholder relations*—first point of contact for analysts and fund managers; responsible
   for tours and briefings, distribution of financial information, and liaison. In major
   listed public companies, public relations often has little to do with shareholder
   relations, which comes under the chief financial officer's (CFO) jurisdiction. However,
   there is evidence of increasing emphasis on the importance of financial public relations
   and investor relations, especially since the 2008 global financial crisis that has forced
   organisations to think more carefully about the management of communication with
   their shareholders, who are key stakeholders (Chia & Xavier 2008).
➤ *Public relations*—understand and respond to public expectations of major corporations,
   judge pressures and demands, forecast trends, measure and analyse public attitudes,
   and advise management on response mechanisms. Also guide community investment
   program.

➤ *Publications management*—responsible for content of all external publications, including website content.

➤ *Liaison with head office* (in this country or overseas if a multinational corporation).

➤ *Diplomatic officer*—deal with VIP visitors and protocol issues.

➤ *Industry organisations*—represent the company on designated professional organisations.

➤ *Communication skills*—speak on behalf of the organisation to a wide range of audiences—business, academic, professional, NGO, and media.

➤ *Reputation management*—contribute to customer confidence in the organisation.

While the public relations officer in this environment can aspire to become manager of the public relations department, it is unlikely that they would ever reach the position of managing director, although armed with a second qualification, such as accounting, law, or engineering, such a transition could be possible. In contrast, the consulting environment (discussed below) does provide the opportunity to reach the top of the business.

Issues management is an area of practice in which the public relations role can be of great use to the organisation. As explained in Chapters 3 and 7, the public relations role is a boundary spanner because of the need to understand the views and issues of both the organisation and its publics, and to try and connect those views, for example, to interpret the external view internally so that management can make its decisions with the full knowledge of how those decisions will affect others.

A key task of the public relations practitioner is to undertake environmental scanning, also described as scanning of the macro and micro environments (Heath & Coombes 2006) to find out what is happening outside the organisation that might have the potential to impact the organisation positively or negatively. If a potential issue, such as employee dissatisfaction with the organisation's lack of communication about changing work practices, is identified early the organisation has the opportunity to consider the issue, work around it, or change its plans in some way so that the issue does not build into a problem for the organisation or its publics. An issue can escalate into a crisis if it is not managed effectively (see Chapter 10).

At a more junior level, such as the role of a community relations officer at a minesite, a day at the office is likely to include:

➤ dealing with a raft of emails, often internal, when the CRO is asked to report progress on specific programs

➤ meetings, either with site management to discuss specific issues or programs, or with another function to discuss a project both might be working on

➤ some walking around time in boots, safety glasses, and hard hat, to get information for internal communications activities, such as information for the staff newsletter

➤ dealing with phone calls from the local community on such issues as a potential sponsorship, details about a forthcoming presentation to the shire council, or complaints about odour from the plant

➤ attendance at community reference group meetings, possibly combined with taking the minutes
➤ organisation of community relations activities, such as presentations at the local school, a display at the local library
➤ hosting visitors to the site, which involves liaison about the arrangements, organising transport onsite, organising personal protective equipment, planning the route, advising managers and staff about the visit, lining up the site manager to welcome guests, and preparation of information slides and handout material
➤ continuing to progress with regular communications projects and programs.

REFLECT AND DISCUSS

Identify five well-known corporations that operate in your city. Look on their websites, and then answer the following:

➤ What is mentioned about communication practices and priorities?
➤ What sponsorships do they provide?
➤ What resource material about the organisation do they provide?
➤ Do they have a section on new media releases?

The public sector

The public relations role in the public sector is to deliver government messages about programs, services, and initiatives. Many public sector programs relate to community services that people need to know about, for example, expansion to rail networks, changes to health claims procedures, or to social campaigns such as TravelSmart, drink driving, and quit smoking campaigns.

The public sector is aligned to the government of the day. Any government has as its goal the desire to be re-elected, so the communication is often undertaken to position the government and its decisions in a positive light. The public relations role is related to delivering government messages, and the work is often constrained by protocols, culture, and processes.

While research has found that government public relations is more likely to practise a public information model than two-way communication (Grunig & Jaatinen 1999), government public relations has recognised the importance of community input and increasingly incorporates a community engagement component (OECD 2003).

A typical government public relations function is staffed by a senior practitioner, often at director level, who presides over a team of practitioners, with well-defined roles, who work in different communication streams. The government director of communications sets the communication objectives, manages budgets, resourcing, and staffing. The more senior practitioners in the team tend to work on strategic elements of the communication programs, while the more junior practitioners tend to do the implementation.

The likely communication streams

➤ *Internal communications*—This role has strategic and implementation elements, from counselling managers on communication techniques and how to deal with a particular issue with staff, to producing newsletters, running CEO forums, overseeing the intranet, working with human resources on staff inductions, and producing the communication tools to support organisational issues and changes.

➤ *Media relations*—This role also has strategic and implementation elements. The more senior strategic role maintains close daily contact with the minister's office and the minister's press secretary to plan media activity and to respond when asked for information. Media coverage is monitored closely. If there is an issue with significant amounts of media interest, statements may be generated by the minister's office in response. In this situation, the media relations person will be asked for specific information to help respond on a specific issue, and will liaise with the CEO and policy staff within the department to coordinate the response, which is passed to the minister's office for release. A number of strategic considerations arise during this process. Are we the right agency to respond to this? Who else is involved and who else needs to be part of the response? Does this provide an opportunity to talk about departmental programs and initiatives?

Liaison with the minister's office is also undertaken in relation to ministerial events where the department may be required to provide speech notes, media releases, identification of photo opportunities, and organisation of third-party endorsements. This type of media relations work is usually handled by a senior practitioner who understands the media well, is highly organised, has good research skills, and good interpersonal skills to ensure high levels of cooperation in the process of coordinating a quick response to the minister's office.

➤ *Media relations (proactive)*—While much of the media relations work described above is reactive, the department needs to maintain a proactive communication program to build knowledge and awareness in the community and with other audiences about its programs across the whole area of its operation. This role requires good writing skills to develop features, backgrounders, speeches, website material, and to create photo opportunities. Removed from the reactive element of day-to-day response to media issues, this practitioner is able to follow a developed program of activity to achieve specified objectives for the department.

➤ *Events management*—This is a proactive role to plan and manage events that support the achievement of the organisation's objectives. The Western Australian Department of Education and Training runs the Career Choices Expo to help final year school students understand the range of further educational and training opportunities available to them. A quick scan of the range of events listed on the Tourism Western Australia website will show you the diversity of events possible. This role requires good organisational capabilities and an eye for detail because the promotional impact of a well-planned and well-run event can be significant.

➤ *Issues management*—This role has strategic and implementation elements and is the role where traditional public relations campaigns can be developed with specific messages and tools for target publics and audiences. The issues management practitioner may be part of a project team on an issue with the project manager, technical staff, HR, and staff with specific expertise, where the strategy is developed, implemented, monitored, and, if necessary, adjusted. If more than one public relations practitioner is involved, the senior person will be responsible for developing the strategy, the junior person for implementation.

➤ *Internet*—A key promotional and information tool for the department, the internet site must be kept up to date, fresh, and interesting. The role requires good liaison within the department to source information for the website and to ensure that the flow of updated information is continually provided. It also requires database management capabilities, and a creative mind to develop new ways to keep relevant people interacting with the site. Social networking applications are starting to appear on some government websites as an important component of a communication program.

➤ *Marketing support*—In some agencies this is a separate function, particularly when a large amount of marketing support work is required. This work supports the creation and maintenance of corporate profile and positioning, and social marketing and behavioural change programs such as the QUIT campaigns, drink and drive campaigns, and Keep Australia Beautiful. It is a role that requires liaison with graphic designers, advertising agencies, and market research companies.

➤ *Other communication functions*—The area of electronic and new media communication may be staffed by a specialist in some agencies and departments. Usually a junior position, the role involves looking after the corporate databases and handling podcasts, YouTube, and other business-to-business communication. The communications branch may also have a dedicated person to produce the annual report, or may manage customer service roles, including call centres and information centres.

One of the decisions faced by the government director of communications is whether to build up the internal communications branch with a potentially sizeable team, or whether to outsource the work to contractors and consultants. Contractors and consultants could be used on an individual project, or could be used to provide a specific service, such as speech writing, event management, design work, or issues management on an as-needs basis. The benefits of having the capabilities inside the agency include better control of the work and the ready availability of someone to do the work. The benefits of outsourcing include paying for the role only when it is needed and having access to expertise that is constantly being honed by consultants on a range of projects. Outsourcing requires the internal person to manage the consultant.

For Sheryl Fewster, a day at the office of the Western Australian government is likely to touch on the following activities:

➤ Liaison with the CEO, Sheryl sees her role as a strategic spear carrier: she alerts the CEO to what is happening in the external environment that could impinge on or link with organisational plans and priorities, what is relevant and strategically interesting in the media, and what is current with issues for the organisation.

➤ Staff management, which includes team meetings, staff development, training, succession planning, multiskilling, forward planning, and recruitment.

➤ Preparation of tender documents.

➤ Attending whole of agency meetings.

➤ Provision of advice at the strategic level on potential projects and issues and how to approach them. Providing an internal feasibility information check on proposed behavioural change programs. It is important to ask the questions up front while the project is being scoped to determine:

  • what can realistically be achieved on the awareness–attitudinal–behavioural change hierarchy
  • what resources are needed and how are they obtained
  • what do people think
  • what is our starting point
  • should some research be done to establish that before proceeding
  • who needs to be involved.

➤ Reflection to gather threads of ideas from a range of sources and research into allied cross-over areas, and to quietly reflect about whether these ideas could be used to improve the projects she's developing for her organisation.

REFLECT AND DISCUSS

Choose a government department and find out about its public affairs or public relations branch.

➤ How many staff does it have?
➤ What outputs is it responsible for?
➤ What outcomes does it aim to achieve?

Gae Synnott

The consultancy

Consultancies (also known as agencies) are stand-alone businesses. They generate income by providing public relations services to clients and satisfying those clients' needs. This generally means that people working at management level in consultancies must be both competent practitioners and business managers. Consultancies compete against other consultancies to gain business, and to do this they must demonstrate a wide range of knowledge and skills, particularly industry-specific knowledge. To retain the business they must do a good job, achieve the outcomes specified, and meet client expectations. At stake is the potential loss of earnings and loss of business that result from dissatisfied clients, which places issues of client satisfaction and profitability at the forefront in a consultancy.

Attractions of the consultancy environment include:

➤ the variety that comes from working for a number of different clients
➤ the competitive nature of the business, and the thrill of the chase involved in bringing new clients and projects into the consultancy
➤ the fantastic learning environment provided by the variety of work, and the ability to simultaneously develop good business skills, such as time management and budgeting
➤ the perception of having control over your own destiny.

Consultants work in a professionally tough and competitive environment. There is a strong focus on achievement, performance, successful billings, and the ability to generate new work, all of which provide clear goals in terms of success. This entrepreneurial business aspect, the commercial driver, is what makes the consultancy environment different from working anywhere else. As a consultant, your fees are earned through your efforts to deliver outcomes within the time and budget available.

The challenges of the consultancy environment come from:

➤ budgets that are often restricted, and time and other project constraints that mean you cannot always follow through on a project to the extent you would like to; you work within the project boundaries specified by the client and negotiated at the commencement of the project
➤ your role and the level of power may not be what you want; often, the client is the one who decides what is needed and the consultant is hired to deliver.

The top tier of consultancies may become known for their expertise in a specific niche, but most consultancies are more likely to be generalists who undertake multiple tasks for multiple clients. Consultancies try to establish a point of difference so they can stand out in the marketplace, such as their technological base, standalone products, value-adding capabilities, and the ability to provide integrated solutions. Clients buy the consultant's expertise, systems, methodologies, and personal style.

Typical structures for consultancies follow the lines of advertising agencies, with account managers (more senior) and account executives who work at different levels, and at different hourly rates, to undertake the work. There are also a number of smaller consultancies built around the skills of the owner-operator.

While new graduates might gravitate more easily into public sector or not-for-profit positions, the consultancy environment provides a good level of professional excitement, and is often seen as a means of further career development after a few years of experience. Marie Howarth, Senior Consultant, looks for these traits in someone coming in to the consultancy:

➤ experience and the ability to do the job
➤ a cultural fit with the consultancy
➤ talent, spark, and enthusiasm
➤ specific skills in planning and project management, dealing with deadlines, dealing with complex jobs, writing, and contributions to the team.

As in the other public relations environments, there is also no such thing as a typical day in a consultancy. Each day is likely to have variety, pace, lots of talking and building relationships, being accessible, and being prepared to act on opportunities. The differences between the roles of a junior, middle and senior consultant are:

➤ junior—works on specific projects with defined activities; less room for decision making and less client contact
➤ middle—increased level of responsibility and more client contact
➤ senior—has primary responsibility for the client's work and is the first point of contact for the client with the consultancy; is aware of the importance of business generation and actively works to secure new business.

BOX 6.1 \ SOME GOOD ADVICE

It's about the outcomes and not the outputs.

Sheryl Fewster, senior public sector practitioner

Learn from your mistakes. We all make mistakes. Things don't always go as planned. Use it and build on it.

Graham Lovelock, senior corporate practitioner

It is important to have a predetermined process that you can apply to whatever you are doing. Allows you to determine the steps, ask the *what if* questions, and develop a way of working that can be charted and tested. The benefit is that you are always in control. If it's written down, you can measure it, and you can improve on it.

Brian Wills-Johnson, retired senior corporate practitioner

Gae Synnott

> Don't listen to the solution. Find out more about the problem.
>
> Marie Howarth, senior consultant
>
> Work out what everyone wants to achieve, and work for a win:win:win.
>
> James Best, former corporate practitioner and consultant, current mayor, South Perth

Organisations and their grassroots connections

A theme in this book is the growing acceptance of the inter-relatedness of organisations and communities, with practitioners increasingly looking to achieve mutually beneficial results rather than to work for the one-sided interest of an organisation. This approach comes from the belief that organisations are part of communities and that there is an interdependence between all parties within a community, in that the actions of one will affect others. From this acknowledgment of interdependency, the next step is to embrace the principles of community democracy, which suggests that people affected by a decision should have some input into that decision. By extension, if people in a community are affected by the actions of an organisation, then they should have some input into those decisions that will affect them.

Connection with community is an area of real importance to all organisations—government, commercial, and not-for-profit. Often identified as the community relations component of a public relations program, significant effort to build relationships at the grassroots and community level is a growth area in public relations practice. Edmund Burke calls this becoming a 'neighbor of choice' (1999). Community relations is part of the broader concept of corporate social responsibility (CSR) (see Chapters 7 and 8). Here is a useful definition of CSR:

> In essence, the focus of the issue of corporate social responsibility is on the way in which the affairs of companies are conducted and the ends to which their activities are directed, with particular reference to the environmental and social impact of their conduct. A responsible company, like a responsible individual, is one that acknowledges and takes responsibility for its actions (CCPA 2007: 6).

Organisations that have a need to build strong community relationships often develop a community relations policy that outlines the values and principles they will adopt in working with communities.

Mining companies, for example, base their community relations programs on the premise that to maintain their social licence to operate, they must develop and sustain productive relationships with communities in close proximity to mining operations and with a wider set of publics and audiences, including indigenous communities who may control access to land. Good relationships will smooth the way for future industry development, including land and resource access, and ensure a stable, long-term operating environment. There are strong economic and social drivers for the approach that lead to a mutual beneficial outcome. Other good reasons for developing and maintaining meaningful community relations include:

➤ the belief that strong communities with strong economic and social capital provide a more sustainable environment within which to operate

➤ the concept of obligations of citizenship, which means that those who succeed in free markets have an obligation as citizens to give back to the community through individual and corporate philanthropy

➤ the community expectation that companies will act sustainably, which leads companies to act in ways that meet community expectations; this in turn gives companies their social licence to operate.

Community relations is built on strong community relationships that require a commitment to effective engagement with many sectors of communities. Consider this statement by Nexen, a Canadian-based global energy company: 'While government can grant a company a permit to operate, it is the community that gives permission.'

BHP Billiton's approach is that:

Critical to our long-term success is our ability to build relationships and work in a collaborative and transparent way with business partners, governments, non-government organisations and host communities. Wherever we operate, we commit to engaging regularly, openly and honestly with the people interested in and affected by our operations.

Specifically, on community engagement, BHP states that:

Without effective community engagement strategies and programs, our operations may be left vulnerable to project approval delays, business disruptions and increased costs that can result from mistrust, disempowerment and a lack of information within local communities and other stakeholder groups.

The Alcoa approach to community engagement aims high:

Alcoa aspires to be the best company in the world and to do this we must be the best neighbour in each community where we operate. Alcoa is committed to building capacity within our own operations and the communities in which we work to create sustainable operations and sustainable and stronger communities with a shared future. Stronger communities create opportunities for people and organisations to work together to bring about economic, social and environmental benefits for all of us.

In a broader sense, this means managing the business in a way that enhances social and economic benefits to society while striving to minimise the environmental impacts associated with resource development. Late Nobel prize winning US economist Milton Friedman's notion of responsibility is argued to be 'only for individuals' (Theaker 2004: 136) as he suggested that it was wrong to expect organisations to participate in social responsibility as their greater responsibility is to shareholders. However, meeting the social, environmental, and economic expectations of employees, shareholders, customers, communities, governments, and advocacy groups has been shown to create a solid foundation for increasing shareholder value.

REFLECT AND DISCUSS

> ➤ What do you think of the concept 'social licence to operate'? Could it apply to other organisations apart from mining companies?
> ➤ What could threaten a company's social licence to operate?
> ➤ Identify two ways that having strong community-level relationships might help an organisation.

Consultation and communication

Integral to the process of building strong community relationships is a sound understanding of the views, concerns, and aspirations of the communities. This requires an engagement approach to gauge communities' and key stakeholders' understanding, awareness, and attitudes, to identify issues, and to understand local concerns and identify ways the company can contribute to ameliorating them.

A number of companies are explicit in their intention to engage with communities and the way in which the dialogue will occur. Alcoa, for example, commits to establishing and working with community at each site. On its website it details the community engagement mechanisms for each of its facilities in Australia. OZ Minerals states that all of its operations have mechanisms for gaining and understanding the views, concerns, and aspirations of the communities it is part of.

The deliberative democracy context is part and parcel of the democratic system of government. Governments require project proponents to demonstrate that they have consulted with the community, have made an effort to understand the issues, and have attempted to resolve or manage those issues in the development of the proposal. The Mindarie Regional Council case study at the end of this chapter demonstrates the level of influence communities can have on a project, and the win–win outcome that is possible through solid engagement (see Chapter 5 for a description of the International Association of Public Participation (IAP2) Public Participation Spectrum, which sets out the range of ways in which the community can become involved in discussions with organisations, with increasing community involvement in decision making as you move along the continuum).

A variety of tools can be used to engage the community and provide feedback channels back into the organisation. Shell Geelong Refinery's Community Advisory Panel (CAP) was established in November 2005 and is a key part of the refinery's community engagement program. CAP members have expertise in a range of areas including environment, health, education, human services, commerce, and industry. The CAP's role is to help monitor the refinery's Environment Improvement Plan (EIP) and provide advice on key strategic documents, including the Social Performance Plan and Community Engagement Plan. The CAP's advice has included how to best reach a broader audience to hear concerns and communicate to the community the work being done.

REFLECT AND DISCUSS

> ➤ Choose two high-profile companies in your region and look at their websites. Do they have a community relations policy? What does it contain? Do both companies have similar policies? Which is more effective? Why?
> ➤ Log on to www.corporateregister.com, which is a study of social performance reports. Look at the reports of two companies of interest and see what opportunities they provide for community involvement.

Community corporate investment

A lot of companies enhance their community relationships through sponsorships and donations. But there is a distinction between community giving (sponsorships and donations) and community development. While the intent of community giving is related to supporting business goals, the intent of community development is strengthening the communities in which companies operate to ensure long-term sustainability of the community and of the organisation. This is often achieved through partnering with community organisations and government agencies to enhance the social, human, and economic capital of a region.

According to the report *Corporate Community Investment in Australia* (CCPA 2007), the business case is the main driver for community corporate investment. Equally important, however, are the relationships that can be established through these programs, which are a good means of:

> ➤ winning and maintaining community trust and the licence to operate
> ➤ building and maintaining positive reputations; corporate community investment is seen as a demonstration of corporate values
> ➤ creating a clear market differentiation
> ➤ building relationships with key stakeholders, including corporate critics.

An organisation's community investment strategy might have an emphasis on health or education and training. Newcrest Mining Limited works closely with Indigenous communities near its mine at Telfer in the Pilbara region in Western Australia on a range of projects that are important to the communities. One of these has been to establish a respite dialysis facility for Martu people in the Jigalong community. Having a fully functional and safe facility in Jigalong enables Perth-based patients from the Pilbara to return to their own community for dialysis treatment for planned and regular periods of respite care. This provides physical and social benefits to these patients and their families.

Aboriginal Australians have the highest rate of kidney disease in the country—twenty to forty times higher than for non-Aboriginal people—which can lead to kidney failure and the need for dialysis (ESRD). For Aboriginal Australians, the need for dialysis occurs, on average, twenty years before it does for non-Aboriginal Australians (at 40 rather than 60), affects women and men equally (compared with more males in non-Aborigines), and they have poorer survival rates and lower rates of transplantation than do non-Aborigines (*Feasibility Study* 2007).

The community donated a house for the facility and Newcrest facilitated funding support from a variety of corporate and government sources, including Lotterywest. The house has been refurbished and equipped and will operate on a three-year trial. The facility will also provide a base for a Western Desert Healthy Lifestyle program designed to assist with the prevention of diabetes and associated renal failure.

REFLECT AND DISCUSS

> Look at how Alcoa and Rio Tinto describe their activities in this area. What criteria do each of them use to determine which activities to support?

Reporting community relations performance

Tracking and reporting community relations, or CSR performance, is based on the premise that companies are accountable to their communities and have mechanisms in place to achieve this. Reporting on corporate social performance has been growing rapidly since the mid 1990s. Most major corporations now report in some form (CCPA 2007: 10), many with a separate sustainability or triple bottom line publication.

The key to effective reporting of performance is to be able to report against targets, which requires an agreed plan for community relations activity against which performance can be tracked, monitored, and assessed. According to the CCPA report (2007: 10) around one-third of reports are prepared according to guidelines such as the Global Reporting Initiative (GRI).

Reports cover social and community, environmental, sustainability, corporate social responsibility and citizenship, philanthropic, and health and safety performance.

The title of the report communicates the company's approach to this area:

➤ Alcan: *A Sustainable Approach to Business*
➤ Argyle Diamonds: *Sustainable Development Report 2007: Innovation brings rewards*
➤ BHP Billiton: *Resourcing the Future Sustainability Summary Report 2008*
➤ Newmont: *Beyond the Mine: The journey towards sustainability 2007*
➤ Nexen: *Proven Values.*

Public relations practitioners are required to contribute to reports such as these.

REFLECT AND DISCUSS

Look on the websites of five companies from different industry sectors.

➤ What information do they provide about social performance indicators used by the organisation?
➤ What community partnerships are they involved in? To what extent do these partnerships contribute to achieving a social licence to operate?

Day-to-day challenges and pressures

Regardless of your work environment, you are likely to come face to face with all the operational challenges discussed in this section.

Good relationships

One of the main things you need to develop early on is a good relationship with the people you are working with in the organisation (your workmates), and between yourself and the person you are working for (your manager or your client). These relationships rely on effective verbal and written interpersonal communication, and on a positive attitude.

Good processes

Every practitioner develops processes and frameworks for their activity, including:

➤ reporting processes to confirm decisions and actions agreed at meetings
➤ sign-off and clearance processes
➤ processes to follow for distributing media material
➤ checklists to follow for organising events.

The aim of such systems and processes is to achieve a good consistent result every time. In public relations, these are a critical part of your tool bag.

Gae Synnott

Avoid trying to reinvent the wheel: just look and listen to what is going on around you and learn from it.

Time management

A reality of life in public relations is the rapid pace at which people work. Public relations is seen as a pressure business, where there is lots to be done, deadlines to be met, meetings to attend, the unexpected happening, highs and lows.

You may be working on a number of projects at one time, all of which may have set deadlines for completion. We often feel that we are juggling to get everything done. Understand that deadlines are non-negotiable. Fix deadlines for all jobs and stick to them.

Many agencies or consultancies charge on the basis of the amount of time taken to do a task, so they require their employees to keep a timesheet that records the tasks and the time taken.

Effective budgeting

Everything has a price: whoever is paying you to get the work done (your manager or the client) will want to know that their money is being spent to maximise the results. The client will usually want to know how much a particular project is going to cost and will only proceed if they believe the value of the intended results matches their investment in the work.

Once the project has been approved your aim is to manage the budget so that you do not overspend.

In your career you will be asked to develop program budgets or cost estimates as part of the planning process. You might have a fantastic idea to, say, develop an education centre attached to a manufacturing facility. Your proposal to management needs to include a good rationale for the need for the centre, its strategic fit with the goals of the organisation, its communication objectives, and a well-developed budget that accurately identifies what it will cost to set up and to operate.

If you are a consultant, you will need to estimate how many hours the project will take; that fee is added to the set-up and operating costs.

Sometimes the budget relates to a specific event, such as the launch of a new service; sometimes it is an annual or ongoing program. Either way, the process of budgeting is the same:

➤ Identify all the cost components that will be involved.
➤ Seek quotes for each item so you can estimate the overall cost.
➤ Add all the quotes for all the cost items to establish a total estimate for the project.
➤ Time needs to be costed as well, so estimate the tasks involved, then estimate how much time each task will take, and who will do each task.

➤ Multiply the hours for each staff member by their hourly rate. The total is the fee estimate for the project.

➤ Add the fees and the cost estimates to get a total price for the project.

Annual or ongoing programs use the current year's budget as a guide for next year's budget.

Keeping good records

Good planning requires a paper trail that documents client instructions, decisions made, timelines, budgets, responsibilities, and information required and received. At a minimum, you will be producing proposals (that detail what action you will be taking), minutes of meetings or contact reports (an official record of what was agreed at a meeting), progress reports, and monthly accounts. In addition, you might be producing research reports, or recommendations about options, or lists of suppliers and what you have found out about each one. It is a useful discipline to take notes of key points during meetings; they can be very useful in jogging your memory afterwards, not only about what was said, but also about the thinking behind the decisions. Always record the date of the meeting and who attended.

Being proactive rather than reactive

Public relations is about proactive communication and it is good to have a forward looking as well as a 'can do' mindset. As a practitioner, your interest is in getting things done, achieving goals, managing problems, and moving projects forwards. To achieve change you have to set out to achieve it. To build awareness you have to set out to achieve an increase in awareness. Make things happen. Do not wait to be told that something should be done, and do not be forced into fixing a situation that might not have eventuated had you taken action earlier.

Keeping clients and managers happy

One of the best ways to keep clients and managers happy is to achieve the planned results and to come in on time and on budget.

An important point to remember is that clients and managers rarely enjoy surprises: keep your client and your manager informed. Let them know what you are doing. Let them know if a problem has arisen, and perhaps jointly find a way around the problem. Seek help or advice in areas where your skills are lacking or you do not have the answers.

One of the rules in public relations pertains to confidentiality. Everything that happens at work should be treated as confidential. This means that you do not discuss any aspect of the clients' projects you are working on with people outside the organisation.

Building and maintaining good networks

As a problem solver, it helps to have a supply of sources to go to for information. The longer you work, the larger your network will become of people who work in different environments and who are connected to different types of information. For example, a colleague from another city calls you for recommendations about top-line venues for a forthcoming function. You may not hold events regularly, but if you know someone who does it becomes very easy to locate the information and satisfy the enquiry. Networking is one of the benefits of belonging to your professional association.

Keeping up with changes

Technology is a tool, and as a communicator it is our job to choose which tools will be most effective to reach a specific public or audience for a specific purpose. Keep yourself up to date on the pros and cons of new developments, and build up a network of people who have used the tools and can guide you through how and when to use them. Then you will be ready with the right recommendation. You could, for example, find out about stakeholder management software systems, or how to generate a Twitter campaign.

Understand the contribution of research

Better decisions come about when you have good information, and good information is gathered through research. Rather than guessing, it is better to find out the actual situation before you develop a plan to deal with it. As discussed in Chapter 5, your research does not need to be expensive and formal, but you do need to work out what you need to know to be able to plan effectively.

CASE STUDY \ COMMUNITY PARTNERSHIP AGREEMENTS

Mindarie Regional Council (MRC) is the largest waste management authority in Western Australia. It disposes of waste for a community covering seven local government authorities that comprise 500 000 people who produce 350 000 tonnes of waste per year. While traditional waste disposal has been to landfill, the MRC embarked on a program in 2002 to introduce resource recovery to the region, based on the premise that waste is a resource and that a more sustainable and responsible approach would be to recover the value from the waste by turning it into compost, while at the same time diverting 70 per cent of waste from landfill.

The site of the resource recovery facility (RRF) was a largely undeveloped industrial park, the Neerabup Industrial Estate, next to semi-rural communities in Perth's northern suburbs, who were concerned that the RRF could lead to noise, odour, traffic, and emissions and amenity impacts. Soon after the siting decision was made, a community engagement advisory group (CEAG) was established, which worked with the MRC to ensure that the community concerns were well understood. Jointly, the project team and CEAG devised the concept of a community partnership agreement (CPA). The CPA details the conditions under which the community would support the facility and identifies conditions the facility operator must meet in constructing and operating the facility to ensure that community amenity is protected.

The overall goal was to achieve endorsement of the CPA by the MRC with a commitment to enshrine its conditions for the life of the project.

The outcome objective was to develop a document that identifies the social issues associated with the RRF, shows how these issues will be addressed, and achieves a high level of community support.

The process objective was to develop a process that gives the community sufficient opportunity to become involved in developing the CPA.

RESEARCH

Formal and informal research was undertaken to ensure that community views, issues, and concerns were understood. At the start of the CPA process, MRC knew that the local community valued the semi-rural lifestyle, the bushland and wildlife, low traffic volumes, and the quietness of the neighbourhood. This was its starting point and these were the issues that went into the development of the CPA.

COMMUNICATION STRATEGY AND ACTION

An extensive period of discussion about the facility, which involved community meetings, dialogue with community groups and residents associations, multiple feedback opportunities, door knocking the closest residents, presentations, newsletters, and displays, provided good information about ways in which the project could proceed with the community's interests protected.

Critical activities included community planning workshops that worked progressively through the development of the CPA. The workshops focused on key aspects as follows:

1   to obtain input on the issues the community thought were important in construction and operation of the RRF
2   to address specific issues
3   to identify and develop outcomes that would help resolve the issues of concern.

The draft CPA was emailed to all participants for comment. CEAG reviewed the working draft and the document was then put out for a period of public comment. CEAG reviewed and modified the final draft, which was then tested and validated through formal market research with the wider MRC community.

Results from the research achieved a high level of support for the concept of the CPA and a high level of confidence that it would deliver what it promised. The CPA was endorsed by the MRC for the life of the facility and was incorporated into the tender documentation for the facility. This meant that the bidders to build, own, and operate the facility were aware of the importance of the community's concerns about the facility, and were required to respond to the content of the CPA in their bids.

The CPA comprises twenty objectives related to a range of factors such as odour control, water control onsite, traffic routes, landscaping, and appearance, with the detail included in sixty clauses within the document. Two examples are given below.

OBJECTIVE 1—MAINTAIN STRONG COMMUNITY INVOLVEMENT AND COMMUNICATION THROUGHOUT THE LIFE OF THE PROJECT

OUTCOMES

1 The continued operation of CEAG to oversee and advise on the community engagement process for the project throughout its life.
2 The maintenance of clear channels of communication, including a complaints management system with a defined response time.
3 Regular appropriate communication bulletins.
4 The facility to be open for tours and inspections by community groups.
5 Regular reporting to the community on key performance indicators after commissioning.

OBJECTIVE 9—ENSURE THROUGH MONITORING THAT ALL EMISSIONS ARE BELOW ACCEPTABLE LEVELS

OUTCOMES

1 A key tender assessment criterion.
2 A proven history for the type of facility and equipment proposed using best practice such as a negative air pressure odour control system.
3 Demonstrated ability to meet environmental assessment, approval, and licensing conditions.
4 Approved process control and monitoring system.
5 Develop procedures to continually improve the process by incorporating experience from the facility and relevant research and technology developments.
6 Monitor the condition of the building, particularly the concrete slab.

The contractor has undertaken to abide by the CPA, and is required to report its performance to the community on these social conditions in addition to the environmental conditions set by the Environmental Protection Authority, and the economic conditions set by the MRC and its member councils. The CEAG will continue to monitor performance against the CPA, and the contractor attends CEAG meetings to ensure good dialogue.

The roles of community engagement and public relations were split in this project. Both practitioners were part of a multidisciplinary project team comprising engineering, environmental, and project management expertise. The community engagement adviser's role throughout this project has been to keep the MRC connected with the community, to understand the issues and to bring them into the planning process, to run the community planning workshops and the public comment process that led to the development of the CPA, to liaise with the market research company to test the CPA, and to work alongside CEAG throughout the project.

The public relations adviser developed the communication material and maintained media contact, particularly with local media who saw this as an important local issue. All members of the team contributed to strategy, which culminated in praise from the Environmental Protection Authority in its report on the project's Public Environmental Review:

> In progressing this proposal, the MRC has undertaken a comprehensive consultation program which has set new standards for involving the community in the decision-making process (12 July 2004; see Web resources).

> Key lessons learned: the benefits of a partnership approach, allowing community input, and the necessity for top-level endorsement.

CHAPTER **SUMMARY**

➤ Public relations is an important job because of its ability to bring people together in improved understanding, mutual benefits, and joint action.

➤ The essence of the job, when practitioners understand the big picture and the operating context, is to use communication—better communication—to support organisations in the achievement of their objectives.

➤ Public relations aims to build good working relationships between organisations and their stakeholders and communities.

➤ Community relations and community engagement are important and growing facets of the job.

➤ Public relations skills are required across a range of different organisations..

FURTHER READING

Department of the Premier and Cabinet 2002, *Consulting Citizens: A Resource Guide*, Citizens and Civics Unit, Department of the Premier and Cabinet, Perth.

Department of the Premier and Cabinet 2003, *Consulting Citizens: Planning for Success*, Citizens and Civics Unit, Department of the Premier and Cabinet, Perth www.citizenscape.wa.gov.au.

Department of the Premier and Cabinet 2005, *Consulting Citizens: Engaging with Aboriginal Western Australians*, Citizens and Civics Unit, Department of the Premier and Cabinet, Perth www.citizenscape.wa.gov.au.

Gae Synnott

Grunig, J E, Dozier, D M, Ehling, W P, Grunig, L A, Repper, F C & White, J 1992, *Excellence in Public Relations and Communication Management*, Lawrence Erlbaum, Englewood Cliffs.

Rice, R E & Atkin, C K 2001, *Public Communication Campaigns*, 3rd edn, Sage, Thousand Oaks.

Sriramesh, K & Vércîc, D (eds) 2003, *The Global Public Relations Handbook: Theory, research and practice*, Lawrence Erlbaum, Englewood Cliffs.

WEB RESOURCES

Alcoa, at www.alcoa.com.

Argyle Diamonds, at www.argylediamonds.com.au.

BHP Billiton, at www.bhpbilliton.com.

Citizenscape at www.citizenscape.wa.gov.au.

Community-Based Social Marketing (CBSM) literature and listserve, at www.cbsm.com.

Corporate Register, at www.corporateregister.com.

Mindarie Regional Council's Community Partnership Agreement, at www.mrc.wa.gov.au.

Nexen (Canadian company), at www.nexeninc.com.

Shell, at www.shell.com.

Tourism Western Australia, at www.westernaustralia.com.

TravelSmart, at www.travelsmart.gov.au.

REFERENCES

Adkins, S 1999, *Cause-Related Marketing: Who Cares Wins*, Butterworth-Heinemann, Oxford.

Botan, C 1993, 'Introduction to the Paradigm Struggle in Public Relations', *Public Relations Review*, 19(2): 107–10.

Burke, E 1999, *Corporate Community Relations: The Principle of the Neighbor of Choice*, Greenwood Publishing Group, Abingdon.

Centre for Corporate Public Affairs 2007, *Corporate Community Investment in Australia*, retrieved from www.accpa.com.au/downloads/cci_report_07.pdf, 15 February 2009.

Chia, J & Xavier, R 2009, 'Financial Public Relations', in *Public Relations Campaigns: An Australian and New Zealand perspective*, Oxford University Press, Melbourne.

Coombes, T W, Holladay, S, Hasenauer, G & Signitzer, B 1994, 'A Comparative Analysis of International Public Relations: Identification and Interpretation of Similarities and Differences Between Professionalisation in Australia, Norway, and the United States', *Journal of Public Relations Research*, 6(1): 23–39.

Featherston, T 1995, *Using Repertory Grids in Classrooms: A Tool to Enhance Understanding*, Monograph, Series No. 3, MASTEC, Perth.

Grunig, J E 2000, 'Collectivism, Collaboration, and Societal Corporatism as Core Professional Values in Public Relations', *Journal of Public Relations Research*, 12(1): 23–48.

Grunig, L A, Grunig, J E & Vércîc, D 1998, 'Are the IABC's Excellence Principles Generic? Comparing Slovenia and the United States, United Kingdom and Canada', *Journal of Communication Management*, 2: 335.

Grunig, J E & Jaatinen, M 1999, 'Strategic, Symmetrical Communication in Government: From Pluralism to Societal Corporatism', *Journal of Communication Management*, 3(3): 218–34.

Grunig, L A, Toth, E L & Hon, L C 2000, 'Feminist Values in Public Relations', *Journal of Public Relations Research*, 12(1): 49–68.

Hazleton, V & Cutbirth, C 1993, 'Public Relations in Europe: An Alternative Educational Program', *Public Relations Review*, 19(2): 187–96.

Heath, R & Coombs, T 2006, *Today's Public Relations. An Introduction*, Sage, Thousand Oaks.

Hofstede, G, Neuijen, B, Daval Ohayv, D & Sanders, G 1990, 'Measuring Organizational Cultures: A Qualitative and Quantitative Study Across Twenty Cases, *Administrative Science Quarterly*, 35: 286–316.

Kelly, G A 1955, *The Psychology of Personal Constructs* (2 vols), W W Norton, New York.

Organisation for Economic Cooperation and Development 2003, 'Engaging Citizens Online for Better Policy Making', *Policy Brief*, March, retrieved from www.oecd.org, 15 February 2009.

Sriramesh, K & White, J 1992, 'Societal Culture and Public Relations', in J E Grunig (ed.), *Excellence in Public Relations and Communication Management*, Lawrence Erlbaum, Hillsdale.

Synnott, G 2001, *Values and Identity in Public Relations Practice in Malaysia*, Murdoch University Digital Thesis Program, Perth.

Taylor, M & Kent, M L 1999, 'Challenging Assumptions of International Public Relations: When Government is the Most Important Public', *Public Relations Review*, 25: 131–44.

Tracey, P, Phillips, N & Haugh, H 2005, 'Beyond Philanthropy: Community Enterprise as a Basis for Corporate Citizenship', *Journal of Business Ethics*, 58(4): 327–44.

Theaker, A 2004, *The Public Relations Handbook*, 2nd edn, Routledge, Milton Park.

Toth, E L & Grunig, L A 2000, 'Public Relations Values in the New Millennium', *Journal of Public Relations Research*, 12(10): 1–2.

Chapter 7

PUBLIC RELATIONS MANAGEMENT IN ORGANISATIONS

Amisha Mehta and Robina Xavier

PRACTITIONER PROFILE CAROLYN McCANN

Carolyn McCann is currently Head of Group Corporate Affairs and Investor Relations at Insurance Australia Group (IAG), Australia's leading general insurance group and a top 20 publicly-listed company.

Carolyn's role is to ensure the company's reputation is protected and enhanced, while maximising opportunities to demonstrate IAG's desired leadership position. The role is responsible for corporate affairs, brand integrity, organisational communications and investor relations.

Carolyn says communication professionals are most effective when they understand the operational side of the businesses they work in.

To make a real difference, communicators need to have a seat at the table where decisions are made, and (making a difference) won't happen unless you have a deep understanding of all aspects of the business you work in.

This knowledge allows you to have greater influence on and input into operational decisions which affect reputation. It also helps you educate your internal customers on the value of communication and reputation management.

During the past sixteen years, Carolyn has been the communication and investment marketing advisor on more than fifteen initial public offers and privatisations, and has managed the ongoing investor relations programs for several publicly-listed companies.

CHAPTER **AIMS**

By the end of this chapter, you should be able to:

➤ see public relations as a link between organisations and their environments
➤ use systems theory to guide your understanding and practical application of public relations
➤ define the roles and key areas of focus for the public relations team within an organisation
➤ understand the differences between internal and external publics and audiences
➤ identify and understand how a range of external forces, including conflict, activism, and corporate social responsibility, affect the practice of public relations.

Introduction

Do you turn off the lights when you are not in the room, switch off your computer and television at the wall, keep the airconditioner's temperature at the recommended level of 24 degrees, and offset the carbon footprint of your air travel?

You might take these actions at home, but do you do the same at your workplace? To what extent does your employer require your commitment to more sustainable practices? Communities and stakeholders have high expectations of organisations. Organisations have to consider the way their operations impact the environment and must be responsive to community expectations while, at the same time, managing the business to achieve organisational goals. As a public relations professional, climate change is just one of the external forces or issues that has the potential to affect the health of your organisation.

For some organisations, the need to deal with the climate change issue is more immediate or high profile; for others, the need may be less. Only 22 per cent of Australian businesses with turnovers of more than $150 million have adopted climate change initiatives (PricewaterhouseCoopers 2008). The one industry sector that has taken climate change seriously is the resources sector, with 95 per cent of businesses already taking action. Most businesses are waiting for more information about how to respond to climate change. While you have some luxury to reflect on your personal choices, experts argue that time is up for business. Business has no choice but to join the carbon economy (PricewaterhouseCoopers 2008). Investors, customers, and employees expect it. Employees

Amisha Mehta and Robina Xavier

themselves play a big part in delivering on climate change initiatives by changing work practices and supporting organisational programs, which makes them socially responsive and active on issues management. Compliance is a way to build social capital inside the organisation (Chia & Peters 2008)—a true win–win.

Public relations is uniquely placed to identify and understand the needs and expectations of the organisation's environment such as those related to climate change and filter these through decision-making processes to generate a response or action that meets the combined needs of the organisation and its environment. In the past, it might have been acceptable for public relations to simply create a favourable image of an environmentally aware organisation, but today, publics and audiences are not satisfied with anything less than real action and real outcomes (see Chapter 2). This chapter introduces you to the challenges facing the public relations management role in organisations and the employees' role and position. We start by describing what public relations management is before moving on to what it is informed by and how it works.

The practice of public relations in organisations

Public relations is practised in many different organisational contexts, from inhouse government or public affairs roles to corporate communications roles in small, medium, large, listed, and not-for-profit organisations. Through their communication planning and management, public relations practitioners build and enhance organisational reputation and build and maintain relationships that are important to the organisation and its goals. Most public relations departments are responsible for monitoring and responding to changes in the external environment, including issues, expectations, relationships, and reputation, and at the same time, also contribute to maintaining effective working environments within the organisation through employee communication. Effective employee communication explains organisational priorities and shares organisational information about what is happening so that employees understand and accept the need for change and commit their efforts and ideas to helping the organisation achieve its mission and goals.

In some organisations, the public relations department is also known as the corporate communication department. Corporate communication offers a framework and vocabulary for the effective coordination of all means of communications with the overall purpose of establishing and maintaining favourable reputations with stakeholder groups upon which the organisation is dependent (Cornelissen 2004: 23).

To be effective at managing reputations and relationships with internal and external stakeholders, students and practitioners of public relations need a guiding theory. In the next section, we apply the systems perspective (introduced in Chapter 3) as a guide to the practice of public relations.

Considering theory: a guide to practice

Whether it is about climate change or planning an anniversary event for an organisation, public relations managers use theory to guide decisions and choices. Theory provides a model for the practice of public relations: 'All who attempt to solve problems, make recommendations and predict the future, need theories, models, and as a starting point, concepts' (Skyttner 2001: vi). Over time, the theories you learn, and especially those related to public relations, will mesh with the key learnings and decisions you experience through practice to create your own working theory for public relations. For the student who is new to public relations, this chapter provides a starting point to help you identify, analyse, and resolve public relations problems.

Understanding systems theory

Systems theory provides a framework through which to view organisations and their relationships with the environment. It is firmly established as one of the guiding theories for public relations theory and practice. It is used to explain how public relations helps understand and manage the relationships an organisation has with its stakeholders and publics who make up its environment.

Systems theory developed from the study of biological systems. Following a similar perspective, the seminal public relations text, *Effective Public Relations*, introduced the concept of ecology to public relations in 1952. In the authors' view, ecology emphasised the need for organisms to adjust and adapt to changes in the environment (Cutlip, Center & Broom 2006) as, similar to ecological systems, organisations depend on their environment for support, growth, and, ultimately, survival (Morgan 1998). Ecological environments translate to the social environments of organisations that include governments, competitors, neighbours, customers, employees, the media, and investors.

BOX 7.1 \ **ECOLOGICAL SYSTEMS**

If we were to adopt a systems approach to examine the Great Barrier Reef, we would see it as a system of many parts—coral and other marine life—that interacts with and depends on other systems, including the river systems throughout northeast Queensland, farming trends, the temperature of the ocean, and even scuba divers. An increase in the water temperature or an influx of toxic chemicals from the river systems has the potential to harm the coral and marine life of the reef. The life and beauty of the Great Barrier Reef depend greatly on its environment.

Amisha Mehta and Robina Xavier

Defining systems

Whether taking a life science or public relations perspective, the definition of a system remains the same. The public relations literature defines a system as a 'set of interacting units that endures through time within an established boundary by responding and adjusting to change pressures from the environment to achieve and maintain goal states' (Cutlip, Center & Broom 2006: 176). In this way, the organisation is seen as a system that exists to create and achieve goals that are beneficial to the organisation and the environment. These goals might include increased profits and sales, support from investors, increased employment, the creation of new products, or a lower carbon footprint.

Organisational systems are not static but rely on a series of exchanges of inputs and outputs between environments and organisations. In organisational systems, inputs are likely to come in the form of resources to an organisation (materials, capital, people, and information). Once received, these inputs are transformed via a range of organisational activities, such as production lines and even boardroom meetings. The transformation process may be affected by the degree of interaction among the different departments within the organisation. Ultimately, the inputs become outputs that include:

➤ products
➤ services
➤ plant closures
➤ job cuts.

Although each part is important, systems theory takes a holistic view and encourages us to look outside the organisation or organisational department to see the bigger environment (Modaff, Delvine & Butler 2008). The basic premise behind this whole view is that a change to one part affects the whole system.

Types of systems

Within each system there are a number of subsystems that are involved in the transformation process:

➤ production or technical, which are concerned with transforming inputs into outputs (the production line, for example)
➤ supportive subsystems that ensure the availability of inputs (the finance or procurement departments, for example)
➤ maintenance subsystems that focus on maintaining social relations (public relations, for example)
➤ adaptive subsystems that monitor and respond to the environment (public relations, for example)
➤ managerial subsystems that coordinate and control the other subsystems (Katz & Kahn 1978).

Public relations is part of the adaptive and maintenance subsystems (Modaff, De Wine & Butler 2008). By understanding what is happening within the environment and how environmental changes might affect organisational goals (Cutlip, Center & Broom 2006; Everett 1990; Spicer 1997), public relations can drive adaptation to better suit stakeholder needs.

Qantas is a major Australian airline with a rich tradition and history. One of the key environmental factors affecting all airlines is the rising cost of aviation fuel. Responses to these rising costs include the reduction of available flights and increases in ticket prices. For Qantas, public relations concerns also include damaging media reports about a range of incidents on the ground and in the air. All airlines are affected by safety incidents but what differentiates our reaction to the mass media reporting of Qantas safety incidents and flight delays as opposed to those of Virgin Blue or other carriers? How can public relations be effective in such cases?

Boundary spanning and public relations

Early systems theory (von Bertalanffy 1968) suggested that an organisation and its environment were separated by a boundary through which information and resources flowed. Spanning this boundary was seen as a critical role for public relations professionals, who would provide information to the environment about the organisation and bring information about the environment back to the organisational decision makers. The practitioner monitored the boundary on an ongoing basis, with 'one foot in the organisation and one foot outside' (Grunig & Hunt 1984: 9).

Both these roles continue in today's organisations. Public relations professionals use formal and informal research mechanisms to gather information about key publics and issues and feed them back into the organisation. Knowledge of the attitudes and behaviours of key publics are important to organisations as they plan their goals and strategies. We envisage that Qantas public relations managers are actively engaged in communicating with the public but find that their strategic intent is being tested by ongoing incidents and sustained media interest. In late 2008, for example, Qantas public relations activities involved publicity around the first Qantas A380, which was a planned activity, at around the same time as managing unexpected and certainly unplanned media and public interest in flight delays and safety incidents.

Public relations practitioners undertake an important analytical function in considering the source and value of the information gained, information that may be relevant to the short-term plans of the organisation and therefore acted on in the immediate future, or it may influence its longer-term plans. Forward-looking organisations establish sophisticated databases of information on issues and stakeholders to help them identify issue-specific and sector-wide trends, and inform their long-term planning. By supporting this role, public relations professionals become the eyes and ears of the organisation, staying well connected to key stakeholders to ensure that the

Amisha Mehta and Robina Xavier

organisation is always well informed of events in its environment. Thus, for example, during pay negotiations, employees may threaten strike action. If an organisation is aware of this threat, it may be able to prevent it or at least be prepared for its consequences. When nurses threaten to strike, their actions may affect the delivery of health care services. While governments and other health care providers may not be able to resolve the nurses' demands around pay and conditions, it can at least prepare for this action and prepare patients for potential disruptions.

The outward flow of information from an organisation, which the public relations practitioner develops and distributes, happens through direct and mediated communication channels such as websites, presentations, media releases, interviews, community meetings, and hotlines. The public relations professional tells and sells the organisation's story, ensuring that all key groups are informed about the organisation's actions. Just as important is the information flow back into the organisation and the opportunities for dialogue and discussion so that views external to the organisation are relayed back to the decision makers and are understood.

A mine manager in a remote location, say, may need to communicate directly with local residents about potential impacts during mine upgrades. Both the mine manager and the public relations professional are likely to be involved:

➤ both will plan the discussion and agree how to present the information
➤ the public relations practitioner will prepare communication material, including backgrounders, a PowerPoint presentation, and likely questions and answers
➤ the mine manager might take the lead in the meeting with local residents, as the person responsible for actions onsite
➤ the public relations practitioner might help to answer questions, observe reactions and responses, and take notes of key issues raised by the community
➤ both will be involved in debriefing as the process unfolds.

Straddling the edges of an organisation is not always an easy role as conflicting positions in the environment arise and the strategy of the organisation changes. Just as the idea of a true organisational boundary was considered problematic when it was first suggested (Aldrich & Herker 1977), with more and more organisational partnerships changing the traditional nature of organisation–environment relations it continues to be challenged today. The divide between members and non-members of an organisation is becoming less clear, which is leading to changing roles for public relations practitioners:

➤ Public–private partnerships see clients and suppliers partner together and are rewarded on the performance of all.
➤ Activists are sitting on organisational advisory boards helping organisations negotiate difficult issues, whereas earlier they would have tried to use their organisational power to push through their position.

➤ Community engagement invites communities who are affected by organisational decisions to discuss how decisions will impact them and to offer ideas or jointly plan how to minimise potential impacts.

Public relations professionals are focusing on better understanding of the key drivers of the organisation–environment relations to help navigate this changing setting and provide effective outcomes for their organisations.

REFLECT AND DISCUSS

> ➤ Find two organisations where you think it would be helpful for an activist to be involved on an advisory board. What issues could the activist help the organisation understand better?
> ➤ Find an example of community engagement where community input has modified an organisational decision.

Adjustment and adaptation

Given the critical role that inputs play to a well-functioning system, considerable emphasis is placed within an organisation on gaining the inputs it needs to operate, such as investor funds. The public relations management role establishes and maintains mutually beneficial relationships that provide inputs to the organisation; however, to secure these inputs, organisations may be required to adjust their policies or actions and adapt to their environment (Cutlip, Center & Broom 2006; Witmer 2006). Adaptation results from 'strategies in the form of organisational and environmental change programs that produce and maintain stability in organisational/environmental relationships' (Everett 1990: 235). Adjustment may be problematic when an organisation faces conflicting needs within their public and audience groups. Adjusting organisational strategy to favour one group may very well disenfranchise another. Thus, the public relations management role must help the senior decision makers within the organisation to navigate this difficult terrain and use a variety of relationship maintenance strategies to achieve the most positive outcomes possible.

The Qantas example discussed earlier shows that this organisation has needed to increase ticket prices to cover the rising cost of aviation fuel. This decision may be perceived as unpopular by customers yet goes some way to protect the profitability of Qantas and the returns to its shareholders. For another organisation, it may be the decision to cut back on Christmas events due to the financial crisis, which may be unpopular with staff but it is a one way to manage finances. In both cases, some explanation about the reasons behind the actions must be given.

Amisha Mehta and Robina Xavier

Employee commitment can also be seen as an input to the organisation. Internal communication management is important to help create effective and enthusiastic staff who undertake their roles—the transformation process—and the effectiveness, transparency, and harmony generated internally contributes to how the organisation is perceived by people external to the organisation.

Open and closed systems

Closed systems and public relations

A closed system is isolated from the environment and other systems. Its boundaries are considered impermeable, which discourages the exchange of information with the environment (Cutlip, Center & Broom 2006). As a result, closed systems are rarely influenced by their environment. In closed organisations, managers operate as if they are autonomous or unconstrained by environmental forces (Grunig, Grunig & Dozier 2002; Witmer 2006). Closed systems are likely to encounter the system state of entropy or deterioration (Morgan 1998).

REFLECT AND DISCUSS

> ➤ Identify an organisation that is not communicating, whose communication is closed rather than open.
> ➤ Why do you think its communication lacks transparency?
> ➤ How could an inhouse practitioner improve communication to and with the public?
> ➤ What would you be interested in knowing about this organisation?

In closed systems, the public relations function has low regard for the environment. Although public relations managers may acknowledge their environment and follow regulatory procedures, they are unlikely to interact with other publics. Instead, public relations departments will adopt a one-way communication perspective without considering environmental input. This type of approach is a functionary one, implemented to preserve the organisation's image (Skinner & Shanklin 1978). Because the organisation is closed to its environment, it is not able to take advantage of opportunities or move quickly to address potential problems. Instead, public relations departments react to crises, and when there is a crisis there is often a cover-up as management denies that there is, or was, a problem (see Chapter 10).

Open systems and public relations

Open systems view the environment as important to survival. Open systems continuously exchange inputs and outputs with the environment through permeable boundaries (Cutlip, Center & Broom 2006; Morgan 1998). Organisations actively seek information from their environment, which is received as input into the organisational system. The open systems approach encourages congruency or fit among the different systems and the identification and elimination of any potential dysfunctions (Morgan 1998).

Open organisational systems identify incongruence and respond to environmental pressures that may affect the viability or survival of the organisation (Witmer 2006). Organisational responses can accommodate or counteract changes in the environment (Cutlip, Center & Broom 2006). The organisation does not need, nor is it able, to address every change, variation, or expectation of its environment. Instead, organisations and their public relations managers must select and prioritise environmental change pressures.

REFLECT AND DISCUSS

> An example of an organisation that adjusts to accommodate the needs of its environment is Virgin Blue's carbon offset program. Recognising the importance of climate change and the carbon economy, Virgin Blue, a low-cost airline with a base in Australia, has not only implemented operational changes to minimise greenhouse gas emissions but also offers customers the opportunity to offset the greenhouse gas emissions related to their individual flight. Look at other airlines in Australia and around the world to see if and how they are trying to address climate change.

In open systems, public relations takes on a functional approach that is concerned with two–way communication between the organisation and the environment. This requires resources for organisations to not only monitor their environments and public opinion but also to build and maintain relationships with key organisations and stakeholders within their environment. These relationships are built on trust and a mutual interest in bringing about a solution that meets the needs of all parts of the system.

Public relations in open systems works with the environment to determine what is being said about issues that affect multiple parts of the system. Virgin Blue anticipated the importance of climate change and the carbon economy to its customers and used this information to create a convenient solution for them. Even when conflict arises, open systems public relations is positioned to resolve the situation by working with the environment. In this way, public relations is actively engaged with the environment and not reactive to it.

Amisha Mehta and Robina Xavier

Expanding the systems perspective

Alternative approaches exist to help us understand an organisation's level of interaction with its environment and the different outcomes that may result. In the public relations literature, Piezcka (2006) provides an extensive review of the equilibrium and homeostatic systems models that can be used to understand organisational relationships. Further detail can also be found in the strategic management literature. More attention is currently being paid to systems complexity, in recognition of the contribution of different perspectives to solving complex problems.

Systems theory is not without its critics. Although it provides a useful way for understanding the relationships between an organisation and its environment, Spicer (1997) believes it ignores issues relating to organisational power that are not addressed during dialogue and exchange. The systems perspective is often criticised for emphasising the pragmatic self-interest of the organisation. Even though an organisational system is open, it is also selective about which parts of the environment it will recognise and accommodate. To address this, Grunig, Grunig & Dozier (2002) contextualised systems theory with other perspectives to better understand organisational effectiveness:

➤ The strategic constituencies perspective prioritises publics and audiences most critical to the organisation
➤ The competing values approach contrasts values of effectiveness against efficiency and quality against quantity to help clarify managerial decisions when organisations are going through change
➤ The goal attainment perspective asserts that effective organisations meet their goals (Robbins 1990, cited in Grunig, Grunig & Dozier 2002).

REFLECT AND DISCUSS

Review a variety of public relations texts and journal articles to find out about other approaches to public relations. You might like to examine the role of complexity or power. Think of one specific example of how you could apply either one of these approaches to public relations practice.

Another extension of systems theory comes from some of our own research, which integrates the adjustment and adaptation with organisational legitimacy (Patel, Xavier & Broom 2005). Organisational legitimacy is defined as stakeholder perceptions that an organisation is operating in a manner that is consistent with the stakeholder's moral, regulative, and pragmatic expectations of it (Suchman 1995). Put more simply, organisational legitimacy provides a baseline of social standards for organisations. Mining organisations, for example, have certain regulatory, safety, and moral standards to which they must comply. When a mining organisation's actions meet these standards, they are considered legitimate. Public relations is tasked with acquiring and preserving organisational legitimacy (Waeraas 2007).

The public relations program and team

Now that the theory that informs the public relations management role in organisations has been set out, we can start to explore what it looks like and who is involved.

Excellent public relations programs must operate at organisation, department, and program levels (Grunig 1992), as described in Table 7.1 on the following page. This chapter is concerned with both the organisational and department levels (see also Chapter 9, which deals with how specific public relations strategies are developed and implemented). The organisational level of public relations programs describes the best organisational approach to achieve excellent public relations outcomes for organisations. The department level examines the structure and focus of the public relations function. Department level characteristics will now be explored.

The type of public relations program implemented depends on the type, size, and structure of the organisation (van Leuven 1991), the degree of openness to the environment (Cutlip, Center & Broom 2006), and the organisational decision-making structure or dominant coalition (McElreath 1993). A family run hi-fi company would have different public relations needs when compared to those of Panasonic, Merck & Co, Yahoo!, a government department, or your local hospital.

When it comes to organising the public relations or corporate communications function, there are three recommended approaches:

1 a centralised department
2 multiple communications departments within the organisational structure
3 cross-functional coordination with other areas such as marketing (Cornelissen 2004).

For the most part, public relations academics believe that the public relations department should be separate from the marketing function (Grunig 1992) and should coordinate all forms of communication to maximise organisational goals (van Riel 2007). Nowadays, the public relations—marketing mix is becoming more common but the specific contributions of public relations must still be recognised and supported (see Chapter 2).

Amisha Mehta and Robina Xavier

TABLE **7.1** \ **Characteristics of excellent public relations programs**

I	**Program level**	
	1	Managed strategically
II	**Departmental level**	
	2	A single or integrated public relations department
	3	Separate function from marketing
	4	Direct reporting relationship to senior management
	5	Two-way symmetrical model
	6	Senior public relations person in the managerial role
	7	Potential for excellent public relations, as indicated by:
	a	Knowledge of symmetrical model
	b	Knowledge of managerial role
	c	Academic training in public relations
	d	Professionalism
	8	Equal opportunity for men and women in public relations
III	**Organisational level**	
	9	Worldview for public relations in the organisation reflects the two-way symmetrical model
	10	Public relations director has power in or with the dominant coalition
	11	Participative rather than authoritarian organisational culture
	12	Symmetrical system of internal communication
	13	Organic rather than mechanical organisational structure
	14	Turbulent, complex environment with pressure from activist groups
IV	**Effects of excellent public relations**	
	15	Programs meet communication objectives
	16	Reduces costs of regulation, pressure and litigation
	17	Job satisfaction is high among employees

Source: J E Grunig, 1992: 1–28

Roles and responsibilities

A typical department is likely to be made up of junior and more experienced practitioners who are responsible for implementing the public relations and media relations programs. When needed, organisations can utilise the services of external public relations consultants.

The roles and responsibilities of public relations practitioners are influenced by two forces: the professionalisation of public relations and the nature of the organisational environment. In the early days of the development of professional public relations, internal departments were often managed by former journalists who translated media skills into public relations by promoting a one-way communication model. As public relations education evolved, so too did the role of a public relations professional. This has corresponded with a shift from one-way to two-way communication to the multiway communication central to online and offline communication exchanges. The state of the organisational environment also influences the make-up of the public relations team. More turbulent environments require more senior practitioners to be aware of the dynamic environment and how changes will affect organisational goals (Grunig, Grunig & Dozier 2002). The complexity and changing dynamics of public relations highlighted in Chapter 2 indicate that tensions exist in practice as public relations is constantly changing.

The work of Broom, Dozier, and their colleagues provides the foundation for much of our understanding of public relations roles. In a series of studies, four primary roles were identified and investigated: communication technician, expert prescriber, communication facilitator, and problem-solving facilitator (Broom 1982; Broom & Smith 1979; Broom & Dozier 1986; Dozier & Broom 1995).

The communication technician is an entry level role for which the practitioner is hired primarily to write or implement activities and, as such, is not part of the decision-making process (Cutlip, Center & Broom 2006). An expert prescriber epitomises authority and is charged by management to make decisions relating to public relations, often by themselves and with limited links to the management team (Cutlip et al. 2006).

In contrast to these roles, the communication facilitator and the problem-solving facilitator adopt a more collaborative approach. Communication facilitators operate at the boundary between the organisation and its environment to facilitate exchange and transfer information, while the problem-solving facilitator collaborates with other managers to define and solve problems (Cutlip, Center & Broom 2006).

A more common categorisation is that of the public relations technician and the public relations manager (Cutlip, Center & Broom 2006).

The public relations technician (whose role equates with the communication technician role outlined above) is responsible for the implementation of public relations activities such as news conferences or events, the production of material such as speeches and news releases, and planning and implementation of projects such as employee involvement in community relations activities.

Amisha Mehta and Robina Xavier

Defining the responsibilities of a public relations manager has been the focus of a group of researchers from the United Kingdom (Moss, Newman & DeSanto 2005), who found that public relations managers retained some of the technical work and also undertook:

➤ monitoring and evaluation
➤ issues management
➤ policy and strategy advice
➤ trouble shooting and problem solving.

An area of less emphasis was the management of people (Moss, Newman & De Santo 2005), which suggests that public relations managers focus more on external communication than team management, although the 'disconnect between managers and employees' (Guth & Marsh 2005: 31) points to the need for greater emphasis on internal communication. Guth and Marsh suggest that communication audits are essential 'to measure how well an organization's communications are fulfilling their stated goals' (36), emphasising the importance of public relations internal communication management.

Public relations, the dominant coalition, and links to other departments

Public relations departments operate alongside others, including marketing, human resources, legal, research and development, and operations. These departments are coordinated by a managerial system that is referred to as the dominant coalition. The dominant coalition comprises a range of representatives from the organisation and in some cases, the external environment, who have the power to determine the organisation's mission and goals (Grunig, Grunig & Dozier 2002).

The role of public relations in strategic decision making is determined by proximity and access to management (Cutlip, Center & Broom 2006). The Excellence Study stresses the need for public relations to be part of the dominant coalition (Grunig, Grunig & Dozier 2002). This strategic positioning brings benefits to the organisation and the public relations profession.

Reality is different. There is no doubt that CEOs value the public relations function (Grunig, Grunig & Dozier 2002); however, when asked to decide what roles should be part of the dominant coalition, a major US study found that public relations managers were least likely to be members and the CEO, the chief financial officer, and the chief operating officer were most likely to be included in the dominant coalition (Grunig, Grunig & Dozier 2002).

At a department level, there are three other functions that relate closely to and in some cases compete with public relations for resources and a place in the dominant coalition. The relationship of public relations departments with marketing, legal, and human resource departments will now be examined.

REFLECT AND DISCUSS

The concept of dominant coalition is important. Think about how your family unit operates—who makes the decisions and how involved is each family member in the decision making? Do you have family meetings to discuss major events? Investigate five company annual reports and see if you can determine where the public relations function is located in each organisation. Is it represented by a director of communications, or is it part of a cluster of functions, for example, within a corporate services branch?

Public relations and the marketing department

There is common ground between marketing and public relations functions in organisations, and in some organisations the two functions are combined. There is some suggestion that this is a trend within communication management (see Chapter 2). But these natural synergies (Proctor & Kitchen 2002) can create confusion. Thus, while public relations and marketing may take a consumer focus, their relationship with consumers comes from a different base. Marketing depends on consumers to purchase goods or services and deliver a profit through an exchange process, whereas public relations see consumers as one part of a complex environment.

The customer versus non-customer orientation is one of the main points of difference between public relations and marketing. Marketing is primarily a customer or sales-oriented function. Although the integrated marketing communication concept has introduced a focus on non-customer relationships, public relations is the only function that specifically considers non-customer publics and audiences, including employees, government, communities, and shareholders.

Public relations is critical when marketing activities and sales are affected by public opinion or crisis events. In some cases, marketing activities can be the cause of such crisis events.

One example of this is Herron Pharmaceuticals, which was the subject of an extortion attempt in 2000. Although the company eventually recalled its products, it initially did not notify the public or police about this extortion attempt. In the meantime, two consumers, a Brisbane doctor and his son, were hospitalised after consuming paracetamol capsules laced with strychnine. During the crisis, goodwill towards and confidence in the brand were damaged. To resolve this crisis, Herron not only withdrew and destroyed its products but it also reviewed manufacturing processes and security arrangements, and developed new tamper-evident packaging. Public relations, in particular crisis communications, and marketing were required to work together to re-establish the brand that is still part of the market today.

Amisha Mehta and Robina Xavier

FIGURE **7.1** | Public relations and marketing activities and their overlap

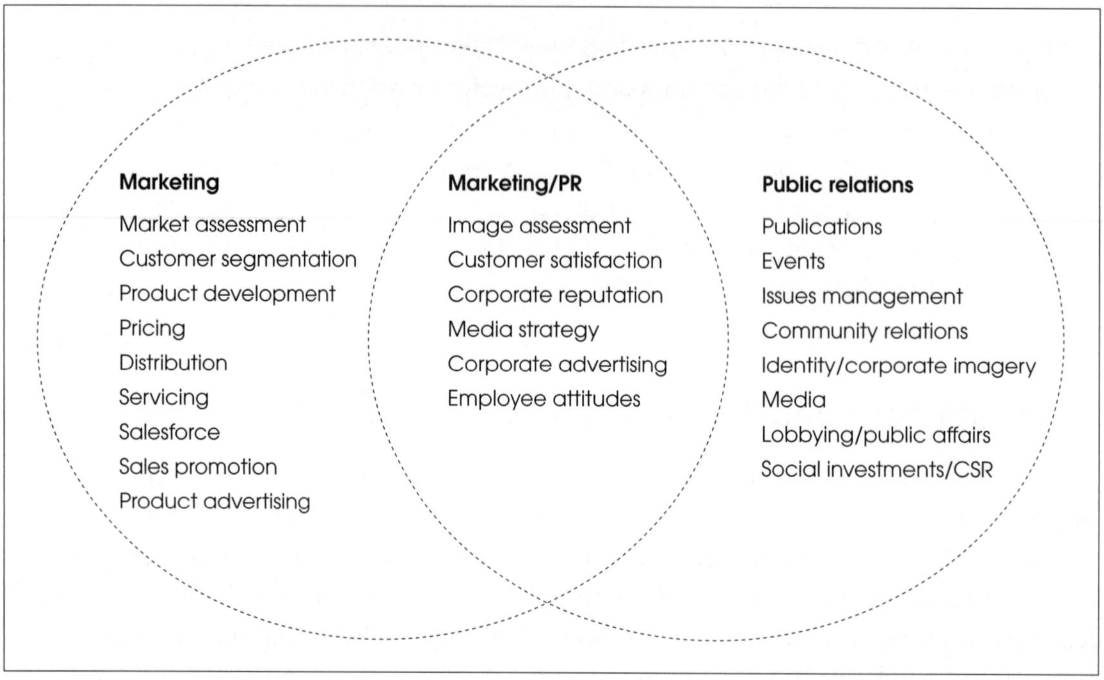

Marketing	Marketing/PR	Public relations
Market assessment	Image assessment	Publications
Customer segmentation	Customer satisfaction	Events
Product development	Corporate reputation	Issues management
Pricing	Media strategy	Community relations
Distribution	Corporate advertising	Identity/corporate imagery
Servicing	Employee attitudes	Media
Salesforce		Lobbying/public affairs
Sales promotion		Social investments/CSR
Product advertising		

Source: Cornelissen 2004: 40

From a structural point of view, public relations academics argue for a separate and centralised public relations department that optimises organisational goals. In reality, public relations is often merged with the marketing department (van Ruler & de Lange 2003). In some organisations, encroachment is prevalent. Encroachment occurs when non–public relations professionals hold senior positions in public relations (Lauzen 1992). The following activity will help you negotiate the differences between public relations and marketing.

REFLECT AND DISCUSS

You are two weeks into your new job as corporate communications manager for a major construction company that is in the process of developing and seeking capital for an innovative design to build a city within a city. You find that there are no plans to include the public relations team in these new developments. There seems to be a marketing frenzy and a focus on marketing the new design.

➤ What contribution do you think public relations would bring to this project?
➤ What can you do to ensure that public relations planning is central to the new city developments?

Public relations and the legal department

The relationship between the public relations department and legal counsel in organisations is mirrored by the tension between the courts of public opinion and the law. While public relations is motivated by open and two-way communication to build relationships and win votes in the court of public opinion, this openness is sometimes seen as a liability (Fitzpatrick & Rubin 1995).

A legal solution to a problem may be a preferred route for some members of society, and while this is not at the levels seen overseas, public relations practitioners may find themselves sitting around the table during issues or crisis management discussions arguing with lawyers about the amount of disclosure that should be given. Lawsuits affect organisational reputations and require public relations managers and lawyers to be part of the strategic decision-making process (Jin & Kelsay 2008, in press).

As a result, it is important for public relations practitioners and lawyers to work together (Lerbinger 2006). Research has shown that lawyers have an accurate view of public relations managers but the converse is not true (Reber, Cropp & Cameron 2001). Common ground between the two professions is that both are important in crisis situations and both should be involved early (Reber, Cropp & Cameron 2001).

Public relations practitioners should apply relationship building strategies to better understand lawyers (Reber, Cropp & Cameron 2001) and the law (Fitzpatrick 1996). Practitioners are encouraged to meet regularly with lawyers to discuss and plan for legal issues that have the potential to affect the organisation (Heath & Coombs 2006; McElreath 1993). Practitioners should also gain an understanding of the different laws or rules that may affect their practice. Public relations practitioners should possess a basic understanding of state, territory, and federal laws relating to their organisation and its industry, rules or codes of conduct of professional associations, privacy, copyright and trademark law, trade practices law, employee rights, and corporate disclosure rules, among others.

Often, companies are reluctant to reveal too much information during legal proceedings. During a crisis, most decisions about the release of information are made collaboratively, with legal counsel in the leadership role (Fitzpatrick 1996), yet it is just as important to manage the court of public opinion. While traditional advocacy strategies might use the media, an effective strategy during litigation is the internet. Reber, Cropp & Cameron (2006) found websites to be a useful dissemination tool for celebrities such as Martha Stewart and Michael Jackson, who both went through major public trials.

Public relations and the human resources department

Unified by a joint interest in employees, the relationship between public relations and human resources departments is important in organisational systems.

Like legal departments, public relations and human resource departments must have strong working relationships during day-to-day operations and crisis situations. Although structural and personnel changes such as job cuts, plant closures, or organisational restructures are accepted organisational behaviours, they still impact the share market and the morale of employees. At an operational level, research into employee benefit programs that are used to recruit and retain employees shows that there are opportunities for collaboration to determine appropriate methods and channels of communication (Freitag & Picherit-Duthler 2004).

When you consider the relationship between public relations and marketing, legal, and human resource departments, all have a role in building and maintaining organisational reputation. Another unifying force is organisational change. Active management of issues generally requires the input of different areas of expertise throughout the organisation. Project teams are often drawn together to coordinate multidisciplinary perspectives and knowledge to focus on a specific project of importance to the organisation. It is important for all departments to build working relationships in good times and bad.

REFLECT AND DISCUSS

Imagine you are part of a project team that is preparing a bid to construct a new highway. You will be providing the communication and community engagement component. Other people around the table include road construction specialists, engineers, environmental consultants, experts in noise control, landscape designers, and financial controllers. Each has a role to play.

➤ Identify the objectives you might aim to achieve in relation to this project.

The practice of public relations in organisations

Publics and audiences

All public relations managers deal with a multiplicity of publics and audiences inside and outside the organisation. Publics and audiences exist because they interact with or are affected by the organisation in some way, or they may develop around an issue, problem, or opportunity (Grunig & Repper 1992). Long-term ongoing public relations programs are developed to maintain the dialogue and communication with publics and audiences such as communities, investors, neighbours, and employees. New programs will be developed to support new initiatives and projects, and may require contact to be established with publics and audiences the organisation has never previously needed to communicate with. Public relations managers try to track the formation of publics as well as their subsequent activities to ensure that the organisation–public relationship can be built from the start. Part of the boundary-spanning role is identifying the emergence of new publics as well as monitoring existing publics.

Public relations programming often starts with the development of a publics or audience map for the organisation, that is, a list of the people who are aligned to or have a stake in the organisation. Edward Freeman (1984) suggests that the manager starts with the typical groups, including owners, customers, competitors, media, employees, suppliers, government, and special interest groups. From here the public relations manager can expand the list to best match their particular organisation and industry sector. The map contains broad categories of people or groups that affect or are affected by an organisation. To be useful to the public relations manager, this map needs to be refined to identify key publics.

Esman (1972) identified four types of organisational linkages that can help public relations managers track their publics:

1   *Enabling linkages* are those that have the authority and resources, such as regulators and owners, to enable the organisation to exist.
2   *Functional linkages* provide input to the organisation and consume its outputs. These include groups such as employees, suppliers, consumers, and clients.
3   *Normative linkages* are those with peer organisations, such as industry associations and professional groups.
4   *Diffused linkages* are those with an interest in the organisation but are not part of a formal relationship, such as the media, activists, and community members. Public relations managers need to be aware that groups with a diffused linkage may influence the groups in the other categories on certain issues, particularly if their environmental power grows. In some circumstances their position may change to one with a formal link.

Having identified the key publics and audiences, public relations managers need to analyse the map to consider alignment with and opposition to the organisation's position on particular issues and within different groups. The food manufacturer who wants to introduce a new line of snack products for children, for example, will need to be aware of publics and audiences, such as health authorities who are concerned with childhood obesity and the promotion of products that lead to it in children. It will also want to attract the attention of retailers and ensure retailer support to stock the product. It is difficult to identify any issue or initiative that will not lead to divided opinion, so the public relations manager knows that they will have to consider the needs of different publics and audiences as organisational strategy is mapped.

The public relations manager also knows that publics are not static. Publics and the environment are constantly changing, so environmental scanning processes need to constantly update the organisational databases.

Amisha Mehta and Robina Xavier

Public relations managers can also use J Grunig's (1989) situational theory of individual communication behaviour to track publics and audiences. The status of publics as latent, active, or aware, or the separate category of non-public provide useful information to the public relations manager when planning their communication campaigns and in monitoring the effect on publics of organisational actions.

At a broad level, public relations departments divide publics and public relations practice into two broad areas: internal and external relations. Internal relations is responsible for employee relations and issues; external relations is concerned with the range of stakeholders external to the organisation.

REFLECT AND DISCUSS

Organisational leaders make difficult decisions that can create conflict between internal and external relationships. When a listed company decides to close a manufacturing plant in Victoria, it must manage the reactions of employees as well as communicate the significance of this decision to shareholders or investors.

➤ Who should the organisation treat as most important?
➤ How should the organisation manage these competing interests?

Internal relations

Internal communication is the public relations specialty dedicated to the building and maintenance of relationships with and among employees. Employees are important and satisfactory employee–employer relationships lead to higher productivity, fewer errors and work stoppages, and less absenteeism (Center et al. 2008).

Some of the key issues that affect this relationship are inadequate communication, the extent of alignment with organisational values and culture, change to industrial relations legislation, unions, globalisation, job cuts or structural changes, and perceived inequities of salary and retirement packages for organisational leaders compared to entry level workers (Lattimore et al. 2006; Seitel 2007). Organisations need to be mindful of these issues and ensure that they are addressed.

Organisational culture

Organisational culture is central to employee relations. Culture is made up of the 'shared values, symbols, meanings, beliefs, assumptions and expectations that organise and integrate a group of people who work together' (Grunig, Grunig & Dozier 2002: 482). The public relations literature talks about two types of culture, authoritarian and participative.

In authoritarian cultures, decision making is centralised and communication is structured, formalised, and largely one-way (Grunig et al. 2002). Participative cultures encourage employees to be part of decision making and share in achievements with communication that emphasises both dialogue and feedback (Grunig et al. 2000). Consider the similarities here with open and closed systems, discussed earlier in this chapter.

Culture is often developed by organisational founders or leaders (Lattimore et al. 2006) and internalised by organisational members. The management literature identifies three different cultures related to different roles in organisations: operators, engineers, and executives (Schein 1996). Sometimes these cultures conflict, as demonstrated in the following operator–executive example:

> [W]hen the operator culture attempts to improve effectiveness by building learning capacity, which requires time and resources, the executives disallow the proposed activities on the grounds that the financial returns cannot be demonstrated or that too many exceptions are involved that would undermine the control system (Schein 1996: 238).

Public relations is one of the departments that can resolve this conflict. Public relations can facilitate and provide opportunities for interaction within organisations and encourage innovation and creativity (Lattimore et al. 2006). Other tools practitioners can use include reinforcement of organisational mission and vision statements, and modelling of appropriate behaviour.

Understanding employees and their information needs

As an internal communications specialist, it is important to understand employees and their information needs. It is also important to understand the differences between employees and external publics. According to Ni (2007), employees are different based on the way their relationship begins with an organisation. Employees enter into relationships to get paid, to gain experience, and to have further career experiences (Ni 2007). Despite these common elements, the position of the employee in the organisation also affects how they evaluate organisational relationships.

Chia and Peters (2008) found that employees are becoming social capital investors because they are taking a key role in growing the organisation's internal and external relationships and participating in community programs such as volunteering for Riding for the Disabled, revegetating the coastline, and supporting the homeless, among many others. This suggests that employees can bring a great deal to the organisation, that they build organisational reputation and relationships, and they become an integral part of a public relations internal and external communication management program.

Because not all employees are the same (Tench & Yeomans 2006) it is not useful to group them together as one public. Employees can be segmented by role or position as well as by their involvement and level of participation in particular issues. Depending on the situation, employees can also become activists.

Amisha Mehta and Robina Xavier

REFLECT AND DISCUSS

In a study of change within a US college, Nance McCown (2007) showed how employees responded to perceived communication gaps by adopting strategies of activists such as defining grievances, rallying and collaborating with other employee groups, engaging in rumours, and using the news media to pressure the organisation. In this example, what steps or actions would you recommend to the organisation?

Here is some advice. A clear set of rules for effective employee relations is provided by Center et al. (2008):

➤ Tell employees first.
➤ Tell bad and good news together.
➤ Be timely.
➤ Inform employees on subjects important to them.
➤ Use media trusted by employees.

Adopting some of these steps may prevent employees from becoming activist publics. In response to the situation described above, the college management invited employee participation in the change program and implemented mechanisms for ongoing employee participation (McCown 2007).

The information needs of employees remain fairly constant (Center et al. 2008), in that the top five subjects of most interest to employees are:

1   the organisation's future plans
2   job advancement opportunities
3   instructional information about role or duties
4   information about improvements in productivity
5   new policies and practices (Center et al. 2008).

To ensure an open systems approach, internal communications should respect employees, provide opportunities for the exchange of honest feedback, recognise and encourage employees, and maintain employee wellbeing and safety (Lattimore et al. 2006; Seitel 2007).

Employee communication channels

There is a range of communication channels that operates within organisations. Some of these are formal and led by public relations or organisational leaders; others, such as the grapevine or rumour mill, are created by employees themselves.

In choosing communication channels, public relations practitioners should consider how they build or maintain trust. Trust is built through the provision of information and trust in the source. Some of the trusted information sources in employee communications are the immediate supervisor, executives, and the organisational policy handbook (Center et al. 2008; Ni 2007). Other formal communication channels include the intranet, print publications, such as internal newsletters, bulletin boards, and face-to-face interactions in team or small group meetings. The least trusted media sources in employee relations are the grapevine and the mass media (Center et al. 2008). Always recognise the importance of the relational context, which means that discussion and dialogue are better for communication than intranets and online communication, which are impersonal.

Despite being less trustworthy, the grapevine or rumour mill is a potent communication channel that can emerge during times of change or uncertainty (Cutlip et al. 2006; DiFonzo & Bordia 2000; Seitel 2007). In some organisations, rumours appear during most weeks and relate to job security, job satisfaction, personnel changes, gossip, stock market performance, product or service quality, and organisational reputation (DiFonzo & Bordia 2000). Rumours lower morale, increase bad press, reduce trust, and increase employee stress (DiFonzo & Bordia 2000). Rumours are a normal part of organisations so employee relations specialists such as the public relations practitioner should be alert to their effects and plan to address them (DiFonzo & Bordia 2000).

Strategies to address rumours include:

➤ reinforcement of values and procedures used to guide any organisational changes
➤ establishment of regular communication updates
➤ explanation of decision-making processes
➤ acknowledgement or confirmation of rumour to increase trust (DiFonzo & Bordia 2000).

As with every type of public relations practice, it is important to identify the right channel and distribution method for the right audience. In today's increasingly flexible workplace, employees work onsite, offsite in client offices, or from home, or from offices in different parts of the country or in other countries, where English may not be the employees' first language. The challenges of communicating to everyone at the same time and with equal effectiveness must be met by the public relations practitioner.

External relations: contemporary challenges

Other chapters in this book, as well as specialist books, explain and describe the external relations functions of organisations including events, community relations, and media relations. In this chapter, we examine how corporate social responsibility, conflict, and engagement present contemporary challenges to the external relations function in public relations management.

Amisha Mehta and Robina Xavier

Corporate social responsibility

Since the mid 1980s in Australia, growing demand for business to deliver more than financial returns has led to the emergence of corporate social responsibility (CSR) (Cornelissen 2004). Through CSR, organisations focus on the social, ecological, and financial contributions or impacts they make through their operations. Australian research has shown that CSR was integrated into organisations through philanthropy and respect for the natural environment (Johnston & Beatson 2006). This research also found that social responsibility was emphasised over financial performance.

CSR presents a challenge and an opportunity to the theory and practice of public relations. A longitudinal study of the Australian banking industry showed that as the environment moved to embrace CSR, banks shifted public relations practices from a one-way influence perspective to a two-way perspective (Bartlett, Tywoniak & Hatcher 2007). As climate change, community relations, and other issues relating to CSR shape the community's expectations of organisations, public relations will have a role in ensuring that organisations respond. This is a specialist area in public relations (see Chapter 9).

Conflict

Conflict is an accepted part of organisational and environmental relationships. Organisational environments are typically dynamic and turbulent and filled with active publics and activist groups (Grunig et al. 2002). An activist public is 'a group of two or more individuals who organise to influence another public or publics through action that may include education, compromise, persuasion, pressure tactics or force' (Grunig et al. 2002: 446). While some activist groups, such as Greenpeace and Voiceless, have long histories and focus around high-profile issues such as the environment or animal welfare, in recent times, activists have become involved in many other issues that impact organisational action. Examples include activists who have targeted organisations such as James Hardie Industries NV for compensation as well as more open disclosure on organisational decision making (see Chapters 8 and 10).

Activists' level of involvement in organisational issues varies according to their interest in the issue (Center & Jackson 2003; Cutlip et al. 2006; Grunig 1992a). When activist publics disagree with organisations, they have the potential to constrain organisational operations (Anderson 1992). Activist publics can either work with recognised authorities, such as government, to affect a target organisation's operations (Grunig 1992), or resist dominant power structures, including government (Holtzhausen & Voto 2002). The methods of activist publics often mirror the methods of public relations experts and are becoming more focused around technology-led communication (see discussion on new media in Chapter 12). Managing these conflict areas requires public relations practitioners to not only be aware of their organisational environments but accept the sophistication of activists within their environment.

Community engagement

An extension of the boundary-spanner role discussed earlier is the practice of community engagement, sometimes known as public participation or community consultation. Community engagement practices are used in a variety of public and private projects and are designed to ensure that a diverse range of publics and audiences have input to proposed actions and policies that may affect them. They also play a major role in the reputational legacy of participants after the major projects are complete. Throughout this scholarly text, examples of community engagement indicate its growing importance within public relations relationship management; in this chapter, the open systems approach allows for a context where communities and organisations can jointly discuss and plan projects where they have common interests and interdependent objectives.

Kim Johnston (2007) proposes that a relational perspective to community engagement be considered as it provides a framework through which to accommodate diversity. Engagement relationship strategies incorporate research, information sharing, consultation, and participation processes; and recognise the continuum of practice from advocacy and power-holding positions through to collaborative, power-sharing strategies (see the IAP2 Spectrum, Chapter 5). On major road upgrades, for example, project managers need to identify the major publics or audiences who might have an interest in the project, including:

➤ affected residents whose houses may be affected by the noise of construction and the possible shifts of land surrounding their houses
➤ road users who may experience delays during major works
➤ businesses that may suffer loss of revenue if customers find it difficult to access their business premises.

The engagement relationship strategies used with each of these publics or audiences may be different to each other and may also vary over time as different parts of the project are completed: at times, the project managers may be able to negotiate with business owners to minimise disruptions by changing the scheduled working hours or days, whereas at other times, both parties may find it impossible to negotiate a workable outcome and the project manager may use an information strategy to ensure that the stakeholders are updated on the decisions made.

Community engagement is closest to the community involvement dimension of Hallahan's (2005) three dimensions of community building. Modern organisations are also participating more in the community nurturing and organising dimensions, which place more emphasis on the community's needs over the organisation's and may build more sustainable, rich relationships for the longer term. Development of community capacity and social capital is often a goal of community relations.

Community relations develop organisations' social capital by establishing relationships and partnering with not-for-profit organisations, for example, so that all partners benefit.

Amisha Mehta and Robina Xavier

Chia and Peters (2008) found that the partnership between credit unions and the charitable organisation, the Smith Family, to support young carers, provided benefits for both: the credit unions benefited through the volunteering opportunities for staff and the long-term relationships developed with young carers enabled them to continue their education and develop a career.

The community engagement role is a rewarding one but one that is being challenged in tight financial markets where a focus on profit seems to be challenging credit unions' progress in this area. Chia and Peters (2008) contend though that community engagement is central to organisational development because organisations are community members.

REFLECT AND DISCUSS

> Think about what is happening in your local community or nearest city. Explore three organisations that have a strong interest in community. How are they involved with the community? What relationships are they prioritising? What is the return on their investment?

CHAPTER SUMMARY

➤ The public relations management role in organisations is grounded in systems theory.

➤ To achieve organisational goals, internal public relations practitioners must be aware of the relationships between the public relations function and other corporate functions.

➤ An important role is to build relationships with employees, with specific regard to communication channels and organisational culture.

➤ There is a need to build and maintain relationships with external publics, who have the potential to affect organisations during times of stability and change.

➤ Community engagement and corporate social responsibility are strong trends in current public relations practice.

➤ Contemporary challenges to the public relations management role are driven by changing expectations of publics and audiences.

➤ As operating environments change and new issues emerge, the public relations role will continue to change and to focus more on active involvement in organisational decision making and relational development at all levels.

CASE STUDY \ PREPARING EMPLOYEES FOR CHANGE

Moving house is often a logistical challenge for a family, so imagine trying to move approximately 2000 employees to new premises. This challenge, coupled with the requirement to change the way in which employees use their work environment was the task facing Suncorp. The program required two years of planning and implementation as part of a national workplace change program.

Suncorp, one of Australia and New Zealand's leading diversified financial service providers, realised that if it was to achieve its corporate goals in an increasingly demanding environment, it needed to provide employees with effective work spaces to enable them to achieve at the very highest levels. A review of its office space, however, found that a significant proportion of existing work spaces did not allow for new ways of working, which were required to promote greater collaboration and increase productivity. To address this issue, Suncorp initiated a National Workplace Change Program with the first project being the relocation of a significant number of its Brisbane CBD workforce to Brisbane Square, a new office tower in the heart of the city. Employees were moved from small group-based environments to a 22 000sqm open plan tenancy with interconnecting staircases designed to improve collaboration and team work across and within business groups.

This was a significant change for many employees and the company realised that communication would play a critical role in preparing its employees for the move, by:

➤ promoting the far-reaching behavioural changes required to achieve its long-term goals
➤ maintaining business continuity during the move
➤ creating a communication blueprint for future sites.

Suncorp appointed Synchronous Communication to develop and implement a robust communication strategy to support this significant corporate initiative.

Significant research was used to inform the communication strategy. Research commissioned by Suncorp on new workplace designs and cultural aspirations was reviewed to identify potential issues and challenges. Briefings with key stakeholders focused on areas such as maintaining business continuity while preparing employees for the move as well as the aspirational targets of promoting the collaborative and sharing behaviours the new workplace was designed to foster.

Target publics for the program included:

➤ the employees who would be relocating
➤ the workplace champions
➤ senior and line management
➤ internal support departments such as human resources.

Amisha Mehta and Robina Xavier

Unlike many external communication programs, all of these publics were known to Suncorp and could be communicated with through corporate channels.

To provide a context for the communication program, the positioning statement 'Outside the Square' was used to focus the program and help internal audiences 'tune in' to program-specific communication.

Six specific stages of the change journey were identified to guide the communication program: announce, engage and excite, align and champion, signal and promote, celebrate and embrace, and reinforce and sustain.

Each stage used different tactics to promote the key messages and desired behaviours with a strong focus on visual and participatory mediums to attract interest. For example, one of the key change and communication tools was a stage-based display centre with full scale fit-out prototypes of a typical work area. The display was used extensively throughout the program to give employees a first-hand experience of what the new workspace would look like and how it would support the way they work. Other tactics included specially designed videos for each stage, a dedicated intranet, site tours, more than 200 employee briefings, newsletters, workplace guides, welcome kits and celebratory events to mark key milestones. While much of the program was designed to create a sense of excitement and achievement, it also dealt directly with employee concerns, recognising the overall wariness to change and the challenges the new open plan workspace would bring. By working with employees, these issues were identified and collaborative solutions designed and implemented.

Overall, the program was highly successful: all relocations occurred on schedule and all employees were able to work without issue from day one in the new premises. Post-relocation research highlighted that collaboration had increased and employees and managers across all groups were embracing the new way of working. Employees recognised the importance of the communication program in achieving this output with 70 per cent rating the program as excellent. The overall strategy has now been adopted for all future Suncorp workplace change projects.

FURTHER READING

Center, A H, Jackson, P, Smith, S & Stansberry, F R 2008, *Public Relations Practices: Managerial Case Studies and Problems*, 7th edn, Pearson, Upper Saddle River.

WEBSITE RESOURCES

PricewaterhouseCoopers, at www.pwc.com/extweb/service.nsf/docid/0c334e23eb5d6b3aca25 72e9001c5edc.

Suncorp, at www.suncorp.com.au.

REFERENCES

Aldrich, H & Herker, D 1977, 'Boundary Spanning Roles and Organisation Structure', *Academy of Management Review*, 2: 217–30.

Anderson, D S 1992, 'Identifying and Responding to Activist Publics: A Case Study', *Journal of Public Relations Research*, 4(3): 151–65.

Bartlett, J, Tywoniak, S & Hatcher, C 2007, 'Public Relations Professional Practice and the Institutionalisation of CSR', *Journal of Communication Management*, 11(4): 281–99.

Berger, B K 2005, 'Power Over, Power with, and Power to Relations: Critical Reflections on Public Relations, the Dominant Coalition, and Activism', *Journal of Public Relations Research*, 17(1): 5–28.

Broom, G M 1982, 'A Comparison of Sex Roles in Public Relations', *Public Relations Review*, 8(3): 17–22.

Broom, G M & Dozier, D M 1986, 'Advancement for Public Relations Role Models', *Public Relations Review*, 12(1): 37–56.

Broom, G M & Smith, G D 1979, 'Testing the Practitioner's Impact on Clients', *Public Relations Review*, 5(3): 47–59.

Center, A H & Jackson, P 2003, *Public Relations Practices: Managerial Case Studies and Problems*, 6th edn, Prentice Hall, Upper Saddle River.

Center, A H, Jackson, P, Smith, S & Stansberry, F R 2008, *Public Relations Practices: Managerial Case Studies and Problems*, 7th edn, Pearson, Upper Saddle River.

Chia, J & Peters, M 2008, 'Employee Engagement in Organisations' Social Capital. Does Public Relations have a Role?', *Asia Pacific Public Relations Journal*, 9: 103–20.

Cornelissen, J 2004, *Corporate Communications Theory and Practice*, Sage, London.

Cutlip, S M, Center, A H & Broom, G M 2006, *Effective Public Relations*, 9th edn, Prentice Hall, Upper Saddle River.

DiFonzo, N & Bordia, P 2000, 'How Top PR Professionals Handle Hearsay: Corporate Rumours, Their Effects, and Strategies to Manage Them', *Public Relations Review*, 26(2): 173–90.

Dozier, D M & Broom, G M 1995, 'Evolution of the Manager Role in Public Relations Practice', *Journal of Public Relations Research*, 7(1): 3–26.

Esman, M J 1972, in R Ice1991, 'Corporate Publics and Rhetorical Strategies', *Management Communication Quarterly*, 4(3): 341–62.

Everett, J 1996, 'Toward a Cultural Ecology of Organising', in L Thayes (ed.), *Organisation Communication Emerging Perspectives III*, Ablex Publishing, Norwood.

Fitzpatrick, K R 1996, 'Public Relations and the Law: A Survey of Practitioners', *Public Relations Review*, 22(1): 1–8.

Fitzpatrick, K R & Rubin, M S 1995, 'Public Relations vs Legal Strategies in Organisational Crisis Decisions', *Public Relations Review*, 21(1): 21–33.

Frank, R E, Massy, W F & Wind, Y 1972, *Market Segmentation*, Prentice Hall, Englewood Cliffs.

Freeman, R E 1984, *Strategic Management: A Stakeholder Approach*, Pitman, Boston.

Freitag, A R & Picherit-Duthler, G 2004, 'Employee Benefits Communication: Proposing a PR–HR Cooperative Approach', *Public Relations Review*, 30: 475–82.

Grunig, J E 1989, 'Publics, Audiences and Market Segments: Models of Receivers of Campaign Messages', in C T Salmon (ed.), *Information Campaigns: Managing the Process of Social Change*, Sage, Newbury Park.

Grunig, J E 1992, 'Communication, Public Relations, and Effective Organisations: An Overview of the Book', in J E Grunig (ed.), *Excellence in Public Relations and Communication Management,* Lawrence Erlbaum, Hillsdale.

Grunig, J E 2000, 'Collectivism, Collaboration, and Societal Corporatism as Core Professional Values in Public Relations', *Journal of Public Relations Research,* 12(1): 23–48.

Grunig, J E & Hunt, T 1984, *Managing Public Relations,* Holt, Rinehart and Winston, New York.

Grunig, J E & Repper, F C 1992, 'Strategic Management, Publics, and Issues', in J E Grunig (ed.), *Excellence in Public Relations and Communication Management,* Lawrence Erlbaum, Hillsdale.

Grunig, L A 1992, 'Activism: How it Limits the Effectiveness of Organisations and how Excellent Public Relations Departments Respond', in J E Grunig (ed.), *Excellence in Public Relations and Communication Management,* Lawrence Erlbaum, Hillsdale.

Grunig, L A, Grunig, J E & Dozier, D M 2002, *Excellent Public Relations and Effective Organisations: A Study of Communication Management in Three Countries,* Lawrence Erlbaum, Mahwah.

Heath, R L & Coombs, W T 2006, *Today's Public Relations: An Introduction,* Sage, Thousand Oaks.

Holtzhausen, D R & Voto, R 2002, 'Resistance from the Margins: The Postmodern Public Relations Practitioner as Organisational Activist', *Journal of Public Relations Research,* 14(1): 57–84.

Jin, Y & Kelsay, C J 2008, 'Typology and Dimensionality of Litigation Public Relations Strategies: The Hewlett-Packard Board Pretexting Scandal Case', *Public Relations Review,* 34(1): 66–69.

Johnston, K A 2007, 'Community Engagement: A Relational Perspective', paper presented to the Australian and New Zealand Communication Association Annual Conference, 2007, *Communication, Civics, Industry,* 5–6 July, 2007, La Trobe University, Melbourne.

Katz, D & Kahn, R L 1978, *The Social Psychology of Organisations,* Wiley, New York.

Kotler, P & Andreasen, A R 1987, *Strategic Marketing for Nonprofit Organisations,* 3rd edn, Prentice Hall, Englewood Cliffs.

Lattimore, D, Baskin, O, Heiman, S & Toth, E 2006, *Public Relations: The Profession and the Practice,* McGraw Hill, Sydney.

Lauzen, M M 1992, 'Public Relations Roles, Intraorganisational Power, and Encroachment', *Public Relations Review,* 4(2): 61–80.

Lerbinger, O 2006, *Corporate Public Affairs Interacting with Interest Groups, Media, and Government,* Lawrence Erlbaum, Mahwah.

McCown, N 2007, 'The Role of Public Relations with Internal Activists', *Journal of Public Relations Research,* 19(1): 47–68.

McElreath, M P 1993, *Managing Systematic and Ethical Public Relations,* Brown & Benchmark, Madison.

Modaff, D P, DeWine, S & Butler, J 2008, *Organisational Communication: Foundations, Challenges, and Misunderstandings,* 2nd edn, Pearson, Boston.

Morgan, G 1998, *Images of Organisation,* Sage, Thousand Oaks.

Moss, D, Newman, A & DeSanto, B 2005, 'What Do Communication Managers Do? Defining and Refining the Core Elements of Management in a Public Relations/Corporate Communication Context', *Journalism and Mass Communication Quarterly,* 82(4): 873–90.

Ni, L 2007, 'Refined Understanding of Perspectives on Employee–Organisation Relationships: Themes and Variations', *Journal of Communication Management*, 11(1): 53–70.

Patel, A M, Xavier, R & Broom, G M 2005, 'Towards a Model of the Impact of Organisational Legitimacy on Public Relations Practice', paper presented at the International Communication Association Conference, New York.

Pieczka, M 2006, 'Paradigms, Systems Theory, and Public Relations', in J L'Etang & M Pieczka (eds), *Public Relations: Critical Debates and Contemporary Practice*, Lawrence Erlbaum, Mahwah.

PricewaterhouseCoopers 2008, *Carbon Countdown*, retrieved from www.pwc.com/Extweb/onlineforms.nsf/docid/0EDACFFBA83712AB852573DB000F55FF/$file/CarbonCountdown.pdf, 30 January 2009.

Proctor, T & Kitchen, P 2002, 'Communication in Postmodern Integrated Marketing', *Corporate Communications: An International Journal*, 7(3): 144–54.

Reber, B H, Cropp, F & Cameron, G T 2001, 'Mythic Battles: Examining the Lawyer–Public Relations Counselor Dynamic, *Journal of Public Relations Research,* 13(3): 187–218.

Reber, B H, Gower, K K & Robinson, J A 2006, 'The Internet and Litigation Public Relations', *Journal of Public Relations Research,* 18(1): 23–44.

Schein, E H 1996, 'Culture: The Missing Concept in Organisation Studies', *Administrative Science Quarterly*, 41: 229–40.

Seitel, F P 2007, *The Practice of Public Relations*, 10th edn, Pearson, Upper Saddle River.

Skinner, R W & Shanklin, W L 1978, 'The Changing Role of Public Relations in Business Firms', *Public Relations Review*, 4(2): 40–5.

Skyttner, L 2001, *General Systems Theory: Ideas and Applications*, World Scientific, Singapore.

Spicer, C 1997, *Organisational Public Relations*, Lawrence Erlbaum, Mahwah.

Suchman, M C 1995, 'Managing Legitimacy: Strategic and Institutional Approaches', *Academy of Management Review*, 20(3): 571–610.

van Leuven, J 1991, 'Corporate Organising Strategies and the Scope of Public Relations Departments', *Public Relations Review*, 17(3): 279–91.

van Riel, C B M 2007, *Essentials of Corporate Communication: Implementing Practices for Effective Reputation Management*, Routledge, London.

van Ruler, B & de Lange, R 2003, 'Barriers to Communication Management in the Executive Suite', *Public Relations Review*, 29: 145–58.

Von Bertalanffy, L 1968, *General System Theory*, Penguin, Harmondsworth.

Witmer, D F 2006, 'Overcoming System and Culture Boundaries: Public Relations from a Structuration Perspective', in C H Botan & V Hazleton (eds), *Public Relations Theory II*, Lawrence Erlbaum, Mahwah.

Chapter 8

REPUTATION MANAGEMENT: A DRIVING FORCE FOR ACTION

Nigel De Bussy

PRACTITIONER PROFILE | MARIE-LOUISE SINCLAIR

Based in Western Australia Marie-Louise Sinclair is a communication consultant with a strong reputation for evidence-based, leading-edge practice. She is the recipient of state, national and international industry awards for excellence and is a Fellow (and former President) of the Public Relations Institute of Australia.

Marie-Louise has held senior management roles in leading communications consultancies over the past two decades prior to establishing Sinclair Consulting in 2003. The consultancy provides specialist corporate positioning, communication and social performance services to major Australian and global organisations.

Ours is a stimulating and rewarding industry. We are one of the few business-based professions at the intersection of arts and science. We get to mix creativity with cleverness!

Our work at the consultancy is knowledge-driven, informed by international best practice and (it's) innovative. We look for young consultants with a solid understanding of

---

the craft and theoretical underpinnings of the profession—as well as a flair for fun and the sort of curiosity you need to keep asking: "Is this the best solution for our client?"

Consultants draw holistically on a lexicon of reliable social research, stakeholder engagement, communication and marketing tools, to build support for defined business drivers, in creative and thoughtful ways.

Marie-Louise encourages young practitioners to involve themselves in the industry—to:

make a contribution to the profession by practising ethically and with a bias for excellence, working to inform best practice—and also by putting your hand up to serve on our professional bodies.

The public relations landscape has changed immeasurably over the last decade and today's students are absolutely familiar with the modern communication geography. All you need to add to the mix is solid academic training, passion and an ongoing thirst for improvement.

CHAPTER **AIMS**

By the end of this chapter you should be able to:

➤ discuss the relevance of reputation management for organisations
➤ understand the role of corporate public relations in contemporary organisations
➤ explain the importance of stakeholders to the formation of corporate reputation
➤ distinguish between key concepts such as corporate reputation, image, brand, identity, and culture
➤ apply these concepts to the analysis of real life corporate issues.

Introducing reputation management

Pick up a newspaper or glance at a television news bulletin almost any day of the week, or watch Sunday morning television, and you are sure to notice the prominence given to business-related stories. Today, large corporations and business executives face increasing scrutiny as society demands accountability and transparency from business, especially big business. Following a string of high-profile scandals in Australia and around the world, trust in major corporations is at an all-time low.

These are the trends behind the growing importance of corporate public relations. High-calibre corporate public relations executives are greatly valued and in short supply

Nigel De Bussy

(Murray & White 2005), which has created outstanding career opportunities for those with the right blend of skills and experience. Contemporary corporate public relations sits right in the space where business and society meet. In today's rapidly changing world, there are few more absorbing places to be.

As outlined in previous chapters, the corporate public relations function is complex, multifaceted, and at least partly responsible for what some say is an organisation's most important asset, its reputation. No one would dispute that a good reputation is a valuable asset but the question of whether it should be the central focus of public relations in contemporary organisations is far from settled. Academic (as opposed to practitioner) definitions of public relations are less inclined to mention reputation. Yet it is increasingly common for public relations to be defined in terms of reputation management, especially by practitioners. The British Chartered Institute of Public Relations (CIPR) describes public relations as 'the discipline which looks after reputation' (Chartered Institute of Public Relations n.d.).

'Reputation' is defined in the *Australian Concise Oxford Dictionary* as, 'what is generally said about a person's or a thing's character … state of being well reported of, credit, distinction, respectability, good report'.

Not all corporate entities are big businesses, and many government-owned businesses and agencies have been corporatised. Hospitals, charities, educational institutions, and other not-for-profit organisations often run on corporate lines. All organisations large enough to have some kind of professional management structure need to pay close attention to their stakeholders and should be concerned about how they are perceived by others. Understandably, societal expectations of big business are greater than those of smaller organisations. But it would be a mistake to think the principles and practice of corporate public relations apply only to well-known major multinationals.

Depending on the organisation, corporate public relations may primarily be the responsibility of inhouse managers or external consultants or a combination of both. Some aspects of the function, such as ongoing employee communication, are probably best handled inhouse, as demonstrated by the many examples in this book that point to the growing importance of inclusive employee communication management.

Understanding the world of corporate public relations involves grasping a number of key concepts, such as:

➤ reputation
➤ image
➤ brand
➤ identity
➤ corporate culture.

There is considerable disagreement on how to define these terms, which often appear to overlap and are sometimes used interchangeably.

Public relations scholar James Hutton has raised serious doubts about the appropriateness of using reputation as a guiding philosophy for corporate public relations practice, preferring instead to put the emphasis on relationships (Hutton 1999; Hutton et al. 2001). One of Hutton's key concerns is that reputation can be fickle and is hard to measure reliably.

Scholars from outside the public relations discipline, such as Charles Fombrun and his collaborators, have to a great extent dominated the field of corporate reputation research (Fombrun & van Riel 2004). Indeed, Fombrun has argued that despite appearances to the contrary, corporate reputation management is a separate discipline to public relations. His case rests on the premise that corporate reputation is about substance whereas public relations deals with more superficial concerns (Fombrun 2006). In saying this though, Fombrun does public relations an injustice. Leading public relations scholars have long emphasised the importance of behaviour over mere symbolism alone (Grunig 1993).

REFLECT AND DISCUSS

> ➤ What creates a good (or bad) reputation? Is the reputation of a business or an individual important? Why?
>
> ➤ From what you have learnt about public relations so far, do you think it makes sense for corporate reputation to be considered a public relations function? Why do some people from outside the public relations discipline say that it does not?
>
> ➤ Which is the most important consideration in public relations—reputation or relationships? How are the two connected?

The confusing nomenclature of corporate public relations

Functions described here as 'corporate public relations' are often given a different name in the real world of business. Job titles such as 'corporate communications', 'corporate affairs', and 'corporate relations', among others, are today more common than 'public relations' itself. In one sense, job titles are a trivial matter but unfortunately departmental turf wars are not uncommon and can be fuelled by confusion and conflict over terms and titles. Such organisational politics can be a real barrier to achieving integrated communication, which is essential to ensuring that stakeholders receive clear and consistent messages (Ewing, De Bussy & Caruana 2000). Integrated communication is part of the wider brief of communication management (see Chapter 2).

'Integrated communication' can be defined as '[t]he act of coordinating communications so that the corporate identity is effectively and consistently communicated to internal and external groups' (Cornelissen 2004: 189).

Nigel De Bussy

There is also a trend towards professionals from other disciplines assuming responsibility for particular aspects of stakeholder and reputation management, working alongside colleagues from public relations backgrounds. In many instances, this makes perfect sense for the organisations involved. For example, in the mining and resources industry employing anthropologists and community development specialists seems a sound approach for managing relationships with indigenous communities living in close proximity to resource projects.

Rio Tinto: long-term work with the community

Rio Tinto is one of the world's largest mining companies. The company stresses the importance of long-term, externally monitored plans designed to benefit the communities in which it operates. Rio Tinto uses two-way community and local stakeholder consultation to create these plans, which even consider the economic sustainability of communities after the mine eventually closes and post-mining land use (Rio Tinto n.d.). In 2007, Rio Tinto businesses supported more than 2900 socioeconomic programs and spent around US$107 million on community assistance (Rio Tinto n.d.).

Why would a large, profit-oriented corporation such as Rio Tinto do this? The answer is that reputation matters to running a successful business over the long term. And reputation is determined to a considerable extent by perceptions about the treatment of stakeholders and the environment. In the words of Rio's finance director Guy Elliott, '[C]ommunity issues … [are] becoming more and more important but we now have an evaluation process in place that's formalized and rigorous, and we are refining it all the time. We even have an anthropologist on staff who helps us think about the really long-term issues which can arise in a community' (Brigg 2003).

Hutton et al. (2001) found that some traditional corporate public relations functions, notably, government relations and investor relations, were being transferred in their entirety to other departments. This is of concern, not only from the self-interested perspective of the public relations profession, but also, and more importantly, because it is likely to lead to increasingly *dis*integrated corporate communications (Hutton et al. 2001), a move in precisely the wrong direction.

REFLECT AND DISCUSS

> ➤ Why are there so many different names for the function described in this chapter as corporate public relations? Why are practitioners apparently so reluctant to use the term 'public relations' in their job titles?

➤ The *Compact Oxford English Dictionary* defines anthropology as 'the study of humankind, especially the study of societies and cultures and human origins'. Why would a big mining company such as Rio Tinto employ an anthropologist?

➤ How could the roles of corporate public relations professionals and anthropologists complement one another in the context of local community engagement?

Perhaps the most crucial question is what really determines reputation. Arguably, the critical driver is the quality of an organisation's relationships with its key stakeholders, which in turn are strongly associated with its perceived corporate social performance (CSP). In recent years, 'stakeholder' has become one of the most widely used terms in the worlds of business and government. This chapter suggests that stakeholder management is the heart and soul of corporate public relations from which all else follows. The next section will explain why corporate public relations is such a challenging task in today's business environment. Following that the spotlight will turn to the stakeholder concept.

Wood (1991: 693) defines corporate social performance as '[a] business organisation's configuration of principles of social responsibility, processes of social responsiveness, and policies, programs, and observable outcomes as they relate to the firm's societal relationships'.

The challenge of corporate public relations

For some people, the very word 'corporation' (or 'corporate') conjures up images of greed, exploitation, and environmental degradation. The highly successful 2003 Canadian documentary film, *The Corporation*, based on the book by Joel Bakan, takes the legal status of corporations as 'artificial persons' as its starting point. What if a psychiatrist assessed the personality of the corporation as if it were a real person? What would the diagnosis be?

The subtitle of Bakan's book, 'The Pathological Pursuit of Profit and Power', really says it all. Bakan and his fellow filmmakers claim that corporations, which all sides agree dominate today's global economy, are inherently immoral. If corporations were people, Bakan says, we would call them psychopaths (Bakan 2004). The movie features many interviews with high-profile critics of globalisation and big business, such as author Naomi Klein and filmmaker Michael Moore.

Data collected in Britain by market research company MORI (now Ipsos MORI) underscore the challenges of corporate public relations (Lewis 2003). MORI found 80 per cent of those sampled agreed with the statement that 'large companies have a moral responsibility to society'. Yet 61 per cent said that large companies do not really care about the long-term environmental and social impact of their actions (Lewis 2003: 358).

Nigel De Bussy

MORI's long-term data are particularly interesting:

➤ In the late 1970s, the public agreed two to one that the profits of large companies benefited their customers; today they disagree by the same margin.

➤ In 1998, 28 per cent of those surveyed said that corporate social responsibility (CSR) was very important in forming a decision about buying a product or service from a particular company. In 2002, the proportion had risen dramatically to 44 per cent (Lewis 2003: 359). For consumers, corporate social responsibility seems to be rapidly increasing in importance at the same time as trust in big business is declining.

➤ When asked if companies should make an effort to tell the public about their CSR activities, 72 per cent said yes but that businesses should not spend significant amounts in order to do so.

➤ When asked which professions they trusted to tell the truth, 62 per cent of the survey population said they did not trust business leaders, who were rated as only slightly less dishonest than politicians and journalists. Doctors, who topped the poll, were trusted by 91 per cent of the public (Lewis 2003).

Corporate social responsibility is defined as 'the economic, legal, ethical, and discretionary expectations that society has of organisations at a given point in time,' (Carroll 1979: 500). 'Discretionary' refers to voluntary actions by corporations, for example, making donations to charity.

Corporate public relations is so challenging in part because the community seems to have contradictory expectations of big business. The MORI research shows that the public does not think profit for profit's sake is a particularly good thing but they want companies to use their resources to benefit society. It is hard to see how business can do this unless it is profitable. Equally, the public wants business to tell them about CSR initiatives but without spending much money to do so. And even if the CSR message does somehow get through it probably will not have the desired effect because people do not trust business leaders to tell the truth anyway.

REFLECT AND DISCUSS

➤ Why is corporate social responsibility becoming such a major concern for many consumers and other corporate stakeholders?

➤ Do you think consumers are telling the truth when they say CSR influences their purchasing decisions?

➤ How could you, as a consumer, find out about an organisation's policy on CSR?

➤ It seems that public trust in big business is at an all time low. Why do you think this is the case? What can large corporations do to increase their credibility?

➤ Do you think the public also has a low level of trust of small business? What might be different in the public's attitudes towards small versus big business?

The stakeholder concept

In this book the phrase 'publics and audiences' has been used to denote the other participants in the communication process. The term 'stakeholder' is also widely used by public relations professionals. From relatively obscure beginnings, the popularity of the word has grown exponentially. Media commentators and academics have produced an overabundance of articles on the stakeholder concept. Today, it seems, rarely a board meeting or ministerial briefing takes place without stakeholders getting at least a mention. Yet the precise significance of the stakeholder concept remains embroiled in controversy. Experts can not even agree on a simple definition of who is a stakeholder.

Stakeholder management is often linked to the notion of corporate social performance but there is considerable disagreement about the extent to which corporations should go in satisfying the expectations of their various stakeholders. Aside from the social responsibility debate there is also a strong business case for adopting a stakeholder approach, that is, companies that pay attention to their stakeholders should be more successful financially as well as enjoying a better reputation for CSP.

The 1984 publication of Freeman's landmark book *Strategic Management: A Stakeholder Approach* was the catalyst for the contemporary stakeholder debate. Freeman (1984: 25) defined a stakeholder as 'any group or individual who can affect or is affected by the achievement of the firm's objectives'. This definition is now widely used but is extremely broad. According to Freeman, just about anyone—even a terrorist (Freeman 1984: 53)—can be considered a stakeholder.

Max Clarkson (1995) also put forward a potentially all-encompassing definition of a stakeholder but suggested that primary stakeholders are those without whom the corporation cannot survive, that is (in no particular order of importance):

➤ shareholders
➤ employees
➤ customers
➤ suppliers
➤ governments
➤ communities.

Clarkson's list seems to represent a sensible set of priorities for most organisations.

The traditional idea of a business is to focus solely on making profits for the shareholders or owners of the business. The whole point of the term 'stakeholder' is that management should be responsive to the needs of all those with, in Clarkson's (1995: 106) words, 'rights or interests' in a corporation, not just the shareholders or business owners alone. The word 'stakeholder' was coined as a deliberate counterpoint to the terms 'shareholder' and 'stockholder'.

Nigel De Bussy

The stakeholder view of the firm remains controversial. Milton Friedman (1970) famously wrote that the 'one and only one social responsibility of business … [is] to increase its profits'. The case against stakeholder theory has been stridently argued by the likes of academic business ethicists Alexei Marcoux (2003) and Elaine Sternberg (1999), as well as media commentators such as Janet Albrechtsen (2006). These critics all believe that the interests of shareholders or business owners are more important than those of other stakeholders. Supporters are equally categorical in their claims. In the foreword to one book on stakeholder management, Freeman wrote of stakeholder theorists rescuing business from the 'moral scrapheap' (Freeman 2002). The argument raises fundamental questions about what is the proper purpose of a business organisation.

In part, the controversy results from confusion over a number of different types of stakeholder theory. Those who emphasise the moral superiority of the stakeholder concept are proponents of what is known as normative or ethical stakeholder theory. In contrast, the view that businesses that pay attention to their stakeholders will perform better financially as a result is called instrumental stakeholder theory (Donaldson & Preston 1995).

The benefits of stakeholder management and positive relationships

As mentioned previously, perhaps the most important factor in a good corporate reputation is the quality of an organisation's relationships with its key stakeholders. These relationships are, in turn, strongly associated with perceived corporate social performance (CSP). Ironically, since they come from opposite ends of the political spectrum, Bakan and conservative commentator Albrechtsen are in agreement about corporate social responsibility. Both regard it as essentially a fraud, designed to mask the true intentions and actions of corporations. Right-wing critics of the stakeholder concept such as Albrechtsen and Sternberg are keen to stress the primacy of shareholders' rights as the owners of the business. But if instrumental stakeholder theory is valid, then these critics should actually support taking a stakeholder approach on the grounds that it is in the best long-term interests of shareholders as well as others with different kinds of stakes in the company.

A research study of 626 Australian companies with around 100 or more employees found strong support for the instrumental stakeholder theory proposition (De Bussy 2005). Adopting a stakeholder management approach with regard to four primary, non-shareholder stakeholder groups (employees, customers, suppliers, and the community) was found to make a positive contribution to financial success quadruple that of a narrow orientation focused on shareholders alone.

Applying the stakeholder concept in practice involves treating stakeholder needs as legitimate ends in their own right, not simply as a means to an end. It requires creating value (social as well as economic) for all stakeholders, not just for shareholders alone. It means listening to stakeholders and being responsive, in other words, engaging in a true dialogue. Dialogue is about communication spirit or orientation, not specific techniques. It requires a commitment to open two-way communication, a willingness to change practices where appropriate, and an atmosphere of mutual trust (De Bussy, Ewing & Pitt 2003).

Even if companies are genuine about stakeholder orientation and corporate social responsibility, their true intentions will inevitably be regarded with suspicion by some. That categorically does not mean they should not make the effort. There is a growing body of evidence to suggest that companies that do the right thing, and communicate with sensitivity, will reap a variety of benefits, including reputational and financial. They are also entitled to claim the moral high ground.

BP and corporate greenwashing

In today's cynical and networked world, attempts to fake sincerity are almost certain to end in disaster. So-called greenwashing is a prime example of how this can occur. Greenwashing involves companies proclaiming their environmental credentials while actually behaving very differently. The activist website CorpWatch.org regularly gives out awards to companies it deems guilty of greenwash. In 2002, one of the world's largest oil companies, BP, was given a greenwash award by environmental activists for its 'beyond petroleum' rebranding campaign (CorpWatch 2002). Officially, the letters 'BP', which used to stand for 'British Petroleum', now do not mean anything. But the company said that beyond petroleum was a good way to describe its new approach because it emphasises alternative energy sources rather than traditional fossil fuels, which cause climate change. On its website, BP describes beyond petroleum as a 'summation of our brand promise and values ... It is both our philosophical ideal and a practical description of our work' (BP n.d.). CorpWatch describes talk such as this as 'beyond preposterous'. The debate continues.

REFLECT AND DISCUSS

> ➤ What is a stakeholder?
> ➤ Which stakeholders should corporations pay most attention to and why?
> ➤ Are big businesses sincere when they claim to care about stakeholders and the environment, or is corporate social responsibility just a big con?
> ➤ The Body Shop is often named as a company that walks the talk. Do some web research and see whether you agree.

Nigel De Bussy

How is reputation created?

If, as the evidence suggests, positive relationships with stakeholders lead directly to improved financial performance, organisations with satisfied stakeholders are also likely to enjoy a good reputation, as stakeholder perceptions are crucial to the process of building a reputation. We will now examine in more depth how corporate reputation is created and explain the role played by public relations.

Hutton et al. (2001) raised a number of objections to the adoption of reputation management as a guiding philosophy for corporate public relations, including the question of whether reputation can really be managed in the traditional business sense. Even if it can, how much control does corporate public relations have over reputation compared with other organisational departments? A study of fourteen British CEOs (Murray & White 2005) found that CEOs themselves take overall responsibility for their organisations' reputations; other studies (Gaines-Ross 2000; Weber Shandwick 2007) have also shown that the personal reputation of the CEO has a major impact on overall corporate reputation.

The CEOs in Murray and White's study pointed out that, by itself, public relations can not create reputation. Reputation, the respondents said, is the result of consistently delivering on promises. The task of public relations is to make sure the organisation gets credit for the good things it does. Potentially, everyone in an organisation can contribute to overall reputation, whether positively or otherwise. Negative stakeholder experiences can have an extremely damaging impact on reputation (Murray & White 2005). The CEOs in the study saw the role of public relations as helping organisational leaders to communicate effectively by coaching them and articulating key messages. It is also essential for public relations to be thoroughly informed about the views of stakeholders (Murray & White 2005).

Murray and White's findings are consistent with earlier work and have significant implications. John Mahon and Steven Wartick (2003) discussed the importance of credibility to reputation, and highlighted the need for consistency between what an organisation says it will do (or will not do) and its actual behaviour. In a different context, marketing scholar Evert Gummesson (1991) pointed out that amateur 'part-time marketers' are really responsible for much of a company's marketing, not the full-time professionals. The part timers have a major impact on customer relations (Gummesson 1991). If corporate public relations is concerned with reputation, and a major driver of reputation is the quality of stakeholder experiences with the organisation, then corporate reputation is, in a sense, the responsibility of everyone within the company. Hence, public relations specialists can not, and should not, attempt to directly manage every aspect of a company's reputation.

The role of corporate public relations

The key role of corporate public relations at a strategic level is as a facilitator and adviser, that, for example:

➤ helps to ensure that stakeholder needs are understood and met
➤ encourages consistency in delivering on promises (that is, acting as the corporate conscience)
➤ coaches employees at all levels (but especially senior managers) in communicating effectively with stakeholders
➤ helps to articulate and frame messages that it may well fall to others to deliver.

As Murray and White's CEO respondents noted, the more visible the public relations person is in the communications process—especially when dealing with the media—the greater the likelihood that the message will be perceived as spin. Hence, corporate public relations often works behind the scenes, crafting messages that others (such as the CEO) will deliver publicly and developing partnerships and relationships that add value or credit to organisations.

By now the complexities, but also the appeal, of corporate public relations should be evident. Without doubt it is a challenging field that requires practitioners of the highest calibre and commitment. Corporate public relations professionals (whatever their actual job title) need to be knowledgeable, sophisticated in their approach, open to new ideas, and have a broad range of interests. Sensitivity towards, and an ability to manage, cultural diversity is essential. Personal integrity and ethics are of paramount importance. For those with the right qualities, the opportunities are immense.

The next section will compare the major concepts on which corporate public relations practice is based: reputation, image, brand and identity.

Major concepts in corporate public relations

How does the term 'reputation' differ from other widely used and apparently similar concepts, such as 'corporate image', 'brand', and 'identity'? Together with corporate culture, these terms make up the key concepts central to the practice of corporate public relations.

Corporate reputation

Reputation is an estimation of a person or a thing (Mahon & Wartick 2003). Hence, reputation can be associated with individuals or organisations independently of their human leadership or both. Since reputation can be the estimation of a thing, issues also have reputations (Mahon & Wartick 2003).

Stewart Lewis, research director of the Ipsos-MORI Reputation Centre, listed six facets or dimensions of overall reputation:

1 social responsibility
2 environmental responsibility
3 leadership
4 quality of products or services
5 financial performance
6 treatment of staff (Lewis 2003: 362).

In developing the reputation quotient (RQ), a measure of corporate reputation, Fombrun, and his co-authors Naomi Gardberg and Joy Sever (2000: 253), have identified a virtually identical set of dimensions, namely, emotional appeal, products and services, vision and leadership, workplace environment, social and environmental responsibility, and financial performance.

Corporate reputation (as opposed to reputation in general) can be defined as 'a collective assessment of a company's ability to provide valued outcomes to a representative group of stakeholders' (Fombrun, Gardberg & Sever 2000: 243).

At least four of Fombrun et al.'s six proposed dimensions of reputation clearly relate to specific primary stakeholder groups as follows:

1 financial performance (shareholders)
2 social and environmental responsibility (communities and governments)
3 workplace environment (employees)
4 products and services (customers).

Of course that is not to suggest that employees and customers are not also concerned about the environment—merely that employees are primarily concerned with the workplace, customers with products and services, and so on. Naturally, it is also possible for an individual to be a member of more than one stakeholder group, for example, an employee may also be a shareholder as a result of a company incentive scheme. Community members may also be customers, and so on.

A large-scale Australian study (Porritt 2005) showed that in practice, respondents only distinguish between two dimensions of reputation—relationship reputation and bottom line reputation. Relationship reputation refers to treatment of staff, customers, and the wider community. Bottom line reputation relates to meeting the expectations of investors and financial markets. Moreover, Porritt (2005) found that a company's reputation for financial success can adversely impact its overall reputation. If the organisation is perceived to be making excessive profits at the expense of customers, employees, and the community, a backlash can result.

These findings are consistent with the British research discussed earlier, which also suggested that the public is suspicious of corporate profit making (Lewis 2003). Above all, Porritt's study confirmed the link between stakeholder relationships and reputation. In understanding the drivers of corporate reputation, it is imperative to place the quality of an organisation's relationships with its stakeholders front and centre.

The problem of measuring reputation

As noted previously, Hutton et al. (2001) queried the adoption of reputation as corporate public relations' guiding philosophy partly on the grounds of the apparently fickle nature of reputation. Enron, the company notorious for arguably the most stunning and scandalous collapse in business history, is a textbook example. Of all the measures of corporate reputation, probably the best known internationally is *Fortune* magazine's 'Most Admired Companies' list. In February 2001, *Fortune* listed Enron as number one in America for 'innovativeness' and number two for 'quality of management' (ABC *News*, 25 May 2006).

Less than a year later, Enron collapsed in shameful circumstances. In retrospect, the reasons behind *Fortune*'s spectacularly misleading rating are not hard to find. The listing is based on the opinions of senior managers from other corporations (van Riel and Fombrun 2007: 246). It is a safe assumption that these managers place far more emphasis on bottom line reputation than other stakeholders or the general public. Moreover, the executive respondents were not in a position to know what was really going on behind the scenes at Enron.

Many other measures of reputation are based on surveys of consumers or the general public. The key weakness of this approach is that even though these respondents may be familiar with the companies in question, in the sense of having heard of them, they are not necessarily primary stakeholders. They may not feel particularly connected to or involved with the organisation. Their views are likely to be superficial in the absence of significant personal interaction with the company or indepth knowledge. Hence, it would not take much to sway their sentiments in a different direction. A single negative (or highly positive) media report could be enough.

Such considerations are the basis of Hutton et al.'s (2001: 258) observation that reputation (as it is typically measured) is of far more significance for 'strangers' who have no direct ties with the organisation, as opposed to 'relationships' which are more likely to be applicable to a company's 'friends and associates'. If someone has a relationship with an organisation, they do not judge the company by its reputation but by the quality of their interactions with it. Hutton et al. went on to suggest that brands represent a middle ground between reputation and relationships, relevant to those with direct ties to the organisation and those without. Cornelissen (2004) similarly argued that reputation varies by stakeholder group.

Therefore, in attempting to manage corporate reputation, it makes more sense to measure the opinions of key primary stakeholders rather than simply consumers or the general public. Knowing what key stakeholders think can be a highly effective early warning system. If they are dissatisfied, sooner or later that dissatisfaction will become known to a wider audience through media coverage or word of mouth. At that point, the company's overall reputation may appear to collapse dramatically. If the organisation had been in the habit of measuring its reputation among the general public alone, it may not have seen the problem coming until it was too late.

Corporate image

With the possible exception of 'spin', few words in the field of public relations have been reviled as frequently as 'image'. The most famous of all public relations professors, J Grunig, discouraged his students from even using the term (J Grunig 1993). Many words have multiple meanings but image is especially problematic in this respect. Clearly, one possible usage of the word 'image' is closely related to 'reputation' and the terms are sometimes incorrectly used interchangeably. Hutton (1999, p. 202) bracketed together the expressions 'reputation management', 'perception management', and 'image management', describing their rise as 'an ominous trend'.

Renowned public relations scholar, the late Scott Cutlip, 'loathed' the word 'image'. In contrast to Hutton, Cutlip drew a sharp distinction between reputation and image, endorsing the former while condemning the latter. 'We in PR,' said Cutlip, 'must be concerned with that good old-fashioned word, *reputation*— not image' (Cutlip 1991). Interestingly, Cutlip said this just a few years before Charles Fombrun, whose background is not in public relations, so successfully made the word 'reputation' 'new-fashioned' again.

In the corporate communication literature, typically produced by authors from outside the public relations mainstream who would prefer not to describe their specialism as public relations, image is increasingly defined as a kind of short-term reputation. Image is said by these authors to refer to perceptions held about an organisation at a given point in time, whereas corporate reputation itself is supposedly established over the longer term (see, for example, Cornelissen 2004). While it is true that a good reputation can take a long time to build up, it is equally true that it can be destroyed almost overnight. Not only was Enron's image shattered in a brief period in late 2001 but also, clearly, its reputation.

One sense of the word 'image' is defined by the *Oxford English Dictionary* (*OED*) as:

> A concept or impression, created in the minds of the public, of a particular person, institution, product, etc.; *spec.* a favourable impression; esp. in phr. *public image*.

A draft 2004 addition to the *OED* defines an image consultant as:

> a person or company employed to advise on how to convey a favourable or desired public impression, esp. on how to ensure positive media portrayal and good public relations, on

personal appearance and style, or on how to improve brand recognition through a change of name, logo, product packaging, etc.

This no doubt describes the type of activity viewed with such suspicion by many academics and practitioners alike. Grunig (1993) argued that superficial symbolic action by itself—the quest for a positive image—does not make an organisation more effective. Only when symbolic relationships (image) are entwined with behavioural relationships (substance) can public relations truly succeed (J Grunig 1993).

REFLECT AND DISCUSS

Review the sections in Chapter 3 that talk about the interpretive approach and use of symbolism in organisations. Confirm for yourself that public relations requires a matching of what an organisation says and what it does.

The production versus the consumption of images

Grunig's (1993) critique of the term 'image' distinguishes between two very different meanings of the word, namely, the production versus the consumption of images. It is self-evidently true that corporate public relations involves the production of images; however, Grunig claimed that not only is this activity insufficient by itself but also the terminology is semantically flawed. 'Symbols' and 'messages', Grunig argued, are superior terms to 'image' in this context.

Image in the sense of consumption of images is an entirely different matter. When we pay attention to corporate communication, we create cognitive structures or constructs in our minds in order to deal with those messages. The normal processes of human cognition involve the construction of mental schemas, complex sets of knowledge and attitudes that help people make sense of the world. Image in this sense, and schema, both appear closely related in meaning to reputation. Thus, reputation is, in some respects, simply a euphemism for image, in the same way that some prefer the term 'corporate communication' to 'public relations'.

The danger of the term 'image' for public relations is that it may be viewed superficially. Practitioners may fall into the trap of thinking good relations with stakeholders can be built on the basis of slick and cynical manipulation of corporate image. This is mistaken from an ethical as well as a practical perspective. Further, image in the sense of the 'artificial representation of the external form of something' does matter. And sometimes the right (or the wrong) image can be created accidentally, as the following case studies of James Hardie Industries and the Australian Wheat Board shows.

Nigel De Bussy

CASE STUDIES JAMES HARDIE INDUSTRIES AND THE AUSTRALIAN WHEAT BOARD

Building-products giant James Hardie Industries and the Australian Wheat Board (AWB) are the companies at the centre of the two biggest Australian corporate public relations scandals of recent times. James Hardie tried to shirk its responsibilities towards former workers suffering and dying from hideous diseases caused by exposure to asbestos, which the company used to manufacture. The AWB was involved in bribery and corruption in Iraq, during the time of the former regime of Saddam Hussein, in order to secure markets for Australian wheat.

Both are complex stories with many lessons of critical importance for corporate public relations professionals. Yet both are notable for remarkable images of individual people that did much to influence public perceptions.

The late Bernie Banton was the public face of the fight against James Hardie. Banton was a former company employee whose health had been destroyed by asbestos. By the time of his death in 2007 from the incurable asbestos-related disease mesothelioma, he had become a national hero and was honoured with a state funeral by the government of New South Wales.

Because of his medical condition, Banton had to carry an oxygen tank with him wherever he went. Banton had many admirable qualities and would have been an effective campaigner regardless. But there is little doubt that the image of those ever-present oxygen tubes graphically reinforced Banton's message in each of his frequent media appearances.

Former AWB chairman, Trevor Flugge, unwisely allowed himself to be photographed in Iraq, bare-chested and holding a handgun, which he pointed at the camera. The story of AWB's activities in Iraq was damaging enough without the existence of the photograph. The image itself was not directly relevant to the 2006 Cole inquiry into the affair; it did, however, strongly influence public perceptions of the company at the time and severely damaged Flugge's personal reputation. These two examples illustrate the impact of image on public perceptions, as well as the interplay between image and reputation.

The most important lessons of these two cases for corporate public relations relate to stakeholders and ethics. In 2001, James Hardie Industries established a new parent company based in the Netherlands. Almost $2 billion in assets from James Hardie companies in Australia was transferred to the new entity. Subsequently, these assets were legally insulated from claims for compensation from asbestos victims in Australia. It seems the Netherlands was chosen because it does not have a treaty with Australia that enables the enforcement of civil judgments obtained in Australia (Australian Council of Trade Unions 2004). The compensation fund James Hardie set up to meet the needs of victims in Australia proved to be grossly inadequate and the company had reneged on a pledge that the assets transferred to the Netherlands would still be available to claimants. The whole point of establishing a Dutch parent company and the associated legal manoeuvres had been to save the company money by depriving the asbestos victims of their rightful compensation—legally valid perhaps, but morally reprehensible.

The company seemed completely unprepared for the public furore that swiftly followed. Devastating publicity, the threat of product boycotts, a highly effective union-backed campaign, and government condemnation left James Hardie's reputation in tatters. Eventually, the company was forced by the sheer weight of moral outrage and adverse publicity to do what it should have done in the first place—sit down with the stakeholders and negotiate a fair settlement of the legitimate compensation claims. Had James Hardie done the right thing by the victims at the beginning, the final cost to the company would have been much lower and its reputation would still be intact. As it is, it will take many years for the company and senior executives involved to live down the scandal.

In December 2005, the AWB was facing an imminent judicial inquiry into its murky dealings in Iraq prior to the 2003 US-led invasion of that country. The company hired American crisis management expert Peter Sandman, who provided some sound advice—apologise. Sandman even drafted a letter of apology in the name of then AWB CEO Andrew Lindberg (Elliott 2006). Foolishly, the company decided not follow Sandman's advice. Instead it chose to tough it out and deny everything. The draft letter came to light several months later after the AWB lost a court battle to keep it secret. Once the draft apology was made public, the extent of the AWB's dishonesty was painfully apparent, which made an already horrendous corporate crisis even worse. As is often the case in situations such as this, a ham-fisted attempt to cover up wrongdoing probably caused more damage than the initial bad behaviour, in this case bribery to secure access to the Iraqi wheat market. As in the James Hardie case, the corporate reputation of AWB was utterly shattered. At the time of writing, key executives involved in both scandals still face serious charges.

The role of corporate public relations includes helping to ensure that stakeholder needs are understood, acting as the corporate conscience, and helping to articulate and frame messages. With James Hardie and the AWB, it is apparent that much reputational damage could have been avoided if the advice of high-level public relations professionals had been taken.

Nigel De Bussy

REFLECT AND DISCUSS

➤ How does corporate image differ from corporate reputation? What are the similarities between the two terms? Use the James Hardie Industries and AWB cases as examples.

➤ Think about an organisation with an image that you perceive as bad. What words would you use to describe the organisation? What has led you to forming this image? What could the organisation do to change this image, in your view?

➤ Why do many public relations experts dislike the term 'image'?

Corporate brand and identity

In the words of corporate identity thought leader John Balmer, 'Clearly, there is a considerable overlap between an organisation's identity and its corporate brand,' (Balmer 2003: 308). But there are important differences between the two concepts that are relevant to the practice of corporate public relations. It is also important to understand how corporate brand and identity differ from corporate reputation and image.

There are numerous definitions of corporate identity and they frequently contradict one another. One of the oldest remains, after three decades, perhaps the most useful. Wally Olins, co-founder of legendary corporate identity consultancy Wolff Olins, based his thinking on the idea of the corporate personality, which he defined as follows:

> Corporate personality…embraces the subject [corporation] at its most profound level. It is the soul, the persona, the spirit, the culture of the organisation manifested in some way. A corporate personality is not necessarily something tangible that you can see, feel or touch— although it may be (Olins 1978: 212).

Olins then went on to define corporate identity itself:

> The tangible manifestation of a corporate personality is a corporate identity. It is the identity that projects and reflects the reality of the corporate personality (Olins 1978, p. 212).

Today what Olins referred to as corporate personality is often called 'organisational identity', not to be confused with corporate identity, which is the projection or expression of organisational identity. Notice how Olins refers to the 'reality' of the corporate personality. As noted earlier, attempts to fake sincerity or present a false identity are likely to end in disaster.

Many businesspeople think of corporate identity purely in terms of visual identity, for example, logos, signage, stationery, uniforms, and similar objects. It is true that logos and the like are an important aspect of corporate identity, but they are only one component of a multidimensional concept. The 'corporate identity mix', a term coined to parallel the well-known expression 'marketing mix', has three core elements (van Riel & Fombrun 2007: 68):

➤ *Communication.* What organisations say about themselves through their authorised communication, including public relations messages and advertising.

➤ *Behaviour.* What organisations actually do. Ultimately, this is by far the most important consideration. It is one thing for a company to say it is socially responsible, but do its actions live up to its rhetoric? Companies—and people—are judged more by their deeds than their words.

➤ *Symbolism.* The logos and other symbols an organisation uses to express its personality and differentiate itself from others. When considered in isolation, this element of the overall corporate identity mix can be referred to as 'corporate visual identity' (CVI) (Melewar & Akel 2005; van den Bosch, de Jong & Elving 2005).

An organisation's annual report is a good indicator of whether these three elements are aligned.

The corporate brand promise

The term 'corporate brand' refers to the company behind the products and services, not to the product brand itself. In some cases a brand name can refer to a company and a product, for example Coca-Cola and Nike. There are some key differences between corporate and product brands (Balmer 2003), including:

➤ ultimate responsibility for the corporate brand rests with the CEO, not middle-level marketing managers

➤ managing the corporate brand is a multidisciplinary task, not just a job for the marketing department

➤ corporate brands focus on multiple internal and external stakeholder groups, not just customers or consumers

➤ effective corporate brand communication requires integrated corporate communication, not just marketing communication

➤ the values embedded in the corporate brand must be genuinely based on the culture of the organisation in contrast to the superficial values normally associated with product brands (adapted from Balmer 2003: 303).

A product brand represents the promise of a bundle of attributes that someone buys and that provides satisfaction. These attributes may be real or illusory, rational or emotional, tangible or invisible (Ambler 1992). In short, a product brand is a promise made by a producer to a consumer. A corporate brand is a promise made by an organisation to a stakeholder.

This is essentially the position taken by Balmer (2003: 313), who summarises the notion of the corporate brand as the organisation's 'covenant' with its stakeholders. According to Balmer, creating a corporate brand involves a conscious decision by senior management to distil and make known the attributes of the company's identity in the form of a clearly defined branding proposition. A strong corporate brand should clearly and consistently communicate the promise implicit in this proposition and differentiate the organisation from competitors (Balmer 2003). The brand should also enhance stakeholder loyalty and the esteem in which the organisation is held, thus contributing to an improved corporate reputation (Balmer 2003).

Nigel De Bussy

REFLECT AND DISCUSS

Can you demonstrate these concepts with reference to Coca-Cola or Nike?

Corporate identity structures

The notion of corporate identity structures (Wolff Olins 1995) offers a useful tool for developing and analysing organisational strategy in this field. The corporate identity structure refers to the public presentation of the relationship between the product and the corporate brand. Which approach a company adopts is partly a function of the structure of the organisation itself (Stuart 1999). There are three main alternatives (Wolff Olins 1995):

1 *Monolithic—the single business identity*. The classic example is the Virgin Group. Virgin founder Sir Richard Branson has created businesses in a hugely diverse range of industries, from music to airlines, mobile phones to soft drinks, and many more. No matter what the product, the same monolithic Virgin corporate brand identity is used to communicate the brand values of fun, innovation, and value for money.

2 *Endorsed—the multibusiness identity*. The individual product brand is given the most prominence but the corporate brand of the organisation behind the product is also made clearly visible, in effect endorsing the product in question. A good example is Nestlé, the world's largest packaged food company, which prominently displays its corporate identity in association with most of its famous product brands, such as Milo, Kit Kat, and Carnation.

FIGURE **8.1** | Milo logo

Source: Nestlé/Milo

FIGURE **8.2** | Kit Kat logo

Source: Nestlé/Kit Kat

FIGURE **8.3** | Carnation milk logo

Source: Nestlé/Carnation

3   *Branded—the brand-based identity.* There is no obvious public association of corporate and product brands. One such example is Procter & Gamble, whose famous product brands such as Gillette, Head & Shoulders, and Pantene are not, in their public presentation, linked in any obvious way to the parent company (Wolff Olins 1995).

FIGURE **8.4** \ Gillette logo

Source: Procter & Gamble/Gillette

FIGURE **8.6** \ Pantene logo

Source: Procter & Gamble/Pantene

FIGURE **8.5** \ Head & Shoulders shampoo logo

Source: Procter & Gamble/ Head & Shoulders

FIGURE **8.7** \ Procter & Gamble logo

Source: Procter & Gamble

FIGURE **8.8** \ Olay logo

Source: Procter & Gamble

REFLECT AND **DISCUSS**

➤ Identify two organisations with which you are familiar. What corporate identity do these organisations project to the outside world through their communication, behaviour, and symbolism? Do you consider this identity reflects the reality of the organisation's personality? Why?

➤ Look on the shelves of a retail store or at print media advertisements and find examples of a monolithic, an endorsed, and a branded approach to corporate identity structure. Why do you think these particular companies have adopted their chosen strategy? What are the advantages and disadvantages of each approach?

Nigel De Bussy

CHAPTER **SUMMARY**

➤ Corporate public relations offers outstanding career opportunities for those with the right blend of skills and experience. But it is highly demanding and requires practitioners of the highest calibre. Beginning public relations practitioners can build their expertise through gaining experience in such spheres as local community relations and employee communication.

➤ Corporate reputation management is multidisciplinary. It is based on the skill set of ethical corporate public relations professionals but involves cooperation and coordination across the entire organisation. Support and understanding from the CEO is essential.

➤ The most important driver of reputation is the quality of an organisation's relationships with its key stakeholders. The traditional, narrow emphasis of big business on making short-term profits at all costs to keep the shareholders happy is dangerously outmoded. Companies that build strong relationships with their other primary stakeholders not only enjoy a better reputation, but tend to be more financially successful in the long run as well.

➤ Many of the current techniques used to measure reputation are flawed. The reputation of a company can vary between different stakeholder groups. It is critically important to regularly monitor the opinions of key stakeholders who have a real interest in the business, rather than rely on surveys of the general public.

➤ The greatest mistake a corporation can make with regard to its reputation is to pretend to be something it is not. Public relations professionals have a responsibility to help create corporate identities based on the real culture and personality of the organisation. If the corporate culture is undesirable, the correct course of action is to change the culture through carefully managed strategic communication initiatives, not to try to present a false identity to the world.

➤ The corporate public relations practitioner, in focusing on reputation—and the relationships and communication that build reputation—recognises the importance of three key things: that multiple aspects of what an organisation says and does contribute to reputation, that organisations must have a clear vision of the reputation they aspire to and the nature of the relationships they would like to have, and that this vision must be clearly communicated within the organisation.

FURTHER READING

Balmer, J M T & Greyser, S A 2003, *Revealing the Corporation: Perspectives on Identity, Image, Reputation, Corporate Branding and Corporate-Level Marketing*, Routledge, London.

Davies, G, Chun, R, Da Silva, V & Roper, S 2003, *Corporate Reputation and Competitiveness*, Routledge, London.

Kitchen, P J & Schultz, D E 2001, *Raising the Corporate Umbrella: Corporate Communications in the Twenty-first Century*, Palgrave, Basingstoke.

Post, J E, Preston, L E & Sachs, S 2002, *Redefining the Corporation: Stakeholder Management and Organizational Wealth*, Stanford University Press, Stanford.

WEB RESOURCES

Arthur W Page Society, at www.awpagesociety.com.

Centre for Corporate Public Affairs, at www.accpa.com.au.

Harris Interactive, at www.harrisinteractive.com/services/reputation.asp.

Reputation Institute, at www.reputationinstitute.com.

Wally Olins, at www.wallyolins.com.

Wolff Olins, at www.wolffolins.com.

REFERENCES

Albrechtsen, J 2006, 'Moral Coercion Hoax', *Australian*, 29 March.

Ambler, T 1992, *Need-to-know Marketing*, Century Business, London.

Australian Council of Trade Unions 2004, *Australia's Greatest Corporate Scandal*, retrieved from www.actu.asn.au/Campaigns/PastACTUCampaigns/JamesHardie/Australia8217sGreatestCorporateScandal.aspx, 7 April 2008.

Bakan, J 2004, *The Corporation: The Pathological Pursuit of Profit and Power*, Free Press, New York.

Balmer, J M 2003, 'The Three Virtues and Seven Deadly Sins of Corporate Brand Management', in J M Balmer & S A Greyser (eds), *Revealing the Corporation*, Routledge, London.

Brigg, P 2003, 'Meet Guy Elliott', *Rio Tinto Review*, 63, retrieved from www.riotinto.com/library/reviewmagazine/63/article2 1.aspx, 20 June 2008.

British Petroleum n.d., *Beyond Petroleum*, retrieved from www.bp.com. com/sectiongenericarticle.do?categoryId=90102219&contentId=7019491, 15 March 2007.

Carroll, A B 1979, 'A Three-dimensional Conceptual Model of Corporate Social Performance', *Academy of Management Review*, 4(4): 497–505.

Chartered Institute of Public Relations n.d., *What is Public Relations?*, retrieved from www.cipr.co.uk/direct/looking.asp?v1=what, 21 January 2008.

Clarkson, M B E 1995, 'A Stakeholder Framework for Analyzing and Evaluating Corporate Social Performance', *Academy of Management Review*, 20(1): 92–117.

Cornelissen, J 2004, *Corporate Communications: Theory and Practice*, Sage, London.

CorpWatch 2002, 'Greenwash Academy Awards Announced at Earth Summit', retrieved from www.corpwatch.org/article.php?id=3648, 18 January 2008.

Cutlip, S 1991, 'Cutlip Tells of Heroes and Goats Encountered in 55-year PR Career', *O'Dwyer's PR Services Report*, 5(5): 12, 51–6, quoted in Grunig 1993.

De Bussy, N M, Ewing, M T & Pitt, L F 2003, 'Stakeholder Theory and Internal Marketing Communication: A Framework for Analysing the Influence of New Media', *Journal of Marketing Communications*, 9(3): 147–61.

De Bussy, N M, Ewing, M T & Pitt, L F 2005, *STAKOR: The Development of a Scale to Measure Stakeholder Orientation and its Impact on Performance*, PhD thesis, Curtin University of Technology, Perth.

de Chernatony, L & Riley, F D O 1998, 'Defining a "Brand": Beyond the Literature with Experts' Interpretations', *Journal of Marketing Management*, 14(4/5): 417–43.

Donaldson, T & Preston, L E 1995, 'The Stakeholder Theory of the Corporation: Concepts, Evidence, and Implications', *Academy of Management Review*, 20(1): 65–91.

Elliott, G 2006, 'Master of Sorry Management', *Australian*, 20 May.

Ewing, M T, De Bussy, N M & Caruana, A 2000, 'Perceived Agency Politics and Conflicts of Interest as Potential Barriers to IMC Orientation', *Journal of Marketing Communications*, 6(2): 107–19.

Fombrun, C J 2006, *What is Reputation Management?*, retrieved from novitaic.typepad.com/novitaic/corporate_reputation_management/index.html, 21 January 2008.

Fombrun, C J, Gardberg, N A & Sever, J M 2000, 'The Reputation Quotient: A Multi-Stakeholder Measure of Corporate Reputation', *Journal of Brand Management*, 7(4): 241–55.

Fombrun, C J & van Riel, C B 2004, *Fame and Fortune: How Successful Companies Build Winning Reputations*, Prentice Hall, Upper Saddle River.

Freeman, R E 1984, *Strategic Management: A Stakeholder Approach*, Pitman, Boston.

Freeman, R E 2002, 'Foreword', in J Andriof, S A Waddock, B W Husted & S Sutherland (eds), *Unfolding Stakeholder Theory*, Greenleaf Publishing, Sheffield.

Friedman, M 1970, 'The Social Responsibility of Business is to Increase its Profits', *New York Times Magazine*, 13 September, 32–3, 122, 126.

Gaines-Ross, L 2000, 'CEO Reputation: A Key Factor in Shareholder Value', *Corporate Reputation Review* 3(4): 366–70.

Grunig, J E 1993, 'Image and Substance: From Symbolic to Behavioral Relationships', *Public Relations Review*, 19(2): 121–39.

Gummesson, E 1991, 'Marketing Orientation Revisited: The Crucial Role of the Part-Time Marketer', *European Journal of Marketing*, 25(2): 60–75.

Hutton, J G 1999, 'The Definition, Dimensions and Domain of Public Relations', *Public Relations Review*, 25(2): 199–214.

Hutton, J G, Goodman, M B, Alexander, J B & Genest, C M 2001, 'Reputation Management: The New Face of Corporate Public Relations?', *Public Relations Review*, 27(3): 247–61.

Lewis, S 2003, 'Reputation and Corporate Responsibility', *Journal of Communication Management*, 7(4): 356–64.

Mahon, J F & Wartick, S L 2003, 'Dealing with Stakeholders: How Reputation, Credibility and Framing Influence the Game', *Corporate Reputation Review*, 6(1): 19–35.

Marcoux, A M 2003, 'A Fiduciary Argument Against Stakeholder Theory', *Business Ethics Quarterly*, 13(1): 1–24.

Melewar, T C & Akel, S 2005, 'The Role of Corporate Identity in the Higher Education Sector: A Case Study', *Corporate Communications*, 10(1): 41–57.

Murray, K & White, J 2005, 'CEOs' Views on Reputation Management', *Journal of Communication Management*, 9(4): 348–58.

Olins, W 1978, *The Corporate Personality*, Design Council, London.

Olins, W 1995, *The New Guide to Identity*, Gower, Aldershot.

Porritt, D 2005, 'The Reputational Failure of Financial Success: The "Bottom Line Backlash" Effect', *Corporate Reputation Review*, 8(3): 198–213.

Rio Tinto n.d., *Community Investment*, retrieved from www.riotinto.com/ourapproach/7186_community_investment.asp, 17 June 2008.

Sternberg, E 1999, *The Stakeholder Concept: A Mistaken Doctrine,* retrieved from http://ssrn.com/abstract=263144, 19 January 2003.

Stuart, H 1999, 'The Effect of Organizational Structure on Corporate Identity Management', *Corporate Reputation Review*, 2(2): 151–64.

van den Bosch, A L M, de Jong, D T & Elving, W J L 2005, 'How Corporate Visual Identity Supports Reputation', *Corporate Communications*, 10(2): 108–16.

van Riel, C B & Fombrun, C J 2007, *Essentials of Corporate Communication*, Routledge, Abingdon.

Weber Shandwick 2007, *Safeguarding Reputation Survey*, retrieved from www.webershandwick.com/Default.aspx/Insights/ThoughtLeadership/ResearchInitiatives/SafeguardingReputationSurvey, 13 February 2009.

Wood, D J 1991, 'Corporate Social Performance Revisited', *Academy of Management Review*, 16(4): 691–718.

Chapter 9

STRATEGIES TO PROACTIVELY MANAGE ACTIVITY

Melanie James

Frank, decisive, strategic, and intuitive, Heidi believes it is up to every practitioner to become adept at translating messages.

Developing, protecting and enhancing the brand image and reputation of an organisation requires not only a long-term view but an ability to translate that vision into everyday actions and stories that create clarity and synergy.

Heidi has worked in public relations since 1995 in leadership roles in health, education, and occupational health and safety, as well spending four years as a consultant and coach to the corporate sector. She has a degree in public relations, a graduate diploma, a masters in Professional Communication and is a coach and a neurolinguistic programming practitioner (NLP).

Her passion for continuous learning and communication mastery has fuelled her thirst for best practice. This passion, combined with her technical skills and experience, enable her to assist organisations to deliver high-impact, sustainable business results.

Heidi's advice to new graduates is to:

Work harder on yourself than you do on your job. Your organisation or cause needs you to be a strong, ethical leader. Great professionals don't get there because they are perfect or flawless, they get there because they know their values, strengths and ethics, they stick to them and build on them with gritty determination.

CHAPTER **AIMS**

By the end of this chapter you should be able to:

➤ describe how strategy is an integral part of public relations practice
➤ understand the key concepts of how meaning is constructed in a contested space, intentional representation, and intended meaning
➤ differentiate between functionalist and constructionist approaches to public relations strategy
➤ apply a planning model, from research through to evaluation
➤ develop strategy to achieve specific objectives
➤ describe the major tactics used within public relations and in what settings they might be useful.

Strategy in public relations

This chapter does more than introduce you to public relations strategy and the tactics important to the strategy; it also takes you into the contested space of public relations

Melanie James

practice. It presents the public relations role as one that is highly strategic in the way that communication is planned to support achievement of the organisation's objectives.

When you first encounter some of the language of public relations you might wonder whether you have mistakenly enrolled in military school: words such as 'strategy', 'tactics', and 'target' are commonly used in public relations texts.

While it is simplistic to equate public relations activities to military campaigns, the language used in the field reflects three key concepts in public relations—contested space, intentional representation and intended meaning.

Intentional representation is where we decide how we want the organisation to be perceived and what we would like people to think of when they hear the organisation mentioned. Public relations activities are designed to present this chosen perception, which underpins our work to achieve credible reputations for our organisations.

Not only must the intentional representation be accurate to be effective (that is, it must be real), but it must also survive unscathed when it hits the contested space and seeks to be understood by publics and audiences. This contested space is where meaning is constructed, deconstructed, and reconstructed. Berger (1999: 186) tells us that:

> public relations provides organisations with dynamic and comprehensive methods and processes of intentional representation in contested sites in which information is exchanged, meaning constructed and managed, and consensus, consent, and legitimation gained or lost with others.

Intended meaning, the third key concept, is where the public or audience receives the organisational message and understands the meaning in the way it was intended. With so much competition for audience attention, and so many different frames of reference used by audiences as they construct meaning, successfully landing the intended meaning can be quite a challenge.

Public relations practitioners choose strategies and tactics that they believe will achieve intentional representation and intended meaning. Charities present themselves to potential donors as caring and responsible, computer companies present themselves as innovative. A government initiative to save water will use different strategies and tactics from those used to make a youth festival inviting and worth attending. The strategies and tactics chosen will be the most effective for what it is you intend to achieve, as well as for the publics and audiences you are trying to reach.

Practitioners need to understand what happens in the contested space where public relations operates so they can design activities and campaigns to best achieve their intended outcomes.

REFLECT AND **DISCUSS**

Think about national charitable fundraising campaigns such as the Red Cross and the Salvation Army's Red Shield Appeal. Can you identify the ways that these not-for-profit organisations seek to intentionally represent themselves to the public?

What is strategy?

Strategy is central to the role and function of public relations. The strategic contribution of public relations practitioners develops 'problem-solving strategies for the entire organization' (Newsom, Turk & Kruckeberg 2007: 215) by working with other departments and coordinating problem-solving activities. External public relations activity is undertaken with the strategic intent of gaining some kind of competitive advantage, or to inform and engage with the community, to build reputation, and to achieve positive working relationships.

If a strategy is planned for competitive advantage competitors may not be immediately obvious. If you are promoting a cinema complex, your competitor might seem to be another cinema complex. In fact, the competition is more likely to come from the television or computer in a prospective customer's living room. People are probably not sitting around debating whether to attend one cinema complex or another; more likely they are debating whether to go out at all because the advent of advanced home entertainment systems might make staying home seem like a more desirable option.

Government campaigns urging people to become more active, to lose weight, to vote, or to get their children immunised are designed knowing that people's inertia is the competitor that proves to be most challenging. People's inertia, that is, people's tendency to do nothing or to resist changing their habits, is a major barrier for many such campaigns, even if the advantages of doing what is being promoted are clearly presented.

The spaces where all these campaigns operate are contested spaces. Multiple messages are competing for attention and are viewed in relation to each other. There is competition for attention and there is a strong possibility that the meaning you want to create may be misunderstood. This is where a workable and dynamic public relations strategy can make a difference.

A simple analogy is media strategy. Space for editorial in newspapers is limited—it is a contested space—and many organisations and ideas compete to be picked up and used in journalists' stories. For organisations, the media coverage is important because it puts the message in front of the audience through a credible medium. If, for example, the RSPCA wants people to know about the number of unwanted animals waiting to be adopted, you will use a strategic approach to choose the right media outlets and the right angle to get media interest, and select the appropriate tactics to do so, such as writing style, personal influence, and persuasion so that the public responds to the RSPCA's plea to adopt unwanted pets.

Or if a theatre company's public relations strategy is to develop a better understanding of its new program and its partnership with the Smith Family's Carers' Program, your story will have more success if you write the media release to suit the style of the intended publication—more colloquial language for a street magazine, more formal language for a story pitched to a national daily newspaper.

You might frame your story to best suit a particular journalist's interests. If you know a journalist has been following the career of a certain actor, that journalist would be interested in your story if that actor were in the play. Or perhaps the writer of the play was born in the local area, was supported by the Smith Family, and began a successful acting career as a result: it is an angle you can pitch to a journalist who might otherwise overlook your story.

Interestingly, publishing to the web is not necessarily strategic because the space may not be contested; anyone with the required resources can publish online. More broadly, strategic thinking about the issue will determine whether use of new media has a place in the communication program. What is contested on the web is where your website is listed on major search engines as this can determine whether anyone will ever find and read your information. Many public relations managers invest significant strategic effort into search engine optimisation.

A good working definition of strategy in public relations is this:

Strategy is a plan or method by which you are going to achieve a specific goal in a contested environment.

Every organisation will require a public relations strategy as the basis of its communication programs and plans. Think about a government health department that needs to increase the percentage of children who are fully immunised, or a local theatre company that is trying to achieve a full house for every performance.

The need for public relations strategy is underpinned by goals:

➤ health department goal—to prevent childhood illness through immunisation
➤ local theatre company goal—to be viable.

REFLECT AND DISCUSS

Think about a contentious issue in which public debate is happening or likely to happen, such as the future of Antarctic development. Many different people or organisations would have a view, including national governments, mining companies, environmental organisations, and the tourism industry.

➤ Identify the intentional representation that each organisation would present on this issue.

➤ What goal would each be trying to achieve in relation to the issue?

➤ What messages (intended meanings) would each be trying to communicate?

➤ Develop one strategy that each party could adopt to achieve its intended result.

The space where public relations operates

This contested space is not an easy concept to grasp at first, and in fact does not exist in some models of communication. In transmission (functionalist) models of communication (see Chapter 3), the space that exists between message sender and message receiver is not seen as a place where meaning is negotiated. It is considered to be a gap through which a message, sent by someone, travels until it arrives somewhere and reaches a receiver. There is an assumption that the message will arrive intact and that the meaning will be readily understood by the receiver. With this model, it is also assumed that if awareness of an issue is raised, this will automatically lead to the desired behaviour.

This view, which does not acknowledge the existence of contested space, is slowly losing its dominance as the discourse in public relations.

In contrast, the constructionist approach to communication acknowledges that the construction of meaning is a dynamic process that involves not just a sender but also the intended and unintended audiences, publics, and communities who construct their own meanings from a range of inputs. Constructionism claims that meanings are constructed by human beings as they engage with the world they are interpreting (Crotty 1998). Generation Y, for example, is constructing the meaning of social space on YouTube and MySpace, but it is also finding that meanings change as conflicting views pervade in that space.

This is not to say that the entire world is totally subjective, but constructionism does tell us that there are no universal interpretations; there are instead interpretations that groups of people or communities accept as useful and these stand over interpretations that are judged by people to serve no useful purpose. This aligns with emerging theory in contemporary public relations, in which the concept of publics can best be viewed as 'a continuing process of agreeing on an interpretation because whether a group of people understand that it shares an interest at a particular time determines whether a public exists' (Botan & Taylor 2004).

People receive inputs in the form of messages from an organisation. They may also receive messages from the organisation's competitors, critics, supporters and regulatory bodies. These messages may not just be what the organisation is saying but also what actions it is taking and what expectations it is or is not meeting. Combine these with inputs that people draw from their own experiences and surrounding environment and you can see that many inputs will contribute to the construction of meaning.

Melanie James

REFLECT AND DISCUSS

Imagine you are working for an organisation such as the Australian Red Cross Blood Service and your brief is to encourage more people to become blood donors. Your strategy is to work through community groups so you send a letter to the secretaries of community groups to outline the need for more blood donors. You ask for their support to spread the word and encourage their members to donate blood.

What happens to your intended meaning if the person reading your letter tried to give blood some time ago and found that it really hurt? Or if their neighbour gave blood once and fainted? Perhaps they misheard something on the radio a few years back about people getting diseases from blood donations. Your letter may not deliver your intended outcome and you may never know why, especially if you designed your activities with a transmission-style model of communication. Discuss how you might overcome such barriers in a campaign.

Transmission models of communication assume that the intended audiences, or community members as message receivers, are fairly passive. Whether this was ever the case is debatable but technologies such as the internet, that have only been commonly used in Western countries since the mid 1990s, now require public relations practitioners to assume that intended audiences or publics are anything but passive (for further insight into how online audiences engage with and become the gatekeepers of communication through social media activity, see Chapter 12).

REFLECT AND DISCUSS

Public relations practitioners who work in marketing communication roles in the banking industry have seen a huge change in the approach used to promote home loans to potential customers. Once, the banks held all the information and controlled its flow and access. Now, potential customers are most likely to have done extensive research online before even approaching a bank for a home loan. People have visited blogs and online forums where actual experiences with banks are reported and the possible pitfalls discussed. They have visited educational sites run by governments and consumer groups. This group of people is not passive, but is actively engaged in constructing meaning, deconstructing messages and information, and forming opinions.

➤ What information would a potential loan customer want to find out?
➤ What would be the main factors in choosing which bank to approach?

What public relations strategy can achieve

Public relations works best when it is an integral part of the development of any organisational activity and focused on supporting the achievement of organisational goals. Public relations is more likely to fail when it is *ad hoc* or tacked on at the end of other activity. Relationship management and issues management approaches require a focused program in which strategy is developed, implemented, evaluated, and refined.

Sometimes public relations practitioners play a devil's advocate role or place themselves in the shoes of the organisation's publics or audiences to try to anticipate and alert organisations to possible repercussions of decisions, policies, and actions. By operating in this manner, public relations practitioners bring real value to an organisation. This is often defined as one of the best ways a public relations practitioner can operate strategically, that is, by heading off potential situations that would impact adversely on the organisation, especially in terms of the way it is perceived by its publics.

Developing strategy

In public relations, strategic planning is where you develop a plan in order to achieve a specific public relations goal. The goal may be one that relates to a long-term organisational goal, such as maintaining high levels of community support for an industry over the next five years, or it may relate to a specific campaign with a short timeframe, such as a one-off music festival.

In public relations, the practitioner needs to apply their knowledge and skills to the situation that presents itself. The steps to follow in preparing, implementing, and evaluating a strategic public relations plan are as follows:

1   research
2   analysis
3   goal setting
4   setting objectives
5   identifying publics or audiences
6   developing strategies
7   devising and implementing tactics
8   monitoring
9   evaluation.

Research

If you travelled to a destination in a foreign country without having done any research, you might end up in the right place eventually, or you might not. Either way, you would have wasted time, money, and effort in your struggle to figure things out as you went along. It is the same with public relations strategic planning (see Chapter 5).

Let us take a specific campaign. Assume you are the public relations officer for the RSPCA. Every year the organisation deals with the situation of people giving pets as Christmas presents, only to find them unwanted by the recipient and dumped with the

RSPCA. In planning the program to highlight the issue this year and make people think twice before giving a pet for Christmas, what information do you need to know?

In organisational terms, not only is the return of unwanted pets heartbreaking, but it also puts significant strain on the organisation's resources to feed and house all the animals. If the organisation is unable to feed and house the animals, it faces the prospect of putting down those it cannot keep.

Internal research using organisational records and resources is generally done first. These will tell you whether additional external research is needed.

TABLE **9.1** \ Internal research: the answers are available within the organisation

Question to pose	Why would you ask this?
• Reports of previous Christmas returns. • Is there any socioeconomic data available that tells us who is more likely to return an animal? • When do the returns happen? • Are certain types of animals returned more than others?	• You may have quite recent information on hand. You do not want to waste time doing external research that has already been done. You may want to check the quality of the past research.
• What promotional material has been used in the past? • What tactics have been used? What worked? What didn't? • Are there evaluation reports available?	• On what basis have tactics been selected—past solid research and evaluation or just on a whim?
• Can you identify any potential barriers?	• Does this help to explain why the problem occurs year after year?

TABLE **9.2** \ External research: answers are usually available outside the organisation

Question to pose	Why would you ask this?
• What appeals to people about giving a pet for Christmas? • Who drives the purchase—young children or doting grandparents?	• You need to know why pets continue to be purchased and returned each year. • Why have previous campaigns been unsuccessful?
• What traditional and new media channels are available to you? • What are their deadlines?	• You need to develop an effective communications strategy.
• What other communication channels are available to you?	• Can you utilise existing mailing lists of service organisations? Can you use council rate notices, etc.?
• Has any legislation or regulation changed since the last campaign? Are you still permitted to hang posters in the usual spot?	• No use producing a large banner only to learn that council no longer lets you hang it off your fence.

Source: Melanie James 2008

Some of these questions can be answered by making a few phone calls or through desk research (see Chapter 5 for more on research methods). The first set of questions (Table 9.1) could be answered through a focus group. The time and resources you have available will determine what research can be done.

Analysis

You will need to analyse the results of the research. What is the information telling you that will help you develop the appropriate strategies and tactics? There are many approaches to doing this but one of the popular ways is to undertake a situational analysis and, as part of this, a SWOT analysis. SWOT is an acronym for **s**trengths, **w**eaknesses, **o**pportunities and **t**hreats and offers a way of sorting and evaluating your research results. You're looking to define the situation within which your campaign will be developed, implemented and evaluated. This can also be called an environmental assessment report as you are reporting on both the internal and external environments that could impact on and inform your public relations activities. Environmental scanning has long been seen as an essential first step to developing strategy—the writings on military strategy by Sun Tzu, which date back to the fourth century BC, recommend 'knowing your terrain' (Cleary 2003). Your situational analysis summary might look something like Table 9.3.

TABLE **9.3** \ **The unwanted Christmas pet issue**

Strengths	Weaknesses
• Organisation has a strong track record of caring for animals and providing new homes for pets. • Community response and survey supports the organisation. • Traditionally strong support from the local newspaper, online website active	• People do not consider what is involved in looking after a pet when they make the purchase decision. • Lack of interest in implications of purchase decision.
Opportunities	**Threats**
• Pets are great company, especially for the elderly. • Pets are calming; they are great friends. • Good opportunities for message exposure through various means.	• Busy lifestyles and no time for pets and caring for animals.

Source: Melanie James 2008

Decision making and setting your goal

Experienced practitioners may not consciously think about theory in their practice but their ways of thinking, analytical skills, and decision making have been refined over the years through a combination of theory, experience, and practical knowledge. Beginning practitioners may work alongside people who can look at a situational analysis and see almost instantly what decisions are required and what strategies and tactics are needed. At other times, even the most experienced people need to apply all their efforts to figuring out how to proceed.

One way of approaching this next step is to develop scenarios. Based on your analysis, you develop a range of options that might deliver the desired outcomes for the campaign, such as, in our example, to encourage people to consider their pet purchase carefully. You have no doubt done some similar exercises in other areas of your life. Have you ever thought, 'If I do this, then such and such could happen but if I did that, then something else could result'?

Environmental scanning is important in public relations because by knowing the internal and external environments in which you are operating you can anticipate positive and negative outcomes that could happen in response to certain actions: you will be expected to be able to anticipate what could happen. Your strategies and tactics need to be able to give the best chance possible of meeting the desired outcomes of your organisation or project.

This is often the point of the strategic planning process when the public relations practitioner brings in other people with a stake in the campaign. Who these people will be depends on your organisation but they might include the executive management team, a specific project team, or a steering committee.

Presenting scenarios and your evaluation on how the various situations could unfold enables wider discussions of the pros and cons, and evaluations of risks involved, to take place. Other people may bring new or previously unknown information to the meeting that could impact on the decision-making process. Sometimes it is when everyone brings their own expertise and knowledge to the discussion that new synergies or links emerge and a new or hybrid scenario is proposed.

From these processes, your final campaign goal will emerge, essentially, a broad statement of what you are aiming to achieve. For the RSPCA it might be: To improve the public knowledge and understanding of pet care with a view to encouraging responsible pet ownership.

Setting the objectives and the link to evaluation

Whereas your goal is broad, the objectives you set for your public relations campaign will be specific. The general rule is to set what are known in the popular management literature as SMART objectives—meaning that your objectives should be **s**pecific, **m**easurable, **a**chievable, **r**esults–oriented, and include a **t**imeframe. This approach was originally put forward by management guru Peter Drucker in his book *The Practice of Management* (1954) and it has stood the test of time.

If you apply this approach, you also make the monitoring and evaluation of your campaign or program very straightforward. Setting SMART objectives is one way to ensure that you build in evaluative measures.

Here are two sample objectives:

➤ To have the responsible pet ownership message (specific) available at all (measurable) pet outlets and vet clinics in our catchment (specific and achievable) area during December (timeframe).

➤ To achieve a 50 per cent decrease (measurable, achievable, and results-oriented) in unwanted pets (specific) being returned to us in January (timeframe).

Through having measurable objectives and a timeline for your activities, you can track how the roll-out of your campaign or program is proceeding. Identifying problems as the campaign progresses enables you to intervene and manage them. In the final evaluation, reporting on the degree to which your objectives were met gives you an indication of what was achieved and also provides valuable information to feed into future programs.

Identifying your publics and audiences

The publics and audiences for your campaign are the people with whom a campaign needs to interact. These people may need to be informed, motivated, influenced or persuaded. They will be active in the process of meaning making on the topic you want to communicate about.

For example, the Anti-Cancer Council's SunSmart campaign originally focused on sun lovers because a critical message was to cover up to avoid the risks of direct sunlight and skin cancer. They found that communicating only to sun lovers was too narrow an approach. There is also an important message to communicate to people who cover up too much.

The full range of people the program needs to communicate with includes:

➤ those who are exposed to excessive sun
➤ those who get too little sun
➤ the groups who are affected, perhaps those suffering from skin cancer or from vitamin deficiency
➤ the professional associations supporting and educating the respective groups affected by too little or too much sun.

FIGURE **9.1** \ Planning for a SunSmart campaign

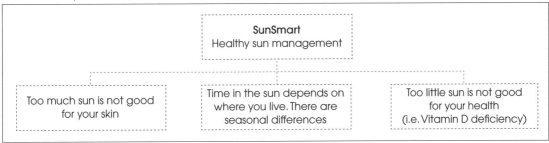

Source: Adapted from Newsom, Turk & Kruckeberg 2007

Setting the strategies

You need to plan your strategies and tactics in ways that will result in your audience constructing only your intended meaning, not other meanings.

You have to think strategically as this is where you encounter the contested space in which all public relations operates. You will be attempting to construct certain meanings within this space and your strategies will aim to intentionally represent your organisation or your offering so that you have the greatest chance of achieving your overall goal. There is no one correct way to develop strategies and as you progress through your studies and career, you will learn other ways to adapt what you are learning here. Ask yourself what seems to have the best likelihood of success based on your scenario planning and identification of the audiences, communities, and publics of the campaign and build your strategies around those. Strategies position the campaign in the contested space and provide an umbrella under which tactics are grouped.

Strategies for the SunSmart campaign group might include:

➤ to partner with other organisations and conduct more general health smart campaigns
➤ to conduct a YouTube sun smart, health smart program for a Generation Y audience.

The main strategy for the unwanted pet issue could be the development of a responsible pet ownership kit that is made available to all outlets where pets are purchased. The kit could contain a pet ownership pledge as well as details on looking after your pet.

Tactics—how you are going to implement the strategies

Tactics—writing, pitching, liaising, arranging, and organising—are how the public relations work gets done and are often seen as the bread and butter skills of public relations. The budget for your public relations activity covers the human, financial, and physical resources needed to implement the tactics, and includes cost estimates for the planned tactics. Often, it is a fine balancing act between the available budget and the strategies that need to be implemented that determines what tactics are finally used.

Outlined below are three categories of tactics that show the range of tools available to you in your public relations practitioner tool box.

Tactics to personally interact with a limited number of people

Personal contact is the most effective way of communicating because it reduces the notion of contested space and allows multiple opportunities for dialogue and feedback. While effective, these opportunities are resource intensive and their use can be limited by physical constraints such as:

➤ the number of people representing your organisation available to interact personally with the community

➤ the number of people who can fit into a venue
➤ the amount of time available within which to interact personally.

Personal contact is most useful when seeking to persuade, influence, engage, convince or win over. These tactics used in public relations to facilitate personal interaction with a limited number of people include:

➤ meetings—one to one, one to several, several to several, and so on
➤ lobbying activities
➤ presentations
➤ small to medium-sized events such as launches, openings, and previews that are planned internally for employees or externally with other organisations
➤ videoconferencing or web meetings
➤ personal correspondence.

An emerging trend among practitioners is to put more available resources into tactics designed for smaller, and in some cases niche, audiences because of the increased effectiveness of these approaches.

When you have completed your situational analysis and examined the available resources you have, you may decide that it would be better to spend your budget on hosting ten influential people at a lunch with your client's CEO than letterbox dropping a flyer to 10 000 homes.

This approach makes sense in a constructionist approach to public relations where you are trying to intentionally represent your organisation or offering in a specific way. With a smaller audience, or for a local community, you can fine tune your tactics based on research findings. You can then tailor your tactics in ways that you ascertain would enable them to construct your intended meaning.

Tactics to interact with large numbers of people

When personal contact is not feasible you need to think differently about how to construct your intended meaning with a large or diverse number of people. The tactics available to practitioners are extensive; selection will be determined not just by suitability but also by the constraints of the project such as budget and available personnel. This list is by no means exhaustive and tactics in this category are only limited by your imagination:

➤ *Printed and digital publications*—annual reports, brochures, flyers, postcards, booklets, posters, fact sheets, websites, newsletters, backgrounders, emails, mass mailouts.
➤ *Media relations*—media releases, media kits, media alerts, media conferences, journalists' tours, and personal contact with editors and journalists.
➤ *Special events*—trade shows, expos, stunts designed to attract broad public or media attention, mass protests and blockades, and events for employees to celebrate their successes.

➤ *Major events*—such as Earth Hour, Biggest Morning Tea, Jeans for Genes Day.
➤ *Created opportunities*—for example, getting your organisation's cause into a soap opera's story line, setting up and maintaining a fascinating blog that generates a committed readership, creating a funny e-Christmas greeting video that ends up being shared worldwide by email or on YouTube.

Directly distributing material or attempting to reach large numbers of people can be expensive and unwieldy. Often you will need to use a conduit to reach intended audiences.

The conduits most frequently used by public relations practitioners to communicate externally from an organisation are the traditional and new media—television, radio, news, business, opinion columns, trade and industry-specific magazines, websites, internet broadcast, and magazines; to communicate internally within an organisation there is the intranet newsletters and meeting face to face. The nature of the conduit can also contribute to the meanings constructed by your audience. Externally, people are more likely to attribute credibility to your story if it appears in what they judge to be credible media.

One of the tools most widely used to convey the organisation's message is the media release. Since the advent of the world wide web in the mid 1990s, corporate websites, chat rooms, email customer response facilities, and electronic news release distribution are now standard online staples of public relations practice (Galloway 2005). Media releases are now used in multiple ways, not just to inform journalists, as they once were, but, through the inclusion of media releases on corporate websites, to provide a record of organisational positions of an array of subject areas, an ongoing history of promotional efforts, and an ongoing narrative of the organisation's activity.

Key points to raise here with regard to media relations (see also Chapter 11) are that while truly newsworthy stories may only need a quick phone call to a journalist to mobilise a full media contingent, many practitioners are not seeking straight news coverage; they work to secure niche coverage in specialist media such as lifestyle magazines, music news websites, newspaper travel liftouts, and more. For these situations, providing a full raft of material to a journalist can assist or even sway them to engage with your public relations efforts.

Even when you are overseeing a genuinely newsworthy story that is almost guaranteed to get media coverage, such as a state election or the appointment of a CEO to a major organisation, having prepared material to give to journalists can assist in having the story covered accurately. This could include:

➤ a folder containing profiles
➤ a CD-ROM with high resolution images of relevant people, logos, or location shots
➤ the latest annual report
➤ other key publications
➤ a background information sheet
➤ a media release.

The kit should be prepared in advance and be available to attending journalists. It can also be sent or emailed to journalists who cannot cover the story in person.

BOX **9.1** \ THE AUSTRALIAN CENSUS

One of the largest communication exercises in Australia is to inform people about the National Census of Population and Housing, which is conducted by the Australian Bureau of Statistics every five years. The exercise usually generates media interest that arises from many angles, such as the large numbers of people needed to work on the census, the fact that every home is involved on one night of the year, and the huge amount of data to be processed. To assist the media to cover the story accurately and help ensure that information reaching households is correct the census communications staff prepare an array of material for the media, including:

➤ background information on why Australia needs a census
➤ information on the history of censuses in Australia and in countries around the world
➤ contact information for media liaison staff around Australia
➤ information on the logistics of conducting the census—tonnes of paper, number of trucks, and so forth
➤ suggested story angles list and timeline of key events around census night
➤ stock video footage and photo CD of images relating to completing the census forms, census collectors in different locations, storage of information
➤ background information on interesting talent for census stories, for example, the oldest census collector, the most remote residents in Australia
➤ prewritten stories that can be adapted for local news
➤ third-party endorsements from users of census data such as health, environmental, and business organisations
➤ celebrity endorsement, particularly endorsement of people from population groups who, traditionally, have been challenging to count in the census, such as youth, Indigenous communities, and people from culturally and linguistically diverse backgrounds.

In addition to these types of resources, various events are scheduled in the lead-up to census night to ensure that the story runs longer in the media, and therefore the necessary information has a better chance of reaching more people. Events can include the launch of the census collector recruitment campaign, the delivery of Australia's first census form, and counting newborns in the census (complete with baby-sized 'I just made the count' T-shirts).

All the events are designed to have people (that is, good talent) available for journalists to speak with and action that news crews can film or photograph. Across Australia, the census invariably gets wide media coverage that plays a vital role in helping inform the population about why and how the census is undertaken.

Source: Australian Bureau of Statistics

Melanie James

Communicating directly with large numbers of people can also be achieved through producing and distributing published material such as brochures, flyers, posters, information sheets, newsletters, and booklets. One of the main challenges in this area is distribution. With today's technology and software programs it is not necessarily difficult or expensive to publish such material but it is vital that this material not be produced in a vacuum. The intended audience must be identified and ways in which the publication will reach these people must be thought through.

It is imperative that tactics such as printed publications are part of the wider strategy to achieve a particular objective and that all costs and logistics involved are considered before production.

Tactics to establish and intentionally represent the organisation within a contested space

This third group of tactics is primarily about how you can represent your organisation through visual means or symbolic capital. Symbolic capital is defined as the investment in symbols and signs that are as important to an organisation as its financial capital (Stanton 2007). These are the signs and symbols that are projected into the contested space where meaning is constructed by internal and external audiences to help the process of creating meaning. The signs and symbols chosen are physical and non-physical and can include:

➤ logos and branding
➤ the quality of paper and stationery
➤ the style of the building or offices
➤ the colour and style of staff uniforms or the fact that there are no uniforms
➤ geographical positioning
➤ virtual and new media positioning, for example, the position on search engine results lists, whether the organisation exists in Second Life
➤ scripts that are followed by staff in their dealings with customers
➤ the model of cars chosen for company representatives.

REFLECT AND DISCUSS

Think about how companies use slogans or taglines to position themselves and help build and consolidate their brand awareness. How many taglines can you think of? Your immediate thought might be Nike's 'Just do it', but can you list ten other company taglines? Can you list fifty?

Consider government-sponsored taglines, such as 'Queensland—Beautiful one day, perfect the next' or '100 per cent pure New Zealand'.

➤ Do you think using taglines is an effective tactic?
➤ What do these taglines achieve?

One example of how meaning was constructed in a way that was never intended by the campaign designers was the classic case of NSWow! Designed to be interpreted as 'New South WOW' it was instead widely interpreted as NSW Ow! It sounded as if the state was in pain. It has been dubbed a 'celebrated failure' and 'the worst campaign that any Government ever ran' (Gibson, in *Hansard*).

➤ Can you think of another instance in which a tagline or slogan has backfired on an organisation?

Corporate and government sponsorship programs are a common way of building symbolic capital for an organisation. The events, organisations, and people that are sponsored by an organisation carry the potential to create all sorts of meanings. Associating your brand with a successful program or athlete, for example, can assist in building your symbolic capital. On the other hand, if the sponsored entity has a fall from grace (imagine your champion athlete is charged with substance abuse or child molestation), then your brand can be severely damaged. This is especially so if the sponsored person has been a visible face for your organisation.

Sponsorship works best when there is a good match between the goals of the sponsoring organisation and those of the sponsored entity. It can fail when an entity is so grateful or desperate for funds that it overlooks the importance of being well matched. If an organisation's goal is to sell cigarettes and a sporting team's goal is to achieve performance excellence, it is hard to see how the sporting team would avoid adverse publicity for accepting tobacco sponsorship.

REFLECT AND DISCUSS

➤ Do you think corporate sponsorship contributes positively to all events?
➤ Should organisations avoid being sponsored by companies that produce products that are known to cause harm, such as gambling or tobacco companies?

Tactics designed to build symbolic capital are notorious for eating up budgets and showing little return on investment unless they are carefully considered and are part of a wider strategy for achieving a specific objective. Developing and managing sponsorship deals is an emerging specialist area of public relations.

Melanie James

Monitoring and evaluation

Monitoring is done during the implementation phase of the public relations program where we are implementing the plan and making things happen. Research at this stage focuses on monitoring the action and implementation of the plan, to check that we are doing what we said we would, and looking for early signs of success or any need to fine-tune or redirect the program (see also Chapter 5).

At the end of the program we want to know whether it worked, whether the strategies and tactics were effective and whether the objectives were achieved. This is where progress against the objectives outlined at the start of the program is reviewed. We have to decide whether sufficient effort has been put into the project and the problem has been resolved, or whether more time and effort need to be invested on it.

In the case of the unwanted Christmas pets two sample objectives were identified:

➤ to have the responsible pet ownership message (specific) available at all (measurable) pet outlets and vet clinics in our catchment (specific and achievable) area during December (timeframe)
➤ to achieve a 50 per cent decrease (measurable, achievable, and results-oriented) in unwanted pets (specific) being returned in January (timeframe).

Now we can find out whether the responsible pet ownership message was effectively distributed to pet stores and vet clinics, and whether there has been a decrease in the numbers of unwanted pets. We will be able to determine whether our main tactic—the responsible pet ownership kit—was utilised: How many were distributed and what response did pet stores receive? Media coverage received will be reviewed to determine whether the message was clear and whether it contributed to the results achieved.

Finally, as the public relations practitioner, you will now have a good grasp of how to run a campaign such as this and a framework for how to do it next year. As you plan the program again next Christmas, you will add additional refinements, perhaps a new strategy, and some new tactics. This becomes an adaptive process of continual improvement and adjustment, based on your research and your understanding of whether the intended meaning has successfully been created.

Being able to adopt a strategic approach is an important skill because it constantly links the public relations programs and thinking back to what is important for the organisation. Reputation and relationship management are built on strategies adopted at all levels within organisations, especially through the communication programs implemented by public relations practitioners.

REFLECT AND **DISCUSS**

➤ Examine a series of public relations case studies, such as those found online in the Golden Target Award database (see Web resources). Look at the case studies' goals, objectives, and communication strategies and identify the links between them. Then read the implementation report on how the selected tactics worked to achieve the desired strategic outcomes. Do the stated results in the evaluation section link directly back to having measurable objectives?

➤ Imagine you need to develop strategies and tactics for a public relations campaign designed to get young people to enrol to vote before the next federal election. Discuss what you think would be the main challenges in engaging young people's interest in such a campaign.

➤ The goal of such a campaign might be to have all eligible people enrolled to vote. Using the SMART approach, write some campaign objectives. Review your efforts to ensure that they are **s**pecific, **m**easurable, **a**chievable, **r**esults-oriented, and that they have a **t**imeframe for completion.

➤ Draft some key strategies that, given your knowledge of young people, might be worth considering. Discuss these strategies and the tactics that would be needed to implement them.

CHAPTER **SUMMARY**

➤ Strategy is a key concept within the public relations field. Practitioners recognise that they are working to create intended meanings in an environment that is a contested space. Often, many others are also working to intentionally represent their organisation's interests and create meaning that may be at odds with your intentions.

➤ Public relations practitioners apply methods and processes of intentional representation in order to try to manage the way publics and audiences construct meaning around a particular topic or issue.

➤ Strategy is developed through analysing the results of thorough research, including scanning the environments internal and external to the organisation. Strategies emerge from the practitioner's assessments as to how best to create intended meanings in a contested space.

➤ Goals and objectives are set to clarify what is trying to be achieved. Objectives are measurable so that campaign monitoring, tracking, and evaluation can take place.

➤ Tactics are selected on the basis that they will be most likely to deliver the intended strategic outcomes, although sometimes constraints such as time, money, and personnel can impact on the selection of tactics.

CASE STUDY \ EDUCATING SCHOOL CHILDREN ABOUT THE CENSUS

The Australia Bureau of Statistics, in a campaign developed by Melanie James, identified a need to educate school-aged children about the census because school children are a conduit to convey general information to their families. Children are often called upon to assist in completing the census, especially to assist parents with disabilities or language or literacy difficulties. The challenge was to find a way to inform Australia's school students about the census and to encourage them to take positive messages about the census into their homes.

The census public relations manager was aware that the strategy of targeting programs at schools was somewhat overused; she also knew that any tactic developed would need to be more interesting, educationally sound, and attention-attracting than the myriad of other project and promotional materials that arrive weekly into schools.

Following a period of intensive research and development, a census CD-ROM, entitled *A Tale of Two Worlds*, that contained educational games for students and excellent resources for teachers, was produced to meet this need. Teachers were engaged to work with the multimedia developers to build the activities and to write lesson plans for various levels of learning.

Focus group testing with teachers and students was conducted at several stages through the development process to monitor reactions and to gather ideas for the fine tuning of the final product.

Copies of *A Tale of Two Worlds* and associated promotional material were sent to all schools in Australia. A support area for teachers and an extended activities area were developed on the website, which was promoted through the media and other resources such as images, editorial copy; line images of the product's characters suitable for colouring competitions were supplied to journalists. It was also promoted through subject-specific teacher associations' publications and conferences.

The product won a number of educational awards and this fact was integrated into the public relations campaign: it was hailed by teachers as an easy to use resource and great fun for students. Because the initiative was based on solid research about what it was that teachers would use in the classroom and on what children enjoyed doing, the CD-ROM had wide take-up in Australian schools.

Read some other case studies that aim to engage school students (see Web resources).

WEB RESOURCES

Apprenticeship or traineeship, at www.lib.uts.edu.au/gta/show.php?id=598.

Case studies and stories from around the world, at http://caseplace.org.

CensusAtSchool program, at www.abs.gov.au/websitedbs/cashome.nsf/Home/Home.

Consumer group-run sites, at (for example) www.consumer.org.nz.

Educational sites run by governments, at (for example) www.fido.gov.au.

Enrol to Vote Week, at www.lib.uts.edu.au/gta/show.php?id=700.

Golden Target Award database, at www.lib.uts.edu.au/gta.

Help to develop SMART objectives, at www.dlsweb.rmit.edu.au/bus/mk100/html/4-smart_examples.html.

Leading Value, at www.leadingvalue.net.

Nuclear Matters in Education, at www.lib.uts.edu.au/gta/show.php?id=698.

Royal Society for the Prevention of Cruelty to Animals (RSPCA), at www.rspca.org.au.

SunSmart campaign, at www.sunsmart.com.au/browse.asp?ContainerID=1917.

Sun Tzu's Art of War Applied to Modern Strategy and Leadership, at www.sonshi.com.

REFERENCES

Berger, B 1999, 'The Halcion Affair: Public Relations and the Construction of Ideological World View' (electronic version)', *Journal of Public Relations Research*, 11(3): 185–203.

Botan, C & Taylor, M 2004, 'Public Relations: State of the Field' (electronic version), *Journal of Communication*, 54(4): 645–61.

Botan, C & Taylor, M 2006, 'Grand Strategy, Strategy and Tactics', in C Botan & V Hazleton (eds), *Public Relations in Public Relations Theory II*, Lawrence Erlbaum, Mahwah.

Cleary, T 2003 (500 BC), 'Preface to *The Art Of War: Complete Texts and Commentaries*, by Sun-Tzu', in *The Art Of War: Complete Texts And Commentaries*, Shambhala, Boston and London.

Crotty, M 1998, *The Foundations of Social Research*, Allen & Unwin, Sydney.

Drucker, P 1954, *The Practice of Management*, Harper, New York.

Galloway, C 2005, 'Cyber-PR and "Dynamic Touch" ', *Public Relations Review*, 31(4): 572–7.

Gibson, P 1993, *Hansard*, 15 September, retrieved from www.parliament.nsw.gov.au/prod/parlment/HansArt.nsf/448b8decbe0283adca2871c1001885bb/ca288d11000bd3aa4a28648d0011875a!OpenDocument, 17 February 2008.

Howell, G, Miller, R & Bridges, N 2006, 'Cardinal Rule of the Media Release—Get Your Facts Straight!' (electronic version), *Asia Pacific Public Relations Journal*, 6(2).

Newsom, D, Turk, J V & Kruckeberg, D 2007, *This is PR*, Allen & Unwin, Sydney.

Stanton, R 2007, *Media Relations,* Oxford University Press, Melbourne.

Chapter **10**

AN ISSUES–CRISIS PERSPECTIVE

Gwyneth Howell

PRACTITIONER PROFILE ANDREW COLLETT

Andrew Collett is Managing Director of Hill & Knowlton Australia. He has more than twelve years' experience in corporate positioning, business-to-business marketing and consumer marketing in the financial services sector. Prior to becoming Managing Director in June 2008, Andrew headed Hill & Knowlton's corporate division and was also appointed Director of Client Services.

Andrew shares his thoughts about working in the PR industry:

> Public relations is a dynamic and exciting profession in which to work. The world of communications is going through a period of great change and PR has a unique opportunity to take the leading role in growing brands and protecting reputation.
>
> Consumers have become a lot more sophisticated, and how they make decisions about brands is much more complicated. The proliferation of media with the advent of social media has led to consumers now being able to access and discuss brands without control. A company no longer owns its brand—the consumer does.

PR has the unique ability to engage a consumer with a brand—whether (that brand) be a product or a company.

What I have loved about working in the industry is the great diversity the profession provides. I have spent more than a decade working in PR consultancies and each day presents new challenges. I have really enjoyed having a portfolio of clients where one minute I am on the phone talking to a journalist about a new product and the next counselling a client on a major issue impacting their brand's reputation. Throughout my career I have worked with some great brands including the Commonwealth Bank, Etihad Airways, Nestlé, BP and Mars.

Having studied PR at university, I was able to gain an understanding of the principles of public relations. While it is a practical profession and much of the learning is undertaken on the job, my degree gave me the opportunity to learn about what PR is, the value of it, how it works with other marketing disciplines and how to approach developing a PR strategy.

It is also important to keep up-to-date with new approaches. PR is constantly evolving, so you should get actively involved in the industry. I am currently President of the Public Relations Institute of Australia (PRIA) in New South Wales and represent New South Wales on the National Board of the PRIA.

CHAPTER **AIMS**

By the end of this chapter, you should be able to:

➤ learn how public relations practitioners respond to and manage issues
➤ explore how proactive issues management can avert a crisis for an organisation
➤ understand the difference between a crisis and an issue
➤ understand the role of public relations practitioners during crisis situations
➤ identify the types of crises organisations can experience
➤ explore how each crisis follows a life cycle
➤ develop an understanding of the impact of new media on issues management and crisis public relations activities.

Introduction

Local, national, and global issues affect every aspect of our lives. Many of these issues not only affect people as individuals, but also the corporations for which people work, the governments we elect, and the multiple groups we are members of. Issues such as global warming, loss of habitat and animal species throughout the world, the ageing population

Gwyneth Howell

in many countries, the war on terror, childhood obesity, waste management in throw-away societies, current farming practices, racial and religious prejudice, excessive alcohol consumption, and the use of child labour have influenced public policy globally. Shifts in public opinion on issues such as these influence how government and business respond, which means that people who feel strongly on an issue and are motivated to take action can quite often bring about change.

Once in the public arena, an issue is typically discussed and debated in traditional and online media forums. Opinions are formed by individuals and groups of like-minded stakeholders joining together to discuss, debate, and engage with the issue. As advocacy groups and key publics affected by an issue attract more participants, the intensity of the debate and the profile of the issue are raised.

Organisations that have a proactive public relations approach recognise the importance to their operational success of sound reputation and community standing, and value the strength of productive relationships with multiple publics and audiences. They also recognise the risks that unmanaged issues could present to these relationships and to their reputation.

This chapter presents the view that issues management requires constant commitment from organisations and public relations practitioners to identify and understand issues, to monitor their growth, and to minimise potential impacts on the organisation.

The links between issues, crises, and public relations management

For an organisation, government, or individual, crises can result when issues are not well managed. Crises are unpredictable events that can impact an organisation's viability, credibility, and reputation. No matter the size of the organisation, history illustrates that crises can and will happen. A study conducted in 2005 (Farmer & Tvedt 2005), identified that 27 per cent of organisations will not be able to recover from a crisis, yet the majority remain unprepared. An organisation's reaction to the crisis, in terms of timing, stakeholder communication, and corporate behaviour, will leave an indelible impression on its publics. The reaction of key publics during the crisis will determine if the company survives and is able to recover.

In April 2006, a mine disaster occurred in Beaconsfield, Tasmania. Of the seventeen people who were in the mine at the time, fourteen escaped immediately following the collapse, one was killed, and the remaining two were freed after two weeks being trapped nearly a kilometre below the surface. The mine had been plagued with problems since 1991, and was closed for eleven months after the disaster. Darby (2006) revealed that a succession of safety failures led to the rock fall that in turn led to the disaster. If these safety issues had been managed correctly and resolved, the entire crisis might have not occurred and loss of life may have been prevented.

Mike Lester from CPR Communications, retained to manage communication throughout the event, relates that the key message that was developed focused on the human element—the spirits of the two trapped miners, their families, and the people of Beaconsfield (ABC Radio National 2006). There were two official spokespeople during the event, the resident manager of the Beaconsfield Mine Joint Venture, Matthew Gill, and Bill Shorten from the Australian Workers' Union. Both were well briefed, credible, and accessible during the two weeks of the rescue. Their responses to media questions typically employed simple language to describe a complex situation. The media were regularly briefed as information became available and the focus from mine management was on the loss of life and human casualties. At no stage were the financial costs of the disaster mentioned.

Public relations practitioners should consider the media's portrayal of events, as they will play a vital role in the organisation's attempt to communicate with their key publics. Given the importance of the media in creating impressions, it is essential to have a cohesive and strategic approach to all organisational communication. Any discrepancy in communication will be exploited by the media. Therefore, strong and effective public relations should occur in a deliberate, precise, and strategic manner. How an organisation undertakes to manage the issues and crises it confronts is a key public relations function, regardless of the size or the industry. Effective online and offline media management is important and online management is on the rise.

The web is an increasingly important component of public relations (see Chapter 12). Organisations use websites to build relationships with publics, and through the web can provide a variety of organisational information and services to a diverse group of stakeholders, audiences, and communities.

The web provides a forum through which information is broadcast around the world by online discussion groups, emails, web logs, and personal and organisational websites. This communication medium creates new challenges for an organisation. The rapidly changing and competitive climates in which companies operate expand the factors to be dealt with. Information technologies, such as webcasting, email, and web logs, add to the level of complexity by changing the communication environment in which public relations practitioners operate.

REFLECT AND **DISCUSS**

There is a range of websites offering information about organisations and individuals all the time. Visit www.truthorfiction.com and http://urbanlegends.about.com. Think about how you would respond if your company appeared in one of these reports.

Gwyneth Howell

Today, the web ensures that information about organisations is instantly available and has become a major tool for emerging issues because it is a communication channel used by individuals who are issues-oriented (Heath 1998). The development of technology and the introduction of new media have amplified the likelihood of the potential for organisations to be subject to damaging information that could create a crisis if not dealt with effectively as an issue. This is because the web is a direct source of rumour content and is a highly successful communication channel for spreading rumours to vast audiences. However, organisations can also use online technologies to quickly disseminate rebuttals (Dr Pepper), corrections (Veuve Clicquot), clarifications (Oracle), and evidence (Ford).

In a climate in which 60 per cent of print journalists report online information with one confirmation and 19 per cent report a rumour directly from a major online source (Middleberg & Ross 2000), the risks incurred by not managing online information are high for public relations practitioners. There are two reasons why negative information that first appears on the web is becoming a problem for many companies. First, because it appears in virtual print, it is deemed to be true (Bordia & DiFonzo 2004). Second, if the mainstream media pick up the story, the information then has an expanded audience (Neil 2000).

Natural disasters such as Hurricane Katrina caused widespread damage, loss of life, and had a huge impact on business operations of organisations located in the path of this destructive event and also those organisations that had business relations with organisations situated in the storm's path. One of the lessons learnt by public relations practitioners who operated in New Orleans during Hurricane Katrina was the importance of setting up online information storage in other parts of the country to enable staff access to company information during and after the event, thereby enabling them to return quickly to productivity after the initial physical damage had been incurred. As most people now rely on the web rather than traditional media for information in times of crisis, your key publics are likely to access it first for information about an event.

Diligence is an essential aspect of effective public relations. Communications strategies will only be successful if all avenues are explored and public relations practitioners are prepared for the unexpected. Effective issues management is based on how rapidly an organisation can respond to and manage an issue, which requires an organisation to act in a proactive manner to best manage potentially damaging situations and issues. A key strategy is to proactively identify and monitor websites that could take an interest in the company's products and services so the organisation can be aware of what is being said and can respond. The web enables customers and stakeholders to be active and selective in their exposure to marketing, advertising, and public relations messages. For public relations practitioners to act effectively on behalf of organisations, they must monitor and track traditional and new media sources for potential issues, and then respond accordingly.

What is issues management?

Issues management is a specific management function that seeks to identify potential, emerging, or actual trends, concerns, or issues likely to affect an organisation and its key publics. Once the issue is identified, the organisation will develop a coordinated response to best manage and influence its progression.

BOX **10.1** \ INSIGHT: LESSON LEARNT

Since the early 1970s, the annual November schoolies phenomenon on the Gold Coast in Queensland has grown to attract 30000 to 50000 young people who are celebrating the end of their high school education. While celebrations occur across Australia, the Gold Coast Schoolies Week (GCSW) receives approximately 80 per cent of all schoolies (Golden Target Awards 2007). Due to the nature of this phenomenon there has been no formal ownership of the event, and, as a result, no management of the issues it generates. In 2006, to take ownership of the event, Surfers Paradise Management appointed a coordinator for the GCSW 2006, and the Gold Coast City Council provided support in the management of the 1200 volunteers (ABC 2006). The primary goal was to improve and enhance community perceptions of the event and positively impact on schoolie behaviour.

The objectives of the communication campaign were to:

➤ improve the proportion of positive media coverage
➤ increase local business satisfaction
➤ increase community involvement with the use of volunteers
➤ ensure schoolies registered for and participated in the safety program.

The central strategy was to position Surfers Paradise Management as the lead organisation on all schoolies issues, establish facts of the event in the media, and provide accurate and consistent information to all media channels throughout the event. It also involved developing a much better relationship with the media covering the event. The results were outstanding: the highest proportion of positive media coverage for the event to date, the largest number of registered schoolies for the event, and the largest number of community volunteers to support the Surfers Paradise Management's program of activities (Golden Target Awards 2007). The campaign received a commendation from the National Golden Target Awards in 2007.

Gwyneth Howell

What is a crisis?

Crises are said to be highly uncertain events in which the causes and effects are unknown. A crisis is a major occurrence with potentially negative outcomes that affect the organisation, company, or industry, as well as its publics, products, and services, and its reputation. Crises interrupt normal business operations and can threaten the existence of the organisation.

BOX **10.2** \ INSIGHT: LESSON LEARNT

Coca-Cola has more than twenty brands of water in over 100 markets around the globe. The launch of Dasani in Britain was intended to challenge the dominance of Europe's bottled water giants, Nestlé and Group Danone. In 2004, Dasani, the tap water bottled by Coca-Cola and marketed as especially pure, was launched and withdrawn from the market within five weeks, after rumours circulated about the product's origins and impurities introduced in the production process. A £7 million public relations campaign was used to launch this product.

The key messages of the product were that:

➤ the water is a purified, still water enhanced with minerals for a pure, fresh taste
➤ the water is produced using a highly sophisticated purification process, based on NASA spacecraft technology (Lawrence 2004).

In the weeks leading up to the launch in February 2004, *The Grocer*, a UK trade magazine, suggested that Dasani brand water was treated tap water from Sidcup (Garrett 2004). This issue was not addressed or managed by Coca-Cola.

By early March, the mainstream media picked up on the story, and reported that Sidcup tap water was being treated, bottled, and sold under the Dasani brand name. Although Coca-Cola never implied that the water was being sourced from a spring or other natural source, a key message used at the launch was that the water was pure, thereby implying that the source was pure or from a natural spring. On 19 March 2004, the product was removed due to contamination after it was announced by the Food Standards Agency that Dasani water contained illegal levels of bromate. Once the information about the contamination appeared in the media, Coca-Cola withdrew its Dasani brand from the market. Regardless of how successful a public relations campaign is, if a product is defective, no public relations can make the product desirable for purchase. For this new brand, there was no established customer loyalty or market share. Poor management of the issue prior to the launch escalated into a full-blown crisis, which ensured that the brand was not relaunched (Garrett 2004).

What is the difference between an issue and a crisis?

An issue arises when there is a gap between what a company does and the key public or audience expectations of the company's behaviour. An excellent example of this is the environmental lobby. In the 1980s, the community at large was not generally concerned about whether products were tested on animals, contained genetically modified ingredients, used sustainable farming, or were dolphin friendly. Today, a vast array of products have key messages such as 'dolphin safe tuna', 'not tested on animals', 'no GM products', 'totally organic', 'no child labour', and 'sustainable farming practices employed'. Each one of these indicates an issue that has grown and developed to the point where organisations have had to adapt and modify their practices. A crisis could occur for an organisation if it ignores the issue or where it promotes a product as 'totally organic' when it is not.

The 2008 documentary titled *Swoosh! Inside Nike* explores Nike's troubled history with labour practices. The film documents the company's activities in the late 1990s, and explores how the company sought to manage the issue. In 2001, Philip Knight, the company's then chairman, in a response to reports that children as young as ten in Pakistan and Cambodia were making shoes, clothing, and footballs, asserted that Nike had only employed children accidentally:

> Of all the issues facing Nike in workplace standards, child labor is the most vexing. Our age standards are the highest in the world: 18 for footwear manufacturing, 16 for apparel and equipment, or local standards whenever they are higher. But in some countries (Bangladesh and Pakistan, for example) those standards are next to impossible to verify, when records of birth do not exist or can be easily forged (Boggan 2001: 5).

Nike continues to face questions about its labour force, particularly in its manufacturing plants in developing countries.

Issues can also be generated and public awareness spiked by organisations who want people to start thinking about and responding to a particular situation. In 2007, the World Wildlife Fund (WWF) sought to raise the awareness of the issue of global warming in a unique way. Earth Hour was a public relations activity designed as a global event to create awareness that, as individuals working together, people could make a positive impact on climate change, no matter who they were or where they lived. Sydney-based public relations consultancy Red Agency was appointed by WWF Australia to manage the public relations for the launch of Earth Hour. This involved increasing awareness about the initiative, gathering support from all types of media, and reaching as many Sydney individuals, households, and businesses as possible using a range of media-based tactics such as a press launch and distribution of media materials. The goals of the event were met (Red Agency 2007) and, building on the pilot program in 2007, the event

Gwyneth Howell

was replicated in over twelve cities worldwide in 2008. The principal aim of Earth Hour was to bring together a diverse group of community, municipal, corporate, and non-government organisations to raise awareness about climate change and to inspire individuals and business to take action to reduce their carbon footprint (World Wildlife Fund 2008).

Issues management in detail

For public relations, issues management focuses on the identification of issues that may affect the organisation, and then the development of a response to best manage the issue. Organisations engaged in socially responsible practice tend to be more successful at anticipating potential public issues and responding to them before the issue becomes politicised (Buchholz 1982). Typically, practitioners need to adopt an assertive and proactive stance in which they seek to meet or exceed public or audience expectations of the organisation's behaviour by developing harmonious relationships with their key publics (Heath 1997), understanding the issues, and recommending organisational adaptation.

According to Heath (1997), there are four key functions in issues management:

1 anticipation and analysis of issues
2 development of the organisational position on the issues
3 identification of the key publics and those whose support is needed for the public policy issues
4 identification of the desired behaviours of the key publics.

Heath (1997) suggests that issues management is a function dedicated to assisting organisations to understand and strategically adapt to their public policy environment. The key role of issues management is to proactively scan, track, and monitor issues. One objective of strategic issues management is to identify, as early as possible, an emerging issue that is promoted by one or more of the key publics. Howard Chase and Barrie Jones (1979) developed an issues management process model to assist practitioners to predict the effect of internal and external environmental changes on the performance of the overall corporate system. This model designates decision-making authority and performance responsibility, and makes possible an objective review and evaluation of issues management performance.

Issue identification

Issue identification involves the organisation deciding whether the issue or concern that exists could affect the organisation's ability to meet its strategic goals. Issues can arise because there are perceived concerns in the marketplace about the company's goods or services, the behaviour of its employees, actions of management, company policies, and even the location of its operations. Concern about the labour practices of multinational organisations, say, appeared as an emerging issue several years before it was linked to Nike. This means that organisations need to keep a watching brief across a broad range of issues and determine whether the issue might have relevance or impact for them.

Issue scanning

Issue scanning has been aided and hindered with the development of online media. It is now much easier for organisations to monitor and scan traditional and online media for content and they have greater access to obscure and niche publications. However, the online environment has also increased the level of coverage that now must be scanned and filtered to measure and gauge potential problems for an organisation.

Issue monitoring

Heath (1997) recommends that an issue should be included in the organisation's issue management system only if it meets the following three criteria:

1 the journalists covering the issue believe it is legitimate and should be discussed in the public arena
2 the issue could either harm the organisation's reputation or operations or benefit the organisation through providing a market advantage
3 the issue is of concern to one or more key publics for the organisation, and the key public has the potential or experience to motivate a legislative agenda.

Heath suggests that once the issue is identified the organisation should undertake to monitor the issue as it develops in the public arena and, if possible, forecast the potential movements and developments of the issue. In Australia the debate about alcohol and sport has been raised in the media in conjunction with the prime minister's announcement of the campaign to alert young people to the dangers of consuming too much alcohol. Alcohol sponsorship of sporting teams and the practice of providing discounted product to young professional players have been raised in media as issues. They present a range of issues for the sporting clubs that rely on the sponsorship to remain financially stable, and issues for the alcohol suppliers, whose products carry the warning notice 'Drink Responsibly', who choose to undertake these sponsorships for product placement in their key markets.

REFLECT AND DISCUSS

You are retained by the Australian Hotels Association (AHA) to manage its media profile in New South Wales, and the New South Wales government has just released the following media statement: 'In an effort to stem a wave of alcohol-related violence on Sydney's streets, authorities will no longer issue twenty-four-hour liquor licences and 50 pubs and clubs will be forced to lock out patrons and serve drinks in plastic glasses.'

➤ Using Heath's four key functions, how would you respond?

Issue analysis

Issue scanning assists in the identification and awareness of the potential issues an organisation may face. Monitoring and analysis of the issue aims to measure the potential financial, social, and political impacts of the issue on the organisation. Consider external factors such as technology and how it could or will change the issue. It is important to consider the best and worst case scenarios for the impact that the issues could have on the organisation and respond accordingly.

There are four key items to consider in writing an issue brief that also provide a useful checklist in issue analysis:

1 Describe the issue and develop a definition.
2 List all publics affected by the issue and whether they are positive or negative.
3 Decide on the possible timing and impact of the issue for the company.
4 Provide the resources to undertake a thorough analysis of the issue (Renfro 1993).

REFLECT AND DISCUSS

You have been approached by the ABC current affairs program the *7:30 Report* to respond on the behalf on the Australian Medical Association (AMA) about the following event: 'The chief executive of McDonald's has just launched National Diabetes Week. The head of the AMA said it was "like inviting Dracula to the opening of a blood bank".'

➤ Using Renfro's checklist, work through all four steps from the perspective of both McDonalds and the AMA.

Crisis management in detail

The key elements in a crisis are:

➤ a crisis must affect the organisation and prevent the company from functioning properly
➤ a crisis will threaten the organisation's reputation and public or audience perceptions of the organisation.

The James Hardie Industries (JHI) case illustrates these two key elements. JHI's core business is the production of fibre cement and other building materials, one of which was asbestos (Jones 2004). In 2002, it was estimated that 7000 Australians had already died from asbestos–related cancers; it is expected that by 2020 there will be 60 000 such deaths. The financial estimates of Australia's total liability for future asbestos claims is about $6 billion.

In 2003, a *Sixty Minutes* report exposed the funding shortfall for the foundation that JHI established to assist those who were affected by asbestos–related disease. Due to public pressure and media scrutiny, the New South Wales government established a special commission of inquiry in 2004 to explore whether victims of asbestos–related disease were disadvantaged when JHI moved its headquarters offshore and made changes to the foundation's funding. The main finding of the special commission of inquiry was that JHI had knowingly underfunded a compensation trust fund established in 2001 to 'limit the assets available to compensate (disease) victims of asbestos products' (NSW Government 2004: 551).

During this crisis, the company experienced a lengthy and damaging public inquiry. JHI shares lost half their face value, and the company experienced boycotts of its products. The company's profitability and financial stability were adversely affected. In late 2007, JHI made an initial payment of A$184.3 million to the newly established Asbestos Injuries Compensation Fund (AICF). The AICF assumed the role of processing asbestos–related personal injury claims made against certain former James Hardie group subsidiaries; the company's ongoing commitment to fund this scheme is over $4 billion. Today the company is now trading strongly and its share value is higher than before the crisis occurred.

William Benoit (1997) suggests that during a crisis 'perceptions are more important than reality' (178). This is important for public relations practitioners because sometimes facts are inconsequential; it is what stakeholders believe that matters.

Types of crises

The first step to responding to a crisis is to identify its type. There is a wide range of crisis typologies that endeavour to differentiate between the kinds of crises that are experienced by organisations. From their research, Thierry Pauchant and Ian Mitroff (1992) found that crises cluster together into five distinct groups. Two dimensions differentiate the clusters: those clusters in the vertical dimension are more technical or economic in nature; those at the bottom of the figure arise more from human or social actions.

FIGURE **10.1** \ Crisis clusters

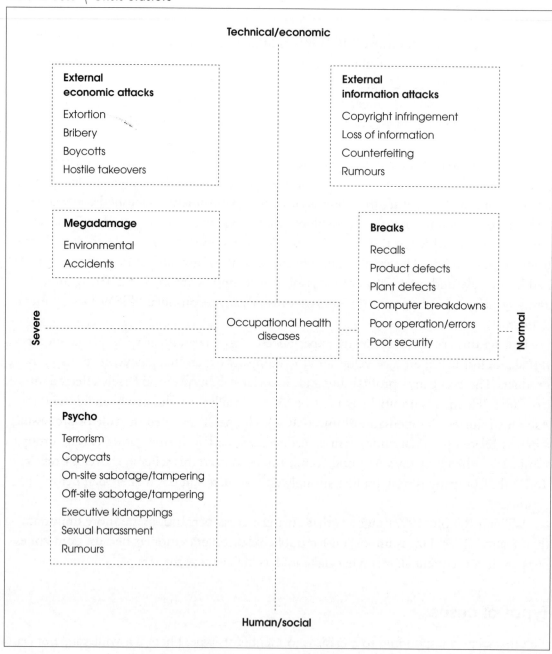

Source: Pauchant & Mitroff 1992: 28

Mitroff and Christine Pearson (1993: 10) established that the array of crises could be limited to a manageable set of 'families'. These types are technical, economic, human, and social. These are consistent with Mitroff and Pauchant's differentiating cluster dimensions.

REFLECT AND DISCUSS

Categorise each of the following crises that received extensive media coverage during and after the event:

➤ Herron paracetamol strychnine poisoning event
➤ 9/11
➤ Barings Bank collapse
➤ Shane Warne SMS sex scandal
➤ ABC Learning Centres placed into receivership
➤ Cyclone Larry
➤ the 2007 worldwide recall of Fisher-Price toys, which represented various Nickelodeon and *Sesame Street* characters.

The life of crises

Researchers have found that crises follow a progression. As marketing researchers used the product life cycle to interpret product and market dynamics, Fink (1986) applied the life cycle model to better understand crisis behaviours. His original model identified four distinct phases of a crisis: prodromal, acute, chronic, and resolution. As reflected in Figure 10.2 (over), Fink's original crisis life cycle was further developed by Mitroff (1996), Fearn-Banks (2007) and others to include an additional and vital (second) phase before the acute crisis stage. This phase, called the probing or preparation phase, has been identified by Alfonso Gonzalez-Herrero and Cornelius Pratt (1996) as the opportunity for 'crisis killing'.

For public relations practitioners, traditional and new media coverage is important as it influences stakeholders' opinions during crises. Figure 10.2 presents the theoretical foundation of the extended crisis life cycle framework and outlines the changing themes in media coverage during a crisis. Each stage of the crisis life cycle contains different themes in media coverage, and each theme exhibits attributes pertinent to the stage to which it is allocated. For practitioners, this life cycle presents a framework of the information the media will seek at each stage of the crisis. Further, the life cycle can inform public relations strategy in terms of the company's response and when data and information should be released.

FIGURE **10.2** \ Crisis life cycle and media coverage over time

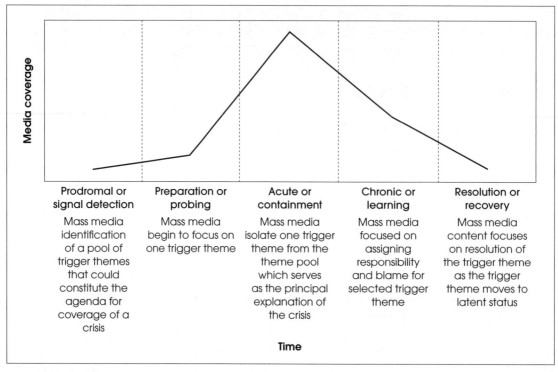

Source: Howell & Miller 2006

Phase 1

Prodromal (Fink and Barton), signal detection (Mitroff), and detection (Fearn-Banks)

The prodromal stage of a crisis is the key in terms of issues management. If an issue is well managed, then crisis strategies will not be required. The first stage of crisis, the detection or the prodromal period, is when organisations experience events that could trigger a crisis. These events are identified as issues that, if managed in a proactive manner, can prevent crisis escalation. If organisations are sensitive to their environment, monitor the media, and explore relevant trends in traditional and new media coverage, they are often better positioned to recognise development of crises, and respond accordingly.

How the issue or potential trigger themes appear in media is the focus for public relations professionals. Typically, issues do not receive indepth analysis or exhaustive scrutiny by the media. They appear in the media as symptoms or precursors to crises, but it is the vital first factor in tracking media content through the crisis lifecycle. If the issue is recognised by the organisation, response strategies can be implemented. Management of the message by public relations professionals can diminish the impact of the impending crisis and lessen the potential impact of the prodromal triggers.

In 2000, a false press release issued by a disgruntled former intern, Mark Jakob, stated that Emulex was restating its earnings, that it faced an US Federal Trade Commission investigation, and had dismissed its chief executive officer. The company lost $2.5 billion in the morning's trade, with most of the damage to the share price evident in the first half hour after the release was issued (Becton & O'Harrow 2000). It took the company more than twenty-four hours to respond to the false media release and reassure the market. Jakob's motivation was a personal profit of $241 000; he claimed he was just recouping $97 000 in losses after selling short. Jakob pleaded guilty to federal securities and wire fraud and is serving fifteen years in prison (Kimmel 2004). Had the company been more proactive in responding to media reports, this situation could have been managed more effectively for the organisation.

Phase 2

Preparation (Barton), probing (Mitroff), prevention (Fearn-Banks)

If organisations undertake to manage issues or trigger themes they can prevent the crisis from progressing, thereby reducing the potential harm and cost to the organisation. The key to crisis management is control of the message. The media's ability to communicate news as soon as it happens has forced organisations to develop crisis strategies that can be implemented quickly. Failure to effectively respond to the crisis can often bring unwanted reactions. Lack of message management by the organisation relinquishes control to the media who will retain control throughout the remainder of the crisis and drive agendas according to specific aims and objectives.

In 2000, traditional media presented a false report about the biscuit manufacturer and retailer Mrs Fields Cookies, in which it said that the company had supplied free products to O J Simpson's celebration party after he was acquitted of murdering his ex-wife. Anti-Simpson websites called for a boycott of the product, which affected company sales. It is interesting that the rumour linking Mrs Fields Cookies to O J Simpson originated in the mainstream media on the television program *Hard Copy*. The rumour gained greater exposure on the web because an anti-Simpson website was used to organise a boycott of the product, which led to a drop in sales (Kimmel 2004).

Phase 3

Acute (Fink), containment (Barton, Mitroff, Fearn-Banks)

This is the shortest and most intense stage of a crisis, when it breaks out of the trigger theme (prodrome) and evolves into an actual crisis. The resulting fiscal, physical, or emotional damage to the organisation and its stakeholders is typically reported in the mass media. Public relations practitioners must prepare to manage mass media coverage that will evolve to extensive discussions on the actual crisis.

The 1989 *Exxon Valdez* oil spill is ranked as the thirtieth worst oil spill in maritime history, yet has the highest profile for an accident of this nature due to the mass media coverage. The organisation failed to adopt an effective crisis public relations campaign immediately after the spill. Exxon provided brief and inaccurate information about the extent of the spill, which led to distrust of the company by the media and influenced the negative perception of the company during the crisis. Furthermore, Exxon did not take responsibility for the spill; rather, the company implicated two of its employees as the reason for the disaster. Today, the *Exxon Valdez* crisis is still cited as the ultimate what not to do of public relations crisis management. A well-prepared and rehearsed crisis public relations strategy would have improved the financial and reputation outcomes for Exxon in relation to this crisis.

Phase 4

Chronic (Fink), learning (Barton, Fearn-Banks, Gonzalez-Herrero & Pratt), damage containment (Mitroff)

During this stage of a crisis, media coverage is driven by criminal and civil charges, government inquiries, litigation, and responses from affected stakeholders. During this post mortem stage it is recommended that the organisation undertakes an audit of the events, activities, mass media coverage of the crisis to date, and seeks to introduce successful management activities and learn from failures. As the effects of crisis can be experienced by organisations for years, management of the message in the media is important as mass media coverage can prolong the effects of the crisis on an organisation. As the crisis will be revisited by mass media during legal proceedings, reminding about trigger themes and revisiting the chronological discussions, public relations practitioners should be prepared to respond to this coverage in a proactive and effective manner.

In 2007, the equine influenza (EI) outbreak in New South Wales threatened the running of the Melbourne Cup and brought the horse racing and breeding industries to a halt in New South Wales and Queensland. The EI outbreak is estimated to have cost the Australian economy up to $1 billion. How government and management bodies reacted to this crisis and their response to the media scrutiny provides an interesting crisis public relations example. Continuing investigations and public hearings into the effect of this crisis have kept this event in the media even though the horse racing industry has recovered and public confidence has returned.

REFLECT AND DISCUSS

Find out what you can about EI and its impact on:

➤ breeders, trainers and owners
➤ racing venues
➤ racing events.

What proactive strategies can you identify that were implemented by each of these stakeholders during the crisis?

Phase 5

Resolution (Fink), recovery (Barton, Mitroff, Fearn-Banks)

In the final stage, media coverage seeks to resolve the trigger theme and summarise how the crisis occurred, who, and/or what was to blame or was responsible for the crisis, and what can be drawn from the events as implications or learning for the future. When organisations are unable to resolve the trigger theme, then the theme moves to latent status and remains there until such time as an event could reactivate the trigger theme and bring it back to prominence. It is in the interest of public relations professionals that trigger themes are not allowed to move to the latent stage because if they do, the potential for a new cycle of damage to the organisation will remain. Crises do not occur in isolation; they occur as one component of the organisational environment. Resolution of trigger themes is directly linked to how management of an organisation manages the crisis; resolution can only be achieved through management action.

Whether you are managing an issue or confronting a crisis, key lessons are that you must:

➤ always put the public first
➤ be honest, do not withhold information from the media or the key publics
➤ establish and maintain strong and effective communication channels with your key publics
➤ prepare information for the media as per the life cycle of the event
➤ be accessible
➤ scan all media—traditional and new—on a regular basis to assess coverage and content of issues and potential triggers
➤ be prepared for the unexpected.

CASE STUDY \ MASTERFOODS PRODUCT RECALL 2005

The MasterFoods case is an interesting example in terms of the life cycle of a crisis. When you read this case, note all the direct types of research the public relations practitioners employed in gathering information about the crisis and how they tested the key messages delivered in the campaign. Practitioners involved in this successful campaign cite research as a key tool in creating that success.

PRODROMAL

On Friday, 8 June 2005, MasterFoods received an anonymous letter claiming that if the demands made in the letter were not met, all Mars and Snickers bars in New South Wales would be poisoned. Included in the package was a Snickers bar that the letter claimed

Gwyneth Howell

was contaminated (Moran 2005a). MasterFoods consulted with the relevant authorities and, with the support of the New South Wales police force and the food safety regulator, the New South Wales Food Authority, MasterFoods elected not to remove its products from the market (New South Wales Food Authority 2005a).

On Friday, 15 June 2005, a second letter from the extortionist arrived at MasterFoods' Ballarat factory. Its contents were similar to those of the first letter. For the second time, in consultation with, and with the support of, the authorities, MasterFoods elected to continue general business operations, as no specific threat was made to the community. MasterFoods and the authorities continued with a low-key investigation to prevent public panic and any copycat extortion bid, be it real or a hoax. The testing of the Snickers bar sent with the first letter remained inconclusive. Later, further testing identified traces of a substance similar to household pesticide in the bar (Safe 2005). The level of contamination was low and provided no health threat to the public.

PREPARATION

MasterFoods instigated the initial activities as outlined in its crisis manual; public relations consultancy Socom undertook the development of generic media releases and prepared question and answer materials should the crisis escalate. But David Hawkins, managing director of Socom, observed a vital flaw in this preparation—MasterFoods had failed to undertake a dummy recall and had not anticipated the behaviour of the New South Wales police force as the crisis unfolded (personal communication, 4 April 2006).

ACUTE

On 1 July 2005, MasterFoods received a third letter. This one claimed that seven contaminated Mars and Snickers bars had been distributed in Sydney (Maley, Needham & Milovanovic 2005). To alert the public of the threat, the New South Wales police called a media conference for 5 p.m. on the same day. The story was leaked to the media; airway coverage commenced from 4.22 p.m.; journalists questioned MasterFoods' motives for not announcing the recall earlier in the day. At the media conference, Andy Weston-Webb, managing director of MasterFoods, announced that the company would begin its recall of Mars and Snickers bars (Sinclair 2005a). The recall of products would require the assistance of 40 000 outlets throughout New South Wales. Between 7 p.m. and 10 p.m. that evening, the MasterFoods crisis hotline received 500 calls; the following day it received 900 calls.

In all, the hotline received over 5300 calls during the crisis from consumers wanting to know what to do with the bars, how to obtain refunds, and complaining of illness (Safe 2005). During the crisis, 158 people complained of illnesses after consuming a Mars or Snickers bar in New South Wales. MasterFoods covered all the medical expenses and Weston-Webb contacted each individual personally (Moran 2005a).

On Saturday, 2 July 2005, Socom released the first of several video news releases that showed the managing director personally removing the recalled products off supermarket shelves. Further, Weston-Webb warned the New South Wales public that 'no one should eat a Mars or Snickers bar that they've bought … it's not safe to eat Mars or Snickers bars' (Weston-Webb, cited in Morri 2005: 2). With the aid of intensive and regular media training (personal communication, 4 April 2006), Weston-Webb was available to media between 6 a.m. and 10 p.m. daily.

The core crisis team established a war room in the offices of MasterFoods' legal organisation, Blake Dawson Waldron, in Sydney (Safe 2005) and held twice-daily teleconferences throughout the crisis, linking MasterFoods operations, especially the Ballarat factory, with the Socom staff in the crisis room, and the logistics staff (Safe 2005).

On Sunday, 3 July 2005, as well as receiving editorial in all major mainstream media publications, MasterFoods produced recall advertisements for broadcast and print media. The cost of publication in the national dailies of the recall letter was A$80 000, but analysis showed that the advertisements were not as effective as the coverage secured by Socom through media releases (personal communication, 4 April 2006).

On Monday, 4 July 2005, Weston-Webb said, 'Nineteen people did call us about feeling ill for a whole variety of reasons—stomach ache, diarrhoea, headaches, vomiting—and two of those visited a hospital but they weren't admitted and I am happy to say they're now back at home' (cited on ABC 2005: 1). Alongside the media relations activities, MasterFoods commenced the collection of the 3 million chocolate bars from 40 000 retail outlets throughout New South Wales (Morri 2005). A team of guardian angels, employees of MasterFoods, was engaged to travel up to 1000 kilometres daily to retrieve the bars in New South Wales (Hawkins, personal communication, 4 April 2006). 'My main concern at the moment is making sure we do this the right way and we protect people,' said Weston-Webb (cited in Bowden 2005).

MasterFoods was questioned and criticised in the media over its delay in recalling the products after the company revealed that it had received two letters in June. Weston-Webb defended the company's procedures and asserted that New South Wales police were contacted on 8 June after the first note and chocolate bar were received. 'This letter was immediately shared with police, who supported our view that there was no risk to the public at that time. For this reason we did not instigate a recall,' Weston-Webb explained (cited in Safe 2005: 19).

On Friday, 8 July 2005, MasterFoods undertook a deep-pit burial of all recalled products at Lucas Height; the video news release and media coverage showed the managing director supervising the burial. Weston-Webb stated: 'We've consulted with the New South Wales health authorities. They're satisfied that this is the best technique' (Weston-Webb, cited in Safe 2005: 20). Socom produced four community service announcements and paid for placement on all commercial television networks to communicate the message relating to the destruction of the product and emphasise how environmentally safe the method of disposal was.

FIGURE **10.3** \ Mars and Snickers bars being buried at a site in Lucas Heights,
8 July 2005

Source: Newspix

CHRONIC

On Tuesday, 12 July 2005, a fourth letter from the extortionist was received. Star City
Casino was identified as the target of the extortion: MasterFoods products were to be
used to extort money from Star City Casino (Kearney 2005). Despite a fifth and sixth final
letter being received in late July, Mars and Snickers bars were back in production on
20 July 2005. Having manufactured and stored the new product in a secure location,
MasterFoods waited for advice from the New South Wales police to determine when the
product would be returned to sale. The threat to the public was deemed negligible, and
so the chocolate bars were returned to the shelves heralded by a state-wide advertising
campaign, 'We're Back', with Weston-Webb as its spokesperson.

On Sunday, 14 August 2005, to promote the 'We're Back' relaunch of the Mars and
Snickers bars, the company distributed free product at locations around New South Wales.

Hawkins suggests that the product giveaways were used as a method of saying thank you to the public for being so patient and supportive (personal communication, April 4 2006; Kelly 2005). On Wednesday, 17 August, MasterFoods announced, with support from appropriate authorities, that products would be returning to retail outlets and were safe and ready for purchase. In conjunction with this announcement, the rollout of the 'We're Back' media and advertising campaign supported the public relations efforts (Sinclair 2005b). Clemenger BBDO, MasterFoods' national advertising agency based in Melbourne, produced television and outdoor advertisements for a national audience, and print and online executions for New South Wales (Sinclair 2005c). On 18 August, the media ran the 'We're back on the shelves' story with a visual of Weston-Webb eating a Mars bar (Safe 2005). The message was clearly conveyed: the product was safe to consume.

RESOLUTION

While the extortionist was never identified, sales of Mars and Snickers bars were 250 per cent higher than average during the product's first week back on New South Wales shelves (Sinclair 2005c: n.p.). Sinclair suggests that these sales figures support the assertion that MasterFoods handled the crisis well by putting public safety first and, as a result, enhanced its products' reputation. However, an analysis of sales figures of Mars and Snickers in 2005 indicates that sales of the products did decline in the last half of 2005 due to the crisis and the product recall. The evaluation and measurement of crisis management outcomes indicate that MasterFoods was successful in its management of the crisis. Various bodies have recognised the success of the campaign internationally with best practice awards, including the International Association of Business Communicators and the Public Relations Institute of Australia.

Some of the reasons for the successful resolution of the MasterFoods case include that throughout the crisis:

➤ MasterFoods was consistent and coherent in its communication; its crisis management plan was guided by the key rules: 'be open, be honest, act quickly and be available' (Socom 2005: 3) with its key publics
➤ throughout the crisis it maintained the same consistent message—public safety was its number one priority.

The overall goal was to 'recall all Mars and Snickers products quickly and safely in New South Wales while protecting the reputation of the company' (Socom 2005: 3).

MasterFoods elected to use only one spokesperson to present the key messages throughout the crisis. Hawkins (personal communication, 4 April 2006) explained that research showed that Weston-Webb was identified as being trustworthy and credible.

CHAPTER **SUMMARY**

➤ Diligence and awareness are essential characteristics of the role as a public relations practitioner.

➤ Issues management is an important component of proactive public relations programs.

➤ Organisations operate in an open environment; they must be responsive to the influences of public opinion and changing societal expectations.

➤ The process of attuning to audience and stakeholder issues and concerns, and being sensitive to the growth of public opinion on an issue of relevance to the organisation, are key functions of the public relations practitioner.

➤ With good management, crisis management may not be needed, which is the aim of many issues management programs—to understand and respond so that issues are managed and risks minimised.

➤ Issues management will contribute to reputation and relationship management.

➤ Issues that escalate towards crises have many opportunities for intervention.

➤ No matter how prepared you are, public relations strategies will only be successful if all avenues are explored and public relations practitioners are prepared for the unexpected.

➤ The most important issue faced by public relations professionals is maintaining control of the message in the public arena.

FURTHER READING

Covello, V T 2004, *Effective Risk Communication*, Springer, New York.

Fearn-Banks, K 2007, *Communications: A Casebook Approach*, 3rd edn, Lawrence Erlbaum, Englewood Cliffs.

Galloway, C & Kwansah-Aidoo, K 2005, *Public Relations Issues and Crisis Management*, Thomson, Melbourne.

Heath, R L 1997, *Strategic Issues Management*, Sage, Thousand Oaks.

Howell, G & Miller, R 2006, 'How the Relationship Between the Crisis Life Cycle and Mass Media Content Can Better Inform Crisis Communication', *PRism* 4(1), retrieved from http://praxis. massey.ac.nz/fileadmin/Praxis/Files/Journal_Files/2006_general/Howell_Miller.pdf, 10 November 2008.

Regester, M & Larkin, J 2004, *Risk Issues and Crisis Management: A Casebook of Best Practice*, 2nd edn, Institute of Public Relations, London.

Newsom, D, Turk, J & Kruckeberg, D 2007, *This is PR: The Realities of Public Relations*, Thomas Wadsworth, Belmont.

WEB RESOURCES

Bernstein Crisis Management, at www.bernsteincrisismanagement.com.

Chartered Institute for Public Relations, at www.cipr.co.uk.

Corporate Reputation Review, at www.palgrave-journals.com/crr/index.html.

International Journal of Strategic Communication, at www.leaonline.com/loi/ijsc.

Issue Management, at www.issuemanagement.org.

Journal of Business Research, at www.elsevier.com/wps/find/journaldescription.cws_
home/505722/description#description.

Journal of Communication Management, at www.emeraldinsight.com/info/journals/jcom/
jcom.jsp.

Journal of Public Relations Research, at www.leaonline.com/loi/jprr.

Management Communication Quarterly, at www.sagepub.co.uk/journal.aspx?pid=105707.

Public Relations Institute of Australia, at www.pria.com.au.

Public Relations Review, at www.sciencedirect.com/science/journal/03638111.

Massey University, at http://praxis.massey.ac.nz/prism_on-line_journ.html.

Sourcewatch, at www.sourcewatch.org/index.php?title=Category:Public_relations_case_studies.

Tourism Victoria, at www.tourism.vic.gov.au/industry-resources/industry-resources/crisis-
management-and-communication.

Truth or Fiction, at www.truthorfiction.com.

Urban Legends, at http://urbanlegends.about.com.

REFERENCES

Arpan, L M & Pompper, D 2003, 'Stormyweather: Testing "Stealing Thunder" as a Crisis Communication Strategy
to Improve Communication Flow Between Organisations and Journalists', *Public Relations Review*,
29(3): 291–308.

Australian Broadcasting Corporation (ABC) 2004, *Lateline*, 'James Hardie Shirking Moral Obligations', transcript
of conversation between G Combet and T Jones (electronic version), 21 July, retrieved from www.abc.
net.au/lateline/content/2004/s1159074.htm, 22 July.

Australian Broadcasting Corporation (ABC) *Premium News* 2005, 'Two Seek Treatment in Chocolate Scare',
retrieved from http://proquest.umi.com.ezproxy.uws.edu.au/pqdweb?index=54&did=862490161&srchM
ode=1&sid=1&Fmt=3&VInst=PROD&VType=PQD&RQT=309&VName=PQD&TS=1153973402&clientId=8429,
18 July 2006.

Australian Broadcasting Corporation (ABC) 2005, *7.30 Report* (transcript), 'Mars, Snickers Threat Aimed at
Unnamed Organisation', 4 July, retrieved from www.abc.net.au/7.30/content/2005/s1406752.htm, 17 July
2006.

Australian Broadcasting Corporation (ABC), Radio National 2006, *The Media Report* (transcript), 'Beaconsfield:
Mining for Heroes' Gold', 11 May, retrieved from www.abc.net.au/rn/mediareport/stories/2006/1635097.
htm, 31 October 2008.

Australian Broadcasting Corporation (ABC) *News on Line* 2006, 'Gold Coast Schoolies Criticised by Alcohol-free Event Organiser', 22 September, retrieved from www.abc.net.au/news/australia/qld/goldc/200609/s1746408.htm, 10 November 2008.

Baker, G F 2001, 'Race and Reputation: Restoring Image Beyond the Crisis', in R L Heath (ed.), *Handbook of Public Relations*, Sage, Thousand Oaks.

Barr, T 2000, *newmedia.com.au*, Allen & Unwin, Sydney.

Barrett, R 2001, 'Ansett's Public Relations', ABC Radio National, *PM* (transcript), 17 April, retrieved from www.abc.net.au/pm/stories/s278468.htm, 7 March 2006.

Barton, L 1993, *Crisis in Organisations: Managing and Communicating in the Heat of Chaos*, South-Western Publishing, Cincinnati.

Becton, N & O'Harrow Jr, R O 2000, 'Arrest in Emulex Hoax Shows Net's Vulnerability', *International Herald Tribune,* 2–3 September: 11.

Benoit, W L 1997, 'Image Repair Discourse and Crisis Communication', *Public Relations Review,* Summer, 23(2): 177–86.

Boggan, S 2001, ' "We Blew It": Nike Admits to Mistakes Over Child Labor', 20 October, retrieved from www.independent.co.uk/news/world/americas/nike-admits-to-mistakes-over-child-labour-631975.html, 16 November 2008.

Bordia, P & DiFonzo, N 2004, 'Problem Solving in Social Interactions on the Internet: Rumor as Social Cognition', *Social Psychology Quarterly,* 67, 33–49.

Buchholz, R A 1992, *Business Environment and Public Policy: Implications for Management,* Prentice Hall, Englewood Cliffs.

Bulik, B S 2000, 'The Brand Police', *Business,* 2 (28 November): 144–55.

Chulov, M & McDonald, A 2005, 'Snickers, Mars in Poison Threat', *Australian: All-Round Country Magazine,* 2 July: 1.

Cincotta, K 2005, 'Less Fluff More Facts, Industry Learns', *B&T: News,* 31 October, retrieved from www.bandt.com.au/news/bd/0c037bbd.asp, 8 May 2006.

Common, G 2005, 'Crisis and Issues Management: Three Recent Examples Show its Impact on Perception and Reputation', *PR Influences,* retrieved from www.prinfluences.com.au/index.php?artId=602, 20 July 2006.

Coombs, W T 1999, *Ongoing Crisis Communication: Planning, Managing, and Responding,* Sage, Thousand Oaks.

Coombs, W T 2004, 'Impact of Past Crises on Current Crisis Communication: Insights from Situational Crisis Communication Theory', *Journal of Business Communication,* 41(3): 265–89.

Coombs, W T & Holladay, S 2002, 'Helping Crisis Managers Protect Reputation Assets: Initial Tests of the Situational Crisis Communication Theory', *Management Communication Quarterly,* 16(2): 165–86, retrieved from ABI/INFORM Global database, 18 July 2006.

Covello, V T, Hyde, R C, Peters, R G & Wojtecki, J G 2000, 'Risk Communication, the West Nile Virus Epidemic, and Bioterrorism: Responding to the Communication Challenges Posed by the Intentional or Unintentional Release of a Pathogen in an Urban Setting', *Journal of Urban Health: Bulletin of the New York Academy of Medicine,* 78(2): 382–91.

Curtin, T, Hayman, D & Husein, N 2005, *Managing a Crisis: A Practical Guide,* John Wiley, Hoboken.

Cutlip, S M, Center, A H & Broom, G M 2006, *Effective Public Relations*, 9th edn, Prentice Hall, Upper Saddle River.

Darby, A 2006, 'A Disaster Waiting to Happen', *Sydney Morning Herald*, 16 May, retrieved from www.smh.com.
au/news/national/a-disaster-waiting-to-happen/2006/05/15/1147545265579.html#, 15 October 2008.

Denton, N 2000, 'How Rumors, Leaks, and News Online have Transformed the Internet's Impact on Business',
Best Practices in Enterprise Content Management White Paper, KM World and Information Today,
retrieved from www.kmworld.com.

Doeg, C 2005, *Crisis Management in the Food and Drinks Industry: Practical Approach*, Springer, New York.

Dr Pepper 2002, 'To Dr Pepper Customers', *Dr Pepper*, retrieved from www.dpsu.com/drpepper_can.html,
26 December 2005.

Fearn-Banks, K 2007, *Communications: A Casebook Approach*, 3rd edn, Lawrence Erlbaum, Englewood Cliffs.

Fernando, A 2005, 'When Rumor Has It (or Not)', *Communication World*, 22(4):10–11.

Fink, S 1986, *Crisis Management: Planning for the Inevitable*, American Management Association, New York.

Garrett, B 2004, 'Coke's Water Bomb', *BBC Money Programme*, retrieved from http://news.bbc.co.uk/1/hi/
business/3809539.stm, 27 May 2008.

Golden Target Awards 2006, *GCSW06 Communication Campaign*, retrieved from www.lib.uts.edu.au/gta/
show.php?id=677, 31 October 2008.

Gonzalez-Herrero, A & Pratt, C B 1996, 'An Integrated Symmetrical Model for Crisis-Communications
Management', *Journal of Public Relations Research*, 8(2): 79–105.

Guth, D & Marsh, C 2005, *Adventures in Public Relations Case Studies and Critical Thinking*, Pearson
Education, Boston.

Hall, A 2005, 'Recalls: How Safe are Your Products?', *Foodbiz*, retrieved from http://foodbiz.net.au/v1i8_
essentials.asp, 10 July 2006.

Heath, R L 1997, *Strategic Issues Management*, Sage, Thousand Oaks.

Heath, R L 1998, 'New Communication Technologies: An Issues Management Point of View', *Public Relations
Review*, Autumn, 24(3): 273–88.

Heath, R L 2001, *Handbook of Public Relations*, Sage, Thousand Oaks.

Hendrix, J 2001, *Public Relations Cases*, 5th edn, Wadsworth, with Thomson Learning, Belmont.

Holloway, P & Betts, J 2005, *A Forethought for Malice*, Freehills Publications, Sydney, retrieved from
www.freehills.com.au/publications/publications_5321.asp, 8 July 2006.

Howell, G & Miller, R 2006, 'The Crisis Life Cycle Model and its Implications for Communication Strategy',
PRism, 4(1): n.p., retrieved from http://praxis.massey.ac.nz/fileadmin/Praxis/Files/Journal_Files/2006_
general/Howell_Miller.pdf, 9 July.

Institute for Public Relations 2006, *Prioritising Stakeholders for Public Relations*, retrieved from
www.instituteforpr.org/pdf/Rawlins_Prioritizing_Stakeholders.pdf, 2 July.

International Association of Business Communicators 2006, 'Winners of IABC's 2006 Gold Quill Awards
Announced', International Association of Business Communicators media release, retrieved from
http://news.iabc.com/index.php?s=press_releases&item=94, 21 August.

Johnson, J & Zawawi, C (eds) 2002, *Public Relations: Theory and Practice*, Allen & Unwin, Sydney.

Jones, B L & Chase, W H 1979, 'Managing Public Policy Issues', *Public Relations Review*, 5(2): 3–23.

Kearney, S 2005, 'July 20 Casino the Prime Target of Mars Bar Extortionist', *Australian*, 20 July: 3.

Kelly, T 2005, 'The Big Idea: There's Life on this Mars', *B&T Magazine*, retrieved from www.bandt.com.au/news/56/0c035b56.asp, 12 July 2006.

Kimmel, A J 2004, *Rumours and Rumour Control: A Manager's Guide to Understanding and Combating Rumours*, Lawrence Erlbaum, Mahwah.

Kumar, S & Budin, E M 2006, 'Prevention and Management of Product Recalls in the Processed Food Industry: A Case Study Based on an Exporter's Perspective', *Technovation*, 26: 739–50.

Lawrence, F 2004, 'Things Get Worse with Coke: Bottled Tap Water Withdrawn after Cancer Scare', *Guardian*, retrieved from www.guardian.co.uk/business/2004/mar/20/medicineandhealth.lifeandhealth, 31 October 2008.

Maley, J, Needham, K & Milovanovic, S 2005, 'Poison Threat Leads to Chocolate Bar Recall, *Age*, 2 July: 3.

Mars 2006, *About Us*, retrieved from www.mars.com/About+us/, 18 August.

Masters, R 2005, 'Product Tampering: The Public's Right to Know vs the Need to Catch an Offender', in C Galloway & K Kwansah-Aidoo (eds), *Public Relations Issues and Crisis Management*, Thomson Social Science Press, Melbourne.

Matera, F & Artigue, R 2000, *Public Relations Campaigns and Techniques: Building Bridges into the Twenty-first Century*, Allyn & Bacon, Boston.

McElreath, M 1997, *Managing Strategic and Ethical Public Relations Campaigns*, 2nd edn, Brown & Benchmark, Dubuque.

Medialink Productions n.d., *Mars Bars and Snickers: Anatomy of a Recall*, retrieved from www.medilink productions.com/casestudies.htm, 10 July 2006.

Michelson, G & Mouly, S 2002, 'You Didn't Hear it from Us But ... : Towards an Understanding of Rumour and Gossip in Organisations', *Australian Journal of Management*, 27 (special issue): 57–65.

Middleberg, D & Ross, S 2000, *The Seventh Annual Middleberg/Ross Survey of Media in the Wired World*, Middleberg Euro RSCG, New York.

Mitroff, I I 1996, *Essential Guide to Managing Corporate Crisis: A Step-by-step*, Oxford University Press, New York.

Mitroff, I I, Shrivastava, P & Udwadie, W A 1987, 'Effective Crisis Management', *Academy of Management Executive*, 1(3): 283–92.

Mitroff, I I & Alpasian, M C 2003, 'Preparing for Evil', *Harvard Business Review*, 81(4): 109–15.

Moran, S 2005a, 'Mars Recall to Cost $2 Million Each Month', *Australian Financial Review*, 5 July: A3.

Moran, S 2005b, 'Nobody Knows the Truffles MasterFoods has Seen, *Australian Financial Review*, 6 September: 61.

Morri, M 2005, 'New Extortion Threat as Poison Found in Chocolate', *Adelaide Advertiser*, 7 July: 29.

Neil, B 2000, 'Crisis Management and the Internet, *Ivey Business Journal*, 64(3): 13.

Newsom, D, Turk, J & Kruckeberg, D 2007, *This is PR: The Realities of Public Relations*, Thomas Wadsworth, Belmont.

New South Wales Government 2004, *Report of the Special Commission of Inquiry Into the Medical Research and Compensation Foundation Volume 1, Part C*, retrieved from www.cabinet.nsw.gov.au/hardie/PartC.pdf, 18 December.

New South Wales Government Food Authority 2005a, 'Food Authority Reminds Retailers that they Must Remove all Mars and Snickers Bars from Shelves', retrieved from www.foodauthority.nsw.gov.au/mr-4-July-05-mars-snickers.htm, 19 August 2006.

New South Wales Government Food Authority 2005b, 'Mars Recall Review', retrieved from www.foodauthority.nsw.gov.au/pdf/the%20food%20chain%20-%20SEPT.pdf#search=%22NSW%20 Government%20recall%20of%20mars%20and%20snickers%22, 19 August 2006.

O'Hagan, J A 2004, 'The Public Relations Target', retrieved from www.bandt.com.au/news/ec/0c0268ec. asp, 10 July 2006.

O'Neil, J 2005, 'Public Relations Educators Access and Report Current Teaching Practices', *Monograph*, 68 (Fall): 1–4.

Olanrian, B A & Williams, D E 2001, 'Anticipatory Model of Crisis Management: A Vigilant Response to Technology Crises', in R L Heath (ed.), *Handbook of Public Relations*, Sage, Thousand Oaks.

Pan, Z & Kosicki, G M 1993, 'Framing Analysis: An Approach to Discourse, *Political Communication,* 10: 55–75.

Patterson, B 2004, 'A Crisis Media Relations Primer', *Public Relations Tactics,* 11(12): 13.

Pauchant, T & Mitroff, I I 1992, *Transforming the Crisis-prone Organisation: Preventing Individual, Organizational, and Environmental Tragedies,* Jossey-Bass, San Francisco.

Retail World 2004, *Retail World 38th Annual Report, Confectionary*, Retail World.

Retail World 2005, *Retail World 39th Annual Report, Confectionary*, Retail World.

Safe, M 2005, 'Bittersweet: Mars Attack', *Weekend Australian Magazine,* 10 September: 18–24.

Saffir, L 2000, *Power Public Relations: How to Master the New PR*, 2nd edn, NTC Business Books, Lincolnwood.

Sinclair, W 2005a, 'MasterFoods Put Public First in Contamination Scare', *B&T Magazine,* 11 July: 3.

Sinclair, W 2005b, 'MasterFoods Puts Public First in Contamination Scare', *Public Relations Institute of Australia: Industry News*, retrieved from www.pria.com.au/news/id/48, 2 July 2006.

Sinclair, W 2005c, 'Mars Unveils Back-to-shelf Strategy', *B&T Magazine*, retrieved from http://bandt.com.au/news/c5/0c035dc5.asp, 2 July 2006.

Socom 2005, 'MasterFoods Mars and Snickers Extortion Threat: June–August 2005', Socom, Melbourne.

Sriramesh, K & Hornaman, L 2006, 'Public Relations as a Profession: An Analysis of Curricular Content in the United States', *Journal of Creative Communication*, 1(2): 155–72.

Stacks, D 2002, *Primer of Public Relations Research*, Guildford Press, New York.

Sturges, D L 1994, 'Communication Through Crisis: A Strategy for Organizational Survival', *Management Communication Quarterly*, 7(3): 297–317.

Red Agency 2007, *The Hour of No Power*, retrieved from www.redagency.com.au/casestudies.php?id=12, 2 November 2008.

Taylor, M & Perry, D C 2005, 'Diffusion of Traditional and New Media Tactics in Crisis Communication', *Public Relations Review*, 31(2): 209–17

Veuve Clicquot 2005, 'Welcome to Veuve Clicquot', *Veuve Clicquot Welcome Page*, retrieved from www.veuve-clicquot.com, 31 January 2006.

Walker, G 1994, 'Communicating Public Relations Research', *Journal of Public Relations Research*, 6(3): 141–61.

Walker, G 1997, 'Public Relations Practitioners' Use of Research, Measurement and Evaluation', *Australian Journal of Communication*, 24(2): 97–113.

Weiner, B 1985, 'An Attribution Theory of Achievement Motivation and Emotion', *Psychological Review*, 92: 548–73.World Wildlife Fund 2008, *Earth Hour*, retrieved from www.worldwildlife.org/sites/earthhour/index.html, 31 October.

Xavier, R, Johnston, K & Patel, A 2004, 'Are We Really Making a Difference? The Gap Between Outcomes and Evaluation Research in Public Relations Campaigns', paper presented at the Australian and New Zealand Communication Association Conference, Sydney, 7–9 July, retrieved from http://conferences.arts.usyd.edu.au/viewabstract.php?id=114&cf=3, 6 July 2006.

Xavier, R, Mehta, A & Gregory, A 2006, 'Evaluation in Use: The Practitioner View of Effective Evaluation', *PRism*, 4(2), retrieved from http://praxis.massey.ac.nz/fileadmin/Praxis/Files/Journal_Files/Evaluation_Issue/XAVIER_ET_AL_ARTICLE.pdf, 6 July.

Chapter **11**

ENGAGING WITH THE MEDIA

Hamish McLean and Richard Phillipps

PRACTITIONER PROFILE REBECCA McCONOCHIE

Rebecca McConochie is the Media and Public Affairs Advisor for Brisbane Airport Corporation Pty Ltd (BAC). She has a Bachelor of Business in Public Relations, and is currently completing her Masters in Governance and Public Policy.

The aviation industry and the business of airports are currently undergoing major change and growth, ensuring Rebecca's day-to-day activities are never the same. Her role encompasses media relations, issues and crisis management, community engagement, and government relations, while working within a Corporate Relations team to protect and improve the company's reputation.

The breadth of activity occurring in this fast-paced environment at Brisbane Airport creates a number of different media opportunities, ranging from promotion of commercial property developments, to educational media campaigns about new security restrictions. BAC's high profile also ensures the company regularly finds it way into the front pages of newspapers in both positive and negative stories. As a result, a major part of Rebecca's media relations role revolves around developing strong relationships with journalists and relevant media outlets to ensure the proactive positioning of the BAC and continuity of corporate messages in the media.

> Relationship-building is key to the community engagement process, which is designed to create open, two-way communication channels with primary stakeholders. It's one of my favourite aspects of the job.

Rebecca oversees the community engagement strategy, which involves a variety of activities from airport tours, to regular newsletters and community forums.

> With the delivery of a $2.5 billion infrastructure program in line with Brisbane Airport's progressive vision to become a dynamic Airport City, this strategy is vital for us to educate and engage the community with developments at the airport.

The issues and crisis management aspect of Rebecca's job means that on any given day, all work may be stopped to deal with potential runway closures, security breaches, traffic incidents and even terrorist issues.

> Due to the high-risk environment and high potential for these incidents to occur, a well-planned crisis management strategy is necessary to ensure a quick and accurate response. It's vital to have clear systems and procedures set up and to follow them at all times.

The variety of the role ensures it is always exciting and satisfying, with strong potential for further diversification of challenges in corporate communications as the company and industry evolves.

CHAPTER **AIMS**

By the end of this chapter, you should be able to:

➤ appreciate the wide range of media available for a campaign
➤ understand the importance of news values and news framing
➤ consider the theories and ethical practices of media relations
➤ write usable news releases and put together media kits
➤ know how to stage a news conference and set up interviews
➤ evaluate campaigns in print and broadcast media.

Introduction

Presenting the public face of an organisation is a key role of the public relations practitioner. Often this is done through achieving media coverage for the organisation. The mass media are important because of their reach, their believability, and their timeliness, although the bombardment of information from them can be overwhelming.

This chapter discusses a wide range of traditional media—newspapers, radio, television, magazines, and newsletters (see Chapter 12 for new media).

The public relations role involves looking for opportunities to publish newsworthy stories about your organisation that will support your objectives—to increase awareness, improve community relations, attract people to an event, even to minimise concern about something that is not working well. In a crisis, you need journalists to be objective. Media strategists are valuable to an organisation because they can anticipate the contested space (see Chapter 9), and can advise on the most effective strategy to achieve the desired media response.

No career path in this fast-evolving world of public and media relations exactly matches another. Some public relations interns have the chance to develop many creative publicity ideas, while others could spend their time on the detail: phoning, emailing, preparing news releases, contacting journalists and editors, arranging interviews, providing background information, meeting deadlines, and monitoring results. Media relations, the cornerstone of most public relations careers, is where public relations practitioners position the organisation as market leader, innovator, or whatever the corporate goal is, and match the image or intentional representation as closely as possible to reality.

Useful theories of communication

It is important to explore theories that can be applied to your work with the media (see also Chapter 3):

➤ *Agenda-setting theorists* claim that journalists and news editors set the agenda for what people think about, not what they think, that is, that the media decide which issues gain prominence in the public mind and which are set aside or buried, but not what people think about them. This theory proposes that people look to the media for direction on what is important and what they should pay attention to.

➤ *Uses and gratifications theorists* downplay media effects in direct contrast to agenda-setting theory. This theory proposes that people have many ways of using the media, many reasons for doing so, and they actively make their own choices to suit their own needs, without being unconsciously influenced to any great extent. Jay Blumler and Elihu Katz (1974) highlighted four areas of gratification: using media for escapism (as in video games), personal relationships as a form of companionship, establishing a sense of personal identity, and surveillance to gain an understanding of the world around them via news and educational material. This theory discounts evidence that the mass media have a strong effect on many people, even with repeated exposures.

➤ *Spiral of silence theory* (Noelle-Neumann 1984) holds that in group discussions, if people think they are in a minority they are less willing to say what they think. This is because of peer pressure or keenness to adopt a consensus view. People go along with what is perceived to be majority thinking for the sake of peace within the group, because they do not want to stand out as being different, or to embarrass themselves. This is similar to the concept of 'groupthink' (see Chapter 3). If the media give the impression that most people are in agreement with a course of action, will people be less willing to say what they really think? The example often used is popular support in the USA for the 1991 Gulf War: did positive media coverage contribute to a spiral of silence that tended to reduce initial opposition to the war? People may be prepared to go along with majority opinion on a minor matter but if an issue surfaces on which they have strong opinions, or on which they are an opinionated discussion leader, they may be more prepared to speak out. An organisation under pressure on an issue needs to find supporters in the media or among the public who are prepared to stand up for what they think is right and are willing to resist this bandwagon effect.

➤ *Two-step flow theory*, first propounded by Lazarsfeld and his colleagues in 1944 (Katz &Lazarsfeld 1955), says that to reach our intended audiences public relations practitioners should first convince the opinion makers the audiences listen to and respect via the mass media they watch, read, and listen to. Put another way, this theory suggests that our publics and audiences gather information from two sources—the mass media, and then, the opinion leaders. People look to opinion leaders to translate, help them interpret the meaning, or guide them what to say and do. Opinion leaders can be quite influential in changing the way people assimilate media information; however, opinion leaders of the twenty-first century may not necessarily pay much attention to the mass media, given that people are engrossed in other pursuits, such as sport or other hobbies, playing computer games, emailing friends and work colleagues, and so on. For public relations practitioners the decline of the mass media in favour of new media helps to reduce the importance of this theory.

➤ *Framing theory* (Tversky & Khaneman 1981) explains that the way something is presented influences how the audience perceives the topic. Framing is where a news story is placed within a specific context that leads us to construct the meaning of that news story within that context. The way in which news is portrayed, including choice of headline in newspapers or the attractiveness or otherwise of a photograph selected for use, or prominence in radio and television bulletins, is a frame created by journalists and subeditors. The choice of language and illustrations used to describe an event are also frames. Public relations media releases frame events in ways favourable to the organisation; as practitioners we frame the story to meet the journalist's criteria of news. If, for example, politicians speak of the war on terrorism they are using framing theory, which employs language, thought, and forethought (Fairhurst & Sarr 1996). Framing is a natural part of human communication, used often in politics, business, and religion. Framing equates to the concept of intentional representation (see Chapter 9).

➤ *Sociological theory and social reality* are an extension of framing theory, which explore, among other things, what is real and what is constructed. Hanah Adoni and Sherrill

Mane (1984), researching with a sample of African American adults, asserted that the reality presented by television is socially constructed. The accepted social tenets of a community, according to these theories, can be a reality constructed in part by advertising, public relations, and the media.

Controlled vs uncontrolled communication

Most media relations work results in uncontrolled communication, in which the public relations practitioner cannot guarantee that the story will be used or in what form. Media relations work has more credibility with the audience precisely because it is uncontrolled.

Controlled communication—a publicity brochure, an annual report, a billboard, an employee magazine, or a shareholder document—is a communication tool that is controlled by the organisation, where total control for the message rests with the public relations practitioner.

REFLECT AND DISCUSS

> ➤ Check whether suburban newspapers in your area offer their major advertisers the opportunity to submit editorial copy for possible use. Does this semi-controlled communication devalue the publication in the eyes of readers? Study your own family and research your neighbours. How many actually read the free newspapers delivered weekly?
> ➤ Research the websites of four major companies in your region that publish an online newsletter. What percentage of stories discuss their firm's success?
> ➤ Do any company newsletter articles cover controversial issues, such as those issues featured on the front pages of daily newspapers? Does the absence or presence of critical and negative news affect their readability?

The foundations of media relations

In this section we discuss some of the basic principles that you need to understand about news and how it is put together.

The important role of gatekeepers

The media gatekeepers are the editors, directors of news, or chiefs of staff who select from among what is on offer—media releases, news tips, letters, emails, web diaries, or blogs—for stories that appeal. The gatekeeper will make a decision on whether to accept or reject your story based on criteria such as:

➤ how interesting it is to the news medium's readers or audience
➤ whether it can be covered; if it is for television, whether it has a visual aspect; if it is a news conference, whether a journalist is available to attend
➤ what the competition is doing; whether this story will be an exclusive
➤ whether it fits in with editorial policy
➤ what the competing news and events are
➤ whether it is more exciting than the news they already have, and if there is space for it.

How journalists in different or even the same media cover one happening or issue will differ widely, depending on the time of day or week, what else is making the news, who is on duty to cover the event, what else is occurring that day, and how much time or space can be freed up for the story.

News values and framing

Each gatekeeper will have different ideas about what are the right news items to select, depending on their news values. Not all journalists and editors will react in the same way to public relations material. Here are a few considerations—news values—they will weigh up:

➤ *Truth*: 'The thought that news reports should be true dawned on journalists only recently. Until well into the twentieth century, most American newspapers [Australian newspapers, too] propagandised on nearly every page' Fuller (2008). Concealing the truth is not an option. Journalists become hostile if you are thought to be withholding information.
➤ *Timeliness*: We expect news to be up to date. Media outlets are in competition with each other to bring the latest news to the public. They do not want old news, or news that someone else has already published.
➤ *Proximity*: The further away from the medium's coverage area an event is, the more earth-shattering and unusual it has to be to make the news.
➤ *Conflict*: Most journalists are taught that conflict makes the news more interesting.
➤ *Eminence and prominence*: Public relations and media relations practitioners aim to boost coverage of a product launch or building opening, for example, through celebrity involvement.
➤ *Consequence and impact*: A tsunami or earthquake is of considerable consequence, but only if it has impact, which means that it affects many people in the region where it occurs.

➤ *Human (or animal) interest*: A dull story, such as information on the effect of rising interest rates and the increase in bankruptcies, can be dramatised by also telling about a family evicted from its home. An article in the *West Australian* (20 December 2008: 72) about the impact of the economic downturn was humanised by relating it to the increasing numbers of dogs being brought to the Dogs' Refuge Home by owners who could no longer afford the expense of keeping them.

➤ *The unusual or remarkable*: There could be something about your company, product, or service that makes it distinctive.

➤ *Fit the focus of each medium*: This news value sounds common sense but is sometimes overlooked by busy media relations staff. Television needs vision, otherwise it is radio without pictures. Financial pages of newspapers need stories involving business and money. Politics at national, state, or local level is an important focus for many daily newspapers, weekly magazines, and radio and television comment programs. Business leaders and politicians become celebrities, the focus of much attention. Women's magazines look for stories of celebrities and their relationships, movie and television stars in particular. Because of longer production times, colour magazines do not often carry up-to-date news of interest to other journalists. But occasionally, one will break a story that generates world headlines, as the example below illustrates.

BOX 11.1 \ PRINCE HARRY POSTED TO AFGHAN WAR ZONE

New Idea website, Australia, January 2008: It took Australian and international journalists a few weeks to realise that the magazine had published the fact that the third in line to the British throne had been posted to an Afghanistan war zone. *Brisbane Times* headline of 29 February 2008 said, '*New Idea* slammed for revealing Prince Harry duty'. The prince wanted to serve the same term as the rest of his unit in dangerous Helmand Province. But he served only ten weeks before he was sent home—he had become a top enemy target.

Pick the right day and hour: How do editors fill a newspaper or broadcast news bulletin if there seems to be just no news about? Slow news days could be a weekend, a public holiday, or a wet sports day when the rain has stopped play. Associated Press (AP) ran a story noting that 'world wide web creator Tim Berners-Lee started a blog just in time for the fifteenth anniversary of his invention'. This lightweight news item got plenty of pick-up (selection by the media as worth using). The fact that this was deemed news in the first place tells us that it was a slow news day and that holidays are a great time to pitch soft news (Dugan 2005).

Media relations strategists also know that if they have a story they must release but want minimal coverage for because it is a bad news story for their organisation, they could try to release it on a day when big events are unfolding, a very busy news time when their story may get overlooked.

Other news values include editors' and readers' fascination with crime, sex, and financial scandals. Motives for homicides are explored—revenge, money, domestic issues, drugs, including alcohol, and racial or sexual vilification. Counteracting this, many editors now realise that too much bad news could be turning away readers, listeners, and viewers. They have begun to reflect on changing reader interests, now emphasising stories about the environment, health, happiness, and spirituality. Stories are often grouped into press lift-out supplements or lifestyle programs on television. These features and programs are well supported by advertisers.

REFLECT AND DISCUSS

Obtain copies of today's major daily newspapers from your region. Compare the front-page items, page 3 stories, business, and sports pages for news values. Do this exercise again in a fortnight, and again in a month to see if the news values have changed.

➤ Record the main television news bulletins on four different channels tonight. Study the first four items and the sports news. Discuss whether television news editors have different sets of news values to those of daily press editors.
➤ List the different news values in order of frequency. Discuss why each editor might have a different view of which values are important.
➤ Research the websites of four major companies in your region that publish their media releases online. Are news values evident in their four latest releases in line with those evident in the daily newspapers?
➤ Decide which of the four companies' news releases match the news values of mass media editors. Which are likely to be published, and where?

The value of media relations

Media releases are the key tool in media relations, but to be effective they must contain real news, not hype. After gatekeepers give them a quick scan, many media releases are consigned to the waste basket because they contain nothing the gatekeeper recognises as newsworthy.

The reality is that the media, to a great extent, rely on public relations practitioners as sources of news. There are fewer resources these days in newsrooms and most journalists have to work quite hard over long hours. Often there is no time for the reporter to go out and chase news in the courts or on the streets.

Public relations people are ready and willing to fill the gaps, as these studies show:

➤ In a US study on newspaper stories on government agencies, Judy VanSlyke Turk (1986) concluded that almost half of the stories about the agencies contained information from a public relations source. Turk's project concentrated on the newspaper-related activities of state government public information officers (PIOs) in Louisiana in 1984.

➤ An Australian study by Jim Macnamara (1993) claimed 'at least 30 per cent of the editorial content of most media—and up to 70 per cent of media content in some small trade, specialist and suburban media—is based substantially or in part on public relations information'. His survey of 417 journalists located in Sydney, Melbourne, Brisbane, and Canberra found more than half admitted to using direct quotes from media releases.

➤ A more recent Australian study by Clara Zawawi (2001) involved the analysis of 1163 articles published by three leading metropolitan newspapers—the *Courier-Mail*, the *Sydney Morning Herald* and the *Age*—to identify the origin of media stories. Her research confirmed the origin of 683 of the articles, of which 251 (37 per cent) resulted directly from public relations activity. Zawawi found that surveys, papers, and submissions sent to journalists with the intent of gaining media coverage could also be regarded as public relations and these accounted for another eighty-eight articles. Zawawi concluded that, in total, 47 per cent of articles in these three capital city dailies were the result of public relations activity.

Is bad news more newsworthy than good?

We tend to think that the media are only interested in bad news, but just how strong is the accent on the negative? Richard Phillipps (2002) assessed a one-week sample of Australian and overseas newspapers, and coded the top ten main stories as positive, negative, or neutral to the person or organisation concerned. The average percentage of positive stories over ten publications for that week was 37 per cent, ranging from 20 per cent for the *Times* of London and 26 per cent for the *Australian*, up to 35 per cent for the *New York Times*, 39 per cent for the *Age*, 40 per cent for the *South China Morning Post* in Hong Kong and the *Sydney Morning Herald*, and 46 per cent for the *Christian Science Monitor*, Boston.

The average percentage of negative stories was much higher: 56 per cent, ranging from 68 per cent for the *Australian* and 61 per cent for the Sydney *Daily Telegraph*, 60 per cent for the *Age*, *South China Morning Post* and the *Observer*, London, 53 per cent for the *Sydney Morning Herald*, and down to 45 per cent for the *New York Times* and 36 per cent for the *Christian Science Monitor*.

A check of political news for the same week revealed an even stronger bias towards the negative: 57 per cent negative political stories, 29 per cent positive, strongest in the

Australian (78 per cent negative, 15 per cent positive), but consistent across all publications except the *South China Morning Post*, where they were balanced with 50 per cent positive and 50 per cent negative. Phillipps concluded that:

> This welter of negative news is likely to drive Australians to even more cynical yet moralistic stances against their politicians, who from time to time display the same human characteristics as the rest of us.

> The figures from this limited sample go a little way towards substantiating political media advisers' claims that journalists tended to seek out negative news (Phillipps 2002: 142).

Where do we get our news?

Those of us who receive our news mainly from established mass media sources may be receiving news and opinion from just a few companies. Ownership of the mass media in Australia, New Zealand, and most countries of the region is restricted to a few big players as outlined below. This does not make it harder to get public relations material published. Ready prepared print and broadcast material on offer from media relations staff at consultancies and companies stands a good chance of being used but only if it fits the news values of the gatekeepers, the editors, and their team.

Singapore: Singapore Press Holdings (SPH) publishes the two dominant flagship daily newspapers, the English-language *Straits Times* and the Chinese-language *Lianhe Zaobao*. It also owns:

- ➤ twelve other newspapers, some English-language, some Chinese, some Malay and one Tamil, with a combined circulation of more than 1 million copies a day
- ➤ two FM radio stations, one Chinese-language, one English
- ➤ ninety or so magazines in Singapore; more than 100, if the region is included
- ➤ 40 per cent of MediaCorp Press, which publishes the free newspaper *Today*
- ➤ 20 per cent of MediaCorp TV Holdings, which operates four free-to-air channels
- ➤ outdoor advertising through the wholly owned SPH MediaBoxOffice, which operates five large LED screens in strategic locations, 400 plasma and LCD screens, and large-format billboards in the heart of the city.

Hong Kong is the headquarters of the Sing Tao News Corporation Ltd, which publishes *Sing Tao Daily*, with its sixteen overseas editions, other newspapers and magazines, including Hong Kong's leading free daily, broadband technology, content and distribution, corporate training and continuing education. Sing Tao also runs book publishing and joint ventures with Chinese government-controlled media companies.

Australia, New Zealand, and the Pacific: In some countries, such as Papua-New Guinea or Fiji, News Corporation dominates the daily press through its ownership of most of the main newspapers. In New Zealand and some states of Australia, the Fairfax company is strong and growing. The Packer group is diversifying out of the media; it seems more interested instead in expanding its gambling interests.

The Australian government has attempted, through Acts of parliament and regulations controlling radio and television, to stop one owner controlling all the daily press, commercial radio, and television in one region. But changes approved by federal parliament in 2006 under the former Howard government look as though the regulations will now allow this. In 2008, Kerry Stokes, who owns Perth's dominant Channel 7, was attempting to win control of the state's major daily, the *West Australian*. By the end of July of that year his Seven Network owned 22.4 per cent of the newspaper's shares and had two representatives on the board of directors.

REFLECT AND DISCUSS

> ➤ Investigate who are the ultimate owners of the main print and broadcast media in your region. Does a web search reveal this?
>
> ➤ If there are only one or two companies with controlling interests in the mass media where you are, is editorial policy similar in each?
>
> ➤ With fewer owners, do you think this makes it easier or harder for public relations practitioners to achieve media coverage?

Convergences are happening fast

The new reality is that public relations professionals do not rely fully on traditional media (see Chapter 12 for a detailed overview of emerging media contexts). In the *PR Week* PR Campaign of the Year 2008: the winner, against stiff competition, was Nintendo's innovative campaign launch of Wii, 'a [video] game for non-gamers' that included a new psychographic for its gaming system. Many different types of media were used but huge press, radio, and television coverage was only a minor part of its success (*PR Week*, 8 March 2008).

GolinHarris, the public relations consultancy involved, decided to make the Wii motion-sensitive controller the feature that made Nintendo's game a stand-out advantage over the popular Sony and Microsoft games.

According to *PR Week* (8 March 2008) Wii's new controller 'makes it possible for anyone to play' so GolinHarris went after the core gaming audience plus 'dabblers, lapsed gamers, and non-gamers', particularly women young and old, and seniors, who in the past have not often played such games.

Hamish McLean and Richard Phillipps

AP was particularly keen to promote the launch because its news is broadcast straight to each Nintendo Wii remote. Players point the remote at a television screen and access the latest news from around the world. The interface on the remote brings up a spinning globe so players are instantly interactive editors, able to select news from Sydney, San Francisco, Shanghai, or Stockholm—almost anywhere it is happening and being reported. This is one example of the remarkable convergence occurring in media relations, marketing and journalism. AP coverage of the midnight launches in New York and Los Angeles was outstanding but the event was also reported extensively on television with fourteen *Today* appearances and a *South Park* skit, as well as plaudits on *Good Morning America*, MTV, and other channels.

Consumers were also targeted on MySpace, where a 'How Wii Play' profile made more than 60 000 'friends', who were also targeted through blogs and an ambassador program to mothers, fathers, grandparents, and mates young and old. The result for Nintendo? 'Wii met or exceeded sales goals, despite early surveys that showed only 11 per cent of consumers intended to purchase it' (*PR Week*, 8 March 2008).

The company shot from being a dismal third in the video game market (behind Microsoft and Sony) to top, outselling Playstation 3 by three to one and Microsoft's Xbox 360 by two to one.

Keys to success

The golden rule for all public relations work, not just media relations, is to under-promise and over-deliver. Over-promising and under-delivering is the best way to lose the confidence and trust of any reporter.

Build relationships with journalists and editors

There are three players in media relations—the media, the client or organisation seeking publicity exposure, and the public relations practitioner.

The media want up-to-date stories and comment from chief executives on the issues of the day. Reporters are mostly short of time and appreciate any help public relations people can give to flesh out a complex story. Unless a very complicated document is being released, the media do not appreciate stories labelled 'embargo' (an announcement with the condition that journalists should not disclose its contents before a certain time).

Clients want media coverage to build their profile and convey organisational news. They can at times have unrealistic expectations based on a poor knowledge of what makes news.

Public relations practitioners match the needs of journalists for news with the needs of organisations for coverage. They clarify the needs and deadlines of each, sorting what is newsworthy from what is not, assessing journalists' profiles to see which ones are interested in developing stories involving their clients' areas of expertise. It is bad practice to hound reporters via phone or email to see if they received a news release or if they are planning to use a client's stories. Such behaviour is a source of much ill-will between journalists and public relations practitioners.

Get to know the journalists

Get to know the journalists who report on areas your organisation is interested in. Face-to-face contacts are much more valuable than those formed via phone or email. If editors know you and what you do, they are much more likely to appreciate you as a news source. Relationships are built up gradually, so keep in touch, follow the careers of the journalists with whom you become acquainted, and always give them good material to work with.

Have up-to-date databases

Up-to-date contact lists are essential. One producer said his pet hate was public relations people who call to speak to a journalist who left five years ago. This is very embarrassing and lacks public relations professionalism. Your news release could get binned just because the address on the envelope is wrong or out of date.

Lists need constant updating because journalists come and go very quickly. Media conglomerates like their staff to have a wide range of experience and shift them around from newsroom to newsroom. Also, editors do not want reporters becoming too friendly with their contacts; an adversarial relationship is encouraged.

Know how newsrooms are organised

Major daily newspapers and capital city television stations will have large editorial teams, including subeditors, reporters, photographers, specialist writers, and commentators; regional newsrooms may have only one or two journalists. In television, subeditors are the producers. With the growth in cross-media ownership it is common for journalists to have to file their stories in different formats to suit several media outlets.

Radio and television channels welcome comments, news tips, and video clips that come to them via the internet. Some journalists issue their email addresses. Editors and subeditors make the decisions about which news tips are followed up and which reporter to assign to stories.

Figure 11.1 (on the next page) demonstrates how the Seven Network solicits feedback and news tips via its website.

FIGURE **11.1** \ How Australia's Seven Network solicits news tips

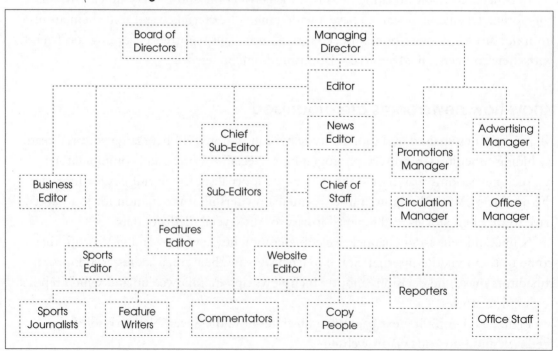

Contact 7 News

Share your views, news, pics and video

At Yahoo!7 News we welcome news story tips from our viewers. Fill in the form below and we will direct it to our newsroom.

We regret we are unable to answer emails personally however if we need your help to follow up a story we will contact you.

* Your name :	
* Your suburb/town :	
* State :	TAS
* Your preferred contact number :	
Your back-up contact number :	
* Your email address :	
* Subject :	
* Your message :	

Would you be willing to appear on Yahoo!7 News? :   No

Please attach your picture or video here :   Choose File   no file selected

Send

Source: http://au.news.yahoo.com/content-upload

FIGURE **11.2** \ How a large newsroom interacts

Board of Directors

Managing Director

Editor

Chief Sub-Editor

News Editor

Advertising Manager

Promotions Manager

Business Editor

Sub-Editors

Chief of Staff

Circulation Manager

Office Manager

Features Editor

Sports Editor

Website Editor

Reporters

Sports Journalists

Feature Writers

Commentators

Copy People

Office Staff

Source: Richard Phillipps

Develop a media strategy

Investigate the story and the proposed outlet to determine which media to target with the story. Does the story match the news values of the media outlet? Tailor your news to suit each medium and each region.

Suppose you are the media relations manager for a big city shopping centre that is about to embark on a major redevelopment. This is important news for the financial pages, even the front pages, of the major daily newspapers and business magazines in your region. Your story will need to cover the following issues:

➤ Who are the financial backers? Can their names be made known at this stage?
➤ Has the proposal received city planning approval?
➤ Who will be the media contacts at state and local government level?
➤ Will you need to organise, publicise, and conduct community meetings?
➤ If competing plazas have redevelopments under way, the media will extend the story to include them. Are they opposing your plans?
➤ What department stores, franchises, and chains are signing up for the complex? How many new specialty shops will there be?
➤ Who can the media turn to for comment?

For television, the cameras need models of the proposal and shots of the complex as it is now. Radio stations will be involved too—they need people to interview, experts to handle talkback sessions and debate. Then there are women's and specialist magazines to cater for at each stage of the redevelopment. Consider the requirements of everything from glossy architectural design journals to fashion magazines, publications for tourists, a host of websites, weekly free suburban newspapers, and community newsletters. Colour magazines need much more notice; check the deadlines of each media outlet.

If there is controversy—objections from neighbours and rival developments, problems with public transport access and car parking, increases in shop rents, political hurdles before approval is given—the story could run over several weeks or months.

Know what is news and what is not

The only good media release is one that is used. 'We throw out 200 times more material than we can publish', claimed *Canberra Times* editor Jack Waterford (Conley 1997). It takes journalists and subeditors only a few seconds to evaluate a news release—they look for who it is from, the headline, and the first sentence. You must have them hooked by then. According to US studies, four news release topics succeed best with editors: coming events, timely issues, interesting research, and consumer information (Guth & Marsh 2000: 276).

Stanton (2007: 81) advises finding 'an angle that localises the issue or event', unless it is a news release from, say, the UN or the World Health Organization about an issue in which the whole world is interested. Here is an example from the Queensland government media release website.

FIGURE **11.3** \ Localising a Queensland news release

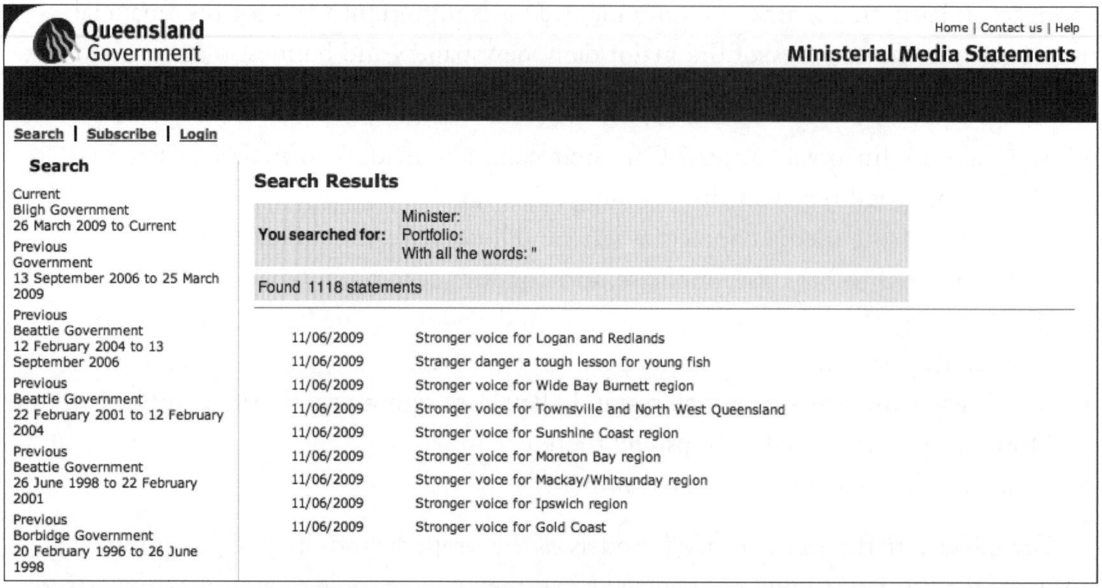

Source: www.cabinet.qld.gov.au/MMS/StatementSearch.aspx

This is a release about community consultation. To increase the proximity news value, the Queensland government's media relations practitioner has localised the release to a particular region or city and provided information relevant to that area while using the framework of a generalised release.

Always meet your deadlines

If you are responding to a media enquiry, make sure you respect the deadline you have been given. If you as a media relations person miss a deadline, you miss an opportunity for your company—and dent your professional credibility.

Tools to attract media attention

Celebrate anniversaries

There is much media mileage to be gained from celebrating noteworthy anniversaries. Companies celebrate staff who have remained loyal for a decade or more; to recognise and appreciate employees is part of good internal communication.

Ten, fifteen, twenty, and twenty-five year anniversaries of an organisation need special planning to make them memorable. With suitable detailed planning and the right amount of excitement generated, plenty of news coverage will flow. Shorter milestones can gain coverage too. The federal Labor government of Australia made a big play of celebrating Prime Minister Kevin Rudd's first 100 days in office early in 2008 by publishing, well before the 4 March date, *First 100 Days* (Australian Government 2008), a forty-page booklet listing eleven of the government's achievements. The event generated much front-page press, as well as first-item radio and television news and commentary.

Writing a really good media release

Keep your release clear and concise. The standard method of writing media releases is the inverted pyramid writing style:

➤ most important news first
➤ background last; the editor should be able to identify the major points of the release by reading the lead or first sentence.

THE TEN COMMANDMENTS OF RELEASE WRITING

1 Headline: do not overplay it, but do not underplay it either; include a verb.

2 Use the active voice with strong, interesting quotes.

3 Have one or two main points of the story in the first sentence.

4 Include the five Ws and an H early in the news release: the **w**ho, **w**hat, **w**hen, **w**here, **w**hy, and **h**ow of the issue or event.

5 Keep it simple—a dozen or so short paragraphs at most, with more information as backgrounders available on request or in the media kit.

6 Standardise dates to the style the outlet uses, most often as in Friday, April 4 2008, or Friday, 4 April 2008. If you refer to 'tomorrow', put in the date.

7 Introduce a new spokesperson before direct quotes; make sure quotes are relevant.

8 Standardise on titles and minimise punctuation, as in: Brisbane Airport Corporation managing director Koen Rooijmans said growth would be addressed through sustainable development. 'This year, Brisbane Airport's focus will shift to efficient energy use,' he said.

9 Localise the release: target the editor's specific audience; address their information needs.

10 Cut out all clichés, jargon, claims of uniqueness, or spectacular success; for most media use common words, not fancy ones, and don't use jargon, except perhaps for trade publications or specialised audiences where jargon is accepted and understood.

Hamish McLean and Richard Phillipps

> Except when writing releases for radio, or for dates and tables, spell out numbers one to nine, then use numerals: 10, 11, 12, and so on. Radio and television news editors spell out everything an announcer might mistake or mispronounce.

Every industry has its own jargon but readers, listeners, and viewers may not be aware of the terms that are commonly used. You will need to translate the information you have been given into words and phrases a reader or viewer would understand.

Make sure you add a headline and a date of issue. Offer a photo or video news clip where possible.

At the end of every release, give your contact details, including email address and daytime and after-hours phone numbers; the release from Bond University in Figure 11.4 shows how it is done.

FIGURE **11.4** \ Bond University news release (for media and public)

For further information or photographs, please contact:
Amanda Elma
Acting Marketing and Communications Manager

Phone: 07 5595 1613
Mobile: 04 2092 7941
Fax: 07 5595 1025
Email: aelma@bond.edu.au

BOND UNIVERSITY NEWS
LATEST NEWS 2009

BOND TO SHINE LIGHT ON FUTURE ICT CAREERS
11 May 2009

Tech enthusiasts eager for a career in Information Communication Technology (ICT) will be given a special insight into the sector's diverse and dynamic world at a free careers day at Bond University tomorrow (Tuesday 12 May).

The **I Choose Technology Conference** will provide students and teachers with exposure to industry leaders experienced in cutting-edge industry elements, including virtual mapping, visual effects, innovative sales and marketing, and artificial intelligence.

Professor Iain Morrison, Head of Bond University's School of Information Technology, said the free seminars will enable students to understand the increasing importance of IT in its everyday applications, its role in the economy, and of the broad range of fulfilling career and employment opportunities enabled by an IT qualification.

'We have over the past few years been hampered in recognising this through historic stereotypes of an "IT" career,' he said.

'The Information Economy is very real and IT career options now range from traditional software design, database and operations through to exciting new areas in Business Intelligence, Media, and Process Automation through Information, Technology and Channel Management.'

The sector can be rewarding in more ways than one, said Professor Morrison.

'The US Government recently predicted looking forward several years that nearly half of all well paid employment opportunities would be in IT.'

Registration for the careers day is at Bond University's Princeton Room at 8.30 a.m. with the seminars starting at 9 a.m.

Mike Jones, an engineer in Google's Sydney Research and Development Centre, will speak at the careers day about what it's like to work at Google, and share some technical information about his specialist area, Google Maps.

Mr Jones will also discuss some significant projects he's been involved with, including Google's Santa Tracker map and Google Australia's Flash map—remarkably developed over one weekend in response to the Victorian bush fires.

Kirsty Garrett, Director of Valintus and chair of the Australian Information Industry Association, said the ICT industry played a major role in the state's economy.

'There's over 7000 registered IT businesses in Queensland,' said Ms Garrett, another guest speaker.

'And there's also a workforce of around 70,000 throughout Queensland that also enables operations to exist in many other areas like mining.

'It's a $29 billion industry for Queensland, and the diversity of roles in IT has changed so much over the last 10 years: it's no longer about programming, bits and bytes and hardwares.

'(IT) is now much more closely aligned with business.'

Professor Morrison said it was difficult to predict key growth areas in ICT, but expected healthcare, community and government service delivery to figure prominently.

Source: www.bond.edu.au

Some classic errors in media releases

Lack of a headline: An obvious error in hindsight, but in the effort to get the text right, the practitioner has forgotten to include a headline. A critical mistake.

No attribution: Any claims in a media release must be attributed to a spokesperson, preferably by name. All media are very reluctant to publish claims that are not substantiated or attributed to someone.

No contact details: Who will the journalist call to follow up the release? Without contact details, preferably twenty-four-hour ones, the opportunity for coverage is wasted—and so is your reputation.

Contacts not available: It can be very frustrating for a journalist to be interested in the topic of the media release only to be told that the spokesperson is not available. Ensure that when the media release is distributed the spokesperson is available for interviews. Make sure your organisation's website has a media contact point.

Not localised: Media outlets like stories from their district so localise your media release to capture the news value of proximity. Rather than issue a media release that has a national focus, localise it to your particular area for a regional outlet.

Illustrate your stories with great photographs

Good photographs and videos can get you and your story on page one, or into the main evening television news bulletins. In the past, newspapers would send a photographer to cover major and minor events; these days the minor events must find their own photographers.

Think outside the box for photograph ideas and look for imaginative ways to portray your subjects. Avoid the same old clichéd scenes of people smiling at the camera, shaking hands, or collecting trophies.

When working with professional photographers, let them choose the best poses for subjects. It is important that, before signing a contract, you clarify whether you are buying worldwide copyright for all photo or video uses, rights for just one use, or for a range of purposes in between. The contract should also set out who is responsible for obtaining clearance from subjects and getting their permission in writing for their photos or vision to be used in the media and company publications.

Pitching your release

Once you have prepared your release you could consider a pitch call, an approach that is usually more successful if you are offering the story to one particular media outlet. The reporter is more likely to be interested in an exclusive story.

Pitch letters or emails and pitch phone calls are made in the hope of convincing an editor or reporter that the story is worth covering because it is newsworthy. Use the one-foot rule that says you should be able to pitch your news item standing on one foot—if your other foot comes down, the pitch is too long (Wilcox & Nolte 1995: 239). You need to get to the point quickly. Offer the evidence that this would make a great story, provide enough facts and story angles, say who the other contacts are and how to reach them, and provide names, phone numbers, email addresses, and website details for extra quotes and statistics.

An emailed pitch, if attractive enough, will produce an instant reply. Keep in mind the volume of emails an editor faces each day. Would a phone call be a better strategy?

News conferences

A media conference can also be effective. Such a conference is a special type of event that needs careful planning. A formal conference should be called for only the most important news. Who is permitted to attend? Certain reporters only, by invitation? Your organisation might need to have security to stop any person who might disrupt proceedings (such as a disgruntled shareholder or an activist) and use the occasion to air their grievances.

We are used to seeing politicians waylaid at the doors of parliament for what is called a doorstop interview. Yet even these can be carefully staged. Former Australian Deputy Prime Minister Tim Fischer, who chaired the rural session of the 2008 Australia 2020 summit, took good care when he was in power to ensure that during these doorstops, the television cameras pictured him against a background of blue sky and gum trees.

Online newsrooms and video news releases

You need a point of contact where journalists can follow up on information twenty-four hours of the day, and these days that place is a media online newsroom on an organisation's website. Media online newsrooms need constant updating—journalists will go there for the latest media release and expect to find it, complete with all the information they need, or someone listed as available on email and phone (with an after-hours or mobile number as well).

Make sure the media section of your organisation's website is easy to access. It must have a prominent link from the home page. As well, journalists appreciate a searchable database of company statements, speeches, media releases, and other key information, as well as short video news releases (VNRs), biographies, and photographs of key personnel.

The Public Relations Society of America (2008) supports the use of VNRs as useful public relations tools if used as follows:

➤ Organisations that produce VNRs should clearly identify the VNR as such and fully disclose who produced and paid for it at the time the VNR is provided to television stations.
➤ The PRSA recommends that organisations that prepare VNRs should not use the word 'reporting' if the narrator is not a reporter.
➤ Use of VNRs or footage provided by sources other than the station or network should be identified as to the source when it is aired by the media outlet.

Offer media kits and case histories

Media kits are packages of information that include everything a reporter needs to know to fill out the story. They could be handed out at a function, mailed out, or offered on CD. Kits usually include some or most of the following:

➤ a covering letter that explains the event or issue
➤ a page of facts about the company, another about the event
➤ background details with more about the organisation and the event
➤ a schedule of future events and who will be involved
➤ maps that show how to get to each event
➤ resumes of the main people and their role in the firm; also photos
➤ a news or feature story, with illustrations or photo opportunity sheet
➤ press clippings about the organisation
➤ product samples (refrain from expensive giveaways)
➤ items such as company caps, key rings, T-shirts, mugs, drink bottles
➤ annual report, poster, brochure, investor newsletter or prospectus
➤ full contact details or business cards for the media relations team.

Media kit items should be packaged for consistency, and branded with the same company colours, logo, and theme. Keep the kits light enough to post or deliver easily, or, if the kits are being handed out at a media event, keep them slim enough to be tucked under one arm.

Train at least one main spokesperson

Media interviews can, at times, be harrowing for the person being interviewed, particularly if that person has had no prior experience of being in the spotlight. Journalists the world over, and particularly in Australia, can be aggressive in pursuit of what they believe is the truth.

The person selected as main media spokesperson needs to be:

➤ media-friendly
➤ well briefed
➤ enthusiastic
➤ cool-headed
➤ familiar with the topic
➤ certain of the objective
➤ able to think quickly
➤ able to act and react calmly.

If the managing director or chief executive does not have the time or inclination to do the required training, then it is likely that that person will not be the best one for the job of media spokesperson. Have one or two back-up people trained and ready for when your main spokesperson is on leave, out of the country, or sick, or for those crises where intensive media attention extends over days and nights or even weeks.

In responding to a question, remember that the grab for television or radio will be no longer than one sentence—that is, about eight to ten seconds. Always avoid yes or no responses because they cannot be used as a grab and a good journalist will then ask 'Why?' to elicit a longer response. Also:

➤ Do not let the journalist put words in your mouth.
➤ The poisoned chalice—is there ever a right answer, when both alternatives in a question are loaded against you? Restate the question in a way that enables you to respond the way you want to.
➤ Hidden agendas—it is wise to check thoroughly (where you have the time to do so) what type of story the reporter is noted for. You might be trapped into defending your company's huge profits and fat executive salaries when the reporter is busy highlighting the injustice of production-line workers with sick families who are on the poverty line.
➤ Questions you regard as private are among the most difficult to avoid. Sticking to your guns and refusing to answer the question may not be viewed by your audience as a fair response. One example of this occurred in 2007 when Queensland Water Commissioner Elizabeth Nosworthy had to announce harsh new water restrictions (at a time when Brisbane dams were down to 16 per cent of capacity): each person on mains water was expected to keep consumption below 140 litres a day. Nosworthy refused to state what her own consumption was and incurred severe media criticism as a result.
➤ The 'What if …?' question: hypotheticals are best rejected as they are asking the person interviewed to foretell the future. Rephrase the question in a positive way.

Minimising media attention

So far efforts to make sure your news is covered extensively, thoroughly, and fairly in the mass media have been discussed. But what if your organisation does not want a topic covered, or wants to delay coverage? Media advisers to politicians, for instance, all rehearse strategies for containing bad news; sometimes they work, at other times, harm can be minimised (Phillipps 2002). If something bad happens and the media get wind of it, advisers will usually tell their ministers to get the story out of the way as quickly as possible:

> One example of a bad-news story was the news that the Royal Commission into the Hindmarsh Bridge was greatly exceeding its budget of $1 million. It needed another $800 000. The *Adelaide Advertiser* reporter who got hold of the story was a former media secretary with the government. We agreed to give them an exclusive on the story but were able to attach certain conditions (South Australian government adviser Lisa Brett, in Phillipps 2002: 121).

Other local and interstate media outlets did follow up the story next day but it died quickly. Another tactic to deflect a bad-news story is to question the facts: 'Are you sure you've got it right?', or promise a tip for a better story.

'Reporters "fall in love" with their bad-news stories. Attempts to deflect them with factual information or even bad-news tips about the opposition are not enough to break off this hot pursuit,' says Phillipps (2002). 'Their minds seem made up before they have even checked with sources, perhaps relying on hearsay,' one Canberra ministerial media adviser told him. 'They can't admit that sometimes there's no story.'

Sanctions such as refusal to talk to reporters or black bans of the entire media outlet have been applied by some irate Australian politicians on occasion but, through intervention of the media adviser, are usually lifted after a time.

What to do if you are not getting a fair go

If a media outlet has used your material and got it wrong, first consider whether it is worth complaining. If it is a minor error, usually the best course of action is to overlook it. But as the public has a right to correct information about your organisation, your company website could be used to highlight the inaccuracy.

Most media relations experts say the best strategy when the media get a story wrong is to phone the journalist first, then, if it becomes necessary, the editor. Some reporters are willing to correct an error. Often this will not be forthcoming. Do not get upset over this or threaten retribution. There will be an occasion in the future when you can set the record straight. You need to stay on speaking terms with the editor concerned.

Former Australian Prime Minister Paul Keating has been accused of conducting 'lengthy, abusive, direct telephone calls to journalists who had crossed him, [also] calls to management to damage the careers of individual journalists' (Walsh 1995: 286).

A short letter to the editor explaining the error sometimes works. Some newspapers have a corner of the publication where errors are listed and corrected; on radio and television, the host of the program on which the error occurred usually announces the apology.

Other avenues open in the more serious cases where the media have injured you or your organisation are appeals to such bodies as the Australian Broadcasting Authority, the Australian Press Council, or the Media Entertainment and Arts Alliance (MEAA).

Your company could take out paid display advertisements to correct an imposition by the media, or insert a paid public notice in the classified advertising columns. Only as a last resort should you decide to take the media outlet to court. You need a very strong case to do this, and if you have a strong case it should be possible to obtain a correction in other less costly ways. The new defamation laws, uniform across all Australian states and territories, now include alternative dispute resolution procedures (Pearson 2007: 242).

Legal and ethical issues

Public relations practitioners need to take special care when dealing with confidential information. If you know that some client information is confidential, do not mention any of it to a journalist. They understand when a matter is on the record, because all information can be quoted and attributed to the spokesperson.

But there are issues with claiming that a matter is off the record; the term can have different meanings for journalists (Pearson 2007: 299). While one may regard it as 'The spokesperson cannot be named, but the information can be used', another may regard all off-the-record information as not for publication.

Off the record also poses problems for confidential sources: there are no shield laws to protect them if the source becomes known. The MEAA has a code of ethics that offers some protection to sources, if journalists decide to abide by it. Courts have sent journalists to jail for not revealing their sources. On the other hand, there have been cases in which the reporter has decided it is important to reveal his or her source. 'Guidance' is a term that is used in the United Kingdom to indicate that the material provided by a spokesperson can be used but not attributed to a person or organisation. Often a journalist will simply attribute the information to 'sources'.

Defamation—watch what you say or write

Be aware that whatever we write or say about someone else, or about a group of people, can result in a legal action known as 'defamation' if the subject believes they have been injured by what has been said or written. Defamation law sets out to balance two competing interests—the protection of free speech and the protection of reputations. In media relations, defamation can arise in many aspects of the role, such as a media release, responding to a question from a journalist during a media conference or even in a letter to the editor, whether or not it has been published. State-based defamation laws across Australia are uniform, which means that what is defamatory in one state or territory, is likely to be in another. Defamation is a tort, or civil matter, between two parties—the plaintiff, who is the person taking the action, and the defendant, the person being sued. There is also provision in criminal law for defamation; however, it is rarely prosecuted. Although a very complex area of civil law, in simple terms defamation has three key components:

1   *Defamatory material*: Communication to a third person is essential for defamation. A person's reputation cannot be damaged by statements made directly to that person. Any words, written or spoken, that damage a person's reputation could be held to be defamatory. Pearson (2007) points out that defamation law is all about imputations, the 'defamatory meaning of the words' (184). The damaging material does not need to be in black and white. Innuendo—reading between the lines—can also harm someone's reputation.

2   *Identify the person being defamed*: It is a grave mistake to assume you cannot be held liable for defamation just because you did not name the person involved. If plaintiffs can show that they are the subject of the material, then an action against you could proceed. Revelation of a person's identity can involve a description of what the person was wearing, their location, or any other detail that can identify them.

3   *Publication*: Another fallacy is that you can be sued only if the defamatory material is published in the media to a large audience. In fact, as Pearson (2007) points out, the plaintiff needs only to prove the material was published to another person. Thus, a media release containing defamatory material that is sent to a journalist can result in a defamation action even if it is not published by the media outlet.

Copyright

Copyright, which has a legal effect on the use of material without permission, must be considered in public relations. The *Copyright Act 1968* (Cth) generally protects the work of an author for seventy years after death. Copyright is automatic and damages can be awarded against anyone who uses material without permission. An example could be the use of copyrighted visual material as part of a video news release or using video or other material from the internet without the permission of the copyright owner, who is usually the author (text), or illustrator (artwork), photographer or filmmaker, or composer of the material.

Other legal issues

Other areas of law that can impact on media relations practitioners include negligence, which arises when the practitioner fails to exercise reasonable care in giving advice to or working on behalf of a client. Practitioners should also consider section 52 of the *Trade Practices Act 1974* (Cth), which provides penalties for misleading and deceptive conduct, such as making false or misleading claims in a media release.

Media relations has moral and ethical aspects

Investigate the codes of conduct for Public Relations Institute of Australia (see Chapter 4) and International Association of Business Communicators members in your country; also read the radio and television industry codes of practice. Some aspects of the Public Relations Institute of Australia code of ethics are contradictory, for instance, there is an obligation to keep client information confidential but there is also an obligation to reveal to the media on whose behalf releases are being issued (see Chapter 4 for the wider ethics perspectives).

Privacy considerations

There is no general right to privacy in Australia but the expectation of private citizens for reasonable exemption from media intrusion must be respected. Media relations people need to ensure that permission forms are completed and signed by people appearing in media materials, such as photographs supplied to newspapers and magazines, and vision for television channels and world wide web outlets.

Evaluate your efforts

The reason that we undertake media relations is to provide information about our organisation as part of the process of building reputation and relationships. The media are regarded as a credible third party and articles in the media are often seen by large audiences who rely on the media for their news and information.

You may have heard the expression 'Any publicity is good publicity', but this is not sufficient for evaluation of professional practice. Although no public relations practitioner is in a position to guarantee coverage in the mass media, over which they have no control, clients are entitled to expect a return on their investment.

Our efforts are evaluated during a campaign and at the end of a campaign (see Chapter 5). Media monitoring companies provide a useful service because they can not only tell you what coverage you received, but they also analyse the coverage on aspects such as:

➤ audience reach
➤ placement of the message, whether it was front page, a lead story, or hidden away
➤ whether the source was clear
➤ whether the organisation that was being promoted actually received a mention or merely a passing comment amid an array of points on several organisations
➤ how the message was portrayed as positive, negative, or neutral
➤ who was quoted
➤ whether your organisation's messages were clear or confused with other messages.

You are particularly interested to see whether the main points you wanted to convey were included, whether your effort to create intended meaning was successful, and whether the coverage contained any inaccuracies that should be corrected. In addition, you would look at this most recent coverage in the context of all coverage received to determine whether, on balance, you are winning the battle of the contested space and gaining the coverage desired. Always evaluating to see if your objectives were achieved is an important part of public relations practice.

To understand traditional and emerging media contexts Chapter 12 provides a fascinating picture of media in action, which complements and invigorates contemporary public relations practice.

CHAPTER **SUMMARY**

➤ The media set the agenda for message dissemination.
➤ Not all media are traditional media although they continue to be important.
➤ Uncontrolled media means that the media are gatekeepers; in controlled media messages are directed to the community, managed by the sender.
➤ News values frame how to work with and get the most out of media.
➤ Working with the media in its various forms is an art that takes skills, creativity and workable relationships that come from knowledge of how the media work and which media are important and appropriate to your organisation or community program.
➤ The tools for effective media relationships are diverse; you need good media releases, photos that add to the story and punchy headlines.
➤ Legal and ethical issues in media management need to be understood and respected.
➤ Media is managed differently in different cultures and political environments.

CASE STUDY \ MEDIA SPECULATIONS

> We do not condone or engage in sledging or any other conduct that constitutes personal abuse.
>
> *The Players' Spirit of Australian Cricket,* Cricket Australia 2008

From a sports public relations perspective, how will the 2008 Border–Gavaskar Trophy Test match series between Australia and India in January 2008 be remembered and recorded in the cricketing annals? As a triumph of great international sportsmanship on the field of play or a bad-tempered and undignified display of sporting rivalry? As an example of how sport is able to transcend the traditional barriers of language and culture or the gulf that persists in international sporting relations?

However history and the cricket archives choose to record the series, one thing is certain, the negative impact of the media and the associated public relations debacle surrounding this much anticipated sporting event is likely to be a significant embarrassment for all concerned.

Before you read further into this discussion, conduct a web search to find out who created the word 'Bollyline'. Why is this word significant within the context of cricket public relations? What is the event we are talking about in this case?

According to Cricket Australia's website, 'Strengthening and protecting the spirit of cricket is one of the four priorities of Cricket Australia's formal strategic plan'. Yet the events that unfolded on many of Australia's iconic cricket grounds and that were played out in front of a global audience during this series raises some questions about this strategic vision and its associated public relations message. It is undoubtedly the case that Australians love their sport. Striving to be the best at whatever sport they engage in is part of their cultural identity which is admired and respected throughout the world.

The fiercely competitive and ruthless methods deployed by the national teams on the world's sporting stage have become legendary and have provided plenty of material for entertaining media coverage whenever Australia is engaged in a sporting contest. The Australian cricket team, particularly, has achieved a status unrivalled by any other national team in that sport. Cricket Australia's dream of making cricket the nation's favourite sport is realised every summer when cricket dominates the sporting calendar, but even a half-interested bystander to the January 2008 Test series might begin to question the ethics behind Cricket Australia and its players' much lauded statements on the *Spirit of Cricket*.

However, it is not just what happens on the field of play that draws attention—both positive and negative—to a sport and its relationships with its publics. The contemporary media have a huge role to play and this case study is a great example. Questions were even raised in the Australian parliament (Harcourt 2008), where genuine concern was voiced about the possible cooling of international and trade relations between Australia and India as a direct result of what has come to be called the 'Bollyline Controversy'.

From the *Sydney Morning Herald* to the *Hindustan Times* and the *Times of London*, cricket has, since the beginning of January 2008, hit the front pages, the back pages and even the business news pages and these publications are only a very few examples of the printed news media that have run the story. If all the associated stories and discussions on social media sites, official and unofficial sports blog sites, television, radio and word-of-mouth conversations were measured and evaluated, the public relations effect of the affair on both cricket and the media would be considerable.

How much of the effect would be favourable and positive, however, is quite another issue—but cricket is only a game after all! Long gone are the days when sport was considered purely a leisure exercise done for fun. In our contemporary society, professional sport is one of the major profit and loss industries, involving countless numbers of individuals as participants or observers and many more in the highly profitable business of satisfying innumerable sports related needs and wants.

Contemporary sports organisations have come to understand that they can differentiate themselves and their offerings and also gain competitive advantage by developing the public relations function as part of their communications and relationship building strategies (Hopwood 2005). Once the dust has settled on yet another transient period of contemporary sports media public relations, one wonders what lessons might be learned for sports media relations management in the court of public opinion.

Source: Maria Hopwood, Senior Lecturer, Leeds Business School, Leeds Metropolitan University, UK; formerly Associate Professor of Public Relations, Bond University

REFLECT AND DISCUSS

> ➤ Do you think the Bollyline incident affected the reputation of Australian cricket?
> ➤ What role do you think the media play in audience attitude formation in contemporary sport?
> ➤ What sports-related public relations issues do you think the Bollyline controversy raise?
> ➤ What media management lessons should be learnt from this case?

FURTHER READING

Bland, M, Theaker, A & Wragg, D 2000, *Effective Media Relations*, Kogan Page, London.

Henderson, D 2006, *Making News: A Straight-Shooting Guide to Media Relations*, iUniverse Star, Lincoln.

Stanton, R 2007, *Media Relations*, Oxford University Press, Melbourne.

Stewart, S 2004, *Media Training 101: A Guide to Meeting the Press*, Wiley, Hoboken.

WEB RESOURCES

Chartered Institute of Public Relations, at www.cipr.co.uk.

Chatham House rule, at www.chathamhouse.org.uk/about/chathamhouserule.

Cricket Australia 2008, at http://cricket.com.au/_content/document/00000056-src.pdf.

Institute of Public Relations Singapore, at www.iprs.org.sg.

International Association of Business Communicators, at www.iabc.com.

International Public Relations Association, at www.ipra.org.

Public Relations Institute of Australia, at www.pria.com.au.

Public Relations Institute of New Zealand, at www.prinz.org.nz.

Public Relations Society of America, at www.prsa.org.

Society of Business Communicators Queensland, at www.sbcq.com.au.

REFERENCES

Adoni, H & Mane, S 1984, 'Media and the Social Construction of Reality: Toward an Integration of Theory and Research', *Communication Research*, 11(3): 323–40.

Arnold, B 2008, Ketupa.net site, retrieved from www.ketupa.net/index.htm, 31 March.

Australian Government 2008, *First 100 Days: Achievements of the Rudd Government*, Canberra, retrieved from www.pm.gov.au/docs/first_100_days.doc.

Bernays, E 1923, *Crystallizing Public Opinion*, Boni & Liveright, New York.

Blumler, J & Katz, E 1974, *The Uses of Mass Communications: Current Perspectives on Gratifications Research*, Sage, Beverly Hills.

Bond University 2009, retrieved from www.bond.edu.au/news/2009/200905-future-ICT-careers.html, 11 May 2009.

Boorstin, D 1961, *The Image*, Vintage, New York.

Brisbane Times editorial 2008, '*New Idea* Slammed for Revealing Prince Harry Duty', *Brisbane Times*, 29 February.

Brooks, D 1999, 'How to Increase Media Coverage for Your Product or Service by Understanding and Meeting Shared Responsibilities with the Media', *Public Relations Quarterly*, 1 January, 2: 6–30, retrieved from www.highbeam.com/doc/1P3-47747272.html, 8 April 2008.

Chatham House rule 1927, retrieved from www.chathamhouse.org.uk/about/chathamhouserule, 4 April 2008.

Conley, D 2002, *The Daily Miracle: An Introduction to Journalism*, 2nd edn, Oxford University Press, Melbourne.

Dugan, K 2005, 'Slow News Day and Blog/Media Relations', retrieved from http://prblog.typepad.com/strategic_public_relation/2005/12/slow_news_day_b.html, 29 February 2008.

Fairhurst, G & Sarr, R 1996, *The Art of Framing*, Jossey-Bass, San Francisco.

Farmer, R 2008, 'Send for the Sound Man', *Political and Legislative Review*, retrieved from www.politicalowl.com, 8 August.

Fuller, J 2008, *News Values: Ideas for an information age*, retrieved from www.columbia.edu/itc/journalism/j6075/edit/Fuller.html, 4 April.

Gardiner-Garden, J & Chowns, J 2006, *Media Ownership Regulation in Australia,* retrieved from www.aph.gov. au/library/intguide/SP/Media_Regulation.htm, 31 March 2008.

Habermas, J 1981, *The Theory of Communicative Action,* trans. Thomas McCarthy (1984), Polity Press, Cambridge.

Harcourt, T 2008, ' "Bollyline" Won't Derail the Australia–Indian trade relationship', retrieved from www.austrade. gov.au/Bollyline-wont-derail-the-Australia-Indian-trade-relationship/default.aspx, 4 April 2008.

Hausman, C 2000, *Lies We Live By,* Routledge, New York.

Herman, E & Chomsky, N 1988, *Manufacturing Consent: The Political Economy of the Mass Media,* Pantheon Books, New York.

Hopwood, M K 2005, 'Public Relations Practice in English County Cricket', *Corporate Communications,* 10(3): 201–12.

Katz, E & Lazarsfeld, P 1955, *Personal Influence: The Part Played by People in the Flow of Mass Communication,* Free Press, Glencoe.

Liu, S 2006, 'An Examination of the Effects of Print Media Exposure and Content on Subjective Social Reality and Acculturation Attitudes', *International Journal of Intercultural Relations,* 30(3): 365–82.

MacCallum, M 1994, *Australian Political Anecdotes,* Oxford University Press, Oxford.

Macnamara, J 1993, *Public Relations and the Media,* Masters thesis, Deakin University, Melbourne.

Noelle-Neumann, E 1984, *The Spiral of Silence: Public Opinion—Our Social Skin,* University of Chicago Press, Chicago.

Pearson, M 2007, *The Journalist's Guide to Media Law,* 3rd edn, Allen & Unwin, Sydney.

Pearson, M & Patching, R 2007, 'Government Media Relations: A "Spin" Through the Literature', research report, Centre for New Media Research and Education, Bond University, Robina.

Phillipps, R 2002, *Media Advisers—Shadow Players in Political Communication,* PhD thesis, University of Sydney, Sydney.

PR Week 2008, 8 March issue, retrieved from www.prweekus.com/PR-Campaign-of-the-Year-2008, 4 April.

Public Relations Society of America 2008, VNRs as Public Relations Tools', retrieved from http://media.prsa.org/ article_display.cfm?article_id=392, 7 February.

Searle, J 1995, *The Construction of Social Reality,* Free Press, New York.

Simmons, P 2006, 'Loath to Admit: Pressures on Ethical Disclosure of News Release Sources', paper presented at the AEJMC Convention, San Francisco.

Singapore Press Holdings 2008, *About SPH: The SPH Story,* retrieved from www.sph.com.sg/aboutus/sph_story. html , 31 March.

Stanton, R 2007, *Media Relations,* Oxford University Press, Melbourne.

Thaindian News 2008, 'No Idea Editors Behind Prince Harry Leak to be Promoted', retrieved from www.thaindian.com/newsportal/world-news/no-idea-editors-behind-prince-harry-leak-to-be-promoted_10023767.html, 4 March 2008.

Turk, J 1986, 'Information Subsidies and Media Content', *Journalism Monographs,* 100: 1–29.

Tversky, A & Kahneman, D 1981, 'The Framing of Decisions and the Psychology of Choice, *Science,* 211: 453–8.

Van Hook, S 2000, *All About Public Relations*, retrieved from http://aboutpublicrelations.net/blrather.htm, 4 April 2008.

Walsh, P 1995, *Confessions of a Failed Finance Minister*, Random House, Sydney.

Wilcox, D, Cameron, G, Ault, P & Agee, W 2003, *Public Relations Strategies and Tactics*, 7th edn, Allyn & Bacon, Boston.

Zawawi, C 2001, *Feeding the Watchdogs—An Analysis of Relationships Between Australian Public Relations Practitioners and Journalists*, unpublished PhD thesis, Queensland University of Technology, Brisbane.

Part **3**

NEW HORIZONS

Chapter **12**

NEW MEDIA AND PUBLIC RELATIONS

Kate Fitch

PRACTITIONER PROFILE PAULL YOUNG

In December 2005, while still a student at Charles Sturt University in Bathurst, Paull wrote his first blog post at Young PR (http://youngie.prblogs.org). Two years later, after travelling around the world he arrived in New York and landed a job with one of the world's leading social media agencies, Converseon, where he worked on award-winning campaigns and was advising *Fortune 500* clients on social media strategy.

What happened in those intervening two years was what he likes to call 'the social media snowball effect'.

Paull started his blog after his academic research had him enthralled with the relationship-building potential created by new online communication tools. He was starting his first job at BAM Media, a sports public relations firm, and wanted to learn some new skills that he would be able to apply to his clients. More importantly, as he learnt the ropes of the public relations profession he wanted to pass on some knowledge to his peers.

To his surprise, he started to get some readers. Then the readers started to become friends. Next thing he knew he was writing and recording podcast interviews for a group blog made up of an international collective of public relations students, practitioners, and educators. The online learning experience was phenomenal, but even better was the friendships that stemmed from his involvement in the blogosphere.

Paull's blog's biggest moment came when a blog post he wrote in July 2006 sparked an international anti-astroturfing campaign that still lives on at the New PR Wiki (www. thenewpr.com). Prominent Australian public relations blogger Trevor Cook and Paull led a global debate about public relations ethics that sparked action from Britain's CIPR and the PRSA in the USA; it also sparked commentary from some of the world's most influential marketing bloggers. By this point Paull knew that his future lay with social media and decided to embark on a worldwide trip to meet the bloggers he had been conversing with online for months to see if he could cut it with the world's best online communicators.

This world blog tour culminated with his dream job with Converseon in New York City, from where he is happy to report that he is thriving, professionally and personally, and extending himself and his clients each and every day. All of which he can attribute to two things: passion, and his involvement in the blogosphere.

Paull's generation of public relations students has the greatest opportunity yet to learn from the best and brightest—all you need to do to take advantage of this opportunity is to get active online.

CHAPTER **AIMS**

By the end of this chapter you should be able to:

➤ understand emerging new media concepts and theories
➤ appreciate the impact of technology on public relations practices
➤ identify the challenges new media pose for the public relations profession
➤ consider the use of social media to develop opportunities for dialogue and two-way and multiway communication
➤ apply ethical practices in relation to new media and public relations.

Introduction

The ways we communicate have fundamentally changed in the last decade. Advances in digital technology have engendered a shift in communication patterns characterised by the shift from the 'one to many' broadcast paradigm of mass media to the 'network paradigm' of 'many to many' communication. Much writing about new media and public relations celebrates the interactivity or conversational nature of new media, which is considered to have the potential to develop relationships and build communities (see, for example, Levine et al. 1999; Holtz 2002). This shift has major implications for traditional public relations practices and concepts.

Not surprisingly, new media is cited by practitioners and scholars as one of the biggest challenges facing the public relations profession (Dougall et al. 2001; Weaver et al. 2003; Zerfass et al. 2007). As Katie Delahaye Paine writes: 'The implications for twenty-first century practitioners are all at once far reaching, terrifying and enormously exciting' (Paine 2007: xiv).

Public relations is concerned with either the management of relationships between publics and organisations or the management of communication between publics and organisations. The advent of the internet causes us to rethink the nature of these relationships and communication. Some academics and practitioners (Gregory 2004; Duhé 2007) are beginning to recognise the potentially transformative impact of technology on public relations and its important contribution to the ability of organisations to be socially responsive.

Internet use in Australia and internationally

The rise of new media has been rapid. Between 2001, when just over one-third of households in Australia had internet access, to 2006, internet use almost doubled, with almost two-thirds (63 per cent) of homes having access to the internet (ABS 2007a: 47). Australia, New Zealand, and Singapore have relatively high rates of internet use, with New Zealand and Singapore recording a similar access to the internet at home (64 per cent in 2006–7 and 66 per cent in 2005 respectively) (ABS 2007a: 48; Lee 2006). However, both countries trail behind the world leader, South Korea, where 94 per cent of households have internet access (ABS 2007: 48).

Technological developments also change how people use the net. Greater access to broadband, for instance, has enabled faster downloads and significantly increased internet use. In one year (2006–7) the number of people using broadband rather than dial-up facilities in Australia doubled (ABS 2007a).

Yet despite the global nature of the internet, it cannot be assumed that access is consistent across or even within countries. In Australia, rural residents have less access and slower services than do their urban counterparts. Many developing countries also lack the appropriate infrastructure for widespread internet access. Indonesia, for example, has an internet penetration of less than 9 per cent, while Malaysia has 38 per cent (Syam 2007); rural Malaysia has relatively low rates of internet access compared to urban areas (Hazelton et al. 2007: 97).

There are other reasons why access to information and services on the internet cannot be assumed. Many countries ban certain sites and services, or searches for and the posting of anything deemed by the authorities to be contentious. China has reportedly banned searches or blogs relating to the candidates for Communist Party leadership positions (Macartney 2007) and is well known for what Hermida (2002) terms the 'Great Red Firewall', where the net is filtered to ensure that access to certain sites such as some foreign news organisations and human rights groups is denied. The Pakistan Telecommunications Authority recently ordered its internet service providers to block YouTube until material they deemed sacrilegious was removed (ABC 2008). The ban was lifted following the removal of the material.

In Australia, 69 per cent of people aged over 15 accessed the internet in 2006–7 (ABS 2007a: 16), which suggests that 31 per cent, or nearly one-third of the population, didn't. Age, income, education, and, to a lesser extent, geographical location appear to determine internet use. According to the Australian Bureau of Statistics, internet use is highest among young people, people with high levels of education, in households with high incomes, and people who live in urban areas (ABS 2007a: 16). It is lowest among older people, the unemployed, and in households with low incomes (ABS 2007a: 16). People living in non-metropolitan areas also have lower than average access to the internet (ABS 2007a: 17).

Some of the figures are startling and emphasise the disparity between those with access to the internet and those without. For instance:

➤ 77 per cent of people aged over 65 did not use the internet in 2006–7, compared with only 7 per cent of people aged 15–17 (ABS 2007a: 21)
➤ 40 per cent of people educated to Year 12 or below did not access the internet in 2006–7, compared with only 8 per cent of people with a Bachelor degree (ABS 2007a: 21)
➤ Aboriginal and Torres Strait Islander households are about half as likely to have internet access compared to non-Indigenous households (ABS 2007b: 55)
➤ only 42 per cent, or less than half, of homes in very remote Australia have internet access compared with 66 per cent, or two-thirds, of homes in cities (ABS 2007b: 17).

REFLECT AND DISCUSS

➤ What implications do these statistics have for public relations practitioners?
➤ If you were asked to develop a campaign to reach people across Australia, what do these statistics tell you that would affect your use of new and traditional media?

Impact of new media

Trevor Barr (2000: 143–4), writing more broadly on the impact of new media, argues that the internet has wrought a major paradigm shift in media and communication studies:

> An inherent strength of the Internet is its anarchy compared to the established modes of ownership and control of traditional media: there are no direct equivalents to the 'gatekeepers' of content and form which characterised the major media of the past few decades, the press and broadcasting. Everyone who has access to the Net can become their own author, expressing their own sense of identity to other Net users scattered throughout the world.

The very idea of public relations as communication management is challenged in a society in which anyone is potentially a producer of information and such information cannot—and, indeed, some would argue should not—be managed or controlled in a top-down sense (see, for example, Holtz 2002; Surma 2005). Rather, the challenge for practitioners and academics is to recognise the full implications of Barr's paradigm shift for public relations and to respond by developing new ways of communicating with, and indeed, relating to, publics.

Certainly, traditional public relations techniques are no longer appropriate in much of public relations practice as they fail to connect with an internet-savvy public (Galloway 2005). Holtz was one of the first writers on public relations to recognise this and writes: 'If communicators understand nothing else about the internet and its impact on the practice of public relations, they must understand this: Everybody is a publisher and everybody is connected to everybody else' (2002: 30).

The advent of new media means the communication environment is more complex and more immediate, with 'instantaneous and far-reaching' consequences for organisations (Owyang & Toll 2007: 1). Significantly, publics are more powerful and can form across geographical boundaries. Their capacity to generate and share information allows them to challenge organisational information, ensuring greater transparency and accountability on the part of organisations. Publics also expect to be consulted and informed about policies and processes that may affect them.

A particular challenge for organisations is the apparent lack of credibility in the information they generate compared with the perception that comments by individuals in an online environment are somehow more authentic and unbiased. There appears to be a tension between organisations that wish to communicate with publics online and what Paull Young (2006) refers to as 'real people'. The challenge for professional communicators is to engage online publics in ways that encourage genuine dialogue and debate without manipulating or dominating with a more powerful corporate or institutional voice.

Kate Fitch

Theoretical approaches

Anne Gregory (2004: 246) identifies two schools of thought regarding the use of technology in public relations. The first sees technology as simply an additional tactic or communication channel, or as an extension of existing tactics (say, where an email is simply the modern version of a letter). This is supported by surveys of practitioners that suggest that the potential of the internet to promote two-way communication continues to remain unrealised (see, for example, Dougall et al. 2001; Sun et al. 2002; Weaver et al. 2003; James 2007). One example might be simply posting information on a company website and assuming this ensures that publics are well informed about decisions that might affect them, rather than using the interactive functions of new media to promote dialogue and discussion in ways that can impact on an organisation's policies and processes. Many practitioners use the internet primarily for the dissemination of information, rather than exploit its potential for fostering discussion and dialogue (Chia 2002: 159; James 2007: 137). Yet, as Holtz points out, 'public relations professionals do not have the excuse of the newness of the internet to explain away the use of the medium as a simple replacement for traditional one-way, top-down communication' (2002: 4).

The second school recognises that technology has brought about a fundamental shift in the balance of power between organisations and publics. While technology can potentially enhance two-way communication through the empowerment of publics, this may mean that information flow is not controlled or even generated by organisations and gatekeepers:

> Organisations are also becoming more porous or leaky, with any number of individuals or groups, external and internal, supplying their own information to those publics. The public relations function cannot control the movement of information and opinion on this scale (Fawkes & Gregory 2000: 122).

One example of porous communication might be the plethora of communication that surrounds corporations: type 'McDonald's' into Google and you will discover not only the multinational corporation's official website, but also links to the *Wikipedia* entry, YouTube videos, news stories, activist websites such as McSpotlight, and so on.

Given examples such as this, which point to the difficulty in managing communications through a coherent, organisational voice (see Chapter 9), the disquiet some practitioners express about technology can be seen in part as a recognition of the challenges posed by new media and their capacity to disrupt traditional communication practices (Owyang & Toll 2007: 2). A European survey of public relations practitioners found that many viewed the application of new technology in communication as a 'disruptive communication innovation', which changes fundamentally the capacity of organisations to communicate in that new media force questions on the 'legitimacy of leadership, the authenticity of communication and the relationships with stakeholders' (Zerfass et al. 2007: 11).

REFLECT AND DISCUSS

> ➤ If you are planning a communication campaign in Australia, how would you determine the effectiveness of new media as a communication channel for reaching your target public(s)?
>
> ➤ How do you define the term 'social media'?
>
> ➤ Review the survey of social media use by practitioners in Europe (Zerfass et al. 2007) and provide a brief précis on the key ways social media are being used by the public relations profession.
>
> ➤ What do you think might change over the next two years? What over the next five? Why?

Industry attitudes

Surveys suggest that despite widespread internet access and use among communication professionals, the internet has not really changed public relations strategies or practices (Dougall et al. 2001; Sun et al. 2002; Weaver et al. 2003). This means that, as a profession, we haven't yet worked out how best to use what the internet offers us, despite the recognition by almost 90 per cent of public relations practitioners in one Australian survey that the internet was fundamentally changing the profession and provided greater opportunities for two-way communication and dialogue (Dougall et al. 2001: 24, 25).

Similarly, a survey of over fifty practitioners in New Zealand concluded that while most did use the internet for public relations purposes, few really exploited the potential of new media to foster dialogic and two-way communication (Weaver et al. 2003). Typically, most used new media platforms such as websites to disseminate information rather than to promote dialogue (Weaver et al. 2003). These findings are replicated in a survey in Taiwan that found that the internet had not really changed public relations practices and that practitioners tended to rely on traditional media relations (Sun et al. 2002: 176). Such surveys confirm earlier research by Michael Kent and Maureen Taylor (1998) who concluded that the internet is underutilised by public relations professions. Holtz (2002) agreed and argues that most public relations professionals fail to exploit the potential of the internet primarily because they see it simply as an extension of more traditional forms of communication. Other research suggests this may be changing. In a European survey of professional communicators, only half the survey participants regularly monitor social media, but this was double the number of the previous year (Zerfass et al. 2007). Given the extraordinary growth of the internet and new media tools, especially over the last five years, we are likely to find a profession that is fully aware of the need to interact more, even if it is not yet doing so.

Kate Fitch

In a series of interviews conducted in Southeast Asia in 2006, the author discovered a high level of discomfort among practitioners when it came to the use of technology. One public relations consultant suggested that the profession was 'scared' of new media and did not know how to use it. Another expressed concern about the loss of interpersonal interaction in mediated communication:

> I think a lot, maybe I'm a bit old school, but I feel that public relations still needs a lot of human touch, still needs a lot of interpersonal feel, [an] interpersonal relationship with the person that you are dealing with and not just leave it to modern technologies to take over.

More recently, Alison Theaker (2008) drew on an online forum to gauge specific barriers to using technology in public relations campaigns. The most cited reasons by contributors were a lack of confidence and a lack of training in new media (Theaker 2008: 353). Public relations practitioner Bernie Charland reports that many participants in his Web 2.0 workshop perceive IT and legal departments as preventing greater use of social media in public relations (2007).

REFLECT AND DISCUSS

> ➤ Why do you think the public relations profession is not embracing new media? List the issues you can identify that the profession needs to address. Can you think of barriers other than those suggested here?
>
> ➤ New media appear to offer greater opportunities for dialogue, two-way communication, and community building. What are the limitations of two-way communications offered by new media?
>
> ➤ How do you correlate the strategy of intentional representation, introduced in Chapter 9, with the lack of organisational control possible in the new media?

Activism and new media

New media offer opportunities for publics to organise around a common issue, regardless of geographical location, time zone, or resources. This has particular importance for activist organisations such as Amnesty International and People for Ethical Treatment of Animals (PETA), among many others, whose websites promote not only online participation but also specific calls to action. These websites demonstrate the advantages of new media to activist groups: low cost communications, the ability to operate through horizontal rather than vertical structures, and rapid dissemination of information across globally dispersed networks.

BOX **12.1** \ PREVENTING CRUELTY TO ANIMALS

PETA, which aims to prevent cruelty to animals though a combination of public education, animal rescue, investigations, protest campaigns, and, in perhaps what has attracted the most media attention, celebrity involvement, claims to have almost 2 million members and supporters around the world (2008).

The organisation is highly interactive and offers a diverse range of activities, information, and links to encourage web users to take personal and public actions to live animal-free lifestyles and prevent animal cruelty. The audience addressed on this website is global and calls to action transcend national boundaries. On a single day, calls for specific action on the home page spanned four countries, in campaigns that ranged from stopping a Korean pop singer wearing fur, encouraging UK supermarket chain Safeway to stop animal cruelty, asking the government of Tamil Nadu in India to stop the cruel game of *jallikattu* (which involves chasing a bull), and pleading with Israel's Knessett (the ruling legislature) to ban horse racing. A click on 'More' takes the viewer to campaigns in Egypt, the Philippines, and the USA.

The implications for organisations who may be targeted by such groups mean that it may be difficult to respond in a timely manner to an issue, or to even contain it. Any inconsistencies in responses tailored for different audiences will be readily shared and communicated through new media networks, which means that transparency, as well as speed, should be paramount in all communications.

BOX **12.2** \ THE KRYPTONITE LOCK ONLINE

The Kryptonite Lock offers one example of how powerful information posted online can be, and how difficult it is for organisations to contain an issue. The Kryptonite Lock is a bicycle lock that is relatively expensive but was generally considered to be secure until a video of someone picking the lock with a cheap ballpoint pen was posted online in 2004 (*Wikipedia* 2008a). This vulnerability was circulated through cyclists' forums and blogs, resulting in a measurable spike in the blogosphere before it made the mainstream news about five days later (Sifry 2004). The initial response from Kryptonite is a textbook case study of what not to do: a slow and inadequate response, and no product recall (Sifry 2004). In this example, new media played a pivotal role in the formation of a geographically dispersed public who came together over a particular issue.

Kate Fitch

REFLECT AND DISCUSS

➤ Choose an activist website such as Amnesty International, Greenpeace, or WWF. How does the organisation you selected engage a globally dispersed public through its website? Is interactivity a feature of the site? How?

➤ Classic textbook crises such as the *Exxon Valdez* oil spill and the Nestlé infant formula boycott happened before the development of the internet. Review each case and discuss the role of internet activism were either scenario to happen today.

Web 2.0 and public relations

Technological developments have the potential to deliver greater interaction and dialogue, but what does this mean for public relations? The term Web 2.0 describes the technology that fosters information sharing, collaboration, social networking, and relationship building among web users; whereas Web 1.0 refers to the web prior to 2004, when most sites were relatively static and simply provided information. Kent and Taylor (1998) view new media as promoting more ethical and democratic public relations because their potential for dialogue and interactivity enable more equal and collaborative relationships between organisations and publics. The challenge for the public relations profession is how to deal with the fact that simply monitoring feedback on a website or responding to specific requests or complaints does not suggest a genuine dialogue or a symmetrical relationship. Rather, ethical public relations requires understanding and dialogue and meeting publics' needs (Kent & Taylor 1998: 322).

As highlighted earlier in this chapter, research suggests that the public relations profession is struggling to use new media in ways that promote interactivity between publics and organisations (James 2007: 138). One reason for this may be that interactivity is ill-defined and often confused with the usability and functionality of websites (Gustavsen & Tilley 2003: 1). Other research suggests that websites tend to lack interactivity and consequently represent asymmetrical rather than symmetrical communication (James 2007: 140).

Thus practitioners cannot assume that by using new media they are engaging or ensuring a symmetrical relationship with their publics and audiences. Karl Herger and Gwyneth Howell (2007: 98–9) believe the limitations in internet access and computer literacy among online publics, the relative anonymity of online users, as well as unequal power in organisational message development mean that not only is the internet 'not a truly symmetrical medium', but it is also one that, with the 'exclusion of certain publics … does not translate into excellent two-way symmetrical relationships'.

A key element of two-way symmetrical communication is equity, and while online dialogue has significant potential to facilitate equity between those involved in the dialogue, it also fails in equity terms to the extent that many people in the audience may not have access to a computer. The implications for practitioners are that until online communication is more widely available, we are likely to continue to need a mix of new and traditional media.

In this mix, the role of new media is to employ technology to create greater opportunities for participation and dialogue rather than be used as a one-way communication tool to promote asymmetrical communication. Greater interactivity and genuine dialogue suggest the potential for real organisational change in response to such dialogue. The implications of this should be considered in relation to the 'Now We Are Talking' case study at the end of this chapter.

BOX **12.3** \ FLOGS

Two well-known fake blogs ('flogs') are the WalMart travel blog, mentioned in the discussion on astroturfing, and the Sony PSP blog, both of which involved public relations agencies. These are interesting examples in that, although they are both interactive and engaging, they are not examples of ethical communication as they fail to allow readers to participate in an authentic conversation.

REFLECT AND DISCUSS

➤ Paull Young maintains that new media such as blogs are successful 'because of their authentic voice and passionate ideas held by real people' (2006). What does this idea of authenticity mean for organisations who wish to engage publics through such media?

➤ How can organisations maintain an ethical stance when they are only one party in the conversation? What guidelines should an organisation adopt to govern its internet interactions?

➤ Evaluate the website of your educational institution. Can you suggest changes to improve the interactivity of the site? What opportunities are there for you to participate online?

Kate Fitch

Legal issues

The impact of new media on professional communication has seen the emergence of new legal and ethical issues. Not only does technology make it easier to plagiarise with its 'cut and paste' culture (Breit 2007: 12–13), but it also exposes legislative grey areas such as the boundaries between personal and professional communication. In one such example, two legal secretaries were fired in Australian in 2005 for an acrimonious email exchange that was copied to other staff members and forwarded to others outside the organisation (*Daily Telegraph* 2005). In an attempt to address the lack of adequate legislation in this area, professional associations such as the CIPR in the United Kingdom and the PRIA in Australia have developed guidelines in the use of new media for their members.

In addition, publishing on the internet means that organisations and individuals can fall foul of national laws. As pointed out earlier, many countries ban access to certain sites and services, or searches for and the posting of anything deemed by the authorities to be contentious. In a groundbreaking ruling by the Australian High Court, libel cases based on material posted on the internet could be mounted anywhere in the world (*Age* 2002). The case that led to this ruling related to Australian mining entrepreneur Joseph Gutnick, who applied to sue the New York-based Dow Jones group in Australia for defamation in relation to an article published online (Breit 2007: 193). The implications for public relations professionals are that they need to be mindful of the global audience for anything online.

eMarketing code of practice

In response to the increasing problem of spam, the Australian government introduced the *Spam Act 2003* (Cth). The Act, which came into effect in April 2004, prohibits the sending of unsolicited commercial electronic messages and the use of software to harvest addresses (ACA 2005). The Act also mandates the provision of accurate information about who sent or authorised a sent message, as well as a functional 'unsubscribe' facility (ACA 2005).

The PRIA worked with the Australian Communications Authority (ACA) in the development of an eMarketing code of practice and is a recognised professional body that can investigate complaints about breaches of the code by its members. This code applies to any organisation that uses email, mobile phone text messages, and instant messaging to promote or market itself or its clients. The code attempts to offer specific guidelines to industries engaged in eMarketing to ensure compliance with the Spam Act.

Interestingly, the code distinguishes between 'commercial' and 'factual' communication, and relates only to the former. Thus, if, say, a water supply company sent an email or electronic newsletter that primarily contained information for customers about how to conserve water, it could be deemed factual rather than commercial communication (PRIA n.d.), which would exempt it from the need for the recipient to have offered consent and the provision of an unsubscribe facility; however, it must still include accurate information about the sender.

Ethical issues

The CIPR has developed guidelines for using social media, partly in recognition that the rapid and dynamic growth of social or new media means that appropriate legislation around the use of such media is not always in place. The institute advocates that the three principles of integrity, competence, and confidentiality should apply to all public relations practices, including the use of new media (CIPR 2007). Integrity in particular demands transparency and openness, so the institute advocates disclosure of one's profession in personal blogs or posts.

Although it does not refer specifically to social media, such a position is also advocated in the PRIA's Code of Ethics, where the first point demands 'fair and honest' dealings with, among others, the media and the general public.

BOX **12.4** \ NETIQUETTE

The public relations office at Alcoa Australia updated a *Wikipedia* entry relating to its alumina refinery at Wagerup in southwest Australia, the site of ongoing concerns about the health of local residents and employees (Martin 2007). Although Alcoa claims it was simply trying to present accurate information, the resulting media coverage in the *West Australian* newspaper suggested that it was dishonest of Alcoa to do so without identifying its vested interest in Wagerup, particularly as the changes included the deletion of any reference to illness (Martin 2007). An important principle of *Wikipedia* is a neutral point of view and as the writing and editing process is collaborative, no one person or organisation owns or controls any entry. A more appropriate response would have been to post a query or comment with evidence of the need to amend the *Wikipedia* entry to the discussion page rather than directly edit the article; however, practitioners obviously need to disclose their professional links.

A recommended first step for organisations contemplating active engagement with online and social media is to develop an organisational policy that provides guidance for employees on how they can use it and respond to it (see the CIPR website for details on how to do this).

Astroturfing

One example of unethical practices, in part engendered by new media, is astroturfing, or the creation of groups that appear to offer grassroots or community support. According to Paull Young (2006), one of the founders of an opposition movement, astroturfing is profoundly unethical: 'Astroturfing is the practice of creating fake entities that appear to be real grassroots organisations, when in fact they are the work of people or groups with hidden motives and identities'. One well-known example is the Working Families for WalMart group, a brainchild of the US firm Edelman PR, which promoted itself as a grassroots organisation and in this guise paid someone to blog about their travels across America meeting with WalMart employees (Goldberg 2007).

Although such practices predate new media, the growth of the internet makes it easy and inexpensive to set up websites and blogs and generate emails to suggest that there is strong support for a cause. Former PRIA president Annabelle Warren states that:

> The web has made it particularly easy for a small group of people to look like a really large group of activists that may be advocating a specific cause. We urge people not to believe everything they read and we continue to encourage organisations to be transparent and accountable (cited in PRIA 2007).

The PRIA (2007) opposes astroturfing and believes it not only breaches the code of ethics in that members shall not disseminate false or misleading information, but also that such behaviour may also breach the Trade Practices Act and other legislation.

Social media

The term 'social media' describes the new technologies that encourage greater participation and interaction on the part of users. They are characterised by being 'easy to access' (Owyang & Toll 2007: 1) yet difficult to define, precisely because of 'the blurring of definitions, rapid innovation [and] reinvention (iCrossing 2007: 11). The CIPR offers this definition:

> 'Social media' is the term commonly given to websites and online tools which allow users to interact with each other in some way—by sharing information, opinions, knowledge and interests. As the name implies, social media involves the building of communities or networks, encouraging participation and engagement (CIPR 2007).

Hazelton et al. (2007: 99) argue that such highly interactive media increase social capital, the social connections that form the basis of relationships, in ways that more traditional mainstream media such as newspapers and television do not. Certainly, the capacity of new media to foster relationships and social connections continues to have currency in public relations theory.

Research from Europe suggests that practitioners, despite initial resistance, may have finally begun to embrace social software sites such as blogs, websites, and wikis, with 37 per cent of practitioners surveyed regularly monitoring the sites of their competitors and pressure groups (Zerfass et al. 2007). The challenge for practitioners is to develop online texts that engage publics rather than simply drawing on such sites for research purposes.

Another difficulty for public relations professionals is how to measure the impact of social media in terms of its capacity to influence and persuade publics and audiences. In fact, Jeremiah Owyang and Matt Toll believe that traditional forms of measurement are not relevant as they do not 'apply to the real-time and conversational nature of social media' (2007: 4). Rather, using blogs as one example of social media, they argue that the most influential blogs have the greatest impact on highly engaged niche publics rather than mass audiences (Owyang & Toll 2007: 6, 7).

New media applications

As new software is developed all the time, it is difficult to survey the full range of new media, or indeed predict the ways in which such media may be used in the future. This section contains a brief survey of some applications that are significant now but which may well be superseded within a couple of years. The next section explores blogs in more detail as just one example that illustrates the challenges and the opportunities new media pose for public relations.

Blogs

Blogs (web logs) are online journals that, with the use of trackback and comments, enable an ongoing dialogue between participants. Blogs on almost any topic can be found by searching the web resources suggested at the end of this chapter. There are approximately 112 million blogs in the world, and the number keeps increasing (Technorati 2008). Their influence spreads to traditional news media, as most news organisations now feature journalists' blogs on their websites.

Podcasting

Although millions of students around the world now routinely download audio and video files, podcasting was first used only in 2004 (Cook & Hopkins 2008: 15). Podcasting (and its video equivalent, vodcasting) is a potentially powerful public relations tool. The CSIRO, Australia's peak government science organisation, podcasts short features of its latest news and research, while the Australian Securities Exchange podcasts presentations on investment advice.

Kate Fitch

Second Life

Second Life is just one example, but perhaps the most well-known, of a virtual world. Although many corporations have a presence in Second Life, its potential in terms of traditional public relations is considered risky and unknown (Saloman 2007). Public relations activities by not-for-profit organisations in Second Life include fundraising and awareness raising. Following the disappearance of young British girl Madeleine McCann in Portugal, virtual billboards were used to raise international awareness of her disappearance (Quinn-Allan & Kirby 2007: 156–7).

Social networking

There are many social networking sites that help people connect online to form vast networks and relationships relatively inexpensively. Sites such as Bebo (launched in 2005), Facebook (2004), and MySpace (2003) are well known in Australia, the United Kingdom, and the USA, while Friendster (2002) is popular in Southeast Asia, and LinkedIn (2003) serves the business community in many countries (Boyd & Ellison 2007). While sites such as Friendster boast up to 30 million active users, there are also numerous niche social networking sites (*Wikipedia* 2008b).

Twitter

Twitter is a microblogging service that allows short posts (up to 140 words) to be sent via mobile phones or computers. It was launched in 2006 and within a year developed a popular following. Hillary Clinton and Barack Obama used Twitter to post short messages during their presidential primary campaigns in the USA in 2007–8. Significantly, Twitter is credited with breaking the news of the 2008 China earthquake before mainstream media and even before the US Geological Survey, which monitors seismic events (Cellan-Jones 2008).

REFLECT AND DISCUSS

Choose an issue that interests you from the daily media and assess the coverage it is receiving. Analyse it in terms of whether it is positive, neutral, or negative, and who appears to be the source.

➤ Now find a range of blogs on the topic and undertake a similar content analysis. Do different angles on the stories emerge via the blogs? How do the blogs add to your understanding of the issue?

Public relations implications of blogs

Given that blogs are a relatively recent phenomenon (the first blog dates back to 1999) and something public relations professionals are only beginning to grapple with, it is surprising that there has been a lack of critical analysis and research about the role of blogs in public relations (Kent 2008). A US study of public relations practitioners concludes that while blogs are recognised by practitioners as important, they are not yet a standard public relations tool (Porter et al. 2007). Recent Australian research suggests the role of blogs in corporate communication remains 'ambiguous and unclear' (Herger & Howell 2007: 102).

Yet blogs can be very useful research tools, particularly in monitoring and environmental scanning, in that they provide direct access to public attitudes (Kent 2008). According to Kent (2008: 36), it is precisely the dialogic nature of blogs that makes them so valuable:

> Blog readers help to construct their own reality in dialogue, rather than simply participating in the symbolic representation of the online poll where visitors 'vote' on issues but never discuss them (cf. Kent, Harrison & Taylor 2006), as is the case with the mainstream news sites (CNN.com, MSNBC.com, etc.). That blog readers actually have an interest in issues, read what others have to say about issues, and have the ability to comment on issues, make blogs genuinely participative.

This suggests that blogs have value as a research tool in public relations in that they offer an insight into the complexity, subtlety, diversity, and the contradictions and lack of cohesion in public opinion. They are democratic in the sense that no voice is privileged over another (except possibly that of the moderator). They allow practitioners to appreciate the depth of feeling and opinion about an issue and in terms of issues management can be valuable qualitative research tools (see Chapter 5).

The blogosphere has its own culture and netiquette, and it is important to remember that blogs are not simply communication tools to help meet strategic organisational objectives. Although blogs appear to offer a 'conversational human voice', and the opportunity for a dialogue between organisations and publics, this does not mean that they are effective in terms of the delivery of public relations messages (Kelleher & Miller 2006). We suggest this may be precisely because corporate objectives and messages are not the conversational human voice that bloggers seek.

The challenges for public relations practitioners using blogs include:

➤ the need for disclosure of one's professional status when posting blogs
➤ the fact that corporate messages in blogs can be viewed with suspicion and seen as 'propagandistic' (Kent 2008: 36)
➤ the recognition that online publics may represent a narrow, niche public that is not representative
➤ the difficulty in evaluating the social impact or influence of blogs.

Kate Fitch

BOX 12.5 \ EQUINE INFLUENZA AND BLOGS

During the outbreak of equine influenza in Australia in 2007, the New South Wales Department of Primary Industries had one media officer and an industry liaison officer monitoring and responding to about twelve external blogs and key websites throughout the campaign that was aimed at managing the outbreak. Hundreds of blog replies were posted to address concerns and clarify issues (Fifield 2008). Director of Public Affairs and Media Brett Fifield believes the monitoring of blogs was invaluable as it enabled the department to quickly identify concerns and respond to issues before they escalated, as well as craft and adapt key messages (2008).

The future

Public relations practices and, to a lesser extent, public relations theories are heavily influenced by asymmetrical and sender–message–receiver models of communication. This means that technological developments and new media tend to be viewed in terms of additional public relations channels or tactics to serve strategic purposes, rather than as something that has the potential to change the nature of communication and, by extension, the relationship between communicators.

In fact, Johanna Fawkes and Anne Gregory (2000: 122) suggest that the apparent shift in power from organisations to the publics is in some ways illusory:

> The over-reliance on the transmission model of communication may have misled the practitioner into an illusion of control, while in reality users have always constructed their own meanings from messages, according to their own social and psychological needs.

Similarly, Herger and Howell argue that the internet only appears democratic, and that it in fact offers a limited notion of a public (2007: 99). Perhaps what the internet does offer, then, is a recognition that communication is not driven or controlled by organisations. This is not the same as saying that technology offers a utopian ideal of greater inclusiveness and social connectedness, but it does have implications for public relations.

New media, in increasing opportunities for publics and audiences to communicate, connect and organise, and indeed to share information in ways which could hardly be imagined even a few years ago, means that organisations can expect to be challenged as the number of alternative discourses to the dominant organisational narrative increases exponentially. What the new media offer are a society in which organisations require not only higher standards of transparency and accountability, but a society in which engagement with publics, audiences and communities is paramount.

The challenge for public relations, then, is less communication management in the top-down sense of controlling debates and discussion, and more communication—or even relationship—management in the sense of creating greater opportunities for participation, consultation and discussion. The onus is on practitioners to embrace new media as a means of actively engaging publics. To view new media as merely additional public relations tactics, or new channels of communication, is to profoundly misunderstand the impact and function of such technology on the communication profession.

CHAPTER **SUMMARY**

➤ Technological advances have the potential to transform the relationships and communication between organisations and publics, audiences and communities.

➤ Internet use varies between and within countries, with factors such as age, education, socioeconomic, and geographical location impacting on levels of access and use.

➤ The rapid development of digital technology makes it difficult to predict how publics and audiences will use new software, and which applications may be useful for public relations professionals in even one year's time.

➤ Public relations practitioners are beginning to use new media in campaigns, but do not yet exploit their potential to promote two-way communication and dialogue.

➤ New media pose legal and ethical challenges; practitioners should always disclose their professional and personal interests.

➤ Social media offer opportunities for greater interaction with publics, but public relations may need to be reconceptualised in terms of the social relationships and connections between organisations and publics.

CASE STUDY \ NOW WE'RE TALKING

Telstra set up its Now We're Talking website as a space for shareholders and the public to jointly explore the social impact of new media (Burgess n.d.). The site includes discussion forums, blogs, podcasts, news, and features. In one way, it can be seen as a brave attempt to embrace new media to promote conversations and dialogue. Alternatively, it can be seen as a somewhat cynical move to promote its own communication technology to consumers.

According to Telstra Group Managing Director, Public Policy & Communications, Phil Burgess (n.d.), the site is designed to increase public discourse around telecommunications and the digital revolution. The site presents blogs from mostly Telstra

Kate Fitch

employees and in doing so offers a diversity of enthusiastic voices that are not the corporate or organisational voice in any traditional sense. For instance, in a post in the news and features section, the chief editor of Now We Are Talking, Jeremy Mitchell (2008), responded to a news story in the *Australian Financial Review* about Singtel (the owner of Telstra competitor Optus). His post is passionate, opinionated, colloquial, and fiercely nationalistic on the issue of foreign ownership of Australian entities. Not only does the website enable Telstra to respond quickly to the news article in a public forum that is not edited or moderated by an external gatekeeper, but the very nature of the site enables it to do so in a very personal, non-corporate way.

Although Burgess suggests the site is a space for all people to share diverse points of view, critics of the site argue that the website is not as democratic as Telstra suggests. Telstra argued that an online poll, in which 97 per cent of respondents blamed Telstra for blocking the growth of broadband in Australia, had been spammed and removed it (Moses 2007). This led to critical articles in mainstream media, with headlines such as 'Now We Aren't Talking' and 'Why We Hate Telstra' (see, for example, Moses 2007; Pesce 2007). The response from some bloggers to Now We're Talking is also less than positive. One blogger wrote: 'There will be no bad news stories about Telstra on there … Ever!!' (Whirlpool 2006).

Given the level of cynicism towards corporate blogs, do you think there is a role for websites such as Now We're Talking? While there are clear advantages in terms of promoting debate among online publics, telling the organisation's point of view and responding quickly—without external gatekeepers—to mainstream news stories and government announcements, there may also be disadvantages, particularly in terms of resistance from online publics.

REFLECT AND DISCUSS

- ➤ Use Technorati, Google blog, or one of the web resources listed at the end of this chapter to explore some public relations blogs. Do you find them a useful resource as a student? As a practitioner?
- ➤ Write a 500 word report on an issue that has the potential to affect a particular organisation. Research your report using blogs to gauge public opinion in relation to the issue.
- ➤ Do you belong to any internet discussion groups? Do you know where the participants are from and how widespread the group's reach is?
- ➤ Research and develop a short presentation for the senior management or board of a specific organisation on the potential impact and opportunities offered by social media applications such as YouTube, Second Life, MySpace, and Facebook.

FURTHER READING

Duhé, S (ed.) 2007, *New Media and Public Relations*, Peter Lang, New York.

Newsom, D & Haynes, J 2008, 'Writing for the Internet', in D Newsom & J Haynes (eds), *Public Relations Writing Form and Style*, 8th edn, Thomson Wadsworth, Belmont, 281–301.

Theaker, A 2008, 'Using New Technology Effectively in Public Relations', in A Theaker (ed.), *The Public Relations Handbook,* 3rd edn, Routledge, Abingdon.

WEB RESOURCES

Chartered Institute of Public Relations, at www.cipr.co.uk/socialmedia.

Constantin Baturea, at www.bloglines.com/public/prblogs.

The New Public Relations, at www.thenewpr.com/wiki/pmwiki.php?pagename=Main.HomePage.

REFERENCES

Australian Broadcasting Corporation 2008, 'Pakistan Lifts YouTube Ban', *Online News*, 27 February, retrieved from www.abc.net.au/news/stories/2008/02/27/2173501.htm?section=world, 28 February.

Australian Bureau of Statistics 2007a, *Household Use of Information Technology*, 8146.0, retrieved from www.abs.gov.au/AUSSTATS/abs@.nsf/DetailsPage/8146.02006-07?OpenDocument, 26 January 2008.

Australian Bureau of Statistics 2007b, *Patterns of Internet Access in Australia 2006*, 8146.0.55.001, retrieved from www.ausstats.abs.gov.au/ausstats/free.nsf/0/1B7DD59C9E8F52ECCA2573A1007EE8DA/$Fil e/8146055001_2006.pdf >, 26 January 2008.

Australian Communications Authority 2005, *Australian eMarketing Code of Practice*, retrieved from aca.gov.au/webwr/telcomm/industry_codes/codes/australian%20emarketing%20code%20of%20 practice.pdf, 28 February 2008.

Barr, T 2000, *newmedia.com.au: The Changing Face of Australia's Media and Communications*, Allen & Unwin, Sydney.

Boyd, D & Ellison, N 2007, 'Social Network Sites: Definition, History, and Scholarship', *Journal of Computer-Mediated Communication*, 13(1): 210–30

Breit, R 2007, *Law and Ethics for Professional Communicators*, LexisNexis Butterworths, Sydney.

Burgess, P n.d., *About This Site*, retrieved from www.nowwearetalking.com.au/about-this-site, 4 June 2008.

Cellan-Jones, R 2008, 'Twitter and the China Earthquake', dot.life blog, BBC *News*, 12 May, retrieved from www.bbc.co.uk/clogs/technology/2008/05/twitter_and_the_china_earthqua.html, 13 May.

Charland, B 2007, *The Barriers to Social Media*, retrieved from http://publicrelationsrogue.wordpress.com/2007/11/15/the-barriers-to-social-media, 20 February 2008.

Chartered Institute of Public Relations 2007, *Social Media Guidelines*, retrieved from www.cipr.co.uk/socialmedia, 12 April 2008.

Chia, J 2002, 'Emails, Educators and Practitioners and Changing Professional Paradigms', *Asia Pacific Media Educator*, 12/13: 156–67.

Cook, T & Hopkins, L 2008, *Social Media, or 'How We Stopped Worrying and Learned to Love Communication'*, 3rd edn, e-book, retrieved from http://trevorcook.typepad.com/weblog/2008/03/cook-hopkins-so.html, 28 March.

Croll, J 2007, 'The Changing Face of the Media', PowerPoint presentation to PRIA (NSW) members, retrieved from www.pria.com.au/sitebuilder/resources/knowledge/asset/files/104/johncrollpresentation.pdf, 14 January 2008.

Daily Telegraph 2005, 'F-email Fury', 9 September, retrieved from www.news.com.au/dailytelegraph/story/0,22049,16536994-5001022,00.html, 23 March 2008.

Dougall, E, Fox, A & Burton, L J 2001, 'Interactivity, Influence and Issues Management', *Asia Pacific Public Relations Journal*, 3(2): 17–34.

Duhé, S 2008, 'Power Resistance and Change Overview', in S Duhé, *New Media and Public Relations*, Peter Lang, New York, 173–4.

Fawkes, J & Gregory, A 2000, 'Applying Communication Theories to the Internet', *Journal of Communication Management*, 5(2): 109–24.

Fifield, B 2008, 'Lessons Learnt from the EI Outbreak', informal presentation to PRIA (WA) members, 10 June, Perth.

Galloway, C 2005, 'Cyber-PR and "Dynamic Touch" ', *Public Relations Review*, 31(4): 572–7.

Goldberg, J 2007, 'Selling Wal-Mart: Can the Company Co-opt Liberals?', *New Yorker*, 2 April, retrieved from www.newyorker.com/reporting/2007/04/02/070402fa_fact_goldberg, 15 February 2008.

Gregory, A 2004, 'The Scope and Structure of Public Relations: A Technology Driven Approach', *Public Relations Review*, 30(3): 245–54.

Gustavsen, P A & Tilley, E 2003, 'Public Relations Communication Through Corporate Websites: Towards an Understanding of the Role of Interactivity', *PRism*, 33(1), retrieved from http://praxis.massey.ac.nz/fileadmin/Praxis/Files/Journal_Files/issue1/refereed_articles_paper5.pdf, 26 January 2008.

Hazelton, V, Harrison-Rexwode, J & Kennan, W 2007, 'New Technologies in the Formation of Personal and Public Relations: Social Capital and Social Media', in S Duhé (ed.), *New Media and Public Relations*, Peter Lang, New York.

Herger, K & Howell, G 2007, 'The Good, the Bad and the Blogger: the Public Relations Challenge of the Noughties', *Asia Pacific Public Relations Journal*, 8: 91–108.

Hermida, A 2002, 'Behind China's Internet Red Firewall', BBC *News*, 3 September, retrieved from http://news.bbc.co.uk/1/hi/technology/2234154.stm, 14 January 2008.

Holtz, S 2002, *Public Relations on the Net*, 2nd edn, AMACON, New York.

iCrossing 2007, *What is Social Media?*, e-book, retrieved from www.icrossing.co.uk/fileadmin/uploads/eBooks/What_is_social_media_Nov_2007.pdf, 12 April 2008.

James, M 2007, 'A Review of the Impact of New Media on Public Relations: Challenges for the Terrain, Practice and Education', *Asia Pacific Public Relations Journal*, 8: 137–48.

Kelleher, T & Miller, B 2006, 'Organizational Blogs and the Human Voice: Relational Strategies and Relational Outcomes', *Journal of Computer-mediated Communication*, 11(2): 395–414 retrieved from http:/jcmc.indiana.edu/vol11/issue2/Kelleher.html, 25 January 2008.

Kent, M 2008, 'Critical Analysis of Blogging in Public Relations', *Public Relations Review*, 5(1): 32–40.

Kent, M & Taylor, M 1998, 'Building Dialogic Relationships Through the World Wide Web', *Public Relations Review*, 24(3): 321–34.

Lee, M C 2006, 'Infocomm Usage by Households and Individuals 2000–2005', *Statistics Singapore Newsletter*, March, Infocomm Development Authority of Singapore, Singapore.

Levine, R, Locke, C, Searls, D & Weinberger, D 1999, *The Cluetrain Manifesto: The End of Business as Usual*, i-book, retrieved from www.cluetrain.com, 5 February 2008.

Macartney, J 2007, 'Internet Ban is Clue to China's New Leaders', *The Times*, 19 October, retrieved from www.timesonline.co.uk/tol/news/world/asia/article2690168.ece, 5 February 2008.

Martin, B 2007, 'Truth on the Internet is in the Eyes of the Writer', *West Australian*, 24 January: 2.

Mitchell, J 2008, 'Breadcrumbs and Flag-flying', 19 May, retrieved from www.nowwearetalking.com.au/news-and-features, 4 June 2008.

Moses, A 2007, 'Now We Aren't Talking', *Sydney Morning Herald*, Tech Supplement, 14 May, retrieved from www.smh.com.au/news/web/now-we-arent-talking/2007/05/14/1178995048612.html, 4 June 2008.

Owyang, J & Toll, M 2007, 'Tracking the Influence of Conversations: A Roundtable Discussion on Social Media Metrics and Measurement', A Dow Jones White Paper, retrieved from www.web-strategist.com/blog/wp-content/uploads/2007/08/trackingtheinfluence.pdf, 14 January 2008.

Paine, K D 2008, 'Introduction', in S Duhé (ed.), *New Media and Public Relations*, Peter Lang, New York, xiii–xiv.

Pesce, M 2007, 'Why We All Hate Telstra', *Age*, 20 May, retrieved from www.theage.com.au/news/business/why-we-all-hate-telstra/2007/05/19/1179497337693.html?page=fullpage, 4 June 2008.

Porter, P, Sweetser Trammell, K D, Chung, D & Kim, E 2007, 'Blog Power: Examining the Effects of Practitioner Blog Use on Power in Public Relations', *Public Relations Review*, 33(1): 92–5.

Public Relations Institute of Australia n.d., *eMarketing Code of Practice Case Studies*, retrieved from www.pria.com.au/documents/item/490, 28 February 2008.

Public Relations Institute of Australia 2007, 'Where the Grass is not Greener, Position Paper on Astroturfing', retrieved from www.pria.com.au/resources/list/asset_id/163/cid/262/parent/0/t/resources, 5 February 2008.

Quinn-Allan, D & Kirby, B 2007, 'Second Life First Hand: A Teacher Perspective', *Asia Pacific Public Relations Journal*, 8: 149–62.

Saloman, M 2007, *Business in Second Life: An Introduction*, Smart Internet Technology CRC, Melbourne, retrieved from www.smartinternet.com.au, 14 January 2008.

Sifry, D 2004, 'State of the Blogosphere: 4.6 Posts Per Second', *Sifry's Alerts*, 11 October, retrieved from www.sifry.com/alerts/archives/000388.html, 14 January 2008.

Sun, S, Lau, T & Kuo, R 2002, 'The Internet as PR Medium: An Exploratory Study of PR Professionals in Taiwan', *Asia Pacific Media Educator*, 12/13: 168–84.

Surma, A 2005, *Public and Professional Writing: Ethics, Imagination and Rhetoric*, Palgrave Macmillan, Basingstoke.

Syam, A 2007, 'Expected Low Internet Rate to Lure More Users', *Jakarta Post*, 31 October, retrieved from www.asiamedia.ucla.edu/article-southeastasia.asp?parentid=80867, 2 February 2008.

Technorati 2008, *About Us,* retrieved from http://technorati.com/about, 12 June.

Theaker, A 2008, *The Public Relations Handbook,* 3rd edn, Routledge, Abingdon.

Weaver, C K, Schoenberger-Orgad, M & Pope, A 2003, 'Public Relations on the Internet: The State of the Art in New Zealand', *Asia Pacific Public Relations Journal,* 4(2): 31–55.

Whirlpool 2006, 'Now We're Talking', forum post by Dr D, 31 August, retrieved from http://forums.whirlpool.net.au/forum-replies.cfm?t=582830, 12 April 2008.

Wikipedia.org 2008a, 'Kryptonite Lock', retrieved from http://en.wikipedia.org/wiki/Kryptonite_lock, 12 April.

Wikipedia.org 2008b, 'List of Social Networking Sites', retrieved from http://en.wikipedia.org/wiki/List_of_social_networking_sites, 12 April.

Young, P 2006, 'Astroturfing: Dark Art of Politics Turned Scourge of the Blogosphere', 31 October, retrieved from http://blogcampaigning.com/2006/10/31/astroturfing-dark-art-of-politics-turned-scourge-of-the-blogosphere, 5 February 2008.

Zerfass, A, Sandhu, S & Young, P 2007, 'Euroblog 2007: European Perspectives on Social Software in Communication Management—Results and Implications', Leipzig/Luzern/Sunderland, retrieved from www.euroblog2007.org/euroblog2007-results.pdf, 14 January 2008.

Chapter **13**

FOCUS ON ASIAN PUBLIC RELATIONS MANAGEMENT

Richard Stanton

PRACTITIONER PROFILE INSOOK KIM

With fifteen years of experience in public relations, Insook Kim is an active, Accredited in Public Relations (APR) professional in Korea. Having joined the Australian Embassy in Seoul in 2000, Insook, as the director of public diplomacy, manages public and cultural diplomacy activities using the full range of global public relations tools. Insook says the embassy work has given her the unique opportunity to develop a specialised expertise in public diplomacy and thereby expand the horizon of her public relations profession.

She believes that effective public diplomacy requires a long-term commitment to winning the hearts and minds of the foreign public.

> I cannot stress enough the importance of ongoing interactive relations with the local media in creating an accurate perception and positive image of a country in the eyes of the local people. The cultural sensitivity and respect for the local culture are equally significant and relevant to public diplomacy strategies and tactics overseas.

Insook says she lives up to the notions of two-way communication and relationships, as the fundamental role of public diplomacy aims to promote mutual understanding between the two countries. 'It is my hope that my work may be an invigorating exercise for other public relations practitioners in search of mutually beneficial two-way public relations practices,' she says.

In Korea, which has the world's highest internet and online interactions, the profession, largely adopted from US models, is constantly evolving with the rapidly changing skills and tools needed to deliver an effective public relations strategy. Proactive and interactive approaches are crucial to public relations in Korea, where technologies stay ahead of the global trends.

Insook believes that successful public relations professionals understand the function and importance of the manager role. In particular, strategic thinking and big-picture perspectives are the most important key features of high-performing public relations professionals. Her advice to public relations students is 'to develop effective communication and people skills with teamwork capacity, which enables one to establish rapport with individuals and groups at all organisational levels'.

CHAPTER **AIMS**

By the end of this chapter you should be able to:

➤ identify the different cultural issues that apply to the practice of public relations in Asia
➤ discuss various aspects of public relations as they apply to different locations
➤ understand the importance of identifying variables in public relations.

Introduction

Imagine a variety of products and services, issues, and events that you might encounter in your everyday lives, whether you wake up in Hong Kong, Hanoi, or Harbin. You check your Samsung mobile telephone for messages, click a computer website for a cheap flight from DragonAir so you can take a holiday in Phuket, then scope the Thai government website to see what is legal and illegal when travelling in Thailand.

All the information you obtain has been designed and constructed using strategic communication by organisations and individuals who want you to focus on them rather than their competitors. Similarly, when people obtain news from media sources about issues and events within Asia, it too has been designed and managed using campaign strategies that have their basis in public relations: Taiwan seeking international support for its claim to sovereignty from China, North and South Korea discussing reunification, or Japan whaling in the Great Southern Ocean. All these issues get coverage in news media because they are managed public relations strategies.

In this chapter we are interested in how public relations is shaped and applied in the countries that comprise the region under investigation. First though, the region needs to be defined, then some of the theories that have been used to influence public relations practice considered. We will then look at particular examples from the primary entities in which public relations is most frequently applied: corporations, governments, and not-for-profit organisations. The question of why public relations is important in Asia is also of interest, given that most of the countries that comprise the region vary enormously in what Van Leuven (1996) describes as 'the three stage process of development':

1   from nation building
2   through market development
3   to establishment and maintenance of a regional interdependence.

This model can be aligned with public relations in which there is an expectation that organisations (governments, corporations, or others) will progress from a non-professional provision of media relations and information supply in the nation-building stage to one of professionalisation in strategic communication that typifies the third stage of development. Part of the answer, as will be demonstrated below, lies in the nature of foreign investment in Asia (from Europe and America) and the need for foreign corporations and other organisations to present particular images of themselves to differentiated stakeholders.

There are many ways to define global regions and for each definition there is a specific reason that underpins the argument for it to be defined that way. For the purposes of this chapter, the geographical areas of north and south Asia, which take in Japan, South Korea, China, Vietnam, Taiwan, the Philippines, Malaysia, Singapore, Laos, Cambodia, Thailand, and Indonesia will be included. For various reasons, India, Pakistan, and other countries in the subcontinent are excluded, despite a well-argued position that a definition of Asia must include all countries through to Turkey if the region is to be defined accurately (Sriramesh 2007). Australia and New Zealand will also be excluded from this discussion, even though some past Australian governments have argued strongly for inclusion due, among other things, to its presence as a member of the Asia Pacific Economic Cooperation (APEC).

Part of the argument for defining Asia in this way lies in the relationship each country has to processes of capitalism and democracy. While China and Vietnam are socialist republics, as is North Korea, China, and Vietnam, they have active stock markets and global trading relationships—factors which drive a large part of the presence of Western-style public relations activities in those countries. They also serve to play a part in the exclusion of North Korea from this chapter. The other major exclusion is Burma, a military dictatorship, and thus devoid of what we might consider orthodox theories and practices of public relations. North Korea and Burma may some day be included, if either they shift towards democracy, or if public relations theory re-unites with propaganda theory.

Applying theories to non-Western cultures

For the present, public relations theory is a separate entity to propaganda theory (see Chapter 3). The importance of the early work of American scholars Grunig and Hunt and how the Excellence Theory has underpinned most US public relations scholarship since the mid 1980s has been described (for an alternative view, see McKie & Munshi 2008). You have also learnt about relationship management theory, organisational theory, persuasion and public opinion, critical theory, rhetorical theory, postmodernism, and stakeholder theory (the latter in Chapter 8). It is the significance of Excellence Theory that is of most interest in this chapter. It provides the ground on which the fast-growing public relations sector in Asia is being built. Similarly, relationship theory plays a significant role in the development of public relations practice in Asia: in South Korea there is a specific term—'*cheon*'—that is applied to business and management relationships, while in China and Vietnam '*guanxi*' is the term applied to a slightly more vigorous method of business and management relationships.

Grunig and Hunt's development of the Excellence Theory at the University of Maryland coincided with a historical shift to capitalist-style mass production in three of Asia's post-Second World War democracies: Japan, South Korea, and Taiwan. The relationship of the USA to the industrial growth of these countries is important. It included long-term cultural and educational exchanges, many of which were developed and fostered by the University of Maryland and other US universities, which in the mid 1980s had created public relations departments to service the exponential growth in demand for undergraduate and graduate courses. Many of the graduates of these courses are now the leading public relations scholars in Asia (Shin, Chen, Sriramesh, and Kim, for example). The Excellence Theory has thus been methodologically applied to public relations teaching in a culturally and linguistically diverse range of countries, the common denominators of which have been industrial growth and trade.

In recent years, an additional theoretical development has emerged from the Grunigian paradigm. As it has in Western industrial democracies, the idea of relationship development has taken shape in Asia. Relationship development and stakeholder theory are being applied in public relations management and practice at a number of different levels in Asia. While relationship building has been a traditional part of corporate culture, it has recently been invested with a level of importance in government that differs from its traditional diplomatic role. Governments have previously viewed the separation between public diplomacy, public affairs, and public relations strategically, with public relations as the events management component of the tricolon. An increased understanding of the role of relationship building between stakeholders other than government to government has begun to shape the acceptance of public relations as something more than events management and to demonstrate that it has value as a strategic management tool. This shift has allowed a number of Asian governments to move a step further, to begin imagining former adversaries—not-for-profit and activist groups—in a more inclusive fashion, in the same way they are being imagined by Western democratic governments.

Oyvind Ihlen and Betteke van Ruler (2007) argue that public relations has a social dimension that is inherently more important than others and that the quest for one great theory to encompass and embrace the field is an impossible dream. They suggest the field of public relations and its epistemological development have been framed historically by US domination, a position from which, as has already been stated, much Asian public relations has developed. But this does not mean all public relations theory development and practice in Asia is controlled by the Grunigian paradigm. In fact some of the most important developments in places such as South Korea, Vietnam, China, and Taiwan are based on the assumption that public relations has a sociocultural dimension within a globalised postmodernity. Specific examples will follow shortly.

Krishnamurthy Sriramesh (2004) argues the importance of understanding and engaging with the sociocultural in a global and regional sense. It is important, he says, for all public relations practitioners to have a multicultural perspective if they are to act effectively. Public relations influences, and is influenced by, culture and cultural practices and most of the recent investigation into cultural practices and their relationship to public relations has been undertaken in Asia (Sriramesh 2004: 12). A body of literature on the relationship between public relations and culture in the former Eastern bloc countries is also emerging.

Sociocultural and sociolinguistic boundaries are evident in Asia, supporting Hazelton's (2006) argument that independent situational variables are embedded elements in all public relations. While the 'united' in United States provides an image of cohesion and the possibility of developing one great theory there is no similar unity within Asia. As China develops its economy to the point of competing with the USA for the title of world's largest, there is nothing in the Chinese sociocultural model that can be taken as the basis for development of a single theoretical Asian model. Nor does such an element exist in Japan or South Korea, the second and third largest industrialists in the region.

REFLECT AND DISCUSS

Begin to imagine the continued development of public relations theory and practice in Asia in the twenty-first century.

➤ What direction might it take?

➤ What models will be used to position the Asian corporation of the future?

➤ What theories will governments apply to their public relationships with existing and emerging stakeholders?

➤ Will activist and not-for-profit organisations take up spaces in the same way they do in Western democracies?

➤ How will practitioners engage with new developments?

What makes public relations important

There are a number of important factors at work in Asia that make the job of public relations more complex than it may be in individual Western countries. In this, the object of globalisation applies as much to the region as it does to the global. In the countries presented here, there are different and competing levels of economic and political activity. The economic position of China outranks all others, while the political position of Thailand as an emerging democracy is less stable than that of Vietnam and China as socialist republics. Economics and politics play important roles in the dynamics of public relations development, but the subtleties of difference are less evident than are the sociocultural and sociolinguistic differences that force situational variable analysis.

Trade

Trade, for example, is paramount in most discussions of global growth and increased economic wellbeing among developing countries, which in Asia are Cambodia, Laos, and Vietnam (for a definition of developed and developing countries, see Dicken 2007). But trade alone is an insufficient measure of the success of economic wellbeing. Education, health, telecommunications, and political stability are also factors in the frame. Of equal if not greater importance is the role of the news media in each country. While Singapore makes a claim to being one of the region's leading business innovators, its news media are substantially controlled by government.

The governments of China and Vietnam control all news media in those countries, while South Korea's government has, at best, a fragmented media relationship. Japan comes closest to the idea of free media and thus the possibility of the orthodox models of public relations working effectively among all potential stakeholders (Stanton 2007). The development of alternative media channels such as the internet has created the possibility of some public relations practices becoming more uniform across the region (distribution of media news statements, for example), but such developments are proscribed by government control of internet access, as in China and Vietnam, Laos, and Cambodia.

Languages

The number of languages in Asia also poses a hurdle for public relations. While English may be the language of business, in many countries with little or no history of association it provides only minimal opportunity for general accessibility. This factor, together with those mentioned in the section above, combine to work against the idea of regionalisation of public relations but they can be overcome.

It is a similar situation to that of the international non-English-speaking background (NESB) student studying public relations overseas. In order to succeed, the student must overcome a number of barriers, including visa applications, finding accommodation, learning to interpret local signs and symbols, and dealing with the emotional impact of relocation. They are then confronted with a number of more complex hurdles, such as the interpretation of meaning of tutorials and classes, the development of relationships with classmates and professors, and ultimately the submission of assessment tasks. As a whole, this would be sufficient to frighten most potential students away but it can be broken down into manageable components. Such is the case of public relations theory and practice in Asia. While there may be no particular model that fits all, there are elements of a number of theories and practices that provide an outline of overall effectiveness.

Government intent

For the most part, governments in Asia control economic and political activity far more than governments do in Western democracies. The role of the private corporation has been limited since the middle of the last century—in Japan, for example—but its emergence in China since the beginning of the twenty-first century and its relationship to government has created a favourable climate for public relations development. For public relations to be effective, governments and corporations need to define who it is they are building relationships with. In other words, they need to understand who their stakeholders are.

Stakeholders

Public relations in Asia, as elsewhere, defines its stakeholders as primary and secondary. But unlike the West, where the news media would be considered primary stakeholders, the media in Asia are far less important. 'Stakeholders' can be defined as those entities who agents and other forces are interested in influencing and persuading. Potentially, there is a large number of stakeholders with a lot of different names—publics, audiences, listeners, readers, shareholders, communities, special interest groups, investors, citizens, and individuals among them (Stanton 2007). In this book, stakeholders are considered as one target public along with audiences and communities, but this chapter presents stakeholders as representing these different groups. Here are some examples:

➤ As China builds vast industrial and housing tracts, the Chinese government considers Western financial backers one of its most important stakeholder groups. It must create strong relationships with these financial backers if it is to continue to fund its developments without using up all its capital reserves.
➤ In South Korea, the government is working to establish a more transparent relationship with its citizens through a greater level of Western-style engagement with the news media. This has positive implications for other governments throughout Asia.

Personal interaction

For public relations practitioners in Asia, the primary source of income and employment is the direct client. Clients, whatever the nature of their issue or event, seek to directly influence and persuade the stakeholder of most interest at the time. Mediated communication is a less important part of the opinion-forming process in Asia than it is in the West. The human channel—discussion and conversations at local level—provides a more valuable opinion-forming mechanism in Asia, especially in China, than in the West (Hung & Chen 2004). Public opinion is the opinion formed by a majority after consideration of an issue or event. In the twenty-first century, it is most often informed by news received from media sources such as television, radio, newspapers, the internet, and magazines; it is reinforced by personal communication between individuals. Public opinion is thus an expression of social, economic, and political will (Stanton 2007).

REFLECT AND DISCUSS

➤ The Asian focus on the importance of personal interaction plays directly into the view, often espoused in the West, that mass media allows many people to be reached and is therefore a cost-efficient communication tool, but that personal contact is more effective. Can you think of examples that you have seen in which personal contact in a public relations program has been particularly valuable to the program?
➤ Using the internet, try to source a public relations case study or example from several different Asian countries.

Public relations and a public sphere

In any attempt to define public relations, especially from a cultural perspective, its relationship to the concept of a public sphere must be considered. For the purposes of understanding the theoretical position of public relations in Asia, you need to understand the need for the existence of a public sphere and, within it, the existence of public opinion and a general public.

French sociologist Pierre Bourdieu's theory of field, in which actors and agents compete for available space (see also the concept of contested space, Chapter 9), can be combined with the concept of the public sphere provided by Habermas. Habermas defined and conceptualised the public sphere within a social science paradigm. In Western democracies the public sphere is viewed from a number of competing positions but in Asia there is no similar image of competitive positions. Habermas' public sphere was defined as a meeting place or public forum—a mediating environment—in which literate and wealthy citizens openly exchanged information and news about relevant political and economic issues and events and with the object of profit (Stanton 2007).

The image of a public sphere has been historically important to the function of journalism and news media in the West (even if it has been more myth than reality), but in Asia, a different importance has been applied to its existence. Public spaces are occupied almost continually, 24/7 by markets, trade, manufacturing, food production and consumption, citizens, and tourists. Public spaces are thus occupied for the processes of living, rather than as designated meeting spaces for the actions of the few. The suggestion that a public sphere in which discursive processes in public spaces embodies the good in a society resonates with us as citizens (see, for example, Schudson 1999). In Asia the embodiment of the good lies in the level of activity on the street, and it is this public expression of culture through street communication that lies at the heart of relationship building and, therefore, public relations in Asia.

For public relations in Asia, relationship building and framing are the main theoretical components, as they are in the West. Framing requires a public relations practitioner to think about an issue or event in a particular way. They must think about the issue or event as part of a wider ideology determined by the cultural context and frame it within that ideological position.

REFLECT AND DISCUSS

> ➤ What makes Asian relationship building different to Western concepts or relationships?
> ➤ How have the histories that exist in Asia contributed to the deep development of relationship building?

Richard Stanton

The ideological position of Samsung in South Korea, for example, might be different to the ideological position of Sony in Japan, even though both corporations are in the business of competitively manufacturing and supplying technologically innovative products. Practitioners also need to understand the ideological positions of stakeholders so the frame they build around the issue or event matches the agenda embedded within the stakeholder ideology. Ideologies vary hugely. The normative ideology of the corporation is return on investment to shareholders, but in recent years some of the world's largest transnational corporations have demonstrated they share that ideological position with one of greater corporate social responsibility and social capital investment (see Chapter 6). The public relations practitioner in Asia, like their Western counterpart, must be pragmatic when framing an issue in ideological terms.

An example of how an Asian government framed an important political issue using effective public relations can be seen in the case of Taiwan and its determination for independence from China. In the summer of 1971, after a protracted struggle, Taiwan lost its seat in the United Nations to the Republic of China. As a country without statehood, Taiwan's image as a satellite of the People's Democratic Republic of China may have appeared hopeless, but since 1993 Taiwan has applied regularly, if unsuccessfully, for UN membership under the name 'Republic of China'. This continuing strategic attempt to overcome diplomatic isolation was reconstructed in July 2007 with a number of initiatives, one of which was described by the *Economist* as being 'backed … with a public relations campaign that will culminate in a mass rally on September 15th, three days before the annual session of the UN General Assembly' (*Economist*, 8 September 2007: 35).

The *Economist*, along with other Western news media, is not shy about imagining Asian governmental issues and events in negative public relations terms, a position that makes it more difficult for those governments to build strong external relationships with Western media. This raises some interesting questions. If national governments such as those in Asia attempt to employ public relations strategies to achieve increased levels of wellbeing for their citizens in a socioeconomic context:

➤ can they expect positive support from Western news media and other stakeholders in attempting to reach their goals?
➤ can they build transparent relationships with global news media, particularly Western news media, in which important issues are framed so that they resonate with citizens?
➤ can public relations ever be imagined by the Western news media as being of value in the pursuit and exercise of transparency?

In the West the news media represent themselves as independent and objective, reporting issues and events as they observe them. They also represent themselves as stakeholders vital to the outcome of many complex and important social, political, and cultural goals and objectives.

The Taiwan case is instructive in that it demonstrates how public relations can be used at government and supranational institutional levels (UN) to attempt to achieve socioeconomic or sociopolitical goals and objectives. The case was reported during the week before the UN decision on 18 September 2007. For example, Hong Kong's *South China Morning Post* described the 500 000 rally participants as 'marching under green and white banners and shouting "Taiwan my country" ' (*South China Morning Post* 15 September 2007). A day later the same newspaper reported threats emanating from Beijing in which it would 'not tolerate any moves to separate Taiwan from the mainland' (*South China Morning Post* 17 September 2007), and referred to the marchers and supporters of the president of the previous day as 'demonstrators'.

The cynical observer of the Taiwanese government strategy—the mobilisation and management of such a large gathering for the purpose of demonstrating collective will—might be tempted to argue that it was a pointless exercise as China's veto power in the UN presented an impasse for any Taiwanese intervention. Such a position was also imagined by the *Straits Times*, which provided a five paragraph opinion on the matter two days after Singapore's ruling Democratic Progressive Party held a rally about the Taiwanese government's strategy and a day before the UN vote. It stated that since 1971 Taiwan has repeatedly failed to rejoin the UN, and that, as had occurred in past attempts, it is 'certain' to be blocked by China (17 September 2007). To balance its cynical observation it provided a glimmer of hope by suggesting that the bid had 'attracted unprecedented attention this year because of the planned referendum' (*Straits Times* 17 September 2007).

Professionalisation of public relations in Asia

The professionalisation of public relations is a global issue with various regional and local discourses. While L'Etang and Pieczka suggest professionalisation requires the triangulation of a body of knowledge with a code of ethics and certification (2006: 270), there can be no doubt that public relations is a very different pursuit to those Western practices that are professionalised: law, medicine, engineering, and accountancy. In this the teaching and practice of public relations in Asia differs little from its Western counterparts.

Just as the theories that dominate Asian teaching are derived primarily from the USA, so too are the practices, although there are some interesting variations in some countries (see over page). The important point is that some countries aspire to professionalisation as it is being pursued vigorously in the West, while others are content

Richard Stanton

to meander along, using different public relations models and technologies with little consideration for long-term implications:

➤ In Japan, for example, public relations is practised in a cultural and economic context that differs little from Western countries.

➤ In Indonesia public relations is directed neither by a code of ethics nor by certification.

➤ In Singapore, the primary purpose of public relations is government propaganda.

➤ In Malaysia it is employed at a variety of levels but fluctuates depending upon the political circumstances of the day.

Initially, public relations organisations set about practising public relations in Asia the way they practised it in the West. Patricia Curtin and Kenn Gaither (2007) cite one of the Western world's leading practitioners, Harold Burson, who, on setting up a practice in Japan, hired an American and an Englishman, who he trained in the methods and culture of the company (Burson-Marsteller) before sending them to Japan (2007: 114). This is diametrically different to how the Japanese approached the manufacture of a motor vehicle for the US market. When the Toyota Motor Corporation considered manufacturing a luxury vehicle for the US market, it sent a dozen of its designers, engineers, and managers to the USA, where they lived for two years, observing and inculcating all the available social and cultural idiosyncrasies. The result was the Lexus (an acronym for **L**uxury **Ex**port **U**nited **S**tates).

REFLECT AND DISCUSS

➤ Is it possible for public relations practitioners to present themselves professionally so they are part of business culture in Asia?

➤ What different approach might you need to take in each country to add value to business decisions?

Country by country practice

China

China, the world's largest country by population and one of the largest by trade and manufacturing, is politically as far removed from the need for orthodox public relations methods and practice as a country could be, yet in measurable terms it is one of the world's biggest consumers of public relations education and training.

Part of the reason for the excessive interest in public relations theory and practice in China can be directed towards its winning of the nomination to host the 2008 Olympic Games in Beijing. For China, whose position had been less than satisfactory for a number of years following the 1989 Tiananmen Square student demonstrations and subsequent killings, the win was an affirmation of its powerful position in world trade and affairs. For twenty years following the crackdown in Beijing, the Chinese government made numerous unsuccessful attempts to ameliorate its human rights position. The 2008 Olympics gave it the impetus to demonstrate its virtues and to do so it was required very quickly to learn media and public relations skills. Chinese government news media followed the lead of Chinese corporations by engaging vast numbers of experts from the West to train them in effective public relations and media techniques.

Ni Chen and Hugh Culbertson (2003) argue that China's long, uninterrupted history of more than 5000 years, a state that requires continuous support from citizens, is in itself a great public relations achievement (2003: 23).

According to Mazhural Haque (2004, following Chen 1996), 1989 proved to be a turning point for the government in its views on Western style public relations and strategic communication as the student pro-democracy movement demonstrated that Western-style public relations was more effective than the traditional Confucian methods of relationship development and loyalty (2004: 358). More recently, the main institutional body representing China's public relations practitioners, China International Public Relations Association, forecast public relations growth around 45 per cent annually (CIPRA 2000). Student enrolments in public relations courses in Western countries, including New Zealand and Australia, support these findings. More than 50 per cent of students enrolled in two Masters courses in public relations and media at the University of Sydney in 2008 originated from China (Stanton 2008).

Public relations and related activity can be separated into geographic zones, though there is no hard and fast rule that delineates them:

➤ In Beijing the emphasis is on government, or public affairs and public diplomacy.
➤ Shenzhen and Shanghai are the focal points for corporate and financial relations.
➤ Guangzhou has developed as a consumer market in which integrated marketing communication plays a more dominant role.

More than 150 associations with a public relations focus exist throughout the mainland, including organisations that have a narrow focus on customer and guest relations and translation services, which are important elements in a country where English is not diffuse.

Hong Kong

Even though it is part of China, Hong Kong is known as a separate autonomous region (SAR). Hong Kong has a special place in Chinese corporate and economic history in that

Richard Stanton

it was once the centre of Western activity in Southeast Asia. Business activity accounts for most public relations practice. Since 1995, Hong Kong has been institutionalised under the organisation Hong Kong Public Relations Professionals' Association (HKPRPA), an independent organisation made up of corporate and public sector members. The HKPRPA has a published code of professional standards.

Public relations pedagogy in Hong Kong crosses public and private institutions, such as universities and colleges. Theory is based mainly on US models but there is a growing body of work that takes account of the peculiar nature of Hong Kong as an autonomous region. Prior to the handover of Hong Kong by the British government to the Chinese government, international businesses operated out of Hong Kong as a link to the mainland and as a hub between Europe and the rest of Asia. Thus it has a well-developed public relations base that operates across all of the recognised public relations activities, including issues management.

As a thriving capitalist base, Hong Kong has provided other Chinese regions with an enthusiastic model for development, most notably Shenzhen and Guangzhou. The mixture of Chinese philosophy and ideology with Western culture in Hong Kong makes the practice of public relations more challenging and more dynamic. On the Chinese side, Confucian philosophy dominates business. Relationship building, particularly human relationships, are crucial to success, but mixed with this is the pragmatism associated with the success of Western individuality that allows the development of business relationships without always needing a concomitant building of personal relationships.

The relative freedom of the news media provides additional access for Western public relations practices as the media is less government-controlled than media in countries such as Singapore, Indonesia, or Vietnam. According to Chen (2004), a peculiar form of *guanxi* known as *renji guanxi* exists in Hong Kong and has an influence on the practice of public relations. This form of social capital (see Bourdieu 1977) comprises the institutions, values, and relationships that make up Hong Kong society (Chen 2004: 100). The networks that sustain *renji guanxi* have, since 1997, begun to extend to Western businesses and corporations, a shift in emphasis from the past in which foreigners and Western public relations practices were less acceptable.

Indonesia

Public relations as a Western form of persuasion and influence is practised narrowly in Indonesia, predominantly on the main island of Java and mainly within the larger cities, particularly Jakarta. Like Malaysia, Indonesia is predominantly Islamic, a situation that has important ramifications for the practice of Western-style public relations.

While it has been noted that Japan, China, Korea, and Vietnam look to the Confucian philosophy of harmony to maintain their sociopolitical institutions, Indonesia draws strength from its ideology of *pancasila* (and Malaysia from *rukunegar*), or shared values and a sense of national identity rather than individualism.

As in Vietnam, Indonesia is in a state of primary engagement with public relations for the purposes of nation building. Indonesia was in political and economic upheaval for most of the twentieth century, with vast stratification of culture, ethnicity, history, and economics from where it is battling to shift politically from a closed authoritarian regime to a democracy (Anato 2004). In this, as noted elsewhere, the development of public relations in a specific environment is framed and paralleled by the development of democracy. The slow rate of development of democracy and the problems confronting government, including large-scale internal corruption, provide almost insurmountable hurdles to the increased professionalisation of public relations in Indonesia (Anato 2004).

A further difficulty for the practice of orthodox Western public relations is government control of the news media. Although measurement of the controlled Asian media systems in terms of freedom is a complex task, it could be said that media control in Indonesia is similar to the control in Singapore but less proscribed than China and Vietnam (Stanton 2007).

Indonesia is a land mass comprising more than 14 000 islands with a population of around 230 million. Most public relations activity occurs in the major business centre of Jakarta, although one could argue that tourism and services from Bali to Borneo contribute significant financial investments. Nonetheless, public relations, practised by marketers and advertisers, is not well defined. The main functions of public relations are nation building by the government, and for market building and trade relations by business (Thomas 2004: 391). Most activity is centred on media relations, charity and social service, corporate advertising, financial relations, government relations, and opinion research (399).

In the aftermath of the struggle for independence by former Indonesian territory East Timor, the Indonesian government employed a number of public relations strategies to gain the support it needed from regional neighbours and global partners for its continued economic and political stability.

By early 2008, as the international market gained more confidence in business in Indonesia, IPOs were becoming more regular. International agencies such as Hill & Knowlton or Burson-Marsteller have been involved directly in the provision of public relations services for initial public offerings (IPOs) where private corporations have listed on the Jakarta stock exchange (IDX).

Japan

Japan is an interesting place for the practice of public relations. It is home to the world's largest advertising agencies and the world's biggest circulation news media, so there is a tradition of using the services of advertising agencies and paid advertising rather than public relations. Western-style public relations has traditionally been viewed as being in conflict with elements of Confucian philosophy.

The Confucian notions of the importance of hierarchical relationships and humility create tensions with the more aggressive elements of Western public relations (Inoue 2003: 69). The possibility of using public relations for issues management in government, especially, is relatively new. According to a 2007 stakeholder survey by Edelman, one of the world's largest public relations consultancies, 85 per cent of respondents said they believed public relations was increasingly important to the corporate sector, while 70 per cent said that media channels were the most trustworthy and believable (Edelman 2007).

Japan has an active institutional presence, the Public Relations Society of Japan (PRSJ), which has been in existence for more than twenty-five years following a merger between the PR Society of Japan (founded in 1964) and the PR Industry Association (founded in 1974). PRSJ membership is predominantly agency and corporate departments centred on Tokyo. Unlike its near neighbours South Korea and Taiwan, Japan does not have a broad availability of scholarship and teaching in public relations at universities and colleges. It does, however, have a similar history for three decades between the 1950s and 1970s when accelerated economic growth brought with it the anticipation of the need for increased public relations activity. A number of agencies were established during this time, though much of the activity undertaken could be described in non-professional and marketing terms.

Japanese governments and corporations tend to differentiate their public relations requirements. They employ inhouse practitioners for everything manageable then turn to agencies during times of turbulence or crisis (Inoue 2003). This appears to be related to the dominant position of advertising of which public relations is traditionally considered a subfield. Japan has a cultural history that has tended to limit the growth of public relations. While Singapore and South Korea particularly have pragmatically merged philosophies with business, Japan has been less enthusiastic, retaining the concept of *wa*, or harmony, a cultural practice in which aims and goals are reached through mutual cooperation rather than competition (Inoue 2003: 77).

According to Toshiya Takata and Robert Magyar (2007) the biggest difficulty for public relations agencies lies in their inability to work across their areas of expertise due to the reluctance of Japanese businesses and governments to outsource major specialist areas such as media relations, investor relations, and issues management. This position began to change in 2003 when a political organisation, the Democratic Party of Japan (DPJ), used a public relations consultancy to help with its election campaign strategy; and the Liberal Democratic Party (LDP) chose to engage a public relations agency to assist it in 2005 with a public information campaign about postal services (Takata & Magyar 2003). Media coverage of these issues led to an increased awareness of the potential role for public relations in politics as well as government and business.

Malaysia

Politically and economically, Malaysia is an interesting place. It is a predominantly Muslim country, with similar structures of government and politics to Indonesia, yet economically more buoyant than its neighbour. The Institute of Public Relations Malaysia (IPRM) has set itself high standards of accountability in the past few years, measuring itself against those in the United Kingdom and the USA, the International Association of Business Communicators, and more importantly, against the Bar Council of Malaysia. It has talked more seriously than other Asian public relations accreditors of the possibility of licensing of practitioners, with the result that it is closer to the establishment of professional identity than most other Asian countries. Another of its moves towards serious recognition is its royal patronage. Such recognition is a reflection of the importance of the royal imprimatur in other countries, such as the United Kingdom.

The most important stakeholders for public relations activities are government, the corporate sector, and the news media. The similarity between these and Western stakeholder importance becomes more obvious when the fact that Malaysia's major trading partners are the USA, Japan, and Singapore is considered (Venkateswaran 2004).

Western public relations has played a vital role in Malaysian development of the sector, but according to Zulhamri Abdullah and Terry Threadgold (2003), it has had difficulty in reaching maturity, and professional status within the sociopolitical sphere. The main elements of practice that Abdullah and Threadgold identify as being critical to the emergence of public relations professionalism in Malaysia are the exclusive jurisdictions of stakeholder relations, reputation management (corporate branding), corporate social responsibility, and consultative and corporate advisory services to management. The extent of public relations activity in governments and corporations has been driven by professionals and public relations has become 'integrated into the overall management policy and practice' (Idid 2004: 207). While public relations is integrating into management policy it is also perceived socially as being 'identified with karaoke singers and social escorts' (Idid 2004: 207), a position not dissimilar to that in China and Singapore.

For Malaysia, and particularly for government policy, the stated intention of reaching critical mass in its industrial strength by 2020 poses challenges and opportunities for public relations practitioners and theorists within Malaysia as well as externally.

The Philippines

The Philippines history invokes a long relationships with the USA and thus provides the basis for active public relations across a number of sectors, including government, business, and industry, not-for-profit, health, education, and services. The Public Relations Society of the Philippines (PRSP), established more than forty years ago, is the institutional umbrella under which public relations practitioners practice. The PRSP provides an accreditation process for potential members that includes written and oral examinations and an adherence to its *Code of Ethical Standards in the Practice of Public Relations.*

Like a number of its counterparts in the region, scholarship and teaching of public relations is centred on the wider field of communication, embracing journalism and media rather than specifically focusing on public relations. The main universities also tend to teach from US-based textbooks rather than culturally relocating material for a domestic student base.

The majority of practitioners in the Philippines are employed by large corporations, such as Manila Water Company, or in the public sector by organisations such as Manila Electric Company.

Journalism and public relations are viewed as activities that are not always free of corruption. According to Maria Zenaida Sarabia-Panol and Caterina Lorenzo-Molo (2004) the reputation of public relations is 'plagued by corruption and unsound practices' (2004: 132). But if a culture of corruption exists in public relations and journalism that amounts to the distribution of gifts to all types of stakeholders (and stakeseekers), then the Philippines differs very little from most other Asian countries or from countries in the West.

Singapore

Singapore is the smallest country by land mass in Asia, yet it is one of the most technologically advanced, although this does not mean it is one of the most advanced in terms of the professionalisation of strategic communication. Government control has limited the obvious practice of public relations, as it has limited the historical freedom of the news media, yet Singapore has an active institutional organisation, the Institute of Public Relations of Singapore (IPRS). The not-for-profit IPRS was established in 1970 to assist the process of public relations growth through the acquisition of knowledge and information, and networking. Unlike many other public relations institutions in Asia, IPRS has a constitution in which is embedded its code of ethics. Interestingly, despite its relatively small population, IPRS has around the same number of members as Japan's PRSJ. But, like most other public relations organisations, the object of its existence is to enhance the reputation of the profession rather than to enforce ethical conduct and the growth of professionalisation. Singapore has a size advantage in that businesses and industries most likely to require the services of public relations practitioners are located in a relatively small area.

Singapore has a strong recent history of public relations teaching and scholarship. It is also a large direct consumer of Western public relations. According to Kate Fitch and Anne Surma (2006), Singapore and Malaysia provide Western Australia's Murdoch

University with up to 60 per cent of students in its public relations programs (2006: 104). Newsom (2004) argues that Singapore, with its government initiative to become a paperless society and its adoption of English as the language of business (coinciding with the language of the internet), has the potential to become a leader in international public relations (2004: 363). Constance Chay-Nemeth (2003) provides an added insight into the practice of public relations in suggesting that it can be best understood when viewed as the relationship between government and geopolitics in all the major areas of development: political, economic, and social (2003: 86).

Tactical methods such as press agentry and information dissemination have embodied public relations in Singapore for so long that it is difficult to see it as being of any more complex value, especially given the government's control and use of public relations' close relative, public diplomacy. As with some of its near neighbours, Singapore suffers from a lack of understanding of a definition of public relations, merging it with advertising, marketing, and publicity. In this, it has an added difficulty in defining the relationship between public relations and the news media. For public relations practitioners in Singapore any media relationship must first be developed as a matter of public affairs with government. This places an unrealistic burden on practitioners who must be seen to have the added skills of the public affairs practitioner.

South Korea

Public relations in South Korea is dominated by the cultural notion of *cheong*. *Cheong* has been given important status as a key to relationship building between journalism and media relations in Korea (Berkowitz & Lee 2004), similar to the importance of *guanxi* in China. South Korea has a dynamic media industry and there are two elements in Korean social relationships that can be extrapolated into media relationship development: *cheong*, that which exists between Koreans, and *no-cheong*, non-developmental contact with others, which appears to be closer in form to the notion of *guanxi*. In this, business and personal relationships are fostered and developed for the period of time necessary. Afterwards, there is little or no contact until necessity again arises.

Public relations pedagogy in South Korea is widespread among public and private universities at undergraduate and graduate level. In some cases it is taught entirely in English, in others in Korean. Despite the spread of learning and teaching in universities and colleges, the practice of public relations is still dominated by *hong-bo*, a Korean term that indirectly refers to the practice of public relations as a subfield of media relations (Kim 2003).

At the end of the 1980s, a shift occurred in the image of public relations, similar to that which occurred in China during and after the 2008 Olympics. Twenty years earlier, the 1988 summer Olympics in Seoul had a similar effect. On that occasion, numerous international public relations agencies were employed by the South Korean government and the measurable value of their involvement provided it with good reason to retain their services for additional large projects.

The level of professionalism in public relations in South Korea remains limited by the dominance of media relations as a hegemonic process, although in late 2007 the government invested a significant amount of funding in research into how it could become more transparent through the complex employment of public relations. This acknowledgement of the important role of public relations converged with a desire by the South Korean government to demonstrate its competitive significance in Asia at a time of increased globalisation.

Taiwan

Taiwan, also known as 'Taiwan, Republic of China', is an interesting and dynamic place for active public relations practice. Its government and its political parties use it for national and international campaign purposes, while business and industry employ every type of public relations practice to gain competitive and comparative advantage. Taiwan's political history is too complex to consider here, other than to acknowledge that it appears to maintain itself as a democracy while it attempts to reconcile with and, at the same time, unfetter its relations with the People's Republic of China.

In cultural terms, Taiwan reflects a Confucian philosophy similar to that of Japan, Korea, Hong Kong, and China, with the additional virtue of building strong business relationships using a mixture of *guanxi* and Western public relations.

Public relations pedagogy in Taiwan follows the US model parallel with Korea, in that the leading scholars have undertaken study in the USA, and then returned to their homeland to teach the theories they learnt and absorbed in the USA. Taiwan colleges began teaching public relations in the early 1960s; by the 1990s a number of national and private universities had begun teaching full-time courses in public relations theory and practice.

Part of the reason public relations practices have flourished in the main economic sectors of government and corporate sectors is that English is the language of business. Mandarin Chinese competes with a number of local languages, some of which are broadcast on Taiwan's relatively liberal media. The news media generally are divided between party loyalists and those who seek to balance news coverage without government or party intervention.

Thailand

Public relations education began in Thailand in 1965 at Chulalongkorn University. From this small beginning public relations is now taught in twenty-one universities at undergraduate and graduate levels. Teaching, which is done in Thai, resembles the US curricula. Most practitioners in Thailand are product and service oriented.

Like most other Asian countries, and indeed, some Western countries, Thailand has its own peculiarities that affect its relationship with Western-style public relations. In Thai culture the importance of the image of self is paramount. Self-face—the image of oneself that is projected into the public sphere—plays a role in all Thai culture to the extent that governments have frequently enacted information campaigns to persuade citizens of the value in altering certain behaviours and attitudes. There is nothing unusual in this as it follows most Western countries that have a duty towards their citizens on issues of health, education, transport, and other socially grounded policies. However, while Thailand has been a constitutional monarchy since 1932 and has seen strong economic development since the mid 1980s, most public relations is practised by governments rather than by the corporate sector. In the early years of the twenty-first century corporate activity has increased but is framed by marketing and advertising rather than issues management, although tourism and the services sector widely apply image building and relationship management strategies throughout urban and rural areas (Haque 2004).

Vietnam

Public relations is in its infancy in Vietnam. By 2008, it had been taught for a few years as an undergraduate program in universities in Hanoi and Ho Chi Minh, and developed as a postgraduate field in Hanoi. It is practised primarily by international organisations with an interest in trade and investment in the Vietnamese stock market. Vietnam is a socialist republic with a single party government that rarely recognises the importance of public relations or differentiates stakeholders. With its entry into the World Trade Organisation in 2006 the government began to acknowledge the necessity of building relationships and identifying stakeholders outside its historical spheres of influence, Russia and China. The government acknowledged that, if it were to engage effectively in a globalised world, the need for skills development in communication would be required.

Vietnam has not yet developed an institutional framework for its practice. It has no umbrella organisation under which to frame ethical and professional practices, nor does the country identify public relations in any way other than as a tool of government to be used for nation building. The problem for Vietnam is that while government is using public relations as a primary nation building tool, it is at once attempting to balance the second stage of action—market development—so that it appears at times to be working in opposition to itself.

Public relations practice in Vietnam manifests in strange ways. While international organisations, including corporations and NGOs, employ public relations strategies and tactics in orthodox ways—image promotion for products and services, building

Richard Stanton

relationships—the media also act as promoters of all types of activities from trade to political information campaigns. In Western terms, it is relatively easy to build media relationships in Vietnam, as it is in China, due to the role of the media in supporting government policies. Newsrooms in Hanoi and Ho Chi Minh City look identical to newsrooms in the West. The difference lies in the role of sources and how journalists report material for broadcast, telecast, and publication. A typical newsroom such as that of *Vietnam News* (English and Vietnamese language versions) takes material from sources in government and publishes long, unexpurgated tracts of copy that announce the virtue of the government policy. This has enormous ramifications for the increased use of Western-style public relations. While the government has control of the media and uses it for its own public relations purposes, agencies and individual public relations practitioners are proscribed within the commercial sector and must compete with government supplied material for space in the news media.

CHAPTER **SUMMARY**

- ➤ One theoretical model does not cover all aspects of public relations in Asia.
- ➤ Different types of practice and management need to be applied in different circumstances in different countries.
- ➤ Culture and language play important roles in developing relationships and framing issues.
- ➤ Public relations has vast potential for all types of strategy developments from nation building to issues management.
- ➤ The contextual influences of government and culture are instrumental in defining how public relations operates in the countries studied in this chapter.

CASE STUDY　　BIDDING CAMPAIGN FOR THE 17TH ASIAN GAMES

SITUATION

In October 2005, Incheon Metropolitan City, the site of Seoul Airport, and, with a population of 2.7 million, the third largest city in South Korea, submitted a bid to the Olympic Council of Asia (OCA), the governing body of the Asian Games (Continental Olympic Games in Asia), to host the 17th Asian Games in 2014. The result, known as the Host City Decision, was made at the 26th OCA General Assembly on 17 April 2007 in Kuwait City. The bid was coordinated by Ms Hyun Jung Lee, chief of the Seoul Office, 2014 Incheon Asian Games Bidding Committee. At the time of publication, Ms Lee was coordinator at the Olympic Council of Asia, the governing body of the Asian Games and forty-five Asian National Olympic Committees.

Incheon was relatively new to the Asian Olympic community, whereas one of its competitors, Delhi, the capital of India, was well known. South Korea was well known as the successful host of major international sport events such as the Asian Games in Seoul (1986) and Busan (2002), the summer Olympic Games in Seoul (1988), and the FIFA World Cup (2002). Yet South Korea's sport diplomacy and leadership in the Asian sporting community was perceived to be not as strong as India's, which exercised diplomatic leadership under Randhir Singh, IOC member and OCA secretary-general.

OBJECTIVES

➤ Raise the profile of Incheon metropolitan city and position Incheon among OCA voters as the best host city for the Asian Games.

➤ Secure voters for Incheon over Delhi (at least twenty-seven votes for Incheon were required for it to be the host city).

TIME FRAME

October 2005–April 2007 (18 months).

PUBLICS AND AUDIENCES

➤ Voters at the OCA General Assembly, and presidents and secretaries-general of National Olympic Committees in forty-five Asian countries, which, for the purposes of the bid, are grouped into five regions: West Asia (fourteen Middle East countries), Central Asia (five countries, including Kazakhstan), East Asia (eight countries, including China and North Korea), Southeast Asia (ten countries, including Indonesia and East Timor), and South Asia (eight countries, including India and Pakistan).

➤ Asian media (sports and general), politicians, businesspeople, and government (ministries of foreign affairs, ministries of culture and sports) as influencers and third party endorsers for Incheon.

➤ Olympic Council of Asia as a silent third party endorser.

STRATEGY

➤ Provide voters with sufficient evidence for them to rationally rate Incheon as the best city to host the Asian Games and to emotionally favour Incheon over Delhi.

➤ Mobilise all possible interlocutors and spokespeople (MPs, South Korean embassies throughout Asia, Korean media) to influence voters to favour Incheon over Delhi.

➤ Use hard power (rational approach) to persuade voters logically that Incheon was ready to host the Games (in terms of infrastructure, climate, environment, general standard of living, sports facilities, and advanced IT systems, for example).

➤ Use soft power (emotional approach; humane and 'skinship') to be personally close to voters and move their minds.

TACTICS

➤ Direct relations with voters.

➤ Develop and cement personally close relations with voters to show sincerity.

➤ Invite voters to South Korea to let them personally experience how the country really is and to build favourable relations.

➤ Key Incheon representatives to personally visit Asian NOCs and demonstrate the sincere preparedness of Incheon to host the Games.

➤ Participate in every overseas occasion (meetings, seminars, other sports) where voters gather to show the professional face of Incheon.

➤ Create breakfast venues and receptions where Incheon representatives can informally meet with voters.

➤ Create personal one-on-one meetings—breakfast, lunch, and dinner—between Incheon representatives and voters.

GOVERNMENT SUPPORT

➤ The minister of culture and sports of South Korea and the president of the Korean Olympic Committee attend major receptions at overseas games where voters gather to support Incheon by showing the South Korean government's strong support for Incheon's bid.

➤ Use South Korean embassies in target Asian countries as venues to host official dinners and luncheons and invite voters to demonstrate the South Korean government's strong support.

ADVOCATE RELATIONS

➤ Undertake research into the friends and influential business associates of voters and attempt to employ them as third party endorsers.

➤ Build favourable relations with voters' family members to utilise them as interlocutors.

➤ Build favourable relations and earn trust from OCA executives (even though they are not voters) in order to carry their silent support.

MEDIA RELATIONS

➤ Invite key influential Asian media (sports and general) to South Korea and Incheon to let them experience Incheon and its readiness.

SUPPORT MATERIAL

➤ Develop well-balanced (rational and emotional) presentations and brochures with state-of-the-art IT equipment to deliver the message 'Why Incheon?' at every official occasion, including at the OCA General Assembly, executive board meetings, and regional fora.

➤ Utilise IT gadgets as strategic gifts for voters and influencers to remind them of South Korea as a state-of-the-art advanced country in IT.

➤ Ms Hyun Jung Lee was one of the key people dealing directly with voters. She was also the official presenter during the bidding process.

OTHER ELEMENTS CONSIDERED

➤ Consistency: key Incheon representatives building relationships with voters.

➤ To better appeal to Asians use Asian English and avoid American English in presentation materials and delivery.

➤ Emphasise Asian values that most Asians share (for example, modesty, sincerity) for tone of presentations and brochures.

RESULT

On 17 April 2007, Incheon won thirty-two votes over Delhi's thirteen at the 26th OCA General Assembly in Kuwait City.

WEBSITE RESOURCES

China International Public Relations Association, at cipra.org.cn.

Edelman Public Relations, at www.edelman.com.

Hong Kong Public Relations Professionals' Association, at www.prpa.com.hk/eng/index.asp.

Indonesia Stock Exchange, at www.bie.co.id.

Institute of Public Relations Malaysia, at www.iprm.org.my/home.htm.

Institute of Public Relations of Singapore, at www.ipra.org.sg.

International Public Relations Association, at www.ipra.org.

Public Relations Society of Japan, at www.prjs.or.jp.

Public Relations Society of the Philippines, at www.prsp. ph.

Richard Stanton

REFERENCES

Abdullah, Z & Threadgold, T 2003, 'Towards the Professionalisation of Public Relations in Malaysia: Perception Management and Strategy Development', Malaysian conference paper.

Ananto, E 2004, 'The Development of Public Relations in Indonesia', in K Sriramesh (ed.) 2004, *Public Relations in Asia: An Anthology*, Thomson Learning, Singapore.

Beng, Y 1994, 'The State of Public Relations in Singapore', *Public Relations Review*, 20(4): 373–94.

Berkowitz, D & Lee, J 2004, 'Media Relations in Korea: *Cheong* Between Journalist and Public Relations Practitioner', *Public Relations Review*, 30(43): 431–7.

Botan, C & Hazleton, V 2006, *Public Relations Theory II*, Lawrence Erlbaum, Mahwah.

Bourdieu, P 1977, *Outline of a Theory of Practice*, Cambridge University Press, New York.

Chay-Nemeth, C 2003, 'Becoming Professionals: A Portrait of Public Relations in Singapore', in K Sriramesh & D Vércîc D (eds), *The Global Public Relations Handbook: Theory, Research and Practice*, Lawrence Erlbaum, Mahwah.

Chen, N 2004, 'Public Relations in Hong Kong: An Evolving Field in a Fast-changing City', in K Sriramesh (ed.), *Public Relations in Asia: An Anthology*, Thomson Learning, Singapore.

Chen, N & Culbertson, H 2003, 'Public Relations in Mainland China: An Adolescent with Growing Pains', in K Sriramesh & D Vércîc (eds), *The Global Public Relations Handbook: Theory, Research and Practice*, Lawrence Erlbaum, Mahwah.

Curtin, P & Gaither, T 2007, *International Public Relations: Negotiating Culture, Identity and Power*, Sage, Thousand Oaks.

Dicken, P 2007, *Global Shift: Mapping the Contours of the World Economy*, 5th edn, Sage, London.

Ekachai, D & Komolsevin, R 2004, 'From Propaganda to Strategic Communication: The Continuing Evolution of the Public Relations Profession in Thailand', in K Sriramesh (ed.) 2004, *Public Relations in Asia: An Anthology*, Thomson Learning, Singapore.

Fitch, K & Surma, A 2006, 'The Challenges of International Education: Developing a Public Relations Unit for the Asian Region', *Journal of University Teaching and Learning Practice*, 3(2): 104–13.

Grunig, J & Hunt, T 1984, *Managing Public Relations*, Harcourt Brace Jovanovich, Fort Worth.

Habermas, J 1989, *The Structural Transformation of the Public Sphere: An Inquiry into a Category of Bourgeois Society*, MIT Press, Cambridge, MA.

Hangpongpandh, P 2006, 'Burson-Marsteller's Depression Awareness Campaign in Thailand', in M Parkinson & D Ekachai, *International and Intercultural Public Relations: A Campaign Case Approach*, Pearson Education, Boston.

Haque, M 2004, 'Overview of Public Relations in Asia', in D Tilson & E Alozie (eds), *Toward the Common Good: Perspectives in International Public Relations*, Pearson Education, Boston.

Hung, C & Chen, Y 2004, 'Globalization: Public Relations in China in the Era of Change', in K Sriramesh (ed.), *Public Relations in Asia: An Anthology*, Thomson Learning, Singapore.

Idid, S 2004, 'Public Relations in Malaysia from its Colonial Past', in K Sriramesh (ed.), *Public Relations in Asia: An Anthology*, Thomson Learning Singapore.

Ihlen, O & van Ruler, B 2007, 'How Public Relations Works: Theoretical Roots and Public Relations Perspectives', *Public Relations Review*, 33(3): 243–8.

Inoue, T 2003, 'An Overview of Public Relations in Japan and the Self-Correction Concept', in K Sriramesh & D Vércîc (eds), *The Global Public Relations Handbook: Theory, Research and Practice*, Lawrence Erlbaum, Mahwah.

Jo, S & Shim, S W 2005, 'Paradigm Shift of Employee Communication: The Effect of Management Communication on Trusting Relationships', *Public Relations Review*, 31(2): 277–80.

Jonsson, G 2006, *Towards Korean Reconciliation: Socio-cultural Exchanges and Cooperation*, Ashgate, Vermont.

Kim, Y 2003, 'Professionalism and Diversification: The Evolution of Public Relations in South Korea', in K Sriramesh & D Vércîc (eds), *The Global Public Relations Handbook: Theory, Research and Practice*, Lawrence Erlbaum, Mahwah.

L'Etang, J & Pieczka, M (eds) 2006, *Public Relations: Critical Debates and Contemporary Practice*, Lawrence Erlbaum, Mahwah.

McKie, D & Munshi, D 2008, *Reconfiguring Public Relations: Ecology, Equity and Enterprise*, Routledge, New York.

Newsom, D 2004, 'Singapore Poised for Prominence in Public Relations Among Emerging Democracies', in D Tilson & E Alozie, *Toward the Common Good: Perspectives in International Public Relations*, Pearson Education, Boston.

Sarabia-Panol, Z & Lorenzo-Molo, C 2004, 'Public Relations in the Philippines: A Cultural, Historical, Political and Socioeconomic Perspective', in K Sriramesh (ed.), *Public Relations in Asia: An Anthology*, Thomson Learning, Singapore.

Sha, B & Huang, Y 2004, 'Public Relations in Taiwan: Evolving with the Infrastructure', in K Sriramesh (ed.), *Public Relations in Asia: An Anthology*, Thomson Learning, Singapore.

Sriramesh, K (ed.) 2004, *Public Relations in Asia: An Anthology*, Thomson Learning, Singapore.

Sriramesh, K 2007, 'The Relationship Between Culture and Public Relations', in E Toth (ed.), *The Future of Excellence in Public Relations and Communication Management: Challenges for the Next Generation*, Lawrence Erlbaum, Mahwah.

Stanton, R 2007a, *Media Relations*, Oxford University Press, Melbourne.

Stanton, R 2007b, 'All News is Local: The Failure of the Media to Recognise World Events in a Globalized Age', McFarland, Jefferson.

Stanton, R 2008a, 'Cheong and Mateship: The Socialization of Media Relations', *Asian Social Science Journal*, 4(5).

Stanton, R 2008b, 'Personal observations of graduate enrolments in strategic communication at the University of Sydney', Sydney.

Takata, T & Magyar, R 2007, 'Embracing PR in Japan', *Outcomes*, 10(3): 3.

Taylor, M & Botan, C 1997, 'Public Relations Campaigns for National Development in the Pacific Rim: The Case of Public Education in Malaysia', *Australian Journal of Communication*, 24(2): 115–30.

Taylor, M & Kent, M 1999, 'Challenging Assumptions of International Public Relations: When Government is the Most Important Public', *Public Relations Review*, 25(2): 131–44.

Thomas, A 2004, 'The Media and Reformasi in Indonesia', in D Tilson & E Alozie, *Toward the Common Good: Perspectives in International Public Relations*, Pearson Education, Boston.

Tilson, D & Alozie, E 2004, *Toward the Common Good: Perspectives in International Public Relations*, Pearson Education, Boston.

Toth, E (ed.) 2007, *The Future of Excellence in Public Relations and Communication Management: Challenges for the Next Generation*, Lawrence Erlbaum, Mahwah.

Van Leuven, J 1996, 'Public Relations in South East Asia: From Nation-building Campaigns to Regional Interdependence', in M Culbertson & N Chen (eds), *International Public Relations: A Comparative Analysis*, Lawrence Erlbaum, Mahwah.

Venkateswaran, A 2004, 'The Evolving Face of Public Relations in Malaysia', in D Tilson & E Alozie 2004, *Toward the Common Good: Perspectives in International Public Relations*, Pearson Education, Boston.

Witmer, D 2006, 'Overcoming System and Culture Boundaries: Public Relations from a Structuration Perspective', in C Botan & V Hazleton (eds), *Public Relations Theory II*, Lawrence Erlbaum, Mahwah.

Chapter **14**

CAREERS AND EXPANDING HORIZONS

Joy Chia and Gae Synnott

Joy Chia and Gae Synnott

PRACTITIONER PROFILE

RACHAEL COCHRANE— LADIES WHO DISCO

Ladies Who Disco is a group of five Perth public relations professionals who wanted to organise some fun nights out and help underfunded charities in Perth at the same time.

It is the natural inclination of people to want to surround themselves with winners, but they felt that, as a group of professional women, it would be too easy for them

Source: Tony McDonough

to align themselves with large, highly visible charities with high-profile patrons.

So, with a wide range of communication and management skills between them, they decided to put their skills to work to support smaller charities that struggled to raise funds or get publicity.

Perhaps the charities did not get the publicity they needed because the media deemed their issues not newsworthy enough. Or they might be engaged with issues that people do not like talking about. Or work that simply does not attract enough volunteers.

Throughout their careers, the Ladies have all worked in a variety of communication roles that include media managers, event coordinators, marketing managers, account coordinators, community relations officers, fundraising officers, and public relations consultants.

With many years of experience in the profession, they had also built up a valuable network of contacts, which enabled them to find a venue that would sponsor the events, and seek out graphic designers, photographers, DJs, hairdressers, makeup artists, and other suppliers who would all donate their time to make the nights possible.

In their free time, Ladies Who Disco coordinate, arrange, and run the nights. In two years they have held eight events and raised over $50 000.

CHAPTER **AIMS**

By the end of this chapter you should be able to:

➤ understand steps important to making students career ready
➤ apply your knowledge about how to prepare for a successful career in public relations
➤ understand the role of internships and placements
➤ understand how to apply yourself once you are working in public relations
➤ appreciate the exciting potential of a grounding in public relations.

Getting started

Your friend is a public relations coordinator for one of the budget airlines. He enjoys his work and suggests that you should think about a career in public relations. He tells you that there are many opportunities to travel and he is thinking of moving to Singapore or Hong Kong and working there. He also says it is hard work, that he had to apply for quite a few positions before he was employed in his current position, and that you have to be passionate about your work. You are ready to embark on your public relations career and you want help in knowing what to do.

By now students should be developing a good sense of the public relations profession and why it works the way it does. While you are still a student, there are many ways to position yourself and make yourself career ready. In order to do so, think about the following ideas:

➤ Is your public relations degree an accredited degree with a recognised public relations professional organisation? Accreditation and recognition of your tertiary studies might also be recognised through alliances with other professional associations so that you can consider employment in other countries (see the PRIA website).

➤ Does your degree major in public relations? Studying only a few public relations courses or subjects provides a glimpse of what public relations is. Courses or subjects such as public relations theory and practice, writing for public relations, strategic public relations, organisational communication management, global and international public relations, issues and crisis management, public relations research and evaluation, ethics and communication management, community relations and corporate social responsibility, and participating in placements or internships are all important. Understanding marketing principles and practice is valuable to the increased emphasis on the public relations–marketing mix.

➤ Gain some experience as a volunteer for an event or for a not-for-profit organisation as it develops its first newsletter, or work as a junior assistant for a public relations consultancy and begin to understand the components of the day-to-day public relations role.

➤ The application of theory is important during your studies, so apply your assignment work, where possible, to real communication and public relations practice.

➤ Become a student member of your public relations association such as PRIA, PRINZ, or one of the associations in Singapore, Hong Kong, South Korea, Taiwan, Thailand, China, or wherever you intend to practise.

➤ Attend functions for young practitioners and begin to network and meet other practitioners. Learn from other junior and senior practitioners as they can offer their insights and share their experiences with you.

➤ If possible have an experienced public relations mentor who will give you suggestions about where you should apply for positions, how to apply, and how to move into the profession. Professional associations may be able to assist you in organising a mentor.

➤ Inform yourself about what is happening in other parts of the world. Consider career opportunities and the conditions for working overseas and speak to other graduates with overseas experience.

➤ Exchange programs at your university might pave the way to an international career or give you invaluable international public relations experience.

➤ Attend university career seminars about writing résumés and preparing for interviews.

➤ Review the applications of successful applicants.

➤ Be prepared to work in all sectors of public relations: government, not-for-profit, corporate, consultancy, and private practice.

➤ Read and research online and hard copy journals, magazines, and newspapers, and attend public relations conferences and seminars to discover what is happening in the profession; many conferences have special rates for students.

➤ Keep informed and be prepared for life-long learning.

Joy Chia and Gae Synnott

Internship and placements

By the time they have completed their degree many students will have completed an internship or placement as part of that degree. Where public relations degrees are accredited with professional institutions such as the Public Relations Institute of Australia (PRIA), one of the conditions for accreditation is to complete an internship or placement in the public relations or communication profession.

An internship is supervised work experience in public relations where the student will undertake public relations tasks in a supervised environment. An internship can be crucial in assisting you to successfully gain your first public relations position.

A placement is similar to an internship but may require a longer period of involvement on the job because it could include, for example, project involvement in an organisation beginning a community program for disadvantaged youth where the supervisor has broader experience in communication management. It is valuable experience and essential to understanding the application of theory to practice.

Ideally, as many students as possible will complete an internship, but whether they do is dependent on the profession and the number of internship places available. The reality of most tertiary public relations programs is that:

➤ the profession has a shortage of qualified public relations educators and practitioners
➤ numbers of students in public relations programs are increasing, which places increasing demand on educators to find suitable internships with trained and knowledgeable supervisors
➤ universities and the public relations profession need to work together to formalise supervision and training and give greater recognition to supervisors' contributions.

Most universities are embedding public relations experience as part of professional majors and public relations subjects or courses. In this way students are applying their learning to the real world of public relations throughout their degree.

The *Report of the Commission on Public Relations Education* found that a survey of students on internships indicated that:

> When asked to name the one factor they believe is important to making an Internship high-quality the overwhelming plurality focused on the internship supervisor and his or her availability, expertise and working relationship with the student. Ranking second as a quality factor was students being given meaningful assignments and not being treated primarily as clerical workers (2006: 60).

The commission identified the need for more regular visits by academics organising placement and internships and the need for a 'high degree of quality control' (61) in administering the internships. Students also need to understand internship expectations and ask for assistance and direction to realise these expectations. Internships need to be managed effectively so that real world public relations experience is beneficial and leads to graduates who are well-prepared and competent public relations professionals from the beginning of their first year in practice. It is apparent that internships, placements, and project management assists students in gaining employment as some students continue their internships as employees of a company and others find employment during project management undertaken as part of their public relations degree program (Guth & Marsh 2007).

REFLECT AND DISCUSS

What would you do if you were on placement or completing your internship and are experiencing any of the following?

➤ You met your supervisor only once, for five minutes ten days ago.
➤ Most of your supervisor's time is spent interstate and overseas, so a junior staff member is supervising you.
➤ You have been answering the telephone, doing odd jobs such as endless photocopying, and are becoming concerned about whether you are learning anything about public relations.
➤ You have been told that the work is confidential, so there is not much that you can do on the project.

Think about supervision contracts, agreed terms of placement, and internships and how the above situation could be managed effectively.

Getting your first public relations job

Imagine that you decide to follow your friend's advice to pursue a public relations career. You have graduated, tossed your mortarboard in the air, sent photos of your graduation to everyone on MySpace, and now you are ready to start working.

According to Ferguson (2007: 11) the possibilities for your career might include positions such as these:

➤ *Press secretary and political consultant*, where you are employed by government officials or ministers of government to promote government officials and the party as well as to take part in policy development.
➤ *Public opinion researcher* with a market research firm, where you explore issues, understand trends, and present reports of possible ways to manage an issue such as credit card debt or the need for low-income housing.

FIGURE **14.1** \ Graduated students tossing their mortarboards in the air

Source: iStockphoto

FIGURE **14.2** \ Applying for your first job

Applying for a position
Read organisations' annual reports
Understand the Public Relations role
If possible speak to someone who has worked for the organisation

Applications should address criteria
Demonstrate your skills through evidence of experience
Ask referees permission, don't just add their name to an application

Interview questions
About your interest in the position and why you applied
What is important to you as a public relations practitioner?
Your team approach to practice
Self tasking and problem-solving skills

Job success
Enjoy it
Regularly update your résumé and keep a record of career development
If you were unsuccessful ask for feedback and seek advice from mentors in applying for other positions

Source: UniSA careers advisor (personal communication)

➤ *Webmaster*, where you are responsible for developing and managing websites, blogs, and new media tools for a range of not-for-profits, government, and corporations. This is a growing area of demand that may well prompt the development of new courses to provide the appropriate training.

➤ *The not-for-profit sector* is the fastest growing sector around the world. Many graduates will find satisfying positions working in this area for organisations such as the Heart Foundation, the Royal Society for Prevention of Cruelty to Animals, or perhaps in programs for disadvantaged young people.

➤ *Financial public relations*, where positions have become more important as stock markets become volatile and 'the next round of corporate fraud has meant a steadily increasing demand for greater corporate transparency and more understandable information about business activity' (Collis 2003: 59, cited in Gregory). The public relations role is to communicate clear and concise information to financial audiences such as shareholders and investors. This is a delicate role and one that graduates may find overwhelming in their early days as a practitioner, which means that it is rarely a position for a new graduate.

➤ *Community relations coordinator* of community activities, where you might work with not-for-profit organisations and schools, follow up on grants and sponsorships, and promote and manage a corporation's image. The community relations coordinator is part of a growing area of public relations practice often connected with corporate social responsibility (CSR) programs. Practitioners have the opportunity to establish alliances and partnerships with not-for-profit sector partners on a range of community-based initiatives.

REFLECT AND DISCUSS

Do some internet research on DHL and its CSR programs with Australian Surf Life Saving Clubs and support for disadvantaged groups.

➤ What benefits does DHL realise through its CSR activities and partnerships?
➤ Through advertisements and online career resources locate community coordinating positions and identify the key skills required.

Ferguson suggests that other career possibilities, such as image consultants who make celebrities and professionals look their best and 'present in a professional manner' (73), or as promotions officers for the music and entertainment industries, may not be readily identifiable as public relations positions. Some graduates will enjoy working in these very different positions where the conventional, specialist role is less prominent. While the context of these positions is different, the principles of practice remain the same: ethical, strategic management underpins all practice.

Joy Chia and Gae Synnott

So many choices

You might see a typical public relations position for a graduate advertised, often online, in the following way.

BOX **14.1** \ COMMUNICATION CONSULTANT/COORDINATOR

➤ Maintaining and building on an organisation's reputation.

➤ Dealing with and researching sensitive issues with internal and external publics.

➤ Developing effective, versatile communication with internal and external publics.

➤ Ensuring consistency and a coordinated approach of organisation's services to the community.

➤ Balancing the demands of proactive and strategic communication strategies with management of issues and crisis that might erupt from time to time.

➤ Ethical and professional management in delivering a service to the community and working collaboratively with stakeholders to constantly improve practice.

BOX **14.2** \ PUBLIC AFFAIRS MANAGER

A COORDINATOR WOULD ASSIST WITH THESE ACTIVITIES AND FUNCTIONS

➤ Exceptional skills in writing for the media, writing for publications, developing news releases, writing speeches, and managing internal communication.

➤ Support and managing the organisation's community programs and involvement.

➤ Leveraging sponsorships.

➤ Developing public relations strategies and tactics.

➤ Managing and building an organisation's brand and reputation.

➤ Skilled in relationship management, developing and maintaining relationships with stakeholders, other organisations, and members of the community.

Where to begin your search

As some jobs may not be advertised you need to think about doing the following:

➤ Register with young practitioner groups and network with young and experienced practitioners. Remember, no one knows you so you have to spread the word about yourself.

➤ Using search engines such as Google and Yahoo, locate employment websites (see Web resources) where you can sign up for job alerts and newsletters.

➤ Attend university career seminars and forums. Many universities bring employers to the campuses.

➤ Your internship or placement may have the potential for your first public relations position.

➤ Send your résumé to prospective employers and follow up with a telephone call.

➤ Ferguson (2007: 11) suggests that graduates develop at least ten samples of their work 'to demonstrate their understanding of both the business and media in which they want to work'. Develop these samples throughout your degree.

➤ Build networks with prospective referees who know your work and know you personally. These people are often aware of new positions or movements in the profession and can alert you to career opportunities.

Remember that successful graduates are those who are competent and have personal skills that they utilise to work effectively within the public relations team and with management.

Starting work

You have received some good news: you have a job as a public relations coordinator at the local council. You are thrilled, but at the same time you feel a little apprehensive and wonder what it is going to be like. The realities of your first job are that:

➤ the salary might not be very exciting but there is good potential for it to grow with experience

➤ you will have to work hard, and it will be demanding, at times stressful

➤ it will be rewarding

➤ it most definitely will not be boring, in fact, you will find the job diverse with a range of tasks that will continue to challenge you

➤ it will draw on your creative skills (creativity is the way you engage publics and other organisations) and make your strategies work for you

➤ it will sometimes be confusing; the diversity of the profession could make you question whether what you are doing is public relations, marketing, fundraising, or project management

➤ it might also be frustrating because the organisation where you are employed may not want to change its culture and may not be keen about some of your ideas to change the way the organisation communicates and engages with its publics.

Karen's story (on page 394) suggests that you can make a difference and be proactive in managing the organisation's public relations.

BOX **14.3** \ KAREN'S STORY

Karen was very excited about her first public relations job but her organisation had little idea about contemporary public relations practice and what it means to an organisation. Until the organisation's image suffered through negative media coverage it had seemed unnecessary to employ an inhouse practitioner. Now that a practitioner was employed there was an expectation that Karen would fix everything and rescue the organisation so that the public would be more accepting of its practices. Initially, Karen was disappointed with her job: it was hard work, budgeting for public relations activities seemed ad hoc, media relationships were strained, and little attention was paid to transparent internal communication with employees or to effective external communication to stakeholders and shareholders. From an organisation of 600 employees, Karen expected much more.

WHAT WAS THE OUTCOME OF THIS SITUATION?

In two years Karen established a public relations team, developed online newsletters with regular employee input, set up a shareholder blog, and developed community networks. Considerable time and energy were invested in community involvement by supporting disadvantaged youth and youth housing projects. It was challenging and media reports were not always encouraging as articles about 'doing it for the brand' appeared in the local newspapers where the media were sceptical of the motives for some of the community-based projects. The public relations team began to take a proactive role. They positively promoted the organisation's services and worked collaboratively with internal and external publics with the aim of creating transparent management of all aspects of the organisation's communication. The public relations team became integral to the management team by taking an increasing role in the organisation's decision making.

Karen's advice: Ask more questions at the interview about the organisation's expectations of the public relations practitioner and its understanding of public relations.

When we begin to explore and build knowledge about public relations our own understanding of public relations and how it should be defined is developed. You need to ask whether your employers have the same view of public relations as you have. Are organisations ready for graduates fresh out of the tertiary sector who are ready to change the world?

BOX **14.4** \ JOY'S STORY

Joy's first public relations job seemed to be almost all event management. Joy quickly learnt that her public relations manager had become very tired of running events so she was very keen to hand over everything to the new public relations staff member.

The good things about Joy's first job were:

➤ that she became very familiar with detailed event lists about what to do, who to contact, what to hire, what it cost, what media to contact, and when to contact the media

➤ that she needed to book venues well in advance and be prepared that she might not find the venue in the desired location

➤ that she was given the opportunity to build the budget into the annual budget plan

➤ that she learnt not to expect that the sponsor she had last year would sponsor the event this year but that new sponsors emerge, often with better support.

Joy learnt on the job that incidents that she did not expect could occur (in other words, that things can and do go wrong):

➤ Keynote speakers can get stuck in the airport due to inclement weather and not be able to make it to the opening of an international event, which leads to the need to reschedule speakers and many very unhappy clients.

➤ A massive thunderstorm, which occurred during a conference, resulted in a total blackout for half a day; the food could not be kept warm, the coffee was cold, and so were all the conference attendees.

➤ For one event, the massive insurance required for expensive artwork displays meant that the expenditure for insurance exceeded the budget for the display.

➤ Having to spend eighteen hours on her feet during exhibitions that seemed to run endlessly.

➤ Having to run a New Zealand exhibition after only fifteen minutes training when the New Zealand manager suddenly became ill.

➤ Catered food did not arrive because it was delivered to the wrong event.

Despite these and other potential hazards, there is no doubt that the bad experiences will be as invaluable as the good. They point to the need to be flexible and show a public relations practitioner that they need to appreciate that even the best laid plans can take an unexpected turn.

Joy Chia and Gae Synnott

Tips for the first job

Swann (2008) gives some good advice for your first job if you want to make your first public relations experience a good one:

➤ Do not make changes immediately.
➤ Understand your organisation and the people working in it.
➤ Be positive when you suggest change.
➤ Create alliances with key people.
➤ Keep learning.
➤ Get a mentor.
➤ Track your accomplishments.

Most of these tips are relevant to other professions as well but networking skills and the need to establish relationships that make communication manageable and beneficial are very important to the public relations practitioner. These relationships include:

➤ relationships with other employees
➤ relationships with the inhouse executive team and decision makers; the new graduate may not be taking a direct role in decision making but will be part of a public relations team who develop policy and strategy important to the organisation and its overall objectives
➤ external relationships with media, which will be extensive for those consultants hired by clients with diverse media needs
➤ relationships with other organisations of similar and opposing interests—the latter points to the need to also develop relationships with those who oppose or challenge an organisation. A public relations practitioner who works for a local council may find that the local constituents are opposed to the council's plans to turn an oval into a housing estate, which will require considerable consultation and communication with the community, which will, in turn, lead to plans based on collaborative decision making
➤ relationships with community leaders, sponsors, and those involved in community projects, or in the not-for-profit sector that an organisation supports or partners with
➤ relationships with academic institutions to foster engagement with formal learning advisers.

According to Guth and Marsh (2007: 548), the following skills are highly valued by the profession for entry-level employees or new graduates of public relations:

➤ media release writing skills
➤ being a self-starter
➤ having critical thinking and problem-solving skills.

The profession often expresses dissatisfaction with graduate skills but because of the diversity of practice and because the profession is developing and establishing itself the profession must also expect that graduates will be on a steep learning curve. The profession needs to facilitate environments of learning where new technology is embraced, practitioners are trained, new and creative ways of managing public relations are considered and the emphasis on emerging areas such as community engagement are recognised and understood.

The following top ten attributes for the successful practitioner come from Sheryl Fewster, a senior public sector practitioner in Western Australia:

1 an enquiring mind
2 project management skills
3 the ability to multitask
4 ability to build rapport and have empathy
5 the ability to distil ideas down to one sentence and communicate clearly
6 confidence
7 knowing when to stop talking and listen
8 knowing when to ask for help
9 having good networks for finding information and to get things done
10 not to be terrified by a blank sheet of paper, and being able to get ideas down in writing quickly.

The following top ten attributes for the successful consultant come from Marie Howarth, a senior consultant in Western Australia:

1 must like people
2 must be able to listen
3 must have the ability to be flexible and to move easily in and out of different environments
4 must be versatile; unless you are a specialist or working in a clearly defined role you will be doing a variety of tasks
5 must have imagination because people are looking to you for answers
6 must have an entrepreneurial spirit
7 must aim to be the trusted adviser, rather than the expert; there are few real experts in any discipline and clients will always know more about their own business than you do
8 must be genuinely interested in the work you are doing
9 must be very accountable because you live and die by your own performance
10 must be a chameleon because with every client the rules of the game change. In each organisation there is a different set of relationships and a different set of politics: you must be able to accommodate to each one.

Joy Chia and Gae Synnott

Celebrity public relations

The growth of celebrity public relations and the celebrity brand is significant. Many female and male film stars seem to have a universal attraction and each country has its celebrity sports stars who promote a range of products and services. The arrival of David Beckham in Japan, Australia, or New Zealand results in a frenzy of media activity, huge media coverage with every form of media that want a slice of the action. The public relations–marketing mix is evident in celebrity promotion when the fame and charisma of a soccer star becomes central to the marketing of aftershave lotion, beauty cream, sports equipment, and clothing labels.

Celebrity branding begins to have its problems if celebrities become embroiled in controversy that results in negative stories and videos appearing on YouTube or other online media. Brand managers may quickly distance themselves and move to the next celebrity for endorsement. But, perversely, brand managers might find that negative publicity promotes the brand and thus will continue to use that particular celebrity, sometimes even more. Celebrity public relations is a fascinating role for the brand manager and the celebrity's manager, who uses careful and strategic management to plan exposure and extensive media coverage. But in terms of overall public relations practice, this is not a primary area of employment or public relations activity even though it is one that seems to be given a great deal of attention in the media.

REFLECT AND DISCUSS

> ➤ Name the stars who are part of celebrity branding and promotion in your state or country, or who have universal appeal.
> ➤ Are you more inclined to buy the products they promote? Why?
> ➤ Would you consider a career as a celebrity public relations manager? Why?

Career progression

As you embark on a career in public relations, it is useful to picture your future career as a series of work role transitions, in which you will go through a constant cycle of moving into a new role, coping with that role, planning for the next move, and then repeating the process. Professional development is ongoing and continual; learning about public relations practice goes hand in hand with experience.

Having a certain number of years of experience implies that some learning has transpired—learning about the nature and professional requirements of the job, learning about the organisation's requirements. It is unlikely that all your learning will occur in the one organisation. Practitioners usually start their career in one organisation and move on, often many times, in the course of their career.

Learning happens as part and parcel of the process of a career, a process defined by Hall (1976: 4) as 'the individually perceived sequence of attitudes and behaviours associated with work-related experiences and activities over the span of a person's life'. Career has an internal focus (the way the individual perceives the career) and an external focus (the series of positions held), and it represents a person's movement through a social structure over time (Hall 1987). A career encompasses many socialisation experiences as the person moves in, through, and out of various work-related roles. It implies continual opportunities or requirement for adjustment on the part of the individual, which over time could lead to personal changes.

As practitioners gain more experience, their capacity to do the work and their appreciation of the role may broaden. This is why we often talk about senior and junior practitioners, and suggest that one point of difference is, for senior practitioners, the more strategic nature of the job. Not only does the strategic capability tend to come from years of experience, but it also comes from a range of other factors related to their maturation as people, such as:

➤ progress through their life cycle, which happens irrespective of their work experiences
➤ the separate impacts of the passage of time and maturation
➤ progress in their careers, including mid-career challenges
➤ changes in self-concept and values
➤ the impact of role transitions and organisational occupational socialisation, which changes skills, abilities, and approach
➤ social aspects surrounding the career.

Simply put, the longer a person has been around, the more likely it is that that person will see things a little differently.

REFLECT AND DISCUSS

> ➤ Think about how you can speed up the process to build the broader worldview needed in public relations practice. What could you do to understand more of what is happening in the world?
>
> ➤ Choose an organisation you would like to work for. Identify three highly visible current social or environmental issues and explore your thoughts about how the organisation could work effectively with these issues.

Joy Chia and Gae Synnott

BOX **14.5** \ HOW TO DEVELOP YOURSELF FURTHER ON THE JOB

A number of senior practitioners were asked their thoughts on this question.

SHERYL FEWSTER'S ADVICE

➤ Get a good understanding of the worldview where you work, that is, the operating environment for the organisation.

➤ Be well read. This means understanding the political environment, what is happening elsewhere in the world, and knowing the big issues of the day.

➤ Know how to harness your thoughts and get them out quickly. Practise writing.

➤ Do not hide your creativity. Employers look for a good grasp of the basics of public relations practice, as well as your creativity.

➤ Talk to a lot of senior practitioners. They have a storehouse of knowledge, are often most willing to share it, and their advice can be a short cut to the basics.

➤ Build relationships widely.

➤ Google widely to gather case studies and different approaches that will help you in thinking about the communication problems you are facing. Recent work or research in the human resources area might be useful in the employee communication program you are developing.

REFLECT AND DISCUSS

Sheryl highlights the importance of reading widely and staying up to date with current affairs and industry trends. Take a moment now to bookmark five useful websites that you can regularly go to. Discuss these websites with your colleagues and discuss something valuable that you have learnt about the profession from each website.

GRAHAM LOVELOCK'S ADVICE

➤ Work on your written and verbal communication skills.

➤ Understand how communication works.

➤ Do not expect to do or have everything at once. You have to get in, get dirty, and get a solid grasp of the fundamentals. While doing this, you will get a chance to apply what you have learnt.

➤ If you are not sure about something, ask somebody. Do not assume that you know. As you progress upwards in your work environment, your advice can have large financial implications. Do not wing it.

➤ Look for opportunities to prove your worth. You can create these opportunities and be proactive in demonstrating the contribution that public relations can make.

➤ Always pay good attention to detail.

➤ Learn where you can create value within your work environment. Sometimes this means knowing how to make other people look good—if they succeed, you succeed.

BRIAN WILLS-JOHNSON'S ADVICE

➤ Be professional: public relations is an attitude and an approach to doing things. A professional attitude comes from the desire to apply a recognised body of knowledge, from your confidence that you possess that body of knowledge, and that you can apply it to deal with public relations issues.

➤ Stay up to date.

➤ Do not take the job personally. You can get bound up in the organisation's reputation, and its ups and downs can affect you. Do not let yourself bruise easily.

➤ Do not just think in terms of outcomes, but also in terms of the process that allows you to get to the outcomes.

➤ Be optimistic that public relations is a lifetime profession. It can lead into other things, such as politics, or some other different work environment; it can also give you some interesting relationships. It can grow you as a person.

➤ Public relations is not an easy option. It can be very demanding, you can work long hours, and there are highs and lows. But it is based on rigour, and as a practitioner you will set the profession back if you do not make that rigour visible.

REFLECT AND **DISCUSS**

Brian's advice is to develop systems and processes that allow you to consistently approach public relations issues. Take a few moments to go through your course notes and extract any processes that you have dealt with in class to add to your professional repertoire. Do you have, for example, a public relations planning framework?

JAMES BEST'S ADVICE

James Best, a former consultant, now in a local government leadership position, offers the following advice:

➤ Work out what level you want to operate at—at the technician level, or in the boardroom.

➤ Get as much variety as you can. Work in a number of different fields to build up your exposure.

➤ Volunteer as much as possible.

➤ Enjoy working with people. It helps you to understand how people organise themselves and what motivates people in groups.

➤ Be hungry for information.

➤ Keep learning. Read articles, attend workshops and conferences.

THE ELEVEN QUALITIES REQUIRED FOR A HAPPY PUBLIC RELATIONS CAREER

Wilcox et al. (2003: 83), quoting Art Stevens, CEO of Publicis Dialog in New York, offer these eleven qualities as important to anyone planning a long and happy career in public relations:

1 Write well, without much editing or supervision.
2 Be skilled at planning; stick to deadlines.
3 Be innovative, imaginative.
4 Be well informed about your clients.
5 Be results oriented.
6 Be a thorough professional.
7 Know how to create publicity.
8 Keep in contact with the media.
9 Keep learning and growing.
10 Be a good manager.
11 Do not be a yes person.

Public relations can lead to many different careers

Public relations is an area of knowledge and application that can take you in many different directions. It is a very versatile discipline, and the communication and strategic skills that practitioners learn and develop can be used in many different ways.

James Best is the mayor of the city of South Perth, a local government authority with approximately 41 000 residents and a $50 million budget. Best spent twenty-one years as a public relations practitioner before successfully moving into local government. Much of his public relations work revolved around community engagement, which involved all the traditional components of relationship management—identifying and understanding stakeholders, knowing your audience, targeting messages, and facilitating people to take action.

From that rich background, Best sees his role now as a 'silo buster' where he puts people in touch with others, and helps people to work together for the good of the community. Some of the most important lessons he learnt through public relations that are critical in his leadership role now are these:

➤ Public relations helps a practitioner understand how society and communities work: what makes people tick, what are their priorities, and how you can package messages that people will listen to and act on.
➤ Public relations is action- and outcome-oriented. It forces the practitioner to think about the intended outcome and what you are trying to achieve.
➤ Public relations progresses by developing plans, strategies, and actions. It enables you to bring ideas together and to plan to achieve outcomes for mutual benefit.

In local government, the focus is very much on the local community. Best engages at the grassroots level, mixing with his community, talking with many people, networking with parents, school councils, and school communities, including school students. By engaging at this level, he learns the community's mood and the different perspectives of its members:

> I understand what's important in people's minds. Collectively we generate some good ideas, and then we move slowly, in micro-mini steps, to achieve the change that people want. Quick changes can lead to resistance. We collectively decide the priority goals, and we work together to make it happen. And periodically I remind everyone how far we've come.

Sound communication skills are evident in this approach.

Best interprets his role as 'being here to help the team'. This is precisely what public relations people do. At the heart of every program, the public relations practitioner needs to think about what can be done to help the corporate reputation, to find ways to open doors to build relationships, and to build third party advocates. A guiding principle for every practitioner to keep in mind is: How can everyone get something out of this that they are happy with?

James offers three fundamentals for good practice: passion, perseverance and possibility. As he explains, you have to believe in what you're doing (passion); you have to aim for continuous improvement because you won't get it right the first time (perseverance); and you have to keep looking for opportunities (possibility).

The final word on this exciting profession

Public relations is an exciting profession at an exciting stage of its development. Not only is there a variety of things to apply your skills to, but the role itself is also legitimised and accepted within organisations. Public relations underpins the sustainability agenda that has

Joy Chia and Gae Synnott

firmly taken hold, because sustainability is all about attitudinal and behavioural changes to the way we live our lives—as individuals and within communities—and communication is the way to achieve attitudinal and behavioural change.

Remember, as with any profession, what you get out of it is determined by what you put in. This is a profession that can take you places, literally. It is a profession that is grounded in people, relationships, and communities. It is a profession that is not about us as practitioners, but is all about what we can achieve for those for whom we are working.

REFLECT AND DISCUSS

In the Preface we talked about public relations education as a process of sense-making in which awareness, knowledge, and appreciation for the profession and its role will be gradually built up.

➤ List five of the most important lessons you have learnt about the practice of public relations that will guide you when you start working.

CASE STUDY REBUILDING AFTER CYCLONE LARRY

THE COMMUNICATION RESPONSE

THE CHALLENGE

On 20 March 2006, Cyclone Larry hit far north Queensland and devastated the town of Innisfail and surrounding communities.

NRMA Insurance and CGU faced a deluge of home claims (6000 in total, at a cost of around $165 million net of reinsurance).

After an event that had caused mass confusion, it was imperative that NRMA Insurance and CGU communicate effectively. The confusion manifested itself in householders who were uncertain about how to lodge claims and make their homes safe. Also, tradespeople and materials were in high demand, which, combined with the need to complete rebuilding before the next wet season, caused shortages. As well, the area had a significant level of under- and non-insurance.

OBJECTIVES

The central goal in responding to these challenges was to demonstrate NRMA Insurance and CGU's commitment to paying claims and helping people get on with their lives.

This goal was supported by three key objectives:

1 Help customers lodge claims and access information about support and assistance being offered by CGU and NRMA Insurance.
2 Ensure that NRMA Insurance and CGU were recognised by customers, the media, and government stakeholders as setting the profession benchmark for other insurers to follow.
3 Manage customer and stakeholder expectations in relation to the scope of insurance cover and claims response in order to minimise potential reputation damage.

COMMUNICATION STRATEGY

Achieving the campaign objectives relied on a five part program.

RAPID PROACTIVE RESPONSE

What we did

Were the first on the ground, proactively seeking out customers.

How we did it

Daily media bulletins were issued under the CGU and NRMA Insurance brands that clearly outlined 24/7 hotline details, claims figures, claims progress, and what NRMA Insurance and CGU were doing to help customers. The bulletins were issued every day for the first week.

On the customer front, hotlines were live from day one, 90 per cent of customers with critical claims had been identified and assessed, and more than 50 per cent of building and contents total losses had been paid out.

Within seventy-two hours IAG companies had:

➤ made emergency accommodation available in Cairns
➤ paid over $3.2 million in total losses
➤ provided more than $7000 in Coles Myer vouchers.

DIFFERENTIATING THE APPROACH

What we did

Highlight aspects of IAG's response that set it apart from other insurers.

How we did it

As the first insurers visible on the ground in Innisfail, NRMA Insurance and CGU were likely to attract media attention. To ensure customer-facing staff in the disaster zone were not distracted by media enquiries, a customer service manager was identified to double as a media spokesperson for the first two weeks. This frontline spokesperson was also available to identify positive customer case studies for media.

One of the most important tasks was to ensure that customers who had lost much of their infrastructure had the ability to lodge claims. Two vans, branded 'Help Vans', were mobilised to the disaster zone, where they became vital channels of communication for affected customers.

USING ALTERNATIVE COMMUNICATION CHANNELS

What we did

Found ways to connect with customers who had lost access to phone, mail, and internet.

How we did it

With many mainstream communications down, radio and print advertising were used as key channels to establish customer contact. Cyclone Larry media bulletins, which were issued daily, updated the community on claims progress and how to lodge a claim.

Existing major claims incidents advertisements were tailored for the Cyclone Larry Response; the initial advertisements (those that appeared in first five days) focused on the customer hotline and the claims lodgement process. Once the first Help Van was set up, we placed advertisements that provided its location details; we also used the Help Van itself as a communication channel.

DEMONSTRATING PROGRESS THROUGH TANGIBLE ACTION

What we did

Use the media to demonstrate progress and mark key milestones.

How we did it

Throughout the process the media update bulletins continued, focusing on progress made and building on the success of the initial response bulletins. This was backed up by continued advertising.

Regular meetings, often daily, were held with a range of community stakeholders and government advisers.

IAG formed partnerships with key local building suppliers in order to speed up the progress of repairs and to demonstrate support for the local community.

It was also important to demonstrate progress to our own people, which was achieved through a series of internal bulletins and face-to-face meetings with key internal stakeholders.

HELPING BEYOND THE CLAIM PAYMENT

What we did

By providing emergency assistance and rebuilding support, we demonstrated that CGU and NRMA Insurance did more than just pay claims.

How we did it

As the emergency abated, it was clear that many customers—indeed, the whole community—had questions about the next steps in the recovery process. The communication response culminated in funding and coordinating a free community Help Expo two months after the cyclone to help equip our customers and the wider community with the right advice on rebuilding their homes and lives. More than 700 residents attended the Help Expo.

RESULTS

Despite having one-third of the total claims, independent media analysis found that, industry wide, NRMA Insurance and CGU generated 70 per cent share of voice. Of all branded coverage, 82 per cent featured our key messages.

Analysis found that 99 per cent of branded coverage was net positive (32 per cent demonstrable).

Source: Carolyn McCann, Insurance Group, Queensland and Susan Hawkins, NRMA Insurance, Queensland

CHAPTER **SUMMARY**

➤ Career preparation begins when you begin your public relations degree.
➤ Internships and placements are important to your career preparation.
➤ Career opportunities are diverse.
➤ Managing your first public relations job requires skilled, flexible graduates who are enthusiastic and can solve problems.
➤ Developing your career is a life-long experience.

WEB RESOURCES

Report of the Commission on Public Relations Education 2006, at www.commpred.org.

CAREER WEBSITES

www.seek.com.
www.careerone.com.au.
www.comjobs.com.au.

Joy Chia and Gae Synnott

REFERENCES

Ferguson, J 2007, *Careers in Focus: Public Relations*, Ferguson, New York.

Gregory, A 2003, 'Communication and the Machine of Government', *International Journal of Communication Ethics*, 1(1): 20–5.

Guth, D, Marsh, C 2007, *Public Relations. A Values-Driven Approach*, 3rd edn, Allyn & Bacon, Boston.

Hall, D T 1976, *Careers in Organizations*, Scott, Foresman, Glenview.

Hall, D T 1987, 'Careers and Socialization', *Journal of Management,* 13(2): 302–21.

Swann, P 2008, *Cases in Public Relations Management*, McGraw Hill, New York.

Wilcox, D, Ault, P, Agee, W & Cameron, G 2003, *Public Relations. Strategies and Tactics,* 7th edn, Allyn & Bacon, Boston.

INDEX